The Muvipix.com Guide to
Photoshop Elements & Premiere Elements 14
Steve Grisetti

The tools in Adobe's amazing suite of programs, and how to use them together to create professional-looking movies and great-looking photos on your personal computer.

About Muvipix.com

Muvipix.com was created to offer support and community to amateur and semi-professional videomakers. Registration is free, and that gets you access to the world's friendliest, most helpful forum and lots of ad-free space for displaying your work. On the products page, you'll find dozens of free tips, tutorials, motion backgrounds, DVD templates, sound effects, royalty-free music and stock video clips. For a small annual subscription fee that we use to keep the site running, you'll have unlimited downloads from the ever-growing library of support materials and media.

We invite you to drop by and visit our thriving community. It costs absolutely nothing – and we'd love to have you join the neighborhood!

http://Muvipix.com

About the author

Steve Grisetti holds a master's degree in Telecommunications from Ohio University and spent several years working in the motion picture and television industry in Los Angeles. A veteran user of several video editing programs and systems, Steve is the co-founder of Muvipix.com, a help and support site for amateur and semi-professional videomakers. A professional graphic designer and video freelancer, he has taught classes in Photoshop, lectured on design and even created classes for lynda.com. He lives in suburban Milwaukee.

Other books by Steve Grisetti

Adobe Premiere Elements 2.0 In a Snap (with Chuck Engels)
The Muvipix.com Guides to Adobe Premiere Elements 7, 8, 9, 10, 11, 12, 13 and 14
The Muvipix.com Guides to Photoshop Elements & Premiere Elements 7, 8,
9, 10, 11, 12, 13 and 14
Cool Tricks & Hot Tips for Adobe Premiere Elements
The Muvipix.com Guide to DVD Architect Studio 5
The Muvipix.com Guides to Vegas Movie Studio HD 10 and 11
The Muvipix.com Guide to Sony Movie Studio 12 and 13
The Muvipix.com Guide to CyberLink PowerDirector 12, 13 and 14

An Introduction

With versions 14 of Photoshop Elements, Premiere Elements and the Elements Organizer, Adobe continues to improve its already excellent photo and video editing bundle with some nice, new features.

Photoshop Elements' biggest improvement is a complete overhaul of its Guided Edits library. Rather than simply list the Guided Edits, the program now displays each step-by-step edit as a thumbnail showing its before-and-after effect. The package of very powerful Photomerge effects has been moved into this library along with a cool new Speed Effect Guided Edit.

You'll also find a couple of new photo enhancement tools. The Haze Removal tool helps cut through fog and haze in your pictures, and the Shake Reduction tool helps remove some of the effect of camera shake or motion blur.

Premiere Elements, meanwhile, gets a complete overhaul of its Export & Share workspace, making the process of selecting the best output format and resolution much more intuitive.

A couple of new Guided Edits have been added to the Premiere Elements library also. It now includes step-by-step instructions for using Hollywood Looks to add some stylish color effects to your movie as well as instructions for creating fast and slow motion effects using the Time Remapping tool.

There's also been a lot of work put into making the People Recognition tool more powerful in the Elements Organizer. The program is better than ever at recognizing faces in your photos and helping you identify and catalog your photos based on the people in them.

In short, Adobe has done a pretty good job, overall, of making a good suite of programs even better.

As always, our goal with this book (as well as our web site) is to make all of the great tools in these programs as easy as possible to learn and understand.

And, if you still have questions, please drop by our Community Forum at Muvipix.com and ask. Our community of helpful fellow videomakers is eager to help.

Muvipix.com was created in 2006 as a community and a learning center for videomakers at a variety of levels. Our community includes everyone from amateurs and hobbyists to semi-pros, professionals and even people with broadcast experience. You won't find more knowledgeable, helpful people anywhere else on the Web. I very much encourage you to drop by our forums and say hello. At the very least, you'll make some new friends. And it's rare that there's a question posted there that isn't quickly, and enthusiastically, answered.

Our learning center consists of video tutorials, tips and, of course, books. But we also offer a wealth of support in the form of custom-created DVD and BluRay disc menus, motion background videos, licensed music and even stock footage. Much of it is absolutely free – and there's even more available for those who purchase one of our affordable site subscriptions.

Our goal has always been to help people get up to speed making great videos and, once they're there, provide them with the inspiration and means to get better and better at doing so.

Why? Because we know making movies and taking great pictures is a heck of a lot of fun – and we want to share that fun with everyone!

Our books, then, are a manifestation of that goal. And my hope for you is that this book helps *you* get up to speed. I think you'll find that, once you learn the basics, making movies on your home computer is a lot more fun than you ever imagined! And you may even amaze yourself with the results in the process.

Thanks for supporting Muvipix.com, and happy moviemaking!

Steve
http://Muvipix.com

Section 1: Adobe Photoshop Elements 14

Table of Contents

Table of Contents

Table of Contents

Section 2: Adobe Premiere Elements 14

Part V: Editing in Expert View

Chapter 18

Start a Premiere Elements Project 237
Creating and opening your video projects

Chapter 19

Add Media to Your Project 245
Capturing video and importing video, audio and photos into your project

Chapter 20

Explore the Project Assets Panel 257

The parts that will form your movie

Chapter 21

Edit Your Video in Expert View 267

Where your movie comes together

Chapter 22

Create an InstantMovie or a Video Story. 281

Quick and easy ways to create movies

Table of Contents

Chapter 32
Export & Share Your Video Projects 401
Outputting from Premiere Elements 14

Chapter 33
A Premiere Elements Appendix 419
More things worth knowing

Section 3: The Elements Organizer

Chapter 34

Manage Your Files with the Organizer...... 431

Getting to Know the Media Browser

Chapter 35

Create Fun Pieces... 451

The Organizer's project templates

Chapter 36

Share Your Photos and Videos 465
The Organizer's output tools

Section 1

Adobe
Photoshop Elements 14

Pixels & Resolution

Raster vs. Vector Graphics

Image Size vs. Canvas Size

Selection

Layers & Alpha

RGB Colors

The Option Bar

Native PSD files

Chapter 1

Things You Need to Know
Principles of photo and graphic editing

Photoshop Elements is a surprisingly powerful photo and graphics editor that borrows a large number of tools from its big brother, Photoshop, the industry standard for photo and graphics work. In fact, both programs can even open and edit the same types of files.

The few limitations Elements does have, in fact, might well be things you'll never even miss (unless you're preparing files that will ultimately go onto a printing press).

But before we go too deeply into the tool set of this fine program, there are a couple of basic principles you'll need to understand.

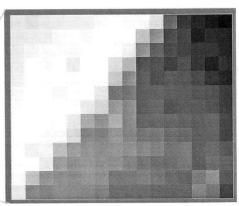

The building blocks of all digital photos are rectangular (usually square) blocks of color known as pixels.

Pixels

Pixels are the building blocks of all digital graphics and photos. Whether you can see them or not, all digital photos as well as photos and graphics created in Photoshop Elements are made up of these little squares of color. Even a tremendously rich, detailed digital photograph, if you blew it up large enough, would reveal itself to be little more than thousands (or millions) of little squares of solid color, each one some mixture of red, green and blue.

This is easier to see on a low-resolution image, such as a graphic created for a web site. Zoom in as far as Photoshop Elements will let you go and you'll soon see that even in the apparently smoothest gradation of color is actually made up of little blocks of solid color.

An understanding of pixels is vital to developing a deeper understanding of how Photoshop Elements works. In order to fully comprehend how virtually any tool does what it does or how any setting affects your image – or how to measure the relative size of your images – you must learn to see your images not merely as pictures of people, animals and places but as compositions of thousands and thousands of little blocks of color.

Non-square pixels – and more than you probably want to know

Like all digital photo devices, video camcorders paint their on-screen images with pixels. But, unlike in a digital photograph, video pixels in some video formats often aren't square blocks of color – they're rectangular.

Even more confusing, the shapes of these rectangular pixels vary, depending on the nature of the medium.

Standard definition NTSC, the television and video format used in North America and Japan, uses pixels that are only 90% as wide as they are tall.

Square (photograph) pixels   Narrower NTSC non-square 4:3 pixels   Wider NTSC non-square 16:9 pixels

Standard definition PAL, the TV format used in most of Europe, uses pixels that are 107% as wide as they are tall. Because of this, a 720x480 pixel NTSC image and a 720x576 pixel PAL image both produce a video frame that is in the same proportion – a 4:3 ratio!

Widescreen standard definition TV uses the same number of pixels to create a video frame as standard TV. The pixels are just proportioned differently. (The pixels are 120% as wide as they are tall in NTSC and 142% as wide as they are tall in PAL.) In other words, there are exactly the same number of pixels in a 4:3 video frame as there are in a 16:9 video image, as illustrated above.

Even some high-definition video camcorders use non-square pixels. In 1440x1080 hi-def TV, the pixels are 133% as wide as they are tall, so that 1440x1080 pixel image produces a 16:9 image. (Though more and more hi-def camcorders are also shooting in 1920x1080, a square pixel format.)

All of this is related to technology dating back to the origins of television. And, unless you're creating graphics for video, it pretty much falls into the "nice to know" rather than "need to know" category. But it *is* nice to know – in case anyone ever asks you why a 720x480 video file becomes a 640x480 web video.

In most cases, as you're designing artwork for your videos, you won't need to concern yourself with whether your pixels are square non-square. This is because Premiere Elements will automatically adapt your square pixel images to the non-square pixel video environment. Just use these **square pixel** equivalents for creating full-screen graphics:

Standard Definition 4:3 NTSC video	640x480 pixels
Widescreen Standard Def NTSC video	855x480 pixels
Standard Definition 4:3 PAL video	768x576 pixels
Widescreen Standard Def PAL video	1024x576 pixels
High Definition 16:9 video	1920x1080 pixels

Resolution

Resolution means, basically, how many of these pixels are crammed into how much space. Standard definition video, like images created for the Internet, doesn't require a particularly high resolution image. Print, on the other hand, can require a pixel density of two to four times that of an on-screen image.

High resolution photo

Same size photo, at much lower resolution (fewer pixels per inch)

Just as digital photos are made up of pixels, printed images are made up of little dots of color or ink. A good, press-worthy image may need 300 dots of color per inch (or more) in order to appear to the eye as a smooth color image. Home printed pieces, like the kind you'd print off your desktop printer, can have as few as 150 dots or pixels per inch. Graphics that will be used on-screen (for the Web or in a video) are about 72 pixels per inch. This is why, if you download a graphic from a web site and print it out, you'll often find that the picture prints fuzzy, jagged or "pixelated."

In order to get a good, high-resolution print-out of a 4" x 3" photo, you'd need a photo that measures as much as 1200 pixels wide and 900 pixels tall. That's a lot of pixels when you consider that a standard TV frame measures only 640 x 480 square pixels. In other words, that 1200 x 900 photo you used for your print-out has four times as many pixels as an equivalent full-screen image on a standard definition TV set!

And that's why we say video is a relatively low-resolution medium. High-definition video needs a bit more image data – but only a fraction of what print artwork requires (and less than half of the resolution produced by a 5 megapixel digital still camera).

Video images are measured in pixels. In other words, as you're working on images for your videos, their dimensions, in pixels, are the only relevant measurement.

The measurements of any graphics and photos you prepare for video are *never* expressed in inches or centimeters. Even the resolution of your images, in terms of pixels per inch, isn't really relevant.

Why doesn't linear measurement (like inches and centimeters) matter in the world of video graphics? Well, basically, it's because you never know how big the TV is your video is going to be shown on!

TVs and computer monitors come in a variety of sizes and screen settings. A graphic may appear to be 2 inches across on a 17" computer monitor, 4 inches across on a 22" TV set and 30" across on a big screen TV! But the graphic itself is always the same number of *pixels* in size. Those pixels are as large or as small as the screen you're viewing them on.

So, when you're creating your graphics for video (or for the web), always think in terms of measurements in pixels. That's the only constant measurement in on-screen graphics.

Just for convenience sake, most people still do use 72 ppi (pixels per inch) as their resolution setting when creating their on-screen graphics. But ultimately the resolution setting makes no difference in this case. When you create an image for video or for the Web, a 640x480 pixel image is still the same size whether it's 72 ppi or 600 ppi.

Raster vs. vector graphics

All computer-created graphics fit into one of two categories – raster graphics or vector graphics – each behaving in its own unique way.

Raster graphics are graphics or photos that are composed of pixels. Digital photos and videos are both composed of pixels. The graphics files you'll be working with and importing into Premiere Elements will be composed of pixels. And, as we've discussed, all raster art requires a certain density of pixels – or resolution – in order for those pixels to be perceived as a smooth blend of colors. If you stretch or enlarge a photograph so much that its pixels show, it will appear jagged and blurry.

Vector graphics, on the other hand, are defined not by pixels but by shape, outlines and fill colors. Programs like Adobe Illustrator, for instance, create graphics in vector. Vector graphics can be as simple as a square or a circle or nearly as complicated as a photograph.

But vector graphics, because they are defined by *outlines and fill colors rather than pixels*, don't have any resolution. They can be resized indefinitely – even scaled to many times their original size – without breaking up into pixels. They remain simply outlines and fills. If you've used a simple drawing tool, such as the one in Microsoft Word, to draw a circle or square, you've worked with vector art.

Photoshop Elements is predominantly a *raster* art program. It is generally concerned with pixels of color. However, there are a few features in the program that behave as if they were vector art:

Shapes. The **Shape Tools** in Photoshop Elements can draw a variety of useful shapes – from circles and squares to lines and arrows and splashes. The shapes it creates, however, have some unique characteristics, as you'll see once you start using them.

Like vector art, these shapes can be easily resized and stretched without concern for resolution. And, if you'll look at a shape layer in the **Layers** panel (as illustrated to the right), you'll notice that they don't even *look* like most Photoshop art. They also won't share their layer with any other graphics. These shapes are *pseudo vector graphics*. They have all of the editing advantages of vector graphics, and they remain as such until you output your Photoshop Elements file as a graphics file or you select the option to manually render or simplify the shape layer.

Text. We usually don't think of text as vector art, but it essentially behaves the same way. You can stretch or resize text as needed in your Photoshop Elements document without concern for resolution. The text will also remain editable until you output your Photoshop Elements document as a graphics file or you select the option to manually render or simplify the text layer.

Text and shapes in Photoshop Elements, like vector art, can be resized without regard for the layer's resolution.

7

Once you output your Photoshop Elements file as a graphics file other than a PSD (a JPEG, TIF or GIF, for instance) or you import the file into Premiere Elements, all of the elements in your graphics file will become raster art. It all becomes pixels. And, because of that, the size (measured in pixels) of your file will determine how large the graphic or photo will be.

Image Size vs. Canvas Size

As you resize your photos or graphics files (under the **Resize** tab, as we'll discuss in **Chapter 7**), it's important to understand the difference between resizing the **Image Size** and the **Canvas Size**.

The distinction is an important one:

As illustrated below, when you resize the **Image Size**, the entire image gets bigger or smaller; when you resize the **Canvas Size**, on the other hand, the image remains the same size but you either add more space around the image or, if you size your canvas smaller, you crop the top, bottom and/or sides off the image.

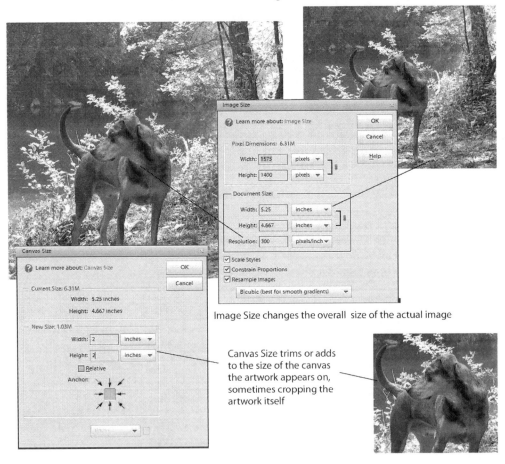

Image Size changes the overall size of the actual image

Canvas Size trims or adds to the size of the canvas the artwork appears on, sometimes cropping the artwork itself

Selections

Selection is a key concept in both Photoshop and Photoshop Elements. A number of the tools in this program are designed to enable you to select – or isolate – areas of your photo or image file and then either remove, add to or add an effect to that area only, without affecting the rest of the image.

Because your photo or graphics work will often involve precise adjustments, understanding how to select areas of your image and then add to, remove from or refine that selection is one of the keys to accessing the program's power.

We'll spend considerable time discussing how to select areas and then use those selections in **Chapter 6, Select and Isolate Areas in Your Photos.**

Many of the tools in Photoshop Elements are designed to allow you to select and isolate areas of your photos so that effects are applied only to your selection.

Layers

The biggest difference between a native Photoshop PSD file and virtually all other photo or raster graphic formats is that PSD files can include layers. These layers can include images, text, shapes or effects – some semi-transparent, some opaque – and it's important to understand how their order affects how they interact with each other.

Think of your layers as a stack of images and other elements. The topmost layers will be entirely visible, while the layers below will be visible "behind" the upper layers or quite possibly obscured completely by them.

Layers can be rearranged. They can also be hidden or made partially transparent or even made to react to certain qualities of the layers below them. And, when the background layer is removed, you can even produce non-rectangular graphics that import into Premiere Elements.

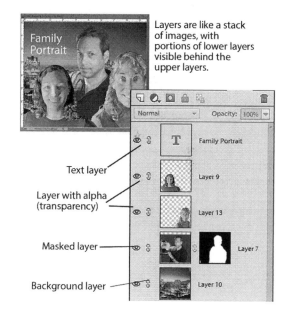

Layers are like a stack of images, with portions of lower layers visible behind the upper layers.

Text layer

Layer with alpha (transparency)

Masked layer

Background layer

Editable text is always on its own layer. Likewise, shapes, until rasterized, are always on their own layers. Layers also give you the advantage of working on your image files in portions, which you can combine, adjust and position in a variety of ways.

In addition, layers and layer groups play a vital role in creating and customizing Movie Menu templates for Premiere Elements, as we'll discuss in **Chapter 13, Advanced Photoshop Elements Tools**.

Alpha

Alpha means, essentially, transparency. However, in order for your graphic file to communicate from one program to another that an area of your image file is transparent, it needs to do so using an "alpha channel." An alpha channel is sort of like a color channel except that, in this case, the color is transparent.

Transparency, represented by default as a checkerboard background in Photoshop Elements, can be carried with the PSD file to Premiere Elements as an "alpha" channel.

Transparent GIFs (see **Chapter 9**) use an alpha channel so that, unlike JPEGs, when used on a web site, GIF graphics can be other-than-a-square shape, allowing the background of the site to display through them.

Likewise, alpha allows you to create graphics for your videos that have non-rectangular shapes or are text only, with no background.

Some graphics formats can carry alpha channels and some can not. We'll show you how to use alpha channels and which graphics file formats can carry alpha channel information in **Create non-square graphics** in **Chapter 9, Work with Photoshop Elements Layers**.

RGB Color

Virtually every graphic or photo you work with in Photoshop Elements will use either the **Grayscale** (black & white) or **RGB** color mode – meaning that every pixel in that image is a mixture of levels of red, green and blue, the three primary colors in video.

Each red, green and blue in each of those pixels is one of 256 levels of intensity, mixing together to produce a total of 16,777,216 possible color combinations. As we work with colors (**Foreground/Background Colors** in **Chapter 5, The Photoshop Elements Toolbox**), you'll see the R, the G and the B and those 256 levels of each at work.

No matter how "real" a digital photo looks, it is merely composed of pixels, each pixel a mix of one of 256 levels of red, green and blue.

Colors can also be designated with hue, saturation and brightness or with a six-digit, alpha-numeric "hex" code.

The **Color Picker** (illustrated on the bottom of the facing page), which launches when you select the option to create a color, builds colors by mixing **red** (R), **green** (G) and **blue** (B) values; or by setting its **hue** (H), **saturation** (S) and **brightness** (B); or by designating the color's six-digit **Hex** value – a color format most often employed when with working with HTML and Web site design.

When the Tool Options Bin is toggled on, the space beneath the Editor will display options for whichever tool you have selected in the Toolbox.

A single button on the Toolbox could hide several tool options, each of which appears as a button on the left side of the Tool Options Bin.

The Tool Options Bin

The **Tool Options Bin** shares the space below the Editor workspace with the **Photo Bin**. To view your **Tool Options** in this area, click on the button in the lower left of the interface, as illustrated above, or simply select a tool.

Virtually every tool you will use in Photoshop Elements is customizable. When you select a tool in the **Toolbox** panel, its settings and options will appear in the **Tool Options Bin**.

Even something as simple as a line drawing tool can include a myriad of options. The line drawing tool, for instance, includes settings for the width of the line and options for adding arrowheads on either or both ends.

Drop-down menus along this bar allow you to select colors and even unusual textures, like glass, plastic and chrome for your shape.

In addition to settings for each tool, the panel also includes options for switching to other tools, so that more than one tool is available under each button on the **Toolbox** panel.

In other words, as illustrated above, when the **Blur** tool is selected in the **Toolbox** panel, the left side of the **Tool Options Bin** displays not only the **Blur** tool but also the **Sharpen** and **Smudge** tools.

Most buttons on the **Toolbox** access two, three or more tools.

The **Tool Options Bin**, then, greatly extends the function and versatility of every tool. And, in **Chapter 5**, we'll discuss the many options available in this bin for each of the individual tools.

What is a native PSD file?

The basic working file for both Photoshop and Photoshop Elements is the **PSD file** (so named, of course, because that's the suffix the file is assigned on your computer).

There are unique characteristics to PSD files – namely that they can include layers, editable text and pseudo-vector shapes. (The word "native" simply means that it's in a native state, the format that all Photoshop files are saved in.)

Photoshop and Photoshop Elements can also export or save your photos and graphics files in a number of other graphics formats, from TIFs to JPEGs to GIFs to PNGs (and a dozen others). These formats, however, don't allow for re-opening layers and text for further editing, as PSDs do.

In the ancient days of technology (like, 15 years ago), Photoshop users had to export their image files to one of these graphics formats in order to import them into another program. But, as Adobe has become the leader in pretty much all facets of print and video production, it's become possible to move graphics files from program to program in their native Photoshop (PSD) state.

In other words, you can import your native PSD files directly from Photoshop Elements into your Premiere Elements project. All of the artwork becomes flattened and the shapes and text become rasterized once the file is added to your video. But any transparent areas in the PSD will remain transparent in your video (which makes them the ideal format for bringing unusually-shaped graphics into Premiere Elements, as we discuss on page 121).

Just as importantly, the original, native PSD file – including the text and layers – remains editable in Photoshop Elements. And , if you are using a PSD file in your Premiere Elements project, whenever you save the file, any updates you've made to the photo or graphic file in Photoshop Elements will automatically be reflected in your graphic in Premiere Elements.

Chapter 2

Get to Know Photoshop Elements 14
What's what and what it does

Welcome to Photoshop Elements – a terrific, affordable photo retouching application and graphics editor that just seems to get better and more feature-packed with every generation!

This is a program that seems to offer more wonderful surprises the deeper you dig into it. It provides not only the obvious tools for cleaning, stylizing and creating images, but also lots of not-so-obvious tools for managing your image files, outputting a variety of print projects and even sharing your work online.

Elements Live

The first time you launch any of the Elements programs, the interface will default to **eLive**, a link directly from the programs to an exclusive web site full of exciting ideas, tutorials and other content especially for Elements users.

eLive (Elements Live) can be accessed from any computer with a live internet connection by clicking the **eLive** link at the top center of the program's interface.

In this chapter, we'll look at the various workspaces in Photoshop Elements – and then we'll dig deeper, looking at the tools Adobe has added in version 14 to make the program even more fun to use.

Launch the Photoshop Elements Editor.

Launch the Elements Organizer.

The Welcome Screen

The **Welcome Screen** is the panel that greets you when you launch the program. (There's a similar **Welcome Screen** for Premiere Elements.)

There are three workspaces that can be launched from the Photoshop Elements **Welcome Screen**.

- **The Photo Editor button launches the main Editor workspace**, where you'll likely do most of your photo and image file editing.

- **The Organizer button launches the Elements Organizer,** a media file management program that also includes tools for cleaning up photos, creating photo projects and sharing your photo and video projects. We discuss the Elements Organizer and its many powerful tools in **Section 3.**

- If you also have Premiere Elements installed on your computer, the launch screen will also include a button for launching the **Video Editor.**

You can, by the way, re-open this **Welcome Screen** at any time by selecting the option under the Photoshop Elements **Help** menu.

Bypass the Welcome Screen

If you'd prefer not to be greeted by the **Welcome Screen,** you'll find options for launching directly into the Editor workspace by clicking on the cog icon at the top right of the screen.

Menu bar   Edit Modes   Panel Bin   Create &
                                                    Share Options

Toolbox

Tool
Options
Bin

Photo
Bin

Layout

The Editor workspace

The Editor workspace in Photoshop Elements 14 is actually *several* photo editing workspaces, each with its own set of tools and features. Its three main workspaces can be accessed by clicking on the tabs at the top center of the interface.

- In the **Quick Edit** workspace, you'll find a simplified set of tools for cleaning up or enhancing your photos. We'll show you how to use the tools in this workspace in **Chapter 3**.

- In the **Guided Edit** workspace, the programs walks you, step by step, through the editing process. The **Guided Edit** tools can do some pretty advanced things too! Not only will the **Guided Edits** walk you through simple clean-up of your photo, but it will also take you through some pretty high-level photo tricks, like creating a photo that seems to be standing on a reflective surface, an image with a **Tilt-Shift** effect applied and a photo in which someone seems to be popping right out of the frame! We'll show you how these cool edits work in **Chapter 4**.

- The **Expert Edit** workspace (illustrated above) includes a comprehensive photo editing and graphics creation **Toolbox**. This is likely where you'll do most of your "serious" editing. It most closely resembles the workspace in the professional version of Photoshop. Needless to say, it's the workspace most of this book is about.

Additionally, the Editor workspace shares a number of tools for creating fun photo pieces with the Elements Organizer under the **Create** and **Share** tabs in the upper right of the interface. We discuss these tools and how to use them in **Chapter 35, Create Fun Pieces** and **Chapter 36, Share Your Photos and Videos**.

By default, all open files are "docked" and appear as tabs along the top of the interface.

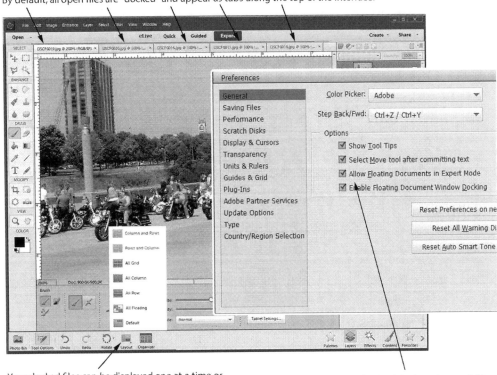

Your docked files can be displayed one at a time or in a variety of arrangements by selecting an option from the Layout menu.

The option to have Floating Windows in your Editor workspace is set in the program's Edit/Preferences.

The Expert Edit Workspace

The **Expert Edit** workspace is modeled after the interface in the professional version of Photoshop.

As illustrated at the top of the facing page, in Photoshop Elements, you have the option of displaying your open photo and image files as a single tabbed set, each photo filling the Editor workspace panel and each open file represented by a a tab at the top of the workspace – or displaying your open photos as floating windows, a stack of open files that you can drag into any position around your workspace as you edit them.

To float your windows, you must have **Enable Floating Documents** checked on the **General** screen under **Edit/Preferences**, as in the illustration above.

The option to display your files in either mode – as well as a number of optional tabbed arrangements – is found under the **Layout** menu button.

The **Layout** menu button appears along the bottom of the interface, as seen in the illustration.

As many veteran Photoshop users know, there are advantages to displaying your photos as floating windows rather than a tabbed set.

By default, all open photos display maximized in the work panel. You can switch between your photos by clicking on the tabs along the top of the panel.

By dragging on its tab, you can undock a photo from the tabbed set and make it a floating window.

To dock or re-dock a floating window back into a tabbed set, drag it to the top of the tabbed set by its docking header (the top of the frame) until it becomes semi-transparent and a bright blue line displays around the photo. When you release your mouse button, the photo will dock with the rest of the tabbed set.

For instance, when your files are displayed as floating windows, you can copy images, portions of images and even entire layers from one image file to another simply by dragging these elements from one open file to another.

As in the illustration above, there are two ways to switch between displaying your photos as a docked, tabbed set and displaying them as floating windows:

- **Set the Arrange menu to All Floating.** When you click on the **Arrange** button and select **All Floating**, all of your photo files will display as floating windows.

- **Undock a photo from the tabbed set by dragging on its tab**. When you pull the photo file by its tab from the others in a tabbed set, it becomes a floating window.

Floating windows, by the way, *always float over tabbed photo files*. This means that, in order to get to the photos in your tabbed, docked set, you may have to either minimize any floating windows or drag them out of the way.

To dock or re-dock a photo into a tabbed set, simply drag the floating window by its docking header (the top of the window) to the top of the Editor workspace. When the photo file becomes semi-transparent (as illustrated above) release your mouse button and the photo will dock to the tabbed set.

Photoshop Elements can optionally display Rulers and Guides over your image files to help you with placement and measurement of your imagery. To create a guide line, drag onto your photo from one of the rulers.

Guides and Rulers

Optionally, Photoshop Elements will display **Guides** over your image files. These horizontal and vertical lines don't show up on your final piece, of course. But they can be a great help for placing elements and text and ensuring that they are properly lined up.

The program can also display **Rulers** which, like **Guides**, can be very helpful in measuring and placing your imagery.

To display **Rulers**, select the option from the **View** drop-down on the Photoshop Elements Menu Bar.

To create a new **Guide**, click and drag onto your photo from one of the **Rulers** running along the tops and sides of your image files. (Drag from the **Ruler** along the top of your photo to create a horizontal guide or from the **Ruler** along the left of your photo to create a vertical guide.)

To toggle between displaying and hiding the guides on your image files, press **Ctrl+;** on a PC or ⌘**+;** on a Mac or select the option from the **View** menu.

The Toolbox

Along the left side of this workspace is the program's **Toolbox** (as illustrated on the left). The tools in this panel serve a number of functions, from selecting areas in your image file to creating graphics and text to patching and cloning areas of your images. As each tool is selected, that tool's individual settings are displayed in the **Tool Options Bin** that runs along the bottom of the editing workspace.

We'll spend considerable time getting to know the tools in the **Toolbox** and how to use their settings and options in **Chapter 5, Get to Know the Photoshop Elements Toolbox**.

The Panel Bin

To the right of the editing workspace is a column known as the **Panel Bin**, which includes a number of tools and panels that vary, depending on whether you're in **Quick Edit, Guided Edit** or **Expert** mode.

When you first open the program's Expert edit workspace, this **Panel Bin** will be in **Basic Workspace** mode. In **Basic Workspace** mode, you can view the **Layers, Effects, Graphics** or **Favorites** panels in this bin by clicking on the buttons in the lower right of the program's interface.

If you click on the arrow to the right of the **More** button, you will find the option to set the **Panel Bin** to **Custom Workspace**, which opens the **Layers, Effects** and **Graphics** panels (and their respective sub-panels) in the **Panel Bin** in a tabbed set, as illustrated below

You can click and drag on any tab in the **Panel Bin** to make its panel a separate, floating panel. (It's common for experienced Photoshop Elements users to make the **Layers** panel a floating panel so that it is always available.)

Clicking directly on the **More** button will open an additional bundle of tabbed panels, including **Info, Navigation, History**, etc. These panels can likewise be accessed by clicking on the appropriate tab or, by dragging on the tab, can be made a separate, floating panel.

In default Basic Worskpace mode, buttons along the Action Bar access individual panels. Clicking the arrow to the right of the More button allows you to switch to Custom Workspace mode, in which more panels are available in a tabbed set.

The panels of the tabbed Panel Bin in Custom Workspace mode.

Layers   Picture Effects   Filter Effects   Style Effects   Backgrounds & Graphics   Create Options

When the Photo Bin option is selected, the area below the Editor worskpace wil display all of the photos you have open in your Photoshop Elements editor, all of the photos you have selected in the Elements Organizer's Media Browser or any photos you've saved to individual Organizer Albums.

The Photo Bin

Running along the bottom of the Editor workspace and sharing space with the **Tool Options Bin** is a small but powerful panel known as the **Photo Bin**.

When the **Photo Bin** button is selected in the lower left of the program's interface, all photos and image files you have open in your Editor workspace will appear as thumbnails in this bin.

To open a file in your **Photo Bin** in the Editor workspace, **double-click** on its thumbnail in the **Photo Bin**.

Although this is the default and most common way to use the **Photo Bin**, it is certainly not its only function. The **Photo Bin** also interfaces with a number of other workspaces.

To access and change the **Photo Bin's** display options, click on the bin's drop-down menu, which reads **Show Open Files** by default, as in the illustration above.

> **Show Open Files.** Displays, as thumbnails, all of the image files you currently have open in your **Editor** workspace.

> **Show Files Selected in the Organizer.** If you have both Photoshop Elements and the Elements Organizer open, and you have files selected in the Organizer's **Media Browser**, selecting this option displays those files in the **Photo Bin**. These photos or image files can then be launched in the Editor workspace by **double-clicking** on them.

> **Organizer Albums.** If you've created **Albums** in the Organizer (see **Chapter 34, Manage Your Files with The Organizer**), you can select the option to display the photos in a particular **Album**.

What's new in Photoshop Elements 14?

Adobe continues to build out the world's most popular consumer photo editor with some nice, new enhancement.

New presets for graphic sizes

You'll find a number of new options available when creating a graphic or Photoshop Elements from scratch in version 14.

To access these presets, select **File/New/Blank File** and then select the **Web, Mobile App Design** or **Iconography** option from the **Preset** drop-down menu. In each of these categories you'll find a number of presets under the **Size** menu for creating graphics for icons for mobile device and phone apps.

Quick editing enhancements

A **Straighten** tool (see page 85) has been added to the **Quick Edit** toolkit. Additionally, when in **Quick Editing**, the **Effects** panel will display nearly a dozen categories of **Auto Smart Looks**, each with a number of variations, stylish effects which can be applied to your photo with just a click.

We'll look at these new features in depth along with the other tools available in the **Quick Edit** Workspace in **Chapter 3, Quick Fixes**.

Redesigned Guided Edits interface

The **Guided Edits** workspace has been completely redesigned in Photoshop Elements 14. The new interface displays the **Guided Edits** library as a series of before-and-after thumbnails, making it easier than ever to see the results of each effect or process.

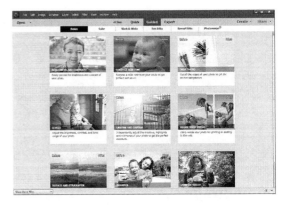

A cool new **Guided Edit** is the **Speed Effect**, which adds a motion trail behind any person or object you select in your photo.

We'll show you the interface and explain each effect available in **Chapter 4, Guided Edits.**

Precise selections with Selection Edges tool

Further improvements have been made to the **Selection Tool**, making the selection of even fine details like hair and feathers even easier.

We'll show you this tool at work on page 64 of **Chapter 5, Get to Know the Photoshop Elements Toolbox.**

New photo enhancement tools

Two new photo cleanup tools have been added to the **Enhancement** menu in version 14.

The **Haze Remover** increases contrast and sharpens your pictures, effectively removing the effects of fog and haze in your pictures.

Shake Reduction sharpens your pictures, effectively removing unwanted blur caused motion or shakiness.

We show you how to use these tools in **Chapter 8, Correct Color and Lighting.**

Menu font size control in Preferences

To make Photoshop Elements' menus readable on a wider range of higher density monitor resolutions, the program also includes preferences for controlling the size of the text on the program's interface.

You'll find these settings (on PCs only) under **Edit/ Preferences**, on the **Display & Cursor** page, under **High Density Displays**.

In most cases, you can simply leave the **IU Scale Factor** set to **Automatic**. However, it can also be set to manually to **Small (100%)** or, for higher resolution monitors , to **Large (200%)**. (You'll need to restart the program in order for the new settings to take effect.)

Organizer improvements

Finally, Adobe continues to tune up its Organizer, the file management tool bundled with Premiere Elements and Photoshop Elements.

You'll find even more tools for filing and retrieving your photos and video files, including much more advanced tools for categorizing your photos by location and by the faces of people that appear in your pictures.

We discuss this terrific little program and all of its tools in **Chapters 34, 35 and 36** of **Section 3** of this book.

Need some Basic Training?

Need more help learning the basics of Photoshop Elements?

Check out my free tutorial series **Basic Training for Photoshop Elements** at Muvipix.com.

This simple, eight-part series will teach you the basics of photo resolution and show you how to adjust lighting and correct color in your photos, work with layers, add effects, scan your pictures and even share your photos and videos online. And, yes, it's absolutely free!

To see the series, just go to http://Muvipix.com and type "Basic Training for Photoshop Elements" in the product search box. (We also offer Basic Training tutorials for other products, including Premiere Elements.)

And while you're there, why not drop by the Community forum and say hi! We'd love to have you become a part of our growing city. Hope to see you there!

Adobe Photoshop Elements

Part I
Quick and Guided
Photo Editing

Simple, Quick Fixes

The Quick Fix Toolbox

Quick Lighting, Sharpening and Color Fixes

Chapter 3

Quick Fixes

Easy ways to touch up photos

In addition to its more professional photo touch-up and graphic design tools, Photoshop Elements includes a number of simplified and semi-automatic tools for fixing, enhancing and adjusting your image files.

Many of these are Quick Fixes, with simplified controls and automatic functions.

The Quick Fix Work Area

View   Hand Tool   Touch-Up Tools   Set Before & After View   Smart Looks

Tool Options

The Expert Editor workspace is a full-featured toolkit for fixing your photos, correcting color and creating graphic and photographic effects.

However, if you just need a simple fix – or if you're intimidated by the multitude of tools and options in the Photoshop Elements Expert workspace – the program also offers simplified **Quick Fix** tools for editing your photos and graphic files.

The **Quick Fix** workspace is launched by clicking the **Quick** tab at the top center of the Photoshop Elements interface.

To the left of the workspace is the **Quick Fix Toolbox**, described on the facing page, a simplified version of the **Expert** workspace **Toolbox**.

To the right of the workspace are simplified adjustment controls for changing the color, lighting, color temperature and sharpness of your photos. These adjustments can be made using sliders or by using the very intuitive **Quick Fix Preview** tool, as described on page 31.

A drop-down menu in the upper left of the workspace allows you to set your view as **Before Only, After Only** or **Before and After**.

To leave the **Quick Fix** workspace once you have finished applying any fixes to your image file, click the **Expert** button at the top center of the interface.

You may then choose to save the changes you've made to the image file or discard them.

The Quick Fix Toolbox

The **Quick Fix** work area includes a number of tools for viewing and manipulating your image file. The tools on the **Toolbox** to the left of the interface work similarly to their counterparts in the **Expert Editor Toolbox**. (For more information, see **Chapter 5, Get to Know the Photoshop Elements Toolbox**.)

Zoom Tool

Hand Tool

Quick Selection Tool

Red-Eye Removal

Teeth Whitener

Straighten Tool

Add Text

Spot Healing Brush

Crop Tool

Move Tool

The Zoom Tool (magnifying glass) controls your view.

The Hand Tool allows you to drag your image around in your viewing area.

The Quick Selection Tool selects areas on your image file for manipulation by "painting" to define the selected area. When an area is selected, any lighting or color adjustments will apply only to that selected area.

Red-Eye Removal removes that annoying red reflection eyes sometimes display when you shoot with a flash in a dimly-lit room. Applying it is as simple as selecting the tool and clicking on the red pupils in your picture, as discussed on page 65.

The Teeth Whitener is a **Smart Brush Tool** (as discussed on page 67 of **Chapter 5, Get to Know the Photoshop Elements Toolbox**). Drag your mouse to **Quick Select** the teeth in your photo and the program will automatically bleach and brighten them.

The Straighten Tool can be used to level out your picture (as discussed on page 85 of **Chapter 5**).

The Text Tool will add text to your photo. We discuss adding and working with text on your image files in **Chapter 10**.

The Spot Healing Brush automatically removes blemishes and other flaws using a very effective **Content Aware Fill** system. Removing a blemish is as simple as selecting this tool and then dragging over the blemish, as we discuss in more detail on page 65.

The Crop Tool can be used to crop and reshape your image.

The Move Tool is used to move or drag the elements, selections or text in your image files to new positions.

The Teeth Whitening Tool will bleach and brighten a selected area of your photo.

Drag the Teeth Whitening Selection Tool to define the whitening area.

Use the Add and Remove options to add to or remove from your selected area.

The Tool Options allow you to set the size, shape and hardness of the edge of your selection.

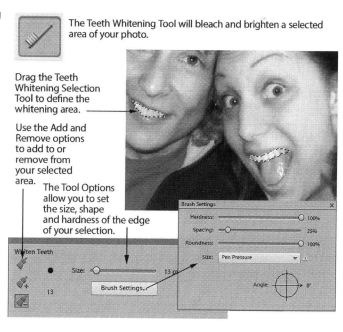

Smart Looks

By default, or when the **Effects** button is selected in the lower right of the **Quick Edit** workspace, the panel bin will on the right of the **Quick Edit** workspace will display the new **Smart Looks** library. **Smart Looks** apply color schemes, tints or filters to your photo with a simple double-click.

Each **Smart Look** category thumbnail will display a preview of its look applied to your photo. Clicking on a **Smart Look** category will open it to reveal variations of this look, as illustrated to the right.

To apply a **Smart Look** to your photo, simply **double-click** on the thumbnail displaying the effect you want to apply in the **Effects** panel.

To remove an effect, apply a different **Quick Effect** or click the ⌂ **Reset** button at the top of the panel.

Adjustments, Borders and Textures

In addition to the cleanup and enhancement tools in the **Quick Edit** workspace, Adobe has included sets of adjustments, borders and textures that can be added to your photos simply by **double-clicking** on them.

Switch between these option panels by clicking on the buttons in the lower right of the interface, as illustrated to the right.

Quick Adjustments

The **Quick Adjustments tools** in the panel bin along the right side of the **Quick Edit** interface (activated by clicking the **Adjustments** button in the lower right of the **Quick Edit** workspace) offer easy, intuitive ways to correct and adjust the color, lighting and sharpness of your photos.

Smart Fix combines adjustments for brightness, contrast and sharpness.

Exposure simulates the adjustments your camera makes, brightening a picture that is too dark or darkening a picture that is too light.

Levels adjusts the saturation and contrast of your picture's color for either shadows, midtones or highlights.

Color adjusts saturation (amount of color), hue (tint of color) and vibrance (intensity of color).

Balance adjusts your photo's color temperature (more blue vs. more red) or tint.

Sharpness increases the sharpness of your image.

The tools in this panel include both a slider, for increasing or decreasing intensity of the adjustment, and a **Quick Fix Preview** tool, which allows you to make an adjustment simply by clicking on one of the variations in the tic tac toe-like interface, as illustrated on the right. (You can even preview a change just by hovering your mouse over any of the variations.)

Some adjustments also include an **Auto** button for making automatic color or lighting corrections.

To undo an adjustment, click on the center square in the **Quick Fix Preview** panel or click the ⌂ **Reset** button at the top of the panel.

If you have used the **Quick Selection Tool** , as described on page 29, to select an area or areas in your photo, your adjustments will be applied only to the selected area.

Quick Textures

Quick Textures apply texture filters to the photo displayed in your **Quick Edit** workspace.

To apply a texture, simply **double-click** on the thumbnail displaying the effect you want to apply.

To remove a texture, apply a different **Quick Texture** or click the ⌂ **Reset** button at the top of the panel.

Quick Frames

Quick Frames create borders around the photo displayed in your **Quick Edit** workspace.

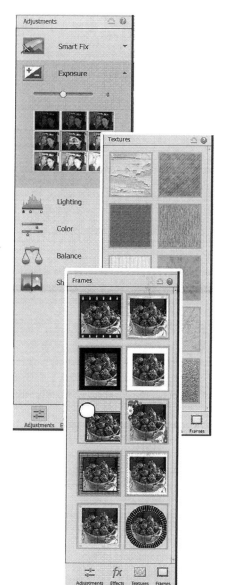

Organizer Instant Fixes

The Elements Organizer includes a similar set of **Instant Fixes** for doing a quick clean-up of your photos. You can access them by clicking the **Instant Fix** button in the lower right of the Organizer interface.

To add a border, simply **double-click** on the thumbnail displaying the border you want to apply.

To remove a border, apply a different **Quick Frame** or click the 🔺 **Reset** button at the top of the panel.

To finalize any new effect, border or texture, click the **Expert** tab at the top center of the program's interface.

Once you are in the **Expert** workspace, you might note that the program has duplicated your original photo, saved it as a new layer and applied your selected effect or border to it. The program has done this so that your Quick change is not irreversible. To remove a **Quick Effect, Texture** or **Frame** and revert to your original photo, simply delete this new layer.

Basic Edits

Color Edits

Black & White Edits

Fun Edits

Special Effects

Photomerge Edits

Chapter 4

Guided Edits

Photo adjustments and cool tricks, one step at a time

Guided Edits, as the name implies, are sometimes very high level photo effects made simple through wizards that walk you through each step of the process.

Guided Edits allow you to get professional-looking results with only a basic understanding of the program.

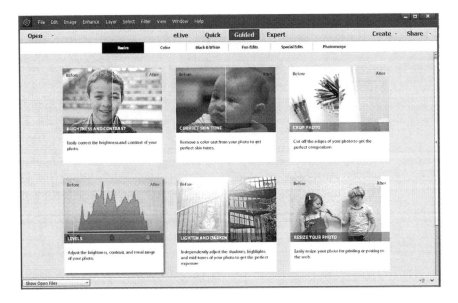

The Guided Edits workspace is opened by clicking the **Guided** tab in the top center of the Photoshop Elements workspace.

Guided Edits, as the name implies, are simplified editing tools that take you step-by-step through a series of adjustments, cleaning up your image or creating special photo effects..

Photoshop Elements walks you through the entire process – explaining how each tool works, offering an automatic fix if available and then giving you the option of either keeping the changes (clicking **Done**) or rejecting the changes and returning to the main menu (**Cancel**).

If you're at all intimidated by the **Expert Edit** workspace, a **Guided Edit** may be the way to go.

The **Guided Edits** appear in six categories, each available by clicking the sub-tab at the top of the interface. Each edit's effect is illustrated with a dynamic before-and-after thumbnail.

Basics clean up your photo's composition or correct its color.

Color effects apply special effects to your photo, giving it an intriguing or surreal look.

Black & White effects desaturate some or all of the color in your photos.

Fun Edits create some very advanced effects, making people in your pictures, for instance, seem to pop out of the photo frame or making your photo look as though it's made from a collage of snapshots.

Special Effects create camera-like photo effects include vignetting, depth of field and tilt/shift.

Photomerge effects combine imagery from two or more photos to add or remove elements to a scene.

Once you've worked through a **Guided Edit**, you'll have the choice of clicking **Done** or **Cancel**.

If you've applied an effect and you'd like to remove it, you can click the **Undo** button in the lower left of the interface or press **Ctrl+z** (⌘+z on a Mac) on your keyboard or by clicking the **Reset** button at the top of the panel.

Basics

Like the **Quick Fixes** discussed in **Chapter 3**, **Basics** are designed to offer you simple workspaces for doing color adjustments, cropping and sharpening.

Brightness and Contrast adjust the blackest and whitest levels of your photo and the contrast between them. This edit includes an **Auto Fix** adjustment button.

Correct Skin Tones is a step-by-step walkthrough of the tool described on page 116.

Crop Photo walks you through the process of trimming down or reshaping your photo.

Levels adjusts the dark, light and mid-tone levels of the red, green and blue in your photo (A similar effect to **Brightness and Contrast**). However, rather than physically changing the photo, these adjustments are made to an **Adjustment Layer** (as described on page 119).

Lighten and Darken opens tools for adjusting your photo's **Shadow**, **Highlights** and **Midtones**.

Resize Your Photos guides you through the process of optimizing the size of your photos for posting to the web or printing.

Rotate and Straighten guides you through the process of straightening a crooked photo.

Sharpen increases the contrast between pixels, sharpening the look of your photo.

The Vignette Effect makes your photo look as if it were shot with a pinhole camera, brighter in the center and darker around the sides.

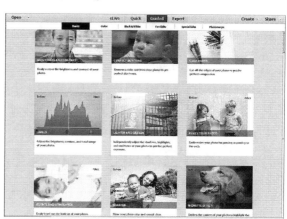

Color Guided Edits

Color edits increase or reduce the intensity or vibrance of the color in your photos.

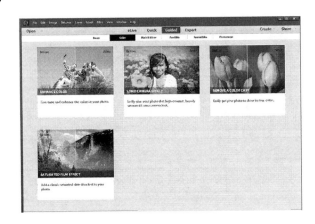

Enhance Colors offers tools for adjusting your photo's **Hue, Saturation** and **Lightness**. This edit includes an **Auto Fix** adjustment button.

The **Lomo Camera Effect** makes your photos look as if they were shot with a LOMO, a primitive, Soviet-made camera whose weird color and exposure results have given it something of a cult following.

Remove Color Cast guides you through the process of correcting the color in your photo.

The **Saturated Film Effect** enriches the color in your photo.

Black & White Edits

Black & White edits guide you through the process of removing all or some of the color in your photos.

Black and White strips the color from your photo, then enriches the black & white based on the preset you select.

B&W Color Pop removes all of the color from a photo except the color you designate.

B&W Selection strips the color from the areas in your photo that you designate with your **Selection Brush**.

High Key washes the color out of your photo and softens its focus to give your picture an ethereal look.

Line Drawing creates the effect that your photo has been hand-drawn in pencil or charcoal.

Low Key increases the black levels in your photo, giving it a dark, mysterious look.

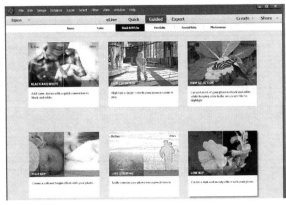

Fun Edits

The **Fun Edits** category of **Guided Edits** includes fix fun walkthroughs for creating highly-stylized photographic effects.

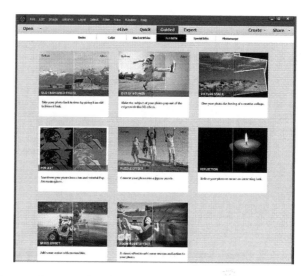

> **Old Fashioned Photo** makes your picture look like an old black & white photo.
>
> The **Out of Bounds Effect** lets you crop your photo, excluding certain elements, so that, say, a person's head, hand or foot extends beyond the borders of the picture. Instructions for using this tool are described below.

Picture Stack breaks your photo into four, eight or twelve photos, making your picture look as if it's been pieced together from several photo segments. For more information on how to use this tool, see page 40.

Pop Art creates a colorful photo series, a la Andy Warhol's famous Marilyn Monroe portrait.

Puzzle Effect cuts your photo into a jigsaw-like pattern – which you can then move or remove, one piece at a time. We'll show you how it works on page 40.

> **Reflection** creates a reflection of your picture, which you can customize so that it appears to be shining off a floor below your photo, a sheet of glass or even rippling water.

The **Speed Effect**, new to version 14, adds trails behind a person or object in a photo, making them appear to be flying across the scene.

Zoom Burst Effect guides you through adding a zoom blur around the focus of your photo.

The "Out of Bounds" Guided Edit effect

Creating an **Out of Bounds Effect** involves basically two steps. The first is redefining the frame of your photo, which will be cropped down from its current size. The second is designating which elements in the photo will not be affected by this cropping.

For my example, I've chosen an action shot of a young girl doing a tae kwon do high kick. To make this shot more interesting, we'll crop the photo's frame around the girl so that her kick seems to be popping right out of the picture.

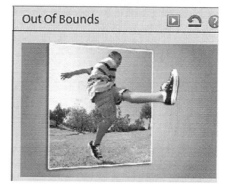

Out Of Bounds

1 With the photo open in the **Guided Edits** workspace, select **Out of Bounds** on the option panel.

The **Panel Bin** will display the **Out of Bounds Effect Guided Edits** options panel.

At the top of this panel is a photo showing an example of the finished effect. If you roll your mouse over it, you'll see the "before" picture that the **Out of Bounds** effect was created from.

2 Click the **Add a Frame** button.

A box will appear over your photo. Drag the corner handles of this box to define what will be your photo's newly cropped frame.

When this cropping box is in your desired position, lock it in place by clicking the green check mark or by pressing the **Enter** key on your keyboard.

The photo will now appear with its new cropping displayed as a semi-opaque overlay, as illustrated above.

3 Click the **Quick Selection Tool** button on the **Guided Edits** panel. (You may need to scroll down the palette to see this button.)

As we show you on page 63 of **Chapter 5, Get to Know the Photoshop Elements Toolbox**, the Quick Selection Tool works like a paintbrush, selecting areas as you "paint" over them.

Click and drag the tool over the elements in your photo you'd like to extend beyond the photo's newly cropped frame. In my case, this will be the girl and her foot. As you drag the tool over your photo, your selected area will be displayed with a moving dotted line around it (commonly called "marching ants").

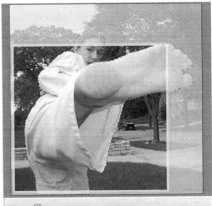

If it adds more than you'd like to your selection, you can always un-select these areas later.

In the **Tool Options Bin** below your photo, you'll find the settings for the **Quick Selection Tool**.

The **Brush** settings allow you to set the size of the tool's selection brush. (You can also quickly widen or narrow your brush's size by pressing the **[** and **]** keys on your keyboard.)

To add to your selection, select the **+** tool from the **Tool Options Bin** or hold down your **Shift** key as you continue to paint with the **Quick Selection Tool**.

To de-select a selected area, select the **-** tool in the **Tool Options Bin** or hold down the **Alt/Option** key on your keyboard as you paint with the **Quick Selection Tool**.

4   When you're satisfied with your selection, click the **Out of Bounds Effect** button on the **Panel Bin**.

The program will crop your photo per your settings, except for the areas you've selected.

As you can see on the **Guided Edit** panel, there are some additional effects which can be added to your photo effect in this workspace, including a **Drop Shadow** and a **Gradient background**.

If, after you've clicked **Done,** your results still seem a bit rough, you can return to the **Expert Editor** and use some of its tools (the **Eraser**, for instance) to clean up and refine the edges of the effect.

If, in **Expert Edit**, you look at the **Layers** panel, you'll see that this simple trick actually involves a number of high-end tools and effects, including **Layer Masks** and multiple copies of your photo on separate layers.

In fact, if you look at one of the bottom-most layers, you'll see that your **Original Image** is still down there, unchanged.

Just in case you want to throw out the whole effect and start again from scratch!

Create a Picture Stack

A fairly automatic effect, the **Picture Stack Guided Edit** breaks your photo into four, eight or twelve pieces, making it look as if it's assembled from a collage of several photos.

1   With the photo open in the **Guided Edits** workspace, select **Picture Stack** on the option panel.

    The **Panel Bin** will display the **Picture Stack Guided Edits** panel.

2   Customize your effect.

    Select the **Number of Pictures** you would like your photo broken into, the **Border Width** you'd like around each picture and the **Background Color** the photos will be stacked on.

    Click **Done**.

The Photo Stack Guided Edit turns your photo into a photo collage.

Create a Puzzle Effect

The **Puzzle Effect Guided Edit** walks you through the semi-automatic process of overlaying your photos with a jigsaw puzzle-like pattern – and then, for added effect, gives you the option of moving or removing the individual pieces!

1   With the photo open in the **Guided Edits** workspace, select **Puzzle Effect** on the option panel.

    The **Panel Bin** will display the **Puzzle Effect Guided Edits** panel.

2   Click to select your puzzle piece size.

    As illustrated on the following page, you have the option of creating a puzzle with small, medium or large pieces.

Select a puzzle piece with the Magic Wand Tool.

When you click the Extract Piece button, the piece separates from the rest of the "puzzle."

The tool will overlay a jigsaw puzzle pattern over your photo.

3 Select a puzzle piece.

Click on the **Select Puzzle Piece/Magic Wand** tool on the panel.

When you click on the photo with this **Magic Wand** tool, it will select a puzzle piece.

4 Extract a puzzle piece.

Click on the **Extract Puzzle Piece** button.

The tool will separate the selected piece from the rest of the puzzle.

With the **Move Tool** you can then drag the piece to any location or, by dragging around its corner handles, rotate the piece.

Note that a drop shadow automatically applied to your photo gives the illusion that you're working with three-dimensional puzzle pieces.

Continue to remove and reposition as many pieces as you'd like.

5 Clean up the extra lines.

If you remove two adjacent pieces from the photo, the outline between them remains in the empty space. Click to select the **Eraser Tool** and clean up any unwanted lines.

Special Effects

Special Effect Guided Edits change the look of your photo in intriguing or surreal ways. As with all **Guided Edits**, the program walks you through the process of creating them, step-by-step. In addition, this workspace includes walk-throughs of some advanced photo correction and re-compositing tools, including the **Recompose** tool (discussed in detail on page 81).

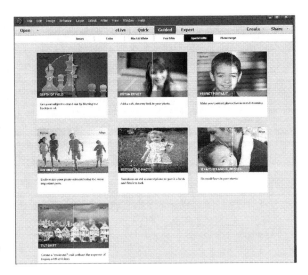

Depth of Field sharpens the subject in your photo and blurs the background, giving your photo the illusion of being shot with a very short depth of field. We demonstrate this edit on page 43.

The Orton Effect softens your photo to give it a gently blurred, dreamy look. You can increase or decrease the effect by custom-adjusting the blur, noise and brightness levels.

Perfect Portrait is a simple, all-purpose guided cleanup with step-by-step instructions for softening or sharpening your photo, adjusting contrast, healing blemishes, removing red-eyes and enhancing eyes and eyebrows.

Recompose is used to move people or elements in a photo closer together without changing their shapes. This tool is discussed in detail on page 81.

Restore Old Photo guides you through the process of repairing a worn photo.

Scratches and Blemishes includes tools for softening flaws and erasing blemishes.

Tilt-Shift, illustrated to the right, adds a blur to the top and bottom of a photo shot from an oblique angle, creating the illusion of exaggerated depth of field and making your photo look as if it were composed of miniatures.

The Tilt-Shift effect gives your scenic photos the exaggerated depth of field of photos of miniatures.

The Depth of Field Guided Edit

The **Depth of Field Guided Edit** uses a blur and layer mask to create a focused center and blurred background for your photo.

To use the **Depth of Field Guided Edit**:

1 With the photo open in the **Guided Edits** workspace, select **Depth of Field** on the option panel.

2 On the **Depth of Field** panel, select either the **Simple** or **Custom** workspace.

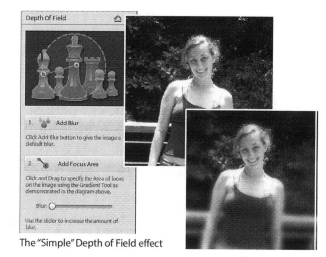

The "Simple" Depth of Field effect

A **Simple Depth of Field** effect will add a blur around the outside of your photo, leaving it unaffected in the center, as in the illustration to the right.

If you select the Simple option.

3 Click the **Add Blur** button, as illustrated above.

Your entire photo will blur.

4 Click the **Add Focus Area** button.

Click on the focal object in your photo, then drag. The program will mask the effect on your focal object, removing the blur from it – then gradually add blur around the rest of your photo, based on the area defined with your mouse drag.

In Custom Depth of Field mode, use the Quick Selection Tool to draw a selection around your focal object...

...then click Add Blur. The program will automatically add a blur outside of the selection. You can increase or decrease the blur level with the slider.

In a **Custom Depth of Field** effect, illustrated at the bottom of page 43, you designate the area of your photo that the blur will not apply.

If you select the Custom option:

3   Click the **Quick Selection Tool** button.

Drag the tool over the subject of your photo, "painting" to select the area you want to keep in focus.

4   Click the **Add Blur** button.

The area outside of your selection will blur.

If you'd like, you can increase the level of blur around your focal point by dragging the slider at the bottom of the panel.

5   Click **Done** to finish your photo effect.

Photomerge

Photomerge Guided Edits combine elements from two or more photos in order to either create an enhanced picture or to create a brand new photo composition.

Photomerge Compose is a tool for grabbing elements from one photo and placing them into another. We explore it in detail on page 45.

Photomerge Exposure is a tool for compositing the best-lit elements from two or more photos. We demonstrate it on page 47.

Photomerge Faces is a tool for creating a perfect portrait by combining the best elements from several photos of the same face.

Photomerge Group Shot is a tool for creating a composite shot in which a person or people who appear in one photo can be painted into another.

Photomerge Scene Cleaner combines elements from two photos of the same scene, borrowing the best elements from each shot, so that you can remove unwanted elements – or even unwanted *people* – from an otherwise perfect shot!

Photomerge Panorama arranges several photos of and around a scene to create a panoramic photo. We look at it in more detail on page 49.

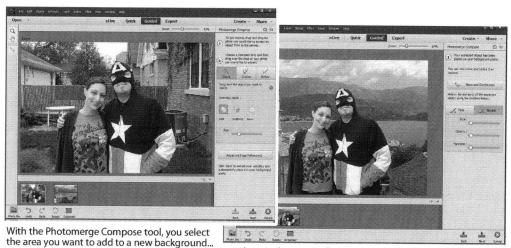

With the Photomerge Compose tool, you select the area you want to add to a new background...

...then, in the new background, you can refine your selection and tint the pasted imagery to match the background.

Paste between photos with Photomerge Compose

Photomerge Compose makes cutting people or other elements from one photo and pasting them into another very easy.

To use **Photomerge Compose**, first ensure that you have at least two photos open in your Photoshop Elements Editor workspace.

1   With the photos you want to cut and paste between open in the Photoshop Elements Editor, select the **Guided** tab and select **Photomerge**, then **Photomerge Compose**. If you have more than one photo open in the Editor, you'll be prompted to select the two you want to **Compose**.

2   Following the prompt, drag the photo you want to cut people or elements from up into the **Compose** workspace, as illustrated above.

3   Follow the prompts in the panel to the right of the workspace to draw a selection around the people or elements you want to cut from your photo using the panel's **Quick**, **Outline** and **Refine** tools individually or in combination.

The best workflow is to do most or your selection work using the **Quick Selection** tool (page 63). By painting along the edges of your selection with the **Outline** tool, you can further define it. Then, if further shaping of the selection is necessary, use the **Push** feature on the **Refine** tool (see page 64).

The size of your selection tool's brush can be controlled with the slider on the tool's panel or by using the bracket open **[** and bracket closed **]** buttons on your keyboard. The **Snap** level controls how automatically the selection tools follow color breaks in your picture.

If the **Mode** on the panel is set to **Add**, any selections you make will be added to the current selection. If the **Mode** is set to **Subtract**, the selection tools will remove from the current selection.

4   To refine your selection, click the **Advanced Edge Refinement** button on the panel.

In the **Advanced Edge Refinement** panel, you can **Set Background As Black**, **White**, **Transparent** or as your **Source** Image (the default). Setting your background to display as a different color can help you see more clearly if you've made a good, accurate selection.

With the background set to **Black, White** or **Transparent**, you can continue to use the panel's selection tools to refine your selection.

5   When you've got a good, accurate selection, click the **Refine Edge** button.

As discussed on page 64, the **Refine Edge** tool can be used to detect and select fine elements (like hair) as well as to create a slightly feathered, more natural edge so that your cut-and-pasted element won't look so cut-and-pasted.

When you're happy your selection, click the **Next** button at the bottom of the panel. Your cut image will be automatically pasted into your second photo.

But the beauty of the **Compose** tool is that – because the transparency behind your selection is created with a **Mask** (see page 128) rather than by actually deleting the old background – you can continue to refine your selection even after you've pasted it into its new background. You can even re-add things that you've deleted!

6   Click the **Move and Resize Tool** button to scale and position your pasted image onto its new background.

If necessary, you can further refine your selection by using the **Reveal Brush** and **Hide Brush**.

Paint over your selection with the **Reveal Brush** to add to your selected area. For instance, if in cutting and pasting from your original image you accidentally omitted your subject's ear, using the **Reveal Brush**, you can "paint" the ear back into your pasted area.

Paint over your selection with the **Hide Brush** to remove elements you inadvertently cut and pasted over.

Sliders under these brushes control the **Size, Opacity** (transparency) and **Hardness** (of the edge) of the elements you add or remove.

When you're happy with the results, click **Next**.

7   On the final panel for this tool, adjustments will be made to the color of your pasted element so that it is more naturally integrated into its new background.

When you click the **Auto Match Color Tone** button, the program will match the color tone of your pasted element to the background.

You may also manually tweak the **Luminance, Contrast, Color Intensity** and **Saturation** using the sliders.

When you're happy with the results, click the **Done** button.

Combine the best-lit elements from two photos with Photomerge Exposure

Another **Photomerge** tool is **Photomerge Exposure**, a tool for taking the best elements of two or more photos and combining them into one great-looking picture.

This is a terrific tool for combining the best parts of several shots taken with a flash at night or in which the subject is standing in front of a window or other brightly-lit background.

It works similarly to **Photomerge Faces** and **Photomerge Scene Cleaner** in that you select acceptable elements in each photo and the program combines them into a best-of composite photo.

Above are two photos. The first was shot with a flash – lighting the foreground but over-lighting the view out the windows. The second photo was shot with natural lighting, the result being that the background (the view through the windows) is perfectly exposed but the furniture in the foreground is too dark.

1   Open both of photos in the Editor workspace.

    You need at least two photos to create a **Photomerge Exposure** – although you can potentially use several photos, combining the best elements from each to create your **Final** photo.

2   Select the Photoshop Elements **Guided** tab and select **Photomerge**, then **Photomerge Exposure**.

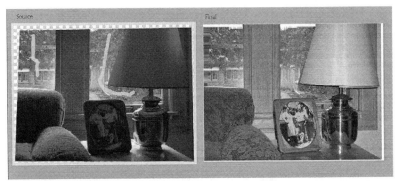

It only took a couple of scribbles drawn through the window area to select these elements for Photomerging onto my Background photo. The second photo shows the results of the Photomerging of elements.

In **Automatic** mode, which the program opens into by default, **Photomerge** will automatically make its best guess at the ideal blending of the two photos. Sometimes **Automatic** mode will give you the results you need – although it may also benefit from some tweaking by moving the sliders in either **Simple Blending** or **Smart Blending Mode**.

I prefer to work in **Manual** mode. It gives me more control of the result. So I clicked on the **Manual** tab on the **Photomerge Exposure** panel.

3 The program will use the first photo in the **Photo Bin** (below the Editor workspace) as my **Source**. The **Source** is the photo that **Photomerge** will draw its new elements from.

If you'd prefer to use another open photo as your source, drag it to the first position in the **Photo Bin**.

4 If necessary, drag the photo you want to use as your **Final** – the photo that my **Source's** elements will be added to – from the **Photo Bin** to the **Final** window.

Manually align your photos for Photomerging

If the program does not automatically align your **Foreground** and **Background** photos, you can manually align them by selecting the **Alignment Tool** under the **Advanced Options** button on the **Photomerge** panel.

When the **Alignment Tool** is selected, three alignment points will appear on your **Background** photo. Place those three alignment points on key reference points in the photo. Then click to select the **Foreground** photo. When three similar alignment points appear on it, move them to the exact same reference points as you did on the **Background** photo and click **Align**.

Photomerge automatically adjusted the positions of similar photos to line them up as closely as possible.

5   With the panel's **Pencil Tool**, indicated the elements on my **Source** photo that you'd like to add to your **Final**, as in the illustration on the facing page. (I designated that the **Source's** views out the windows be added to my **Final** photo).

You can adjust the **Pencil Tool's** size with the slider.

As illustrated, you don't need to completely cover the selected elements in the **Source** photo. Drawing over part of an area tells the program to grab all the similarly-colored elements around your drawing.

Use the **Eraser Tool** to de-select selected elements.

To make the combination of elements look more natural, you can select the **Edge Blending** option.

The biggest challenge with the tool is that, because the **Pencil Tool** selects elements in your photos based on pixel color similarity, you sometimes end up taking more from your **Source** photo to your **Final** photo than you'd like. In my example, for instance, when I used the photo with the over-exposed background as my **Final**, every time I selected the lamp shade, I also got the whited-out windows!

The solution for me was to swap the photos I was using as my **Source** and **Final**. Remember, just because you plan to use elements that are in the *background* of your photo doesn't necessarily mean that the photo with these elements won't make a better **Final** source image!

Combine photos with Photomerge Panorama

Sometimes a single photo doesn't capture the entirety of a scene or landscape. The Grand Canyon, the Golden Gate Bridge, Vatican Square – a single snapshot just can't tell the whole story.

Photoshop Elements' **Photomerge Panorama** tool combines several photos of a scene into one complete photo – producing, for instance, a panoramic image of a wide scene from three or four photos taken of adjacent areas of that scene.

The tool works amazingly well in most cases – even compensating for lens distortion and slight color differences between shots. About the only requirement is that there be a little bit of overlap in the photos' contents so that the program can interpret the scene composition and calculate where to combine the images.

In my illustration on the following page, I gathered a number of photos I'd shot while watching a Harley-Davidson "birthday" parade in downtown Milwaukee.

The Photomerge Panorama tool takes a group of photos with overlapping imagery and stitches them together (auto-correcting for lens distortion) into one, large panorama shot!

1   With the photos you want to cut and paste open in the Photoshop Elements Editor, select the **Guided** tab and select **Photomerge**, then **Photomerge Panorama**.

2   In the option screen that appears, browse to select the photo files or photo folder you'd like included in your **Panorama**. (You can also indicate for the tool to use the photos that are currently open in the Editor workspace.)

3   In most cases, the **Auto Layout** setting produces very good results. However, should you need to tweak the composition, the **Interactive Layout** option opens a dialog box for manually repositioning your **Photomerge** elements.

As you can see in my example on the facing page, there is a small flaw. In the center of the picture, you can see the front end of a car that appeared in one photo but not the photo adjacent to it. But, otherwise, the results are nearly perfect.

And, at 32 inches long, it might make a very nice poster!

The Actions panel

The **Actions** panel is a cool feature borrowed from the professional version of Photoshop.

The **Actions** panel offers a number of pre-recorded, multi-step tasks, tasks that can be applied to a photo open in your editor simply by selecting the **Action** and then clicking the **Play** button on the top right of the panel.

The **Actions** panel can be opened by selecting the option under the **More** button in the lower right of the Photoshop Elements interface or by selecting **Actions** under the program's **Window** menu.

There are four categories of **Actions** included with Photoshop Elements:

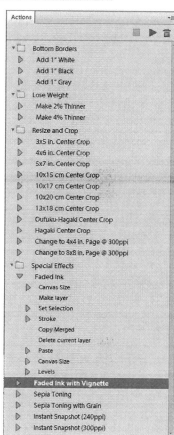

> **Bottom Borders** add a border below your photo onto which you can add text.

> **Lose Weight** narrows your photos, distorting it slightly to make your subject look a little taller and thinner.

> **Resize and Crop** automatically crops and resizes your photo to a specific shape and resolution.

> **Special Effects** automatically give your photo the look of being printed with faded ink, add vignetting or a sepia tint, age your photo or make it look like a Polaroid snapshot by resizing it and adding a white border to it.

If you click on the arrow to the left of any **Action**, you can see the individual steps the program will take in the completion of that **Action**. You have the option of applying the entire **Action** to your photo or, by selecting a sub-task, just one of the main task's individual steps.

Adobe Photoshop Elements

Part II
The Expert Photo Editing Workspace

Chapter 5

Get to Know the Photoshop Elements Toolbox

Your main photo editing toolkit

In Expert mode, the most visible tools in the Photoshop Elements Editor workspace are those gathered into the Toolbox, displayed as two columns of little icons along the left side of the Editor workspace.

Understanding these tools, how they work and how to customize them for your particular needs will take you a long way toward mastering this program.

Quick   Guided   **Expert**

The Toolbox

When Photoshop Elements is set to **Expert** mode, the full Photoshop Elements **Toolbox** will appear along the left side of the Editor workspace. The tools in the **Toolbox** are divided into six categories:

View Tools. Tools for zooming into, out of or changing the view of your image files.

Select Tools. Tools for selecting and isolating areas in your image files.

Enhance Tools. Tools for cleaning up and changing your image files. This category includes the tools for blurring, sharpening, dodging and burning, based on techniques long used by professional photographers.

Draw Tools. Tools for drawing, painting, coloring and erasing. Among the **Draw** tools are tools for adding text. Because working with text is a category all its own, we'll discuss these **Type** tools in depth in **Chapter 10, Create and Edit Text**.

Modify Tools. Tools for cropping, shaping and straightening your image files.

Color Tools. Tools for setting the colors of the elements you will add to your files.

The Tool Options

Tool Options

Sharing space with the **Photo Bin**, below the **Editor** workspace, the **Tool Options Bin** gives you access to the options for customizing how each tool works. (This space is toggled on by clicking the **Tool Options** button in the lower left of the interface.)

Some of these custom settings are so deep that one tool can actually work as several tools. And a few tools even allow you to *add* custom settings of your own!

Tool Options for some tools, for instance, include drop-down menus that list patterns, brushes or effects and sliders for setting specific brush sizes. We'll discuss specific **Tool Options** for each tool as we discuss each individual tool.

Access many tools under one button

Most buttons in the **Toolbox** will grant you access to more than one tool. When the **Blur** tool button is selected, for instance, buttons in the **Tool Options Bin** allow you to optionally select the **Blur, Sharpen** or **Sponge** tools. As we discuss the individual tools in this chapter, we'll indicate which sets of tools share a single **Toolbox** button.

When the Tool Options Bin is toggled on, the space beneath the Editor will display options for whichever tool you have selected in the Toolbox.

A single button on the Toolbox could hide several tool options, each of which appears as a button on the left side of the Tool Options Bin.

Set Foreground and Background Colors

You'll likely refer often to this swatch icon, displayed at the very bottom of the **Toolbox**. The colors that are set here play a role in how a number of your tools function.

Generally, the **Foreground Color** will be the default color in which new items you create will appear.

COLOR

Foreground Color

Background Color

- When a paintbrush, drawing or shape tool is selected, for instance, the brush will paint with or the shape will appear in the **Foreground Color** by default.

- When you use the **Typing Tool,** your text will also appear, by default, in the **Foreground Color.**

- When you use the **Eraser Tool**, the area you erase will be replaced by the **Background Color.** (At least when you're erasing from a background layer or flattened image file. When you erase from a layer [see **Chapter 9**], the area you erase will become transparent.)

- When you use **Fill** or add a **Stroke**, you will have the option of doing so with the **Foreground** or **Background Color.**

- When you use the **Gradient Tool**, the area will be painted, by default, with a gradation or blend of color from the **Foreground Color** to the **Background Color.**

There are a number of ways to set which colors appear as your **Foreground** and **Background Colors.** The easiest way is to simply click on either the **Foreground** or **Background Color** swatch icon on the **Toolbox.**

This will launch the **Color Picker.**

The Color Picker

The **Color Picker** displays a color sampling screen and a slider bar, representing **hue, saturation** and **brightness.** (Hue is your color's shade or tint; saturation is the amount of that hue in your color; brightness is the amount of lightness in your color.)

Your current color is displayed in the lower half of the box, located in the upper center of the **Color Picker**, as illustrated to the right.

Your new color will appear in the upper half of this box.

Current color · New color

Hue slider

Color selection

Constrains to Web Safe Colors

Hue, Saturation, Brightness levels

Red, Green, Blue levels

Hex color

Out of gamut indicator

To adjust the hue for your color, move the white triangles up or down on the **Hue slider** that runs down the center of the **Color Picker**. Then to pick your color, click in the big "picker" box, representing the saturation and brightness of that hue.

By checking the **Only Web Colors** box in the lower left corner of the **Color Picker**, you can restrict the available colors in the picker to only those colors that display consistently on Web pages.

Colors can also be set digitally in the **Color Picker** by typing in numbers for **Hue**, **Saturation** and **Brightness** or for the 256 levels of **Red**, **Green** and **Blue** in the color mix. The alpha-numeric **Hex** numbers for the color, in the lower right, can also be manually designated.

Once you've selected your color, click **OK**. Your selected color will become your new **Background** or **Foreground Color**.

The Eyedropper/Sampler Tool

 Another way to set the **Foreground Color** is by sampling a color from an open photo or image with the **Eyedropper/Sampler** (located among the **Draw** tools) on the **Toolbox**.

To sample a color, select this tool from the **Toolbox** and then click on a color area in an open image file.

The **Tool Options** for this tool includes options for selecting an average color sample from a block of pixels and for selecting colors that appear on either the current layer or all layers of your image file.

The Color Swatch panel

 The **Color Swatch** panel can be opened by selecting it from the Photoshop Elements **Window** menu or by selecting the option from the **More** button in the lower right corner of the interface.

When you click on a swatch in the **Color Swatch** panel, it will become your **Foreground** Color.

The **Color Swatch** panel includes hundreds of color options, categorized in several swatch sets. These various swatch sets can be accessed from the drop-down menu at the top of the panel, as illustrated to the right.

You can even create custom colors for your swatch library.

To do so, set your **Foreground Color** using the **Color Picker**, then click the **New Swatch** icon in the lower right of the **Color Swatches** palette. The color will be permanently added to your swatch library.

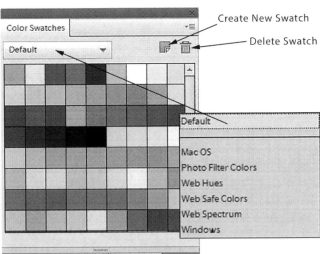

The Foreground and Background Colors can also be set by selecting a chip from the Color Swatches palette. The drop-down menu at the top of this panel offers options for displaying a number of additional color libraries.

The size and number of swatches displayed can be set by clicking the option switch on the upper right of the panel.

Additional Foreground/Background Color options

Swap Foreground and Background Colors. You can quickly switch the **Foreground** and **Background Colors** by clicking on the double-headed arrow to the upper right of the **Foreground/Background Color** swatch icons, or by pressing the **X** key on your keyboard.

Quickly set Foreground/Background Colors to black and white. You can quickly reset the **Foreground** and **Background Colors** to black and white, respectively, by clicking on the black/white icon to the lower left of the **Foreground/Background Color** swatch icon on the **Toolbox**. A keyboard shortcut for setting the colors back to black and white is the **D** key.

Swap Foreground and Background colors

Reset colors to black and white

Move and View Tools

Three tools in the **Toolbox** are for viewing and positioning your image file.

The Zoom Tool

One of two **View** tools, the **Zoom Tool** is represented by a magnifying glass, this tool is used, naturally, to zoom in and out of your image.

Select this tool and click on your image and you will zoom in. (Or you can use the keyboard shortcut **Ctrl+** on a PC or ⌘**+** on a Mac.)

Hold down the **Alt/Option** key and click on your image and you will zoom out. (Or you can use the keyboard shortcut **Ctrl+−** on a PC or ⌘**+−** on a Mac.)

The buttons and checkboxes on the tool's **Tool Options Bin** can be used to 'jump' your view to specific zoom levels.

The Hand Tool

Represented by a **Hand** icon, this **View** tool is useful if you're zoomed in so closely to an image that sections of your image are outside the file's window. When the **Hand Tool** is selected, you can click and drag the image's view around within the viewable area.

A keyboard shortcut for the **Hand Tool** is the **Spacebar** on your keyboard. No matter what tool you're working with, you can always reposition your view by holding down the **Spacebar,** then clicking and dragging your image around in the viewing area.

The Move Tool

The top left **Select** tool in the **Toolbox,** and more or less the default tool in Photoshop Elements, **the Move Tool** is used to move or drag the elements, selections, text or layers in your image files to new positions.

The settings in the **Tool Options** for this tool are useful for arranging the positions and order of objects in your image.

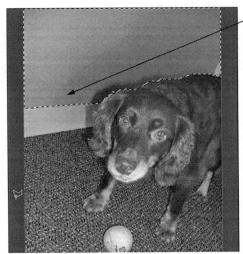

The selected area of your image file will appear surrounded by a moving dotted line, commonly called "marching ants."

Toggles in the Tool Options Bin for the Selection Tools set whether the tool adds to or subtracts from the selection.

New Selection

Add to Selection (or hold down Shift key)

Remove from Selection (or hold down Alt key)

Select Intersection of old and new selections

Selection Tools

The **Toolbox's Select** category are used to select areas of your image files.

A selected area can be cut, copied or pasted. But, more so, a selected area is *isolated*, so that any effects you add to your photo or image file will be applied *only* to the selection without affecting the rest of the image. Selecting and isolating is a very powerful function of Photoshop Elements, which is why we spend an entire chapter (**Chapter 6, Select and Isolate Areas in Your Photos**) discussing it in depth.

Your selected areas will be surrounded by little, moving dotted lines – which are traditionally referred to as "marching ants."

Add to and subtract from a selection

When selecting an area in a photo or image file, you don't have to get the selection exactly right the first time:

- Once you've selected an area, you can add to the selection by toggling **Add to Selection** in the **Tool Options Bin** (as illustrated above) or by holding down the **Shift** key as you continue to select.

- To deselect areas from your selected area, toggle **Subtract from Selection** in the **Tool Options Bin** or hold down the **Alt/Option** key as you drag over the area you want to deselect.

- To select only the area overlapped by your current and your new selection, toggle **Intersect with Selection** in the **Tool Options Bin**.

Using these tools to add to or subtract from your selection, you can hone your selection until it is precisely the area you want to work with.

- To turn off, or **deselect**, all of the selected areas for your image file, press **Ctrl+d** on a PC or ⌘+d on a Mac.

When a Marquee Selection Tool is selected in the Toolbox, you will have the option of selecting either the Elliptical or Rectangular Marquee in the Tool Options Bin

The Marquee Tool can be set to select an area with a feathered edge (see below) and can be set to select a free or constrained shape.

Once a selection is made, you can refine its edge, as described on page 81.

The Marquee Selection Tools

The **Rectangular Marquee Tool** and the **Elliptical Marquee Tool** are both available under the same **Toolbox** button. To switch between them, click on the button for whichever tool is displayed in the **Toolbox,** and then select one or the other tool in the **Tool Options Bin**, illustrated above.

To select an area on your image with either of these tools, click and drag across your image file. As long as that tool remains selected in the **Toolbox**, you can reposition the selected area by dragging it. To deselect the area press **Ctrl+d** on a PC or ⌘+d on a Mac.

Beyond the **Feathering** (discussed below), the **Tool Options** for this tool include a few functions which can also be activated with keyboard shortcuts.

To constrain the tool to select a perfectly circular or square area, select the **Fixed Ratio** option from the **Aspect** drop-down in the **Tool Options Bin** – or hold down the **Shift** key as you drag to make your selection.

When the **Aspect** is set to **Fixed Size**, you can designate the exact size of the area you will select.

Feathering

Most selection tools include an option to allow **Feathering**. This option is available in the **Tool Options Bin** for the **Marquee Selection Tools** as well as a refinement option under the program's **Select** menu.

Feathering means softening the edge of a selected area so that, rather than a sharp division between the selected and unselected areas, there is a soft gradation of selection.

A "feathered" selection has a softer edge so that, when the selection is removed or an effect is added to it, the distinction between the selected and unselected area of your image is a gradation rather than a solid line.

We look at this feature in more detail in the **Feathering** sidebar on page 89.

The Lasso Tool selects as you draw freehand.

The Polygonal Lasso Tool draws a selection from point to point as you click.

The Magnetic Lasso Tool follows the edge of a color break as you drag or click to create points.

Lasso Selection Tools

The three "lasso" tools share the same **Toolbox** button.

To switch between these tools, click the button for whichever tool is displayed in the **Toolbox**, then select the tool you'd like to use in the **Tool Options Bin**.

Lasso Selection Tools define a selected area by drawing a line around it (as if wrapping it in a lasso). There are three **Lasso Tools**, each functioning slightly differently.

The Lasso Tool is a freehand tool for selecting an area. To select an area with the Lasso, you just drag and draw. When you release your mouse button, the defined area will be selected.

The Polygonal Lasso Tool works similarly to the **Lasso Tool** except that, to designate an area to be selected, you click and release to create a series of points, which will be connected by straight lines. To close a **Polygonal Lasso Tool** selection, finish the selection by clicking onto your selection's starting point.

The Magnetic Lasso Tool is also a freehand tool for selecting an area. However, as you draw your selection with this tool, it will try to automate your selection by following the edge of an object, based on its color.

In other words, in the picture above, I dragged around the dog to select it in the photo. As I dragged my mouse around the dog's head, the **Magnetic Lasso** automatically made fine adjustments to my selection (based on the distinction in color between the dog and the background) to more precisely select the dog.

An important **Tool Option** setting for this tool is **Edge Contrast**. This setting defines the tool's tolerance for color contrast between the areas it does and the areas it does not select.

In other words, if the color of the subject you are drawing a selection around is a very different color than that of the background, you can use a high **Edge Contrast** percentage to ensure that the tool finds the edges.

If the subject is not so clearly distinguished from the background, you'll need a much lower **Edge Contrast** percentage. And you'll likely need to be more careful guiding the tool around the selection, or you may need to add to or subtract from the selection to refine it.

The Magic Wand Tool selects everything within a color range, based on the Tolerance level you've set.

The Selection Brush Tool draws a selection as you "paint" an area with its brush.

The Quick Selection Tool combines the the behaviors of both tools, selecting a similar color range as you "paint" across your image file.

Quick Selection Tools

The **Magic Wand, Quick Selection, Selection Brush** and **Refine Selection Brush** tools share the same button in the **Toolbox**. To switch between these tools, click the button for whichever tool is displayed in the **Toolbox**, then select the tool you'd like to use in the **Tool Options Bin**.

The Magic Wand Tool. One of the most useful tools in the **Toolbox**, the Magic Wand Tool, automatically selects an area on your image based on color similarities. (We put it to good use in **Chapter 12, Photoshop Elements Tricks**.)

When you click or drag on your photo with this tool, adjacent pixels of a similar color are automatically selected. By holding down the **Shift** key to add and the **Alt/Option** key to subtract, you can continue to select or de-select areas of your image file to build your desired selection.

The most important **Tool Options** setting for this tool is **Tolerance**. The lower the number, the narrower the range of colors the **Magic Wand** will consider similar. A higher **Tolerance** number widens the range of similar colors the **Magic Wand** will select as you click.

The Selection Brush Tool works just like it sounds like it would – as you "paint" with it, you create a selected area. **Tool Options** include settings for defining the size and hardness of the brush. You'll find more information on brush options in our discussion of **Brush settings and options** on page 72.

The Quick Selection Tool works like a combination of the **Magic Wand** and the **Selection Brush Tool**. As you drag it across your image, it "paints" a selection area, grabbing nearby areas of similar color along the way. This is a great tool for quickly paint-selecting a flat-colored background that you'd like to remove or replace. Its **Tool Options** include settings for the size, shape and hardness of the brush.

The exciting, new **Refine Selection Brush** is discussed in the sidebar on page 64.

The Refine Selection Brush and Push tool

 Given even more precision in version 14, the **Refine Selection Brush**, particularly when combined with the new **Push** setting, is one of the most powerful tools Adobe has designed yet for selecting complicated objects in your photos.

To use the **Refine Selection Brush** and **Push** tool:

1   Make a basic selection using one of the **Selection Brushes** or a **Lasso** or **Marquee Selection** tool.

2   Choose the **Refine Selection Brush** and the **Push** option on the **Tool Options** panel, as illustrated below.

When you select the **Refine Selection Brush,** your cursor will appear over your photo as a gray dot inside a white circle.

3   Click and drag from inside and outside your selection to "nudge" the selection into the precise shape you'd like.

When the gray dot is inside of your selection, dragging will "push" the selection edge out, adding to the selection from areas similar in color to the area under the white circle.

When the gray dot is outside of your selection, dragging will "push" the selection edge in, subtracting the selection from areas similar in color to the area under the white circle.

When the Refine Selection Brush/Push option is selected and the cursor is inside your selection, dragging will add to the selection. When the cursor is outside of your selection, dragging will subtract from your selection.

The size of the brush or gray dot can be set using the **Size** slider on the **Tool Options** panel or by using the bracket open [and bracket closed] buttons on your keyboard.

The **Snap Strength** setting controls the tolerance level for your automatic selection – in other words, how closely the automatically selected areas must match the colors of the areas you drag the gray dot over.

To see a demonstration of this tool, check out my free tutorial at Muvipix.com/pe14.php.

Enhance Tools

Enhance Tools are used to change your image file – whether to clean up a photo or to change it or add a special effect. Some of these tools are simple and almost automatic. Others can do some pretty complex effects!

By darkening and desaturating the areas you click on, the Red Eye Removal Tool instantly tames demonic-looking subjects.

The Red Eye Removal Tool

You know what this tool is for. It's for when you've taken a flash picture in dim lighting and you find that, in the final photo, your best friend or your dog has eyes that glow like those of some evil robot!

To use it, select the tool and then click on the subject's bright, red pupils. The tool essentially strips the color out of the pupil area and darkens it.

Tool Options for this tool allow you to set the **Pupil Size** and **Darken Amount.** You'll also find a checkbox option for fixing **Pet Eyes,** which can sometimes glow red, yellow and even green**!**

The Spot Healing Brush Tool

Sharing a button with the **Healing Brush Tool**, this tool is great for getting rid of unwanted moles, blemishes or other such flaws in your photos, as illustrated at the top of the next page.

When you click an area or "paint" with it, the tool blends the selected area with color information from the surrounding pixels. **Tool Options** include settings for the brush's size and hardness (For more information on brushes, see **Brush settings and options** on page 64) as well as the option to remove objects using **Content Aware Fill** (see the sidebar on page 66).

What is Anti-Aliasing?

Anti-Aliasing is a method of smoothing or slightly feathering the edges of an object or text so that it looks more natural. When **Anti-Aliasing** is turned off, the object or text will have very sharp edges, usually resulting in a very blocky, unnatural look.

Smooth Anti-Aliased edge

Jagged Aliased edge

The Healing Brush Tools

Similar to the **Clone Stamp Tool** (discussed on page 68), this tool borrows color and texture information from one area of your photo (which you've defined by **Alt-clicking** on it) and uses it to paint over another area.

The difference between this tool and the **Clone Stamp** is that the **Healing Brush Tool** then blends this borrowed imagery with the colors of the existing pixels to form a natural "healing patch" over the area.

As with the **Spot Healing Brush Tool**, the **Tool Options Bin** includes settings for the brush's size and hardness.

You can see the **Healing Brush** at work in our **Photo Editing Trick** on page 161.

The Healing Brush uses a Content Aware Fill system to replace blemishes, telephone lines and other unwanted elements in your photos with imagery from the surrounding area!

Using a Content Aware Fill system, the Spot Healing Brush uses nearby imagery to replace blemishes and other flaws in your photos virtually invisibly!

Content Aware Fill

A very exciting enhancement to the **Spot Healing Brush Tool** in Photoshop Elements is something Adobe calls **Content Aware Fill**.

In past versions of the **Healing Brushes**, the tool filled areas that you designated by averaging the colors of the surrounding pixels to create a smooth patch. This was very effective for removing blemishes and small marks in a photo – but it was less so at patching larger areas.

Content Aware Fill essentially looks at the entire area around what you're trying to hide or remove, and it smoothly fills the area you designate with similar, very natural-looking imagery.

This makes it especially effective at removing telephone wires from an otherwise perfect picture of a sunset – or even painting former friends completely out of a scene!

The Content Aware Fill feature in the Healing Brush Tools makes it easy to remove even large objects from many scenes.

The Smart Brush Tools

The Smart Brush Tools Options include a pop-up menu of presets for nearly 100 quick fixes – for everything from making skies bluer to making teeth whiter and lips redder.

The "fixes" are added as semi-opaque layers over your images and can be later changed or deleted.

The **Smart Brush Tool** and the **Details Smart Brush Tool** are part of a great **Quick Fix** tool set built into Photoshop Elements. (To toggle between these two tools, select the button on the **Toolbox** representing the currently active tool and then select one of the two **Smart Brushes** in the **Tool Options Bin**.)

Both tools work similarly, the main distinction being that the **Details Smart Brush Tool** affects only the area you "paint" with the brush (like the **Selection Brush** described on page 63), while the **Smart Brush Tool** expands the selected areas of your picture, based on their similarities to the areas you paint (like the **Quick Selection Tool** also described on page 63).

The **Smart Brush Tools** enhance your photos automatically, using presets available under the pop-up menu on the **Tool Options Bin**. These presets will make grass greener, skies bluer, teeth whiter, lipstick redder, etc. – or they can add color or texture effects to your photos.

To apply a **Smart Brush** fix, select the appropriate preset from the **Tool Options Bin's** drop-down menu, as illustrated above, and then paint over the area in your image file that you'd like to add effects to.

When you finish selecting the area of your photo and release your mouse button, the program will make the adjustments to your picture, as in the illustration above.

Using the **+** and **–** brush icons that appear on your image as you work, you can paint to add to or remove from the selected area (or hold down the **Shift** key to add and the **Alt/Option** key to subtract). The program will update the effect automatically.

The true beauty of these adjustments is that they don't permanently change the image itself! If you look at the **Layers** panel, you'll see that these adjustments are actually just masks added as what are called **Adjustment Layers**, as illustrated above. By clicking on these **Adjustment Layers**, you can reactivate the **Smart Brush Tools** and make further adjustments, or even delete the **Adjustment Layers** completely. The original image remains unmolested! At least until you flatten the layers or save the file as something other than a PSD file.

ENHANCE

A favorite tool for "stunt photo work," the Clone Tool lets you paint over portions of your image file – removing objects or even people – with imagery from another area of your image file (defined by Alt+clicking).

The Clone Stamp Tool

This amazing tool takes imagery from one area of your photo file (an area indicated with an **Alt-click**) and paints it onto another.

The tool is popular for doing special effects, like "erasing" somebody or something from a scene (see pages 162).

In addition to settings for the brush size and hardness, the **Tool Options Bin** includes an **Opacity** setting. Opacity (the opposite of transparency) controls whether the area you paint over is replaced entirely with the new image or whether the new image is blended in semi-transparently with the old to some degree.

The Pattern Stamp Tool

Rather than painting an area in your photo with imagery from another area in your image, the **Pattern Stamp Tool** paints over your image with a pattern, as selected from the pop-up menu in the **Tool Options Bin**.

There are many pages of patterns available for this effect, by the way. And you can see the other categories of patterns by clicking on the flyout menu button in the upper right corner of the option box that appears when you click on the "pattern" drop-down.

An **Impressionist** option turns the pattern into a liquid swirl of paint that intensifies as you hold down on your mouse button.

The Pattern Stamp tool paints over your image with any of dozens of patterns.

The Blur Tool blurs the area you drag across

The Smudge Tool smears your image as you drag acrosss it

The Sharpen Tool increases pixel contrast in the areas you drag across

Blur, Smudge and Sharpen

These three tools, which share the same button in the **Toolbox**, treat your image file a bit like liquid, allowing you to blur, smear or sharpen it.

To switch between these tools, click the button for whichever tool is displayed in the **Toolbox**, then select the tool you'd like to use in the **Tool Options Bin**.

The three tools share similar settings on the **Tool Options Bin** – Brush size, hardness and **Strength** (amount) of the blur, smudge or sharpening. (For information on brush settings, see **Brush settings and options** on page 64.)

The Blur Tool

Dragging this tool across your image softens the pixel edges of the area you drag across, blurring your picture.

The Smudge Tool

This tool treats your image as if it were wet paint. When you drag across it, you smear it!

The Sharpen Tool

The Sharpen Tool increases the contrast between pixels, giving your image a crisper look as you drag across it.

Unlike the general **Unsharp Mask** (discussed in **Chapter 8, Correct Color and Lighting**) which sharpens your entire photo, the **Sharpen Tool** sharpens only the areas of your picture that you drag across.

The Sponge Tool
desaturates, or removes
color from, an area

The Dodge Tool
lightens the area you
drag across

The Burn Tool darkens
the area you drag across

The Sponge, Dodge and Burn Tools

These three tools are sometimes referred to as the "darkroom tools" because they're based on techniques photographers used to use in the darkroom to enhance their prints.

To switch between these tools, click the button for whichever tool is displayed in the **Toolbox**, then select the tool you'd like to use from the **Tool Options Bin**.

The three tools share similar **Tool Options** for setting brush hardness and size.

The Sponge Tool

The Sponge Tool desaturates, or removes color from, an area of your image as you drag over it. (The **Tool Options Bin** includes an option for reversing the process, or increasing color saturation.)

The **Flow** setting on the **Tool Options Bin** determines how much color is removed.

The Dodge Tool

The Dodge Tool lightens the area you drag over, as if it were a photographic print which received less exposure in the darkroom. The **Tool Options Bin's Exposure** settings control how intensely the area is dodged.

The Burn Tool

The Burn Tool darkens the area you drag over, as if it were a photographic print which received more exposure in the darkroom. The **Tool Options Bin's Exposure** settings control how intensely the area is darkened.

Draw Tools

The Brush Tools

The three **Brush Tools** share the same button on the **Toolbox**.

To switch between these tools, click the button for whichever tool is displayed in the **Toolbox**, then select the tool you'd like to use in the **Tool Options Bin**.

The Paint Brush

This tool is your basic paintbrush – similar to the **Pencil Tool** as a line drawing tool, except that the **Brush Tool** includes options for painting soft-edged or even textured lines.

The **Tool Options** for this tool include settings not only for the size and hardness of the brush and the opacity of the paint but also for switching the brush to **Airbrush** mode – which, as you'd expect, paints a stroke that grows more intense the longer you "spray" it on one spot.

In addition, if you click on the **paintbrush icon** in the **Tool Options Bin**, you'll find an option panel for creating your own brush. (For information on brush settings, see **Brush settings and options** on page 72.)

The Brush Tool paints a soft or textured freehand line.

The Impressionist Brush

The **Impressionist Brush** is a pretty cool special effects tool.

When you click and hold or paint with this brush, it "liquefies" and swirls the colors in your image so that it resembles an impressionist painting.

The Impressionist Brush swirls your image.

The Color Replacement Brush

The **Color Replacement Brush** replaces the color of an area you "paint" over in your image file with the **Foreground Color** (although, in **Tool Options**, you can also set it to replace only the hue, saturation or luminosity of your picture).

Because of the way this brush senses the differences in color ranges within your image, it can, amazingly enough, paint the leaves on a tree but leave the sky behind them unchanged or even, as illustrated on the right, tint the darker leaves of a tree in the background while leaving the brighter leaves of the tree in the foreground unchanged!

The Color Replacement Brush overlays color, but only over the range of colors you designate.

The **Tolerance** level you have set in the **Tool Options Bin** determines how much distinction there must be between the areas to be re-colored and those left intact.

Brush settings and options

Many tools behave like brushes. The tool's effects or colors are essentially painted on.

In fact, the size and softness settings in the **Tool Options Bin** for many tools are nearly identical to those of the **Paint Brush Tool**.

There are two basic brush settings: the **Size** of the brush (measured in pixels) and its **Hardness**.

Hardness determines sharpness of the edge of the stroke that the

Brush sub-categories, textures and sizes on the Tool Options panel.

brush paints. The softer the edge, the more feathered the area between the brushed area and the unbrushed area. When using the **Clone Tool**, for instance, a softer edged brush may show a more natural, less abrupt line between your old and newly-added image areas.

Some brushes, called **Scatter** brushes, create an effect like painting with steel wool. Their effect is scratchy and hard.

Brushes can also have shapes. These oblong shapes (included among the **Calligraphy** presets) will paint a wider line when you are painting one direction than they will another, as when you are writing with a calligraphy pen.

Brushes can even be set to paint **patterns**. When a pattern is selected for a brush, the pattern's image will appear again and again as you paint. This can be used, for instance, to paint several stars across a sky in a single brush stroke or to paint a trail of footprints.

In addition to the over 300 preset brushes you'll find in Photoshop Elements, you can also save your own personal brush settings. To do this, once you've set your brush to the shape and size you want, click on the ☰ menu on the upper right of the brush preset drop-down menu and select the option to **Save Brush**.

The **Paint Brush** tool also has some cool advanced brush tool settings in the **Tool Options Bin**, which we discuss on page 74.

Brushes can have soft or hard edges or can even be set to paint patterns

Brush sizes are measured in pixels and can be selected from the presets or set using the slider

The Eraser Tool removes what you drag across, replacing it with your Background Color or, if a layer, transparency.

The Background Eraser erases up to color breaks, based on the Tolerance level you've set in the Tool Options.

The Magic Eraser instantly removes an area you click on, based on its color range and the Tolerance level you've set.

Eraser Tools

Simply put, the **Eraser Tools** remove imagery from your file as you drag across it.

The three **Eraser Tools** share the same button on the **Toolbox**. To switch between these tools, click the button for whichever tool is displayed in the **Toolbox**, then select the tool you'd like in the **Tool Options Bin**.

The Eraser

- If you're erasing from a flattened image or a background layer, what you erase will be replaced with your **Background Color** (see page 57).
- Erasing from a layer creates transparency through that layer.

Tool Options for this tool include settings for brush size, hardness and opacity (transparency level).

The Background Eraser Tool

The **Background Eraser** erases one color or color range and ignores dissimilarly colored areas in your image file.

For example, this tool can be used to erase the background from the photo of a person and yet not erase the person!

The tool determines the color you want erased based on the pixels that are in the tool's crosshairs as you "paint" with it. So, as you erase, if you keep the crosshairs off of what you don't want removed, the tool will erase along the edge of the color break, as in the illustration above, in which it erased the wall but not the dog.

Tool Options include settings for the brush size and hardness as well as **Tolerance** – how much distinction must exist between the area you're erasing and the area you're not in order for the tool to recognize the difference.

The Magic Eraser Tool

Like the **Magic Wand Tool,** this tool selects, and then erases, areas in your image file that fall within a range of colors, based on the pixel you click on or the pixels you drag across.

For example, using this tool, you could easily remove a consistently green background from an image in a single click or simple click and drag.

The **Tolerance** setting, in the **Tool Options Bin**, designates how wide a range of color is considered similar to your selected pixels, and thus is erased. (The higher the number, the more "tolerant" the tool is of variations in the background color.) The **Opacity** level determines if the image is erased completely or simply softened or made semi-transparent.

Advanced brush tool settings

Adobe has included a couple of **Tool Options** in Photoshop Elements that make working with the brush tools even more intuitive. When the **Paint Brush** is selected, these tools appear on the far right of the **Tool Options Bin.**

Brush Settings

Brush Settings allow you to create a brush with whatever characteristics you'd like, including **Fade** (How much the opacity of the paint changes along your brush stroke), **Hue Jitter** (How much the stroke wavers between your selected **Foreground** and **Background**

With Brush Settings, you can create a custom brush with hard or soft edges or even with a non-round shape for creating lines as if drawn with a calligraphy pen.

Colors as you paint), **Scatter** (How much the stroke appears as speckles rather than a solid line), **Spacing** (How much the stroke appears as a series of dots rather than a solid line), **Hardness** (How soft the edges of the stroke are) and **Roundness** (the shape of the brush; an oval brush can be used to make the brush draw variable-width strokes, as if drawn with a calligraphy pen).

Tablet Settings

Drawing tablets, such as those made by Wacom, enable you to draw and paint in Photoshop Elements using a very intuitive pad and stylus. The **Tablet Settings** enable you to use your tablet to create custom brushes.

Tablet Settings control how the program interfaces with devices like the Wacom tablet.

The Paint Bucket (Fill) Tool

When you drag the **Paint Bucket** to your canvas, it paints your image file with the current **Foreground Color**. It does this in one big, even flow of paint.

If you have a **Selected** area on your canvas or on your image file, the **Paint Bucket Tool** will fill only the selection.

There are two keyboard shortcuts that also fill with color, by the way:

Alt+Backspace will fill a selected area with your **Foreground Color**.

Ctrl+Backspace (⌘+**Backspace** on a Mac) will fill a selected area with your **Background Color**.

In the **Tool Options** for the **Paint Bucket**, the tool can be set to fill an area with a selected pattern rather than a color.

The Paint Bucket fills your canvas or your selected area.

The Gradient Tool

The **Gradient Tool** paints your image or selected area with a gradation or blend of one color to another. By default, this gradation will begin with your **Foreground Color** and blend to your **Background Color**.

Tool Options include a number of patterns for your gradients, from linear gradients to radial gradients to pattern gradients. The gradient they create will be a blend of your **Foreground** and **Background Colors**.

The Gradient Tool fills your canvas or selected area with (by default) a gradation from the Foreground to the Background Colors.

The **Gradient Editor** also includes presets for color blends other than the default. You can access them by clicking the **Edit** button in the **Tool Options Bin**.

Tool Options also include a setting for **Opacity**, so that you can set whether the gradient covers your image file completely or blends semi-transparently to some degree with the existing image.

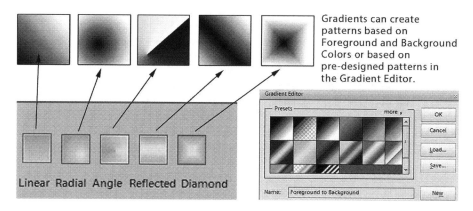

Gradients can create patterns based on Foreground and Background Colors or based on pre-designed patterns in the Gradient Editor.

Linear Radial Angle Reflected Diamond

The Shape Tool includes several common shapes, from lines of varying width to customizable polygons.

The Custom Shape Tool option drop-down menu offers over 550 more, including faces, flowers, plants, animals and funny hairstyles! Each are vector art and can be resized until their shape layer is simplified.

Choose 3D shape style.

Set shape's color.

Heart Card

From Center

The Shape Tools

The **Shape Tools** draw shapes as you drag across your image file. These shapes appear as a new layer on your file, and remain editable until you simplify the layer or flatten your image. (See **Simplify or flatten layers** on page 126 of **Chapter 9, Work with Photoshop Elements Layers**.)

There are about half a dozen common shapes available under the **Shape Tool** button. To switch between them, click the button for whichever tool is displayed in the **Toolbox**, then select the tool you'd like in the **Tool Options Bin**.

If you select the **Custom Shape Tool** option, you will have access to hundreds of more shapes. These custom shapes are available on the pop-up option panel in the **Tool Options Bin**, and include everything from basic snowflakes and arrows to cartoon talk bubbles, animals, flowers, faces and ornaments. (To access more than the default shapes on this pop-up panel, click on the drop-down menu at the top of the option box and select a category or **All Elements Shapes**.)

Using custom settings on the Tool Options panel, the same tool can be used to create many different shapes.

Because shapes are composed of paths rather than pixels, they can be resized and reshaped without concern for their resolution.

When **Add to Shape Area** is selected on the **Tool Options Bin**, you can even combine several shapes to create just about any shape!

Shapes possess some unique characteristics. As you can see, if you look at your **Layers** panel after you've added a shape to your image file, shapes aren't simple raster objects, but are, rather, "masks" with color added to them.

The designers at Adobe have decided to treat shapes this way so that they behave like vector art. In other words, once you've added a shape to your image file, you can resize it and reposition it without any concern for its resolution or pixel depth. You can also re-color a shape just by double-clicking on the shape in the **Layers** panel and then changing its color on the **Color Picker** that pops open.

Some **Shape Tools** have interesting customization settings available in their **Tool Options**. For instance:

The Rectangle Tool, Ellipse Tool and Rounded Rectangle Tool
These tools include options for constraining their shapes to a perfect square or a circle. Additionally, the **Rounded Rectangle Tool** has an option for setting how round its corners are.

The Polygon Tool
The Polygon Tool (illustrated at the top of this page) has options for setting the number of sides on the polygon you will create, how round its corners are and if the sides make it a flat-sided polygon or a starburst-like shape.

The Line Tool
The Line Tool Options panel includes options for setting the line's width and if it includes arrowheads on its start and/or end points.

Typing Tools

Because working with text is a subject unto itself, we've dedicated an entire chapter to it and the **Typing Tools**. For more information, see **Chapter 10, Create and Edit Text**.

The Pencil Tool

As the name implies, this is a freehand line drawing tool. (Unlike the **Paint Brush**, the **Pencil** always draws lines with a hard edge.)

Tool Options for this tool include settings for the size of the pencil and the opacity of the line. The **Auto-Erase** option allows you to toggle the **Pencil Tool** (with a click of the mouse) between working as a drawing tool and working as an erasing tool.

The Pencil Tool draws a hard-edged freehand line.

Modify Tools

Cropping Tools

The **Crop Tool** and the **Cookie Cutter** share the same button in the **Toolbox**. With these tools you can cut or reshape your photos and image files.

To switch between these tools, click the button for whichever tool is displayed in the **Toolbox**, then select the tool you'd like to use in the **Tool Options Bin**.

The Crop Tool resizes your canvas based on your selected area. Once selected, the area can be resized, repositioned or canceled. To finalize your crop, click the green check mark or press Enter on your keyboard.

A dotted line overlay indicates the Rule of Thirds "power alleys" for your photo's composition.

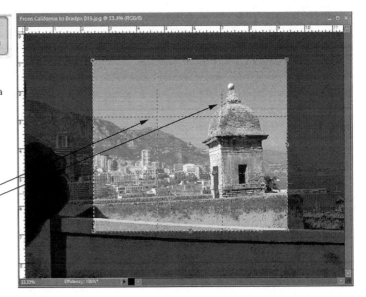

The Crop Tool

The **Crop Tool** is the tool used for cutting both the image and canvas. In other words, this tool changes the canvas size of the actual image file. To use it, click to select the tool, then drag to create a box on your image file.

Crop suggestions

When the **Crop Tool** is selected, it will automatically offer you four suggestions for cropping your photo prior to your creating your own crop. These suggestions are based on the program's analysis of your photo's content – in particular, the faces it identifies in the photos. (To turn this feature off, go to the program's **Preferences** [under the **Edit** menu on a PC] and, on the **General** page, uncheck the option **Enable Crop Pre-Selection**.)

Crop auto-suggestions

To see other crop suggestions, hover your mouse over the thumbnails on the lower right of the **Tool Options** panel, as illustrated above.

You can modify the size and position of the crop by dragging on the corner handles or by dragging directly across the suggested crop. To finalize and crop your photo, click on the green checkmark or press **Enter** on your keyboard.

Crop Tool size/shape presets

The size/shape pop-up menu in the **Crop Tool's Tool Options** (illustrated below) gives you options for constraining the area that you've cropped to specific shapes, sizes or resolutions. When you have a preset selected from this drop-down menu or you have manually typed in a set Width, Height and Resolution, the shape of your crop will be constrained. In other words, although it can be resized, it will remain locked to a specific shape. (To allow you to freely set the size and shape of your crop, set the preset menu to **No Restriction**.)

When **Width, Height** and **Resolution** are set, either by selecting a preset or by manually typing in the measurements, cropping will automatically size your finished photo to these exact specs.

Constrain crop dimensions   Hover over for crop auto-suggestions   Overlay guides   Constrain Resolution

MODIFY

A photo composed with its subject on one of the picture's "thirds" (off-centered) is much more interesting and dynamic than one in which the subject is merely centered (above).

Crop Tool composition overlays

In the lower right of the **Tool Options Bin** for the **Crop Tool**, you will find overlay options for the **Crop Tool**:

None

When you've selected the **None** option for your **Crop** overlay, the program will display no overlay on your potential crop.

The Rule of Thirds overlay

When you've selected the **Rule of Thirds** overlay, your potential crop will be overlayed with guides that divide your photo into three vertical and three horizontal panels, as illustrated on page 78.

Unless you're trying for a certain effect, centering a subject in your photo can make for a fairly boring picture. As many photographers and graphic artists know, pictures are much more dynamic if the focus of the photo is slightly off-center, as above.

Grid overlay

When you've selected the **Grid** option for your Crop overlay, the program will overlay your potential crop with a grid to help you crop an evenly composed photo.

The Cookie Cutter Tool

The **Cookie Cutter Tool** will crop your picture into any of hundreds of custom shapes, from starbursts to butterflies to ragged-edged photos.

(The shaped image will have alpha, or transparency, around it so that, if you save your image file as a PSD, the shaped image will appear with no square background when the file is used in Premiere Elements.)

The Cookie Cutter Tool cuts your image into any of over 550 shapes

The Cookie Cookie Tool Options Bin

Once you've selected the tool, select a shape from the **Cookie Cutter** pop-up menu in the **Tool Options Bin** and then drag to draw the shape onto your image file. Once you click on the green checkmark or press **Enter** on your keyboard, your image file will be cut to that shape.

There are many pages of options for shapes, by the way. And you can access them by clicking on the drop-down menu at the top of the panel that appears when you click on the **Tool Options Bin's Cookie Cutter** pop-up menu, as illustrated above.

The Recompose Tool

The cool and powerful **Recompose Tool** gives you the ability to reshape a photo – re-positioning people or other elements in it nearer together – without distorting these elements in any way.

What's most amazing about this tool is that it does most of what it does automatically (although there are also manual ways to "protect" certain elements in the photo).

With the Recompose Tool, you can make a photo of people sitting too far apart look much cozier.

MODIFY

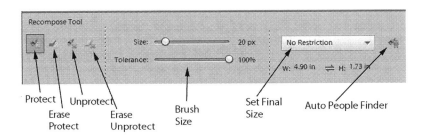

When you **Recompose** a photo, you squeeze it, either from top to bottom or from side to side, compressing the elements of the photo so that they become closer together – *but without changing the shapes of any of the key elements in the picture!*

In many cases, when you're using this tool, the **Recompose Tool** will automatically recognize people in your photo and it will protect them, as much as possible from distorting as you resize your photo. It will also try to keep certain major elements in the background of the photo – trees or cars – from distorting. It merely makes these key elements look closer together.

In our experience, however, the program can often use a little help identifying which elements in the photo you want to preserve. Fortunately, this is very simple to do.

1   With your photo file open, click to select the **Recompose Tool**. (The tool will launch a help screen that explains how to use the tool. You can elect not to see this screen again by checking the box in its lower left corner.)

    In **Recompose** mode, you'll see handles on each corner and in the middle of each side of your photo file. Dragging on these corner handles will resize your photo.

2   Drag one side of your photo in to squeeze your photo. In most cases, people and other major elements in the photo will move closer together – though they may very soon begin to distort.

3   To "protect" the elements you don't want to distort, select the green paint brush from the **Recompose Tool Options Bin** and paint over the elements you want to preserve. As with any brush-based tool, you can enlarge or reduce the size of the brush by setting its size on the **Tool Options Bin** or pressing the **[** (open bracket) or **]** (close bracket) keys on your keyboard.

    In my illustration below, I've painted "protection" over the three people and their chairs.

    To remove protection from an area, switch to the green eraser tool and drag across a "painted" area.

With key elements in your photo designated as protected, these elements move closer together, undistorted, as you resize the photo by dragging on its side handle.

To designate an object or person as something you *want* to see distorted or removed, paint it with the red "unprotect" brush. To remove this indicator, use the red erase brush.

There is also a green "people finder" tool that can often automatically find and protect the people in your photo. It tends to work best when the photo was shot in ideal lighting conditions.

4   With your designated elements protected, drag the handle on the side of your photo in to compress the photo. As you do, the elements and people you've protected will move closer to each other and yet will not change shape.

(There is, of course, a saturation point at which even protected elements will distort.)

You can also change the dimensions of the photo numerically by typing a width or height in the **Tool Options Bin**.

When you are happy with your new composition, click the green check mark or simply press **Enter.** Photoshop Elements will process and re-render your photo.

Note that, because of the way this tool works, your new photo will be layered. So, in order to save it as something other than a PSD or layered TIF, you will need to flatten the layers by selecting **Flatten Image** under the program's **Layer** menu.

When an object in your photo is selected with the Content Aware Move tool and then dragged to a new location, the program will fill the old space with background and blend the object into its new location.

The Content Aware Move Tool

The cool, new **Content Aware Move Tool** expands on concepts put to use in the **Content Aware Fill** aspects of the **Healing Brushes** (see page 66). The **Content Aware Move Tool** fills the area of a moved object with background from the area around it and then blends the moved selection into its new location.

To use this tool, select the **Content Aware Move Tool** in the **Toolbox** and drag to draw a selection around an object or area in your photo – then drag this selection to another area of your photo.

The program will both fill in the space left behind with "content aware" background and blend your selected object into its new location's background. (The **Extend** option will duplicate your selected object and blend the duplicate naturally into its second location.)

Obviously, this tool works more effectively on some photo compositions, with smaller selections and with less defined backgrounds, than it does others. But, when it does work well, the results are really pretty cool!

With the Straighten Tool selected, drag a line to define an object you would like to appear perfectly horizontal. The tool will automatically rotate and straighten your photo accordingly.

The Straighten Tool

I love this tool! It's great for straightening a photo whose subject is a bit crooked.

To use it, just select the tool and then drag to draw a line along an element in your image (a rooftop, a mantle, somebody's shoulders) that you would like to appear perfectly horizontal.

As above, when you release your mouse button, the image will instantly rotate and straighten!

On the **Tool Options** panel for the **Straighten Tool,** you'll find the option to apply **Content Aware Fill** (see page 66) to your straightened photo. **Content Aware Fill** will fill any blank areas around your photo's edges – blank areas created by straightening the photo – with natural background, based on the surrounding imagery.

Making Selections

Refining Selections

Effects and Selections

Cutting & Pasting Selections

Stroking & Filling Selections

Chapter 6
Select and Isolate Areas in Your Photos
Working with selections

A key function in Photoshop Elements – and one which a number of tools support – is selecting.

Selecting means isolating areas of your image file so that effects can be applied to those areas only, without affecting the rest of the image, or so that those areas can be cut or removed completely.

Selections can have hard edges or soft. They can be changed and refined and even saved.

Selecting and isolating make many of this program's most powerful effects possible.

When an area of your image file is selected (surrounded by a moving dotted line), effects and tools applied will only affect the selected area, leaving the rest of your image unchanged.

Why select and isolate?

There are three main reasons for selecting an area of your image file:

To **apply an effect** or adjust the color or lighting of one area of your image file without affecting the rest of the image;

To **protect areas** of your image file so that, for instance, you can paint or erase one area without affecting another area of your image;

To **cut an area** of your image file – cutting a person from a photo, for instance – so that you can either paste him or her into another image file or remove him or her completely.

In **Chapter 5, Get to Know the Photoshop Elements Toolbox**, we discuss a number of tools that can be used to select and isolate areas of your image file.

The **Marquee Tools**, which include the **Rectangular Marquee** and **Elliptical Marquee Tools,** allow you to select a circular or rectangular area of your image file.

The **Lasso Tools**, which include the **Magnetic Lasso, Polygonal Lasso** and freehand **Lasso Tool**, allow you to draw any shape as a selected area.

The **Magic Wand Tool** automatically selects an area of your image that shares a similar color range, based on the tolerance level you've set.

The **Quick Selection Tool** allows you to select an area by "painting" across it, selecting adjacent pixels of similar color as you paint.

A complicated selection may require several passes with several tools to get it exactly right – using the Add to Selection and Subtract from Selection controls to refine the selected area.

As you select an area, it will appear with a moving, dotted line surrounding it – commonly referred to as "marching ants." As we discuss in the individual descriptions of each tool in **Chapter 5**, the selection tools can be used in combination with each other – while selecting the **Add to Selection** and **Subtract from Selection** options (see page 60) – to create or refine your selection into any shape you'd like.

Feathering

Selection tools usually include an option to **"feather"** your selection. **Feathering** means softening the edges of the selection.

For instance, if you were to use the **Elliptical Marquee Tool** to select an area of your image file, this selection would be, by default, a perfect oval or circle, with a clearly defined, hard edge.

But in a number of situations, you'd like that edge softer.

A "feathered" selection has a softer edge so that, when the selection is removed or an effect is added to it, the distinction between the selected and unselected area of your image is a gradation rather than a solid line.

If you're applying an effect to a selected area in a photograph, for instance, you might like the boundary between the affected area and the non-affected area to be softly defined. This can make the effect seem more natural than a hard, abrupt edge might.

Also, when you're cutting a subject from one photo in order to paste him or her into another, a slight feathering around the edge can help blend the pasted image so that it fits more naturally into the new background.

Feathering is measured in pixels. This means that, when working with a low-resolution image, you'll need fewer pixels in your feathering than you will in a higher-resolution image to achieve a similar softened edge effect.

Feathering also plays a role in the **Refine Edge** tool, as discussed on page 91.

The Tool Options for each Selection Tool include settings for adding to or subtracting from your selected areas.

New Selection (Default)

Add to Selection (or hold down Shift key)

Remove from Selection (or hold down Alt key)

Select Intersection of old and new selections

You can add to an already selected area by clicking on the **Add to Selection** button in the **Tool Options Bin,** or by holding down the **Shift** key as you continue to select.

You can remove an area from your selection by clicking the **Subtract from Selection** button in the **Tool Options Bin** or by holding down the **Alt/Option** key as you select.

You can refine your selection so that it includes only the area overlapped by your current and new selections by clicking the **Intersect with Selection** button in the **Tool Options Bin.**

As you build your selected area, two other keyboard shortcuts are worth noting:

To go back a step at any point in the program – even deselecting the most recent area you've selected or removed from your selection – press **Ctrl+z** (⌘+z on a Mac) or click the **Undo** button in the upper right of the interface.

To deselect an area completely, press **Ctrl+d** on a PC or ⌘+d on a Mac.

The Select menu

Once you've selected an area of your image file, the Photoshop Elements **Select** menu (illustrated on the facing page) offers a number of options for refining and changing your selected area.

Select All (Ctrl+a on a PC or ⌘+a on a Mac) selects your entire displayed image. If you are working on a layered file, you will select only the image that appears on the active layer. (For more information, see **Chapter 9, Work with Layers.**)

Deselect (Ctrl+d or ⌘+d) deselects all of your selections.

Reselect (Ctrl+Shift+d or ⌘+Shift+d) re-selects all that you've just deselected – in case you suddenly change your mind.

Inverse (Ctrl+Shift+i or ⌘+Shift+i) switches your selection so that the areas you currently have unselected become your selected areas and vice versa.

All Layers and **Selected Layers** expand your current selection to other layers in your image file, if you are working on a layered file.

Grow expands your selected area to similarly colored adjacent pixels in your image file, based on your current selection.

Similar selects all similarly colored pixels throughout your image file, whether they are adjacent to your current selection or not.

Feather (**Ctrl+Alt+d** or **⌘+Option+d**) allows you to apply feathering to soften the edge, after the fact, of your currently selected area.

Refine the edge of your selection

Once you've selected an area in your image file, you can refine the edge of the selection by using the **Refine Edge** tool, accessed under the **Select** menu or by clicking the **Refine Edge** button in the **Tool Options Bin**. Adobe has made some great improvements to this tool, borrowing some amazing features from the professional version of Photoshop.

Edge Detection

The amazing **Edge Detection/Smart Detection** feature in the **Refine Edge** panel can help you find the edges of a selection that includes very fine details, such as fur or strands of hair. (This is truly an amazing feature!)

Note that you'll get the best results if your subject's background is a smooth color and is distinct in color from the hair, fur or detailed edge of your subject.

1   Using the **Magic Wand, Selection Brush** and/or the **Quick Selection Tool**, select your subject as accurately as possible.

2   Open the **Refine Edge** panel by selecting the option under the **Select** menu or clicking the button in the **Tool Options Bin**.

Selecting fine details along the edge of your selection, like fur or strands of hair, can be very challenging.

The Smart Radius Edge Detection feature makes selecting even fine details like strands of hair possible!

The **View Mode** pop-up menu at the top of the **Refine Edge** panel allows you to see your selected area in a variety of modes. **On White** is a good mode for this process, since it makes everything outside your selected area appear as white, as seen above.

3   Check the **Smart Detection** box and set **Radius** to about 30 px. (You can adjust it later if you need to.)

4   Select the **Edge Detection Brush** to the left of **Edge Detection/Radius** and drag to "paint" the area of your selection's edge that includes details or stray hair, trying to keep the crosshairs on the brush over the background as much as possible. When you release your mouse, your new selection will be visible, as illustrated above, with some very fine details selected!

You can correct any over-selection with the **Selection Eraser Tool**, below the **Edge Detection Brush**.

Refine Edge Adjustments

Other ways to make adjustments and refine the edge of your selection include:

Radius is how detailed any refinements you make in this panel are. The smaller the radius, the finer the adjustments.

Smooth determines how detailed your selection is. The higher you set **Smooth**, the more the fine details in the edge of your selected area will be rounded out.

Refine Edge View Modes

Feather. As discussed on page 89, feathering softens the boundary between your selected and unselected areas, giving a more natural, less abrupt edge to your selection.

Contrast controls how soft or sharp the edge is between your selected and unselected areas.

Shift Edge removes or adds a few extra pixels from around the edge of your selection. This can be helpful if, for instance, you're cutting a person from a background and, in your current selection, some of the background is still showing around the edges. **Shift Edge** and **Feather** are often used in combination to create a very clean, natural edge.

Decontaminate Color replaces any fringe colors that you've selected with colors from surrounding pixels. In other words, if you've selected brown hair and some green background has crept into your selected area, **Decontaminate Color** will tint this green "fringe" brown to match the hair so you don't have any stray color in your selection.

Output gives you options for automatically cutting your selected area into a new layer on your image file, masking your selection on its current layer or copying to a new document.

Checking the **Remember Settings** box will make your current settings your default **Refine Edge** panel settings.

By drawing a selection around the dog, I can isolate him – applying, for instance, color correction to him only, not affecting the background

When I reverse the selection (by selecting Inverse from the Select menu) – my selection becomes everything in the image file *except* the dog. I am now able to apply effects or use brushes – I can even paint a new background with the Clone Tool – affecting everything in the photo *except* the unselected dog!

Use a selection to protect an area

A key reason to select an area of a photo is so that an effect can be applied to the area you've isolated without affecting the rest of your image file.

In the example above, for instance, the dog in the original picture was too yellow for my tastes. However, I preferred that any color corrections I made affected the dog only, and left the rest of the picture as is.

Using a combination of tools – adding to and subtracting from my selection and then refining the edges – I isolated the dog as a selection. I was then able to make color changes to the dog only, without changing the color values of any other part of my image file.

I then inversed the selection (choosing **Inverse** from the **Select** menu) so that the background was selected and the dog was not. Using the **Clone Stamp Tool** (see page 68), I painted in more foliage behind the dog. Because the background was selected and the dog was not, the **Clone Stamp Tool** added these trees and leaves right *around* the dog, as if he were on a whole other layer!

Cut and paste a selection into another photo

As you work with Photoshop Elements, you will likely be doing a lot of cutting and pasting. This is, for instance, a simple way to take a person photographed in front of one background and place him or her in front of another.

Because she was shot against a green screen, the young woman is easily selected by selecting the background with the Magic Wand Tool and then inversing the selection. Once she was selected, I could cut her from one photo and paste her into another.

Because pasting places her on a layer, her image can be refined separately – the edges can be softened and she can be tinted to match the background more naturally.

To cut your subject from a background, draw a selection around him or her by using a combinations of tools – adding to and subtracting from your selection as needed. (If your subject is well defined from the background, you may be able to do most of this with the **Magic Wand Tool**, using the other selection tools and the **Add to Selection** or **Subtract from Selection** options.)

Then, to ensure your selection has a slightly softened, natural edge, use **Refine Edge** to **Shift Edge** and **Feather** it. For detailed edges, you can use the **Edge Detection** tool described on page 91.

To cut your subject from his or her current background, press **Ctrl+c** on a PC or ⌘+**c** on a Mac.

To paste your subject into a new file or onto a new background, press **Ctrl+v** on a PC or ⌘+**v** on a Mac.

Whenever you paste an image into another image file, it will appear as a new layer in that file, as seen in the illustration above. (In fact, even if you paste the image into the *same* image file you cut it from, it will become a new layer.)

This is to your advantage for a number of reasons:

1   If you need to, you can continue to refine the edge of your pasted-in image so that it fits more naturally with its new background (even using the **Eraser Tool**, if you'd like, to remove more of the image). A very effective feature for adding a more natural edge to your pasted image is the **Defringe Layer** tool, which we discuss on page 116 of **Chapter 8, Correct Color and Lighting**;

2   While it remains a layer, you can resize the pasted-in image separate from the rest of the image file.

Resizing a layer is very easy in Photoshop Elements.

When a layer is selected (by clicking on it to activate it in the **Layers** panel), it appears in your image file outlined by a rectangle, defined on each side and on the corners with a "corner handle." (If your layer image is larger than your current image file, these corner handles may appear outside of the image file, and you may need to **Ctrl+−** on a PC or ⌘**+−** on a Mac to see these handles.)

To resize the image on your selected layer, click and drag on these corner handles, as illustrated at the bottom of this page.

As you drag the corner handles, you may notice that the **Tool Options Bin** displays a number of **Transform** options. Using these transform options, you can resize or rotate your layer's image precisely by typing numbers into the spaces in the **Tool Options Bin**.

If **Constrain Proportions** is checked, your image will resize its height and width proportionately – which is usually what you'll prefer. If you uncheck **Constrain Proportions**, you will resize the layer's height and width separately, resulting in a squeezed or disproportionate picture.

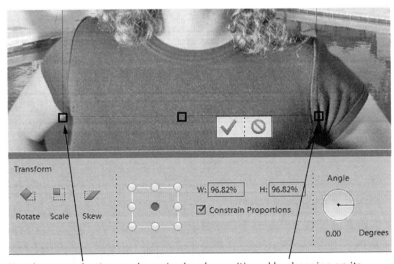

Your layer or selection can be resized and repositioned by dragging on its corner handles or by setting the Transform options in the Tool Options panel.

To finish the resizing, click the green checkmark on your image file or press the **Enter** key.

(While you're in resizing image mode, no other functions in Photoshop Elements will work. So, if you find after resizing your image that no other tool will activate, press **Enter** or click on the green checkmark to complete the resizing.)

If you're enlarging your layer's image by dragging the corner handles, keep in mind the golden rule of raster art: *You can't add details or pixels where they don't exist.*

You can expand the size of your image only so far before the pixels will begin to break up and your image will appear fuzzy or pixelated. For this reason, it's best to cut and paste between image files that are of similar size and resolution.

Your layer will remain a layer until you flatten your layers or save your file as a file format other than a Photoshop (**PSD**) file. (For information on flattening a layered image see page 126 of **Chapter 9, Work with Photoshop Elements Layers**.)

Fill or stroke a selection

Any area that's selected can also be filled or stroked. In fact, even a selected area on an otherwise blank layer can be filled or stroked.

Filling means painting the selected area with color or a pattern.

A selected area can be filled in any one of a number of ways:

The Paint Bucket fills your canvas or your selected area.

1   Dragging the **Paint Bucket Tool** onto the selected area. The selection will then be filled with the **Foreground Color**.

2   Selecting the **Gradient Tool** and dragging a line across the selection. The selection will be filled with a gradation of the **Foreground** to **Background Color** (or however you've defined your gradient), colored from the beginning to the end of the line you've drawn.

3   Pressing **Alt/Option+Backspace**. The selection will be filled with the **Foreground Color**.

4   Pressing **Ctrl+Backspace** (or ⌘+**Backspace** on a Mac). The selection will be filled with the **Background Color**.

5   Selecting the **Fill Selection** option from the **Edit** drop-down on the Menu Bar.

The **Fill** option panel offers a number of possible ways for filling your selection, including: with the **Foreground Color, Background Color** or a custom color; black, white or gray; or a **Custom Pattern** from the dozens of patterns available in the pattern library.

The Gradient Tool fills your canvas or selected area with (by default) a gradation from the Foreground to the Background Colors.

The option to stroke a selection is under the Edit drop-down menu.

Even when a blank layer is selected on your canvas, a stroke can be added to your selected area, outlining it with your Foreground Color or any custom color.

Stroking means outlining a selected area.

A selected area can be stroked by selecting **Stroke (Outline) Selection** from the **Edit** menu.

By default, the stroke color will be the current **Foreground Color**. However, by clicking on the color swatch square on the **Stroke** option panel, you can launch the **Color Picker** (See page 57 of **Chapter 5**), from which you can select any color for your stroke.

The width of the stroke is measured in pixels, by default. And you may set the stroke to appear just outside your selected area (**Outside**), on your selection line (**Center**) or just inside the selection line (**Inside**).

Image Resizing

Canvas Resizing

Chapter 7

Resize Your Images
Image and canvas sizes

Resizing can mean a number of different things in Photoshop Elements.

- You may want to enlarge or reduce the overall size of your image file.

- You may want to enlarge or reduce the canvas your image appears on.

- You may want to trim the edges off your image by cropping.

Each of these functions has methods and challenges for getting the best results.

Image Size changes the overall size of the actual image

Canvas Size trims or adds to the size of the canvas the artwork appears on, sometimes cropping the artwork itself

Image Size vs. Canvas Size

As we discussed in **Chapter 1, Things You Need to Know**, there is a key difference between **Image Size** and **Canvas Size**.

Image Size (page 102) is the overall size of your image file. Changing the **Image Size** changes the size of the entire image file without removing or adding to its basic content. In other words, in changing the **Image Size** of your photograph of a city skyline, the content of the picture will remain essentially the same. The entire skyline image will remain. Only the size and/or resolution of the image file will change.

Canvas Size (page 104) refers to the size of the *canvas*, or background, your image appears on. Changing the **Canvas Size** changes the *content* of the image file, either adding to or subtracting from (essentially cropping) the image itself. Reducing the **Canvas Size** of the photograph of the city skyline, for instance, will *chop off* the edges of the image itself without changing the resolution of the image file.

Cropping is a form of changing the **Canvas Size**. When you crop an image, you don't change the size or resolution of the content. You merely trim the canvas. (For more information on cropping, see the **Crop Tool** on page 78 of **Chapter 5, The Photoshop Elements Toolbox**.)

Both **Image Size** and **Canvas Size** are available under the program's **Image** menu, under the **Resize** sub-menu.

You can't create pixels!

This is a principle we repeat several times in this book.

Your image file is made up of pixels – thousands or even millions of little boxes of color. You can't create pixels where none exist. You can't add more resolution to a low-resolution image.

Well, *sometimes* you can. But mostly you can't. And it's usually not a good idea to try.

See, when you add to the **Image Size** of a file – increasing a 640x480 pixel image to 800x600 pixels, for instance – you're essentially telling the program to create more pixels for that image. Photoshop Elements will do its best to oblige – but it can't work miracles. So what the program does is create new pixels by duplicating existing pixels.

This works to a certain extent. (A rule of thumb is that it will work somewhat effectively for up to about a 10% increase in size.) But, since the result will simply be made of *duplicated* pixels, your image will be larger – but you won't get any more detail.

In fact, if you increase your image's size too much, your image will eventually just look fuzzy and pixelated. (Officially, "over-rezzed.")

Remember that those little blocks of color can only get so big before they start to show. And, if you've ever downloaded a photo or a logo from a web site and then tried to enlarge it and print it, you know exactly what I mean. There's no magic way to increase detail where none exists.

However, there may well be times when you need to *cheat* your image resolution just a bit. Force it up in size – maybe 10%. Going from 640x480 to 700x525 pixels, for instance. And when you do, Photoshop Elements allows you to set *how* it creates these new pixels for the best possible results. This process is called **Resample Image**, and we discuss it in **Image Resizing**, on the following page.

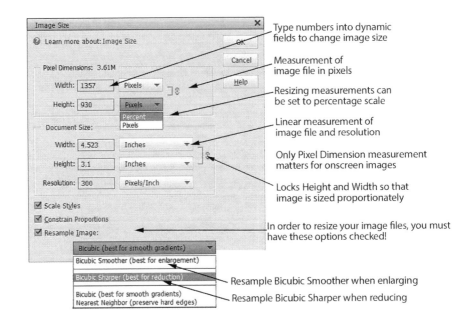

Type numbers into dynamic fields to change image size

Measurement of image file in pixels

Resizing measurements can be set to percentage scale

Linear measurement of image file and resolution

Only Pixel Dimension measurement matters for onscreen images

Locks Height and Width so that image is sized proportionately

In order to resize your image files, you must have these options checked!

Resample Bicubic Smoother when enlarging
Resample Bicubic Sharper when reducing

Image Resizing

The option panel for resizing an image is launched by selecting **Image Size** under the program's **Image** menu, on the **Resize** sub-menu.

Resizing an image means increasing or reducing the size or resolution of the image file itself, usually without substantially changing the photographic content of that image.

In other words, resizing a photograph of a scene from 2048x1536 pixels (the size of an image from a 3 megapixel camera) to 640x480 pixels (the size, in square pixels, of a standard definition video frame) reduces the file size, details and resolution of the photo, but it does not change the essential scene in the photograph itself.

The **Image Size** option screen displays the size of your image file in pixels as well as in linear measurements (inches, centimeters, etc.). It also includes a resolution setting, listed in **Pixels per Inch** (or centimeters, etc.). (For more information on picture resolution, see **Resolution** on page 5 of **Chapter 1**.)

The information listed on the **Image Size** option panel includes:

Pixel Dimensions, a measurement of your image file's size, an actual count of the number of pixels (**Width** and **Height**) that make up your image file.

As we discussed in **Chapter 1, Things You Need to Know**, if you're working on photos or graphics for video or for the Web, these **Pixel Dimensions** are the *only* measurements that you really need to be concerned with. Linear measurements, including resolution, are meaningless in the onscreen image world.

Document Size, a linear measurement of your image file in inches, centimeters, points, picas, etc. (the drop-down menu next to each number allows you to change the measurement method), as well as resolution.

If you are producing photos and graphics for print, these three measurements are very important, since stretching, or "over-rezzing," an image beyond its actual size can produce a poor quality or fuzzy picture. All three numbers are important in the print world because, to produce a relatively clean print image, your photo or graphic will need at least 150-200 pixels per inch and 300 or more p.p.i. for a very high-quality print.

Changing the Image Size changes the size of the photo itself without affecting content.

These measurements are all dynamic fields, and you can change the size of your image by typing new numbers into the boxes. (The **Pixel Dimensions** fields, in fact, can be changed from **pixel** measurements to **percentages** so that you can accurately re-scale your image.)

Note that, as indicated in the illustration on the facing page, **in order to properly change the size or resolution of your photo or image file, you must have the Scale Styles, Constrain Proportions and Resample Image options checked.**

> **Scale Styles.** This checkbox applies to any styles or effects you've added to your image file. (**Drop Shadows**, for instance.) When this box is checked, the size of the **effect** is changed, proportionately, as your image file is resized.

> **Constrain Proportions.** When checked, this feature automatically calculates the **Width** to match whatever **Height** you type in (or vice versa) in order to keep your image file proportionate.

> **Resample Image.** Resampling is a vital function of resizing. Resampling is how Photoshop Elements creates new pixels when you enlarge an image, and how it averages pixel information when you reduce an image 's size.

> If this box is unchecked, with the **Nearest Neighbor** option set, you will not be able to dynamically change your **Pixel Dimensions**.

The **Resample Image** drop-down menu offers a number of options for resampling your image's pixels when you resize a file. Only two are really of value for the vast majority of your work.

> **Bicubic Sharper.** When you are **reducing** an image file's size, select this resampling method. This creates the cleanest-looking reduced image.

> **Bicubic Smoother.** When **enlarging** an image file, select this resampling method. As we've said, there are limits to how much you can increase the size of any image file – but the **Bicubic Smoother** will create the smoothest and most natural blends of color among the new pixels it creates.

Photoshop Elements also includes a function for batch-resizing a number of photos or image files at once. For more information on batching processes, see **Process Multiple Files** on page 174 of **Chapter 13, Advanced Photoshop Elements Tools**.

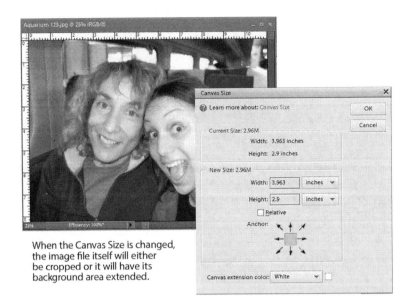

When the Canvas Size is changed, the image file itself will either be cropped or it will have its background area extended.

Canvas Resizing

The option panel for resizing your image's canvas is launched by selecting **Canvas Size** under the **Image** menu, on the **Resize** sub-menu.

The "canvas" is the image file itself, the canvas on which your imagery exists. When you reduce or enlarge the canvas for a photo, you are adding more to the sides or cropping from the size of the image file.

This tool is particularly effective for changing the shape (aspect ratio) of your image file.

The **Canvas Size** option panel displays the dimensions of your image file.

The **New Size** area of this panel contains two dynamic measurement listings, which you can write over. Using the drop-downs, you can set the measurements for these dimensions to any of the standards available in Photoshop Elements. For video, web or other onscreen graphic or photo, you will want to set these measurement standards to **Pixels**.

Though the most common way to resize your canvas is to designate what you want its new **Height** or **Width** to be, you can also simply designate how much you want to be removed instead. Checking the **Relative** option allows you to designate precisely the amount of your canvas that will be added or removed when it is resized. In other words, if you check **Relative** and set the **Width** to -20 (minus 20) pixels, 20 pixels will be cropped from the width of your canvas.

The **Anchor** area of this panel displays a square with arrows that point up, down, right, left and from each corner of the square. This **Anchor** setting represents how and from where your image canvas will be added to or subtracted from when you resize it – as indicated by the directions its arrows point.

Each of these arrows determines which area of your canvas will be affected by the changes to the **Height** or **Width**.

In other words, if you were to set the **Anchor** so that the arrows point down and to the right and then *decrease* the size of your canvas, your image would be resized by cropping from the *top left* of your image file. (Think of it as cropping toward the bottom right).

Because the Anchor is set to the lower right corner, the reduced Canvas Size crops from the upper left of the image file.

Likewise, if you were to set the **Anchor** so that the arrows point up and to the right, increasing the size of the canvas would add space *above and to the right* of your current image, as illustrated below.

If no arrow is selected, the tool will crop from or add to your canvas equally, around all sides.

By default, any canvas added to your image file will appear in the **Background Color**. However, the **Canvas Extension Color** drop-down menu at the bottom of this option panel allows you to set the added canvas to appear in the **Foreground Color**, black, white, gray or any other custom color.

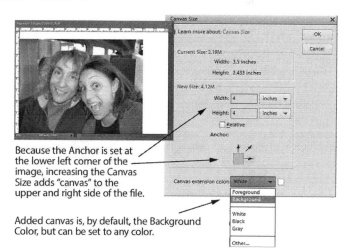

Because the Anchor is set at the lower left corner of the image, increasing the Canvas Size adds "canvas" to the upper and right side of the file.

Added canvas is, by default, the Background Color, but can be set to any color.

Auto Fixing Your Photos

Adjusting Brightness & Contrast

Adjusting Color

Adjusting Sharpness

Adjustment Layers

Chapter 8

Correct Color and Lighting

Adjust and clean up your images

Under the Enhance drop-down menu,
Photoshop Elements includes a number of
tools for cleaning up, correcting color and
adjusting the lighting of your
image files.

Many of these tools are based on advanced
tools in the professional version of
Photoshop. Others are more simplified
"quick fixes."

Whether your goal is to clean up your
photos or to change the colors in your
image files to produce a special effect,
there's likely an adjustment tool for your
general or specific need.

Auto Fixes

Under the **Enhance** drop-down on the Menu Bar, there are seven automatic fixes for your image files. In many cases, an automatic fix may be the easiest way to correct your photo's lighting and color.

But remember that automatic fixes are just math, not magic. Automatic fixes merely look at the lightest spot in your image file and assume it should be pure white, then look at the darkest spot in your image file and assume it should be pure black – and then they calculate the rest of the image's color and light values as a range between them.

So, although in many cases, auto fixes can be very effective – they're still just a best guess.

Photoshop Elements includes a number of "auto" fixes under the Enhance menu.

And, depending on the results, you may want to move on to manual adjustments from there or even **Ctrl+z** (⌘+z on a Mac) to undo the fix and do it entirely manually.

Virtually every auto fix has a manual adjustment alternative.

The nine automatic fixes are:

Auto Smart Tone. We discuss this cool, relatively new addition to Photoshop Elements' "Auto" set in detail on page 110.

Auto Smart Fix. A good, general automatic fix, correcting for poor exposure, contrast problems, color balance and color saturation in a single sweep. (There's also an **Adjust Smart Fix** tool a little further down the Enhance menu list which allows you to control the overall intensity of these adjustments.)

Auto Levels considers the luminance values of red, green and blue in calculating its best color and lighting adjustments.

Auto Contrast considers only the brightness and contrast levels in calculating its best guess settings, without regard to the image file's colors.

Auto Haze Removal automatically enriches the color in your photos to remove the effects of fog and haze. See also the **Haze Removal** tool on page 116.

Auto Color Correction focuses on the mid-tones in the image, correcting the image file's color by presuming the middle range of colors as gray and balancing the other colors based on that. Unlike **Auto Levels**, **Auto Color Correction** does not look at the individual color channels but judges the colors of the image file as an overall mix.

Auto Shake Removal sharpens your photo to remove some of the blur from photos shot with a shaky hand. See also **Shake Reduction** on page 117.

Auto Sharpen increases the contrast between pixels, which can make a photo appear clearer, sharper or more focused. See also the **Unsharp Mask** on page 118.

Auto Red Eye Fix uses its best guess to locate "red eyes" on the people in your photos and then darken and desaturate (un-color) them.

Control what gets changed

When an area of your image file is selected (defined by "marching ants"), any changes made to color or lightness will affect *only* the area within the selection.

The color and lighting adjustments you make to your image files may be applied to the entire file or to isolated areas of your file. You may, for instance, want to brighten or adjust the color of a person in the foreground of a photo but not change the color or lighting for the background. Or you may want to make the sky bluer in a picture but keep the grass a rich green.

There are three ways to control how and where your effects are applied in your image files:

1   **Selection**. As we discuss in **Chapter 6, Select and Isolate Areas in Your Photos**, when you select an area in your image file, only that area will be changed by any added effects or adjustments. This is far and away the most common way to control which areas of your image files are affected.

2   **Brush Tools**. As we discuss in **Chapter 5, The Photoshop Elements Toolbox**, the **Smart Brush** tools are designed for applying effects only to certain areas of your image file. With **Smart Brushes**, you "paint" the effect onto only certain, specific areas of your image file.

   Additionally, the **Red Eye Removal Tool** darkens and desaturates only the area you brush – removing the bright red reflections from your subject's eyes. And the **Dodge** and **Burn Tools** allow you to lighten or darken specific spots of your image file.

   Brushes, as we explained in **Chapter 5,** can be large and wide or very small and fine, and may have hard edges or soft, feathered edges.

3   **Layers**. As we discuss in **Chapter 9, Work With Photoshop Elements Layers**, unless you specifically direct Photoshop Elements to affect several layers at once, any changes you make to an active layer in a layered image file will apply *only* to that layer. As we demonstrate in **Cut and paste a selection** on page 86, this is a very useful function as you work to match a person who has been cut and pasted from another document onto a new background.

Auto Smart Tone

Auto Smart Tone is one of the most advanced of the "Auto" tools in the Photoshop Elements toolkit. This is not only because of its unique interface for adjusting the levels of blacks, whites and midtones in your photos. **Auto Smart Tone** is also a tool which can be set to "learn" from your adjustments.

This means that, as you make adjustments with the **Auto Smart Tone** tool, the tool will essentially record the settings you make and the levels of tone you prefer and, when you next use it to adjust a photo, it will automatically adjust the tool to favor your preferences.

Auto Smart Tone allows you to adjust your photo's tone levels by dragging around a control dot in a very intuitive interface.

Optionally, the tool will remember your usual settings.

The **Auto Smart Tone** tool is very easy to use.

1   Select **Auto Smart Tone** from the program's **Enhance** menu.

The **Smart Tone** workspace will open.

A grid with a control dot in the center will appear over your photo. On each of the four corners of the panel will appear thumbnails representing your photo with various levels of blacks, whites and midtones. (Tone is similar to brightness and contrast, but is somewhat more sophisticated, usually based on the range of individual red, green and blue levels in your photo.)

2   Adjust your photo's tone.

To adjust your photo's tone, simply drag the control dot toward the corner thumbnail that best represents the tone you'd like your photo to have.

To reset your tone back to center, click the **Reset** button along the bottom right of the workspace. To accept your adjustment click **OK**.

In the lower left of this workspace panel is a little menu icon (as seen in the illustration above). Clicking on this icon will give you the option to set the tool to **Learn From This Correction**.

If you elect for the tool to remember your tone adjustment settings, the next time you apply **Auto Smart Tone**, its default setting will be based on the tone levels you've set in the past.

To erase the "learning" history for this tool, go to the program's **Preferences** (under the **Edit** menu on a PC) and, on the **General** page, click the button labeled **Reset Auto Smart Tone Learning**.

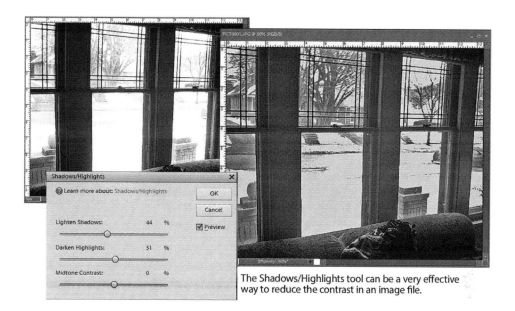

The Shadows/Highlights tool can be a very effective way to reduce the contrast in an image file.

Adjust Lighting

Certainly the most basic adjustments you'll make to your photos will be to adjust their brightness and contrast. As with all adjustments you can make in Photoshop Elements, there are simplified and complex tools for making these adjustments. The more complicated the adjustment, the more control you will have over the results.

These functions are located under the program's **Enhance** menu, on the **Adjust Lighting** sub-menu.

Brightness/Contrast

As basic an adjustment as you'll find in Photoshop Elements, **Brightness** lightens or darkens your photo while **Contrast** determines the difference between the blackest blacks and whitest whites in your image file.

Shadows/Highlights

A personal favorite, this great tool has saved many photos for me. Basically, it decreases the contrast in your image file by enhancing the midtones, as illustrated above. This is helpful if, for instance, you have a photo of a bird in flight, which appears as just a dark silhouette against the bright sky. The tool reduces the contrast between bird and sky and brings out details in the bird that would otherwise be indiscernible. It's great for bringing out details in an image shot on a very sunny or snowy day, a photo with such high contrasts that its lights are too light and its darks are too dark.

The Levels histogram displays a count of all of the pixels in your image file, graphed by level. It can be set to display the color mix or only the red, green or blue channel.

Darkest point

Midtone center

Whitest point

Levels

In my opinion, **Levels** really is more of a *color* adjustment than a lighting adjustment. In fact, it's my favorite go-to tool for color correcting an image file.

The histogram on the **Levels** option screen (illustrated above) maps the pixels in your image from darkest to lightest.

By moving the arrows on either end of the histogram in or out, you define the darkest dark and lightest light points in your image file. The middle arrow defines the center midtone. The **Output Levels** widen the distance between dark and light. In essence, then, this is a more precise way to set your brightness and contrast.

But you can go even deeper in your adjustments on this **Levels** screen. If you drop down the **Channel** menu at the top of the panel, you'll see that you can set these levels for each individual color also. This makes this tool one way to, say, lower the amount of red in a photo or increase the amount of blue.

I show you how to use the **Levels** tool to color correct your photos in the sidebar on page 114.

Quick Fixes and Guided Fixes

Quick Fixes are semi-automatic fixes to color and lighting that Photoshop Elements applies to your image file. These include "red eye" fixes, fixes for enriching the color of the sky or whitening teeth and many simplified and automatic fixes for correcting color and light. We discuss them and how to use them in greater detail in **Chapter 3, Quick Fixes**.

Guided Fixes, as the name implies, are adjustments that are automatically applied to your image file as you work through a list of options. We discuss them and how to use them in greater detail in **Chapter 4, Guided Edits**

Preview changes

When Preview is checked on any adjustment panel, you will see a preview of any adjustments to your image file.

When you launch an option screen for any adjustment or effect, you may notice a checkbox labeled **Preview** on the screen. **Previewing** allows you to see, in real time, how your adjustments will affect your final image.

When this function is enabled, your image file will temporarily display any changes or adjustments you make.

Additionally, by checking and unchecking the **Preview** option as you make your adjustments, you can do a before-and-after comparison of your changes.

If you click **OK**, these changes will be permanently applied to your image file. If you click **Cancel**, your changes will not be applied.

Adjust Color

As every photographer knows, there's almost no such thing as perfect lighting. Natural sunlight tends toward blue while indoor lighting tends toward yellow, and even the best cameras can have a problem adjusting their white balance for every situation. Fortunately, Photoshop Elements offers a number of tools for adjusting and correcting color.

These tools are available under the **Enhance** menu, on the **Adjust Color** sub-menu.

Remove Color Cast

This tool is a smart fix that bases its color correction calculations on a single point that you define. To use it, click on the eyedropper on the panel and then click on a spot on your image file that you'd like to appear as either pure white, pure black or pure gray. The tool will then automatically adjust all the other colors in the image based on that definition.

113

Adjust Hue/Saturation

Hue is the *tint* of a color (essentially the color itself), its levels based on the 360 degrees of a color wheel.

Saturation is the *amount* of color. (The opposite of saturation is no color, or black & white.)

Lightness is how *dark or light* the color is.

Adjust Hue/Saturation is probably less effective as a color correction tool than it is as a color *changing* tool. But it does serve as an alternative to adjusting your image's colors based on red, green and blue values.

Use Levels to color correct a photo

By using the eyedroppers to define the areas of your image you'd like to appear as pure white and pure black, you can very effectively color correct your photo.

Here's a professional trick that I often use to correct color in a photo using this **Levels** panel.

The three eyedroppers to the right of the histogram can be used to define the black, white and midtone points in your image file.

To correct the colors in a photo, click on the first (**Black Point**) eyedropper, then use that eyedropper to click, or "sample," the blackest spot in your photo (as illustrated above).

Then click on the third eyedropper (**White Point**) and sample the whitest spot in your photo.

If you want to further correct color, you can use the center eyedropper (**Gray Point**) to define a spot on your image file you'd like to appear as central gray.

By defining the blackest and whitest areas of your photo, you can usually neutralize any color hues and set a clear contrast level.

Remove Color

Remove Color desaturates your image file, leaving it as pure grayscale (black & white). But it's probably not the best way to get a quality grayscale image from a color photo.

A better, more powerful alternative for creating a grayscale image from a color photo is **Convert to Black and White**, discussed on page 117.

Replace Color

Replace Color uses the same color adjustment tools as **Adjust Hue/ Saturation**, but it applies these changes to a defined area of your image file only.

To define the area of your photo to be changed, create a **Selection** using the eyedropper in the option panel (as well as the add to/subtract from eyedroppers). Your selected areas will appear as levels of white in the preview window. Once you've defined your selection, the mixture of **Hue, Saturation** and **Lightness** you create in this panel will replace the colors in your selected areas.

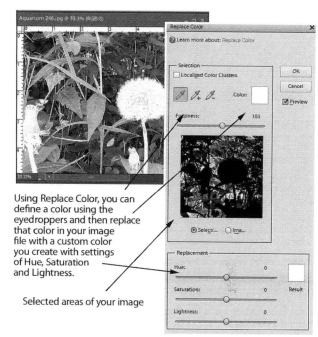

Using Replace Color, you can define a color using the eyedroppers and then replace that color in your image file with a custom color you create with settings of Hue, Saturation and Lightness.

Selected areas of your image

Adjust Color Curves

Adjust Color Curves is a very high-level correction tool that allows you to not only adjust the levels of the darkest and lightest areas in your image file but also, by adjusting the points in the curve or by moving the sliders, adjust the intensity for several color level points in your image, as illustrated below.

Curves adjusts the color for your image files from five separate levels of brightness. The styles listed under Select a Style offer preset curves for making some general adjustments.

The **Select a Style** window allows you to select some color curve presets. Once selected, these settings can be further tweaked by moving the sliders.

Adjust Color for Skin Tone

Skin tones are often the single most challenging element in a photo to color correct. With this tool, you focus on skin tones only, assuming the rest of your photo will follow suit. To use it, click to select a sample of skin tone in your photo, then adjust the **Tan**, **Blush** and color **Temperature** sliders until the skin colors look right.

Defringe Layer

Defringe Layer is designed to work with layered image files. It's particularly effective when you're pasting a person or other subject from one image file into another (which automatically places the pasted image on a new layer, as we demonstrate in **Cut and paste a selection** on page 94 of **Chapter 6, Use a selection to protect an area**). Based on the number of pixels you designate, **Defringe Layer** blends the outline of the pasted layer so that it fits more naturally with its new background.

Haze Removal

New to version 14, the **Haze Removal** too enriches the color and contrast in your photos to reduce the effects of haze and fog. (The **Enhance** menu also includes an **Auto Haze Removal** tool, as discussed on page 108.)

The **Haze Removal** tool offers options for controlling the amount of **Haze Reduction** as well as the **Sensitivity** (or tolerance level) to the fog or haze.

Naturally, there's a limit to how much haze or fog this tool can remove before things just get ugly – but, in most situations, it's very effective!

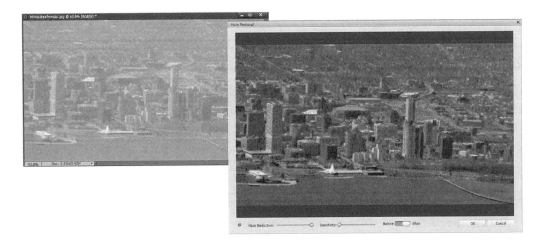

Convert to Black and White

As the name implies, this tool desaturates – or removes the color from – your image file, rendering it as grayscale. But, unlike the simplified **Remove Color** tool discussed earlier in this chapter, **Convert to Black and White** includes options for enhancing the grayscale in your image so that your final black & white image is as vivid as the original color image.

Under **Select a Style**, you'll find half a dozen presets for improving your image. In most cases, one of these presets alone will give you a strong, vivid grayscale. But if you'd prefer, by adjusting the sliders, you can further tweak the image to give you the strongest possible results.

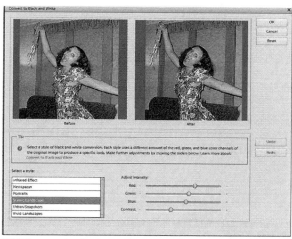

With the proper adjustments (or preset adjustments) a black & white photo can look as vivid as the original color photo.

Adjust Sharpness

A somewhat simplified version of the **Unsharp Mask**, **Adjust Sharpness** uses pixel contrast levels to correct for a certain amount of fuzziness in your photos.

It can't make an out-of-focus picture suddenly look crisp and focused, of course. But, when a photo is just a bit soft or blurred, **Adjust Sharpness** can make it appear crisper and clearer.

As with the **Unsharp Mask**, you can only add so much sharpness to an image before it becomes counter-productive. Too much sharpness can make your photo appear grainy and overly-sharp, its individual pixels too highly contrasted. So remember, the goal with either of these tools is sharpness, not crystal clarity.

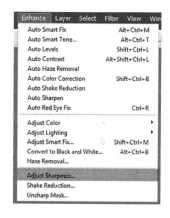

Shake Reduction

New to version 14 of Photoshop Elements is a tool for taking some of the blur out a photo with a bit too much jiggle.

Basically, it's the tool is just a variation on the **Unsharp Mask** – though the **Shake Reduction** tool (as illustrated at the top of page 118) is designed specifically to reduce the blur in a photo shot with a shaky hand.

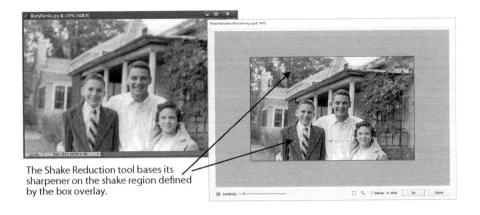

The Shake Reduction tool bases its sharpener on the shake region defined by the box overlay.

Unsharp Mask

Traditionally, the last adjustment made to any photo is to apply the **Unsharp Mask.**

Although the results for **Unsharp Mask** and **Adjust Sharpness** are similar, **Unsharp Mask** is traditionally considered the more "professional" of the two. **Unsharp Mask** increases the contrast in your pixels (dark pixels become darker, light pixels become lighter), the result being a cleaner, sharper image.

As a general rule, **Amount** should not be set to more than 80%, **Radius** is usually set to 1.0 pixels and **Threshold** is set to 0 levels. Although the best settings will vary depending on the needs and resolution of your photo, too much **Unsharp Mask** can result in an overly sharpened, grainy image.

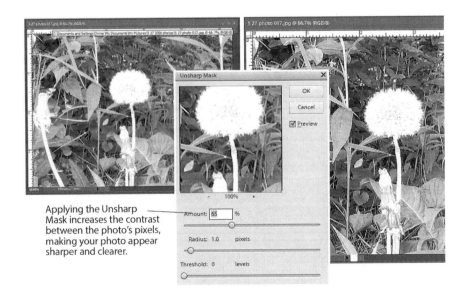

Applying the Unsharp Mask increases the contrast between the photo's pixels, making your photo appear sharper and clearer.

When using an Adjustment Layer, changes to lightness or color appear in your image – but these changes are actually a separate layer and your original image remains unchanged.

Work with Adjustment Layers

When working with most adjustment tools in Photoshop Elements, any changes you make to your image file are permanent. The image itself is changed – the pixels are lightened or darkened or colors are shifted. The only way to remove an adjustment is to undo it (by pressing **Ctrl+z** on a PC or ⌘**+z** on a Mac or using the **Undo** button or the **Undo History** panel) – and then you're also undoing whatever other work you've done since that adjustment.

However, Photoshop Elements also provides a way to keep these changes separate from the original image file. The effect is the same – your adjustments show as changes in the edited image file. But the changes are not permanent until you save the file as something other than a Photoshop (**PSD**) file or you flatten the image.

To launch an **Adjustment Layer** for your image file, go to the program's **Layer** menu and select **New Adjustment Layer** and then, from the sub-menu, whatever adjustment (**Levels, Brightness/ Contrast, Hue/Saturation,** etc.) you'd like to make.

As when you make direct adjustments to your image file, your changes will be displayed on your image file if the **Preview** option is checked.

The difference is that, when you **OK** your changes, the changes are not applied to the original image. Rather, your adjustments show up as a separate layer – an **Adjustment Layer** – in the **Layers** panel.

There are a number of advantages to using **Adjustment Layers** rather than changing the actual image file:

1   **Your changes do not affect the original file.** Remember, once you change your native file and save it, there's no going back. Once you've closed and re-opened your image file, you can't even undo your changes. Using **Adjustment Layers**, your original, native file remains in its original, unadjusted form.

By turning Adjustment Layers on and off (by clicking the eyeball icon), you can do a before-and-after comparision for your adjustments or even compare several adjustments on several Adjustment Layers!

2   **Adjustment Layers can be turned off and on.** As illustrated at the top of the following page, by clicking on the eyeball icon to the left of each layer in the **Layers** panel, you can turn that layer on or off. This is also true of **Adjustment Layers**. By turning your **Adjustment Layers** off and on, you can do a before-and-after comparison of your adjustments.

3   **You can create several alternative versions.** There's no limit to the number of **Adjustment Layers** you can add to an image file and, by turning these layers off and on, you can try to compare several different adjustments (**Levels** vs. **Brightness/Contrast** for instance) to see which gives you the best results.

4   **Adjustment Layers can be re-adjusted.** By double-clicking on the adjustment icon on any **Adjustment Layer** on the **Layers** panel, you can re-launch your adjustment screen for that layer, allowing you to further tweak your settings.

When none of your changes are permanent, you're freer to experiment, to try a variety of changes and even make a few easily-undoable mistakes. And, with **Adjustments Layers**, you're also able to compare your options.

Whenever possible – particularly if you're creating proofs for a client – I recommend your using **Adjustment Layers** to create your variations. The ability to turn any changes off or on, or remove them completely, helps prevent you from making changes to the original photo file that are impossible to undo.

The Layers Panel

Simplifying Vector Layers

The Layer Mask

Copying Layers from One File Another

Creating Non-Square Graphics

Chapter 9
Work With Photoshop Elements Layers
Stacks of images

If you're new to Photoshop Elements, layers may seem a bit intimidating – and maybe even a bit superfluous. But, as you work with them, you'll begin to see how powerful a feature they truly are.

It's not uncommon for an advanced Photoshop user to have a dozen or more layers stacked up in his or her image file at once.

Layers also play an important role in the creation and editing of DVD and BluRay templates for Premiere Elements.

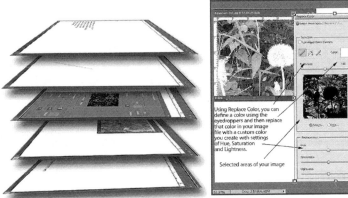

Layers are like a stack of images, with shapes and text on upper layers revealing lower layers through transparent areas.

How layers work

The simplest way to understand how layers work is to imagine them as a stack. The top layer in the stack is completely visible. And, if the top layer is text or does not cover the entire canvas or if there are transparent areas in it, the layers below show around or through it.

One advantage of having elements of your image file on separate layers rather than merged into a single layer is that each layer remains editable, separate from the rest of the image file.

Some other functions of layers include:

- As discussed in **Cut and paste a selection** on page 94 of **Chapter 6, Select and Isolate Areas in Your Photos**, when you cut and paste elements from one image file to another (or even cut from and paste into the same image file) the pasted elements will appear as a new layer. This function allows you to further manipulate and adjust the pasted layer so that it better blends with the background.

- When you add text to an image file (as we discuss in **Chapter 10, Create and Edit Text**) it will appear as a separate layer. The text on this layer remains editable until the layer is simplified or flattened.

- When you create a shape for your image file, it also appears as its own layer (as we discuss on page 76 of **Chapter 5, Get to Know the Photoshop Elements Toolbox**). Like text, shapes remain editable until you simplify or flatten the layer. (See **Simplify or Flatten a Layer** on page 126.)

- As we discuss on page 119 of **Chapter 8, Correct Color and Lighting**, an **Adjustment Layer** allows you to make adjustments to the lighting and color of your image file without actually changing your image file. (The adjustments appear as a separate layer.)

The **Smart Brush Tool** (discussed on page 67 of **Chapter 5, Get to Know the Photoshop Elements Toolbox**) works similarly. The **Smart Brush Tool's** color and lighting adjustments remain separate from the image itself. These adjustments can then be further tweaked – or even removed altogether – without making any permanent changes to your original image file or photo.

Additionally, there are a couple of other functions of layers worth mentioning.

You can duplicate your layers, making several versions of the same layer, each with unique effects or adjustments applied to it. In this way, you can create several versions of your image, comparing them to each other by simply turning the layers on and off.

The easiest way to duplicate a layer is to drag the layer, in the **Layers** panel, up onto the **Make New Layer** icon at the top left of the panel (as illustrated on the following page).

Layers are the key to creating non-square graphics! Non-square graphics include logos, shapes and text-only graphics files.

By removing the background, using layers and saving your files to the proper format, you can create and export graphics in any shape you want, without the constraints of that pesky rectangular background (as we'll demonstrate in **Create non-square graphics** on page 129).

Select a layer to edit

To select the layer you want to work on, click on it in the **Layers** panel. The selected layer will then be highlighted.

In Photoshop Elements, you can also select a layer simply by clicking on the graphic or text in your image file in the **Editor** workspace. (The layer that the graphic is on will automatically be selected in the **Layers** panel.)

This makes repositioning the layered elements in your image file fairly intuitive.

The labels around the Layers panel illustration:

Create Adjustment Layer (see page 109)

Make New Layer

Layer blending options

Currently selected layer (highlighted)

Shape layer

Text layer

Image layer

Disable/enable Layer (eyeball icon)

Background layer

Add Layer Mask   Lock Layer   Delete Layer

Layers | Effects | Graphics | Favorites

Normal   Opacity: 100%

Shape 3
Shape 2
Shape 1
Memories of Summer
Layer 0
Layer 1
Background

The Layers panel

The layers of your image file will appear stacked in the **Layers** panel. Your image file will usually include, at the bottom of this stack, a **Background** layer (unless you've manually removed it).

With the exception of Photoshop (PSD) files (and some rare TIFs), graphic formats (JPEGs, GIFs, PNGs) are flat. When you open them in Photoshop Elements, the only layer that will appear in the **Layers** panel will be a **Background** layer. (This layer is locked by default, indicated by a padlock icon on it. However, it can be unlocked and turned into a layer simply by double-clicking on it.)

As can be seen in the illustration above, the **Layers** panel includes a number of tools for working with and managing your layers:

New layers can be created by clicking on the **Make New Layer** or **Create Adjustment Layer** buttons at the top left of the panel, as illustrated above. As mentioned earlier, some functions – such as cutting and pasting, creating shapes and adding text – automatically create new layers.

Layers can be re-ordered or re-stacked simply by dragging them around in the panel. For instance, if you'd like a shape on one layer to appear *over* rather than *under* the image in another, you can just drag it above the other in the stack on the **Layers** panel.

Layers can be deleted – singularly or several at once – by selecting them (or **Shift-clicking** to select several) and pressing the **Delete** or **Backspace** key on your keyboard or clicking on the trash can icon.

Layers can be linked. When you select two or more layers at once (by **Ctrl-clicking or ⌘-clicking** or **Shift-clicking** to select more than one), any transformation or positioning changes applied to one will apply to *all selected layers*. You can "permanently" link two or more layers by selecting them and then selecting the **Link Layers** option from the pop-up menu in the upper right corner of the panel.

Layers can be locked. Locking a layer (clicking on the padlock) prevents that layer from being edited or moved.

Layers can also be temporarily disabled (made invisible) by clicking on the eyeball icon to the left of each layer. When the eyeball icon is toggled off, your layer will be invisible. Clicking on the eyeball icon again will re-enable the layer.

There are two advanced tools on the **Layers** panel– the first of which is worth knowing well and the other of which is worth merely knowing about:

Blending options are available through the drop-down menu that appears at the top left of the panel, as illustrated on the facing page. By default it reads **Normal** – and it is not available for use with the **Background** layer.

Blending affects how a selected layer reacts with the layers below it. It's a pretty high-level tool, but it can also create some pretty interesting effects. When the **Overlay** blend option is selected, for instance, you can paint on one layer and it will "colorize" the image on the layer below it!

More advanced uses for this feature are beyond the scope of this book, but are worth experimenting with.

Layer Sets are essentially folders on the **Layers** panel that contain groups of layers. They can be turned on or off, moved or manipulated as a group or as individual layers.

Layer Sets can't be created in Photoshop Elements. They're a function of the professional version of Photoshop.

However, depending on how large the file you're working on is, you can often open and edit a **Layer Set** in Photoshop Elements – a key process when you **Create Premiere Elements Movie Menu templates in Photoshop Elements** (as discussed on page 175 of **Chapter 13, Advanced Photoshop Elements Tools**).

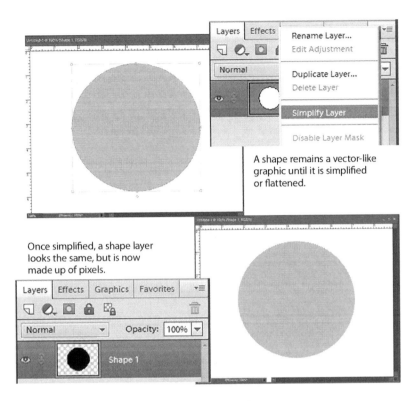

A shape remains a vector-like graphic until it is simplified or flattened.

Once simplified, a shape layer looks the same, but is now made up of pixels.

Simplify or Flatten a Layer

For the most part, the image layers you'll be working on in Photoshop Elements will be raster art. They'll be made up of pixels and, on some layers, may include transparent areas.

Two types of layers, however, are more vector than pixel-based, and include some unique abilities and liabilities.

Shape Layers (as discussed on page 76 of **Chapter 5, Get to Know the Photoshop Elements Toolbox**) are in reality shapes created using something called "masks." (See page 128.) In other words, although a shape may look like a circle, it is actually a colored layer with all the area *except* the circle masked – or made transparent. (You can see this if you look at their representation in the **Layers** panel, as in the illustration above.) This gives shapes some unique characteristics – namely that you can manipulate them like vector art, resizing and reshaping them without regard for resolution.

Text, likewise, is not rasterized, or pixel-based, art. It is a font, which behaves like vector art. In fact, if you click on a block of text with the **Selection Tool**, you can even resize the text block by dragging on its corner handles, just as if it were a shape! Text also remains editable as long as it remains a separate text layer.

These two types of Photoshop Elements objects float as layers over your other layers until one of two things happens:

The layer is simplified. To simplify a text or shape layer, **right-click** on it in the **Layers** panel and select the **Simplify Layer** option, as illustrated on the facing page. Although the shape or text may not appear different, it has now become raster art. It is now made up of pixels and can no longer be edited as vector art.

The file is flattened or layers are merged. You can flatten all of the layers in your image file onto your background, or you can just merge two layers together. The result is the same: The separate layers become one single collection of pixels.

Layers can be merged onto one another or flattened completely.

To merge one layer onto the layer below it, **right-click** on the layer in the **Layers** panel and select **Merge Down** (or press **Ctrl+e** on a PC or ⌘**+e** on a Mac).

To flatten all of the layers in your image file, **right-click** on the **Layers** panel or select from the program's **Layers** menu the option to **Flatten Image**. All of your layers will flatten into a single, rasterized **Background** layer.

Although TIFs can also be forced to maintain layers, only PSDs maintain all of your layers in an editable format. All other formats are flat. That's why, as you work on an image file, it's best to maintain a native, working PSD of your work file in addition to the JPEGs, TIFs or whatever else you are using for your output.

Although other file formats don't maintain layers, certain graphics formats can save transparency information in the form of something called an "alpha channel." That's an important function we'll explain in **Creating non-square graphics**, on page 129.

Copy layers from one image file to another

Layers can be easily copied from one image file to another.

Although you could certainly use **Copy and Paste** to move elements from one image file to another, you can more easily copy layers, layer sets, shapes and text by simply *dragging* the layers from the **Layers** panel of one image file onto another open image file.

By **Shift-clicking** to select several layers at once, you can copy a whole group of them from one image file to another!

This function becomes very useful when you **Create Premiere Elements Movie Menu templates in Photoshop Elements**, as discussed on page 175 of **Chapter 13, Advanced Photoshop Elements Tools.**

A layer, several layers and even layer sets (selected by shift-clicking) can be copied from one image file to another just by dragging it or them from the Layers panel onto the file.

Add transparency with Layer Masks

A high-level feature in Photoshop Elements is the ability to add **Layer Masks** to your image file layers – a feature previously available only in the professional version of the software.

Layer Masks create transparent and semi-transparent areas in your image layers. But, because they do so by *masking* rather than actually removing pixels, they don't actually change or remove any image data from the image itself. The areas are merely hidden or *masked*.

Add a mask to a layer by clicking the Add Layer Mask button. The Layer Mask appears as a white box, linked to the side of the layer in the palette.

1 To create a **Layer Mask**, select a layer in one of your graphics files.

(If you are working with a flat graphic or photo, you can make the **Background** a layer by **double-clicking** on it in the **Layers** panel.

2 Click the **Add Layer Mask** button at the top of the **Layers** panel.

A white box will be added to your selected image's layer, as seen above.

This white box is that layer's **Layer Mask**.

When you paint black on a **Layer Mask**, the corresponding area on the layer will be masked (made transparent). Shades of gray are read as levels of transparency.

3 Click to select this white box on the **Layers** panel, then select a brush from the Photoshop Elements **Toolbox.** Set the **Foreground Color** to black (by pressing **D** on your keyboard) and paint across your image in the **Editor** workspace. (You are actually painting on the **Layer Mask**.)

The areas of the **Layer Mask** that you paint black will mask, or make transparent, the corresponding areas of that layer's image. If you are using a soft-edged brush, the feathered edges of your brush strokes will appear semi-opaque.

In my example, I took a 640x480 pixel photo and, using a 104 px, rough-edged brush from the **Thick Heavy** brush collection, I painted a ragged black frame around the sides of my **Layer Mask**. The result, as you can see, is a photo with a ragged, grungy edge. However, this ragged edge is only a mask. The actual image has not been changed in any way. And, since this is only a mask, it can be easily revised or even removed completely without affecting the original photo.

Create non-square graphics

Most commonly-used graphics formats (JPEGs and TIFs, for instance) are rectangular. They are a certain number of pixels wide and a certain number of pixels tall, and they have four sides and four corners.

However, your graphics (logos, titles, etc.) are often not. And when you have a non-square graphic, you'll want to bring it into Premiere Elements in the shape of the graphic itself. Not square, not rectangular. And with any blank area around it – and even some blank areas through it – transparent.

Using layers, you can create graphics for Premiere Elements in shapes other than rectangular.

This is accomplished by utilizing something called an **alpha channel**.

Because of the way graphic files carry their visual data, transparency has to be communicated from program to program with a separate channel of visual information – the same way that the colors red, green and blue are communicated as individual channels. Transparency, then, is essentially a fourth color – commonly referred to as "alpha." Only a few graphics formats have the ability to carry transparency as an alpha channel.

Use graphics that include alpha channels

Not all graphics formats can carry alpha data. JPEGs and BMP files can not. TIFs and PDFs can, but they aren't typically used for partially transparent graphics. There are five commonly-used graphic formats that can include transparency, and all five will work in Premiere Elements. They are:

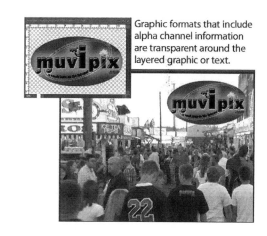

Graphic formats that include alpha channel information are transparent around the layered graphic or text.

PSDs. This is the native Photoshop and Photoshop Elements format. It's far and away the most common way to deliver a non-square graphic to Premiere Elements. This is because, not only do PSDs communicate alpha information between the programs, but the original files also remain easily re-editable (even the text) in Photoshop Elements.

GIFs and PNGs. GIFs (pronounced "jiffs", according to their inventors) are the graphics you see all over the Internet. They're the ones that include animation (like those annoying, flashing Web banner ads). PNGs (pronounced "pings") were designed to replace GIFs, and they do display color much better. Outputting either of them with their alpha channels intact involves a similar process, which we demonstrate later in this chapter.

EPSs and AIs. These are vector-based file formats created by programs like Adobe Illustrator. Though they technically don't carry alpha as a separate color channel, vector art is created by connecting corner points rather than assembling pixels. Because of this, they have no background layers and therefore often include transparent areas.

Create a backgroundless graphic in Photoshop Elements

To create a partially transparent graphic in Photoshop Elements, you need to remove the background layer from the **Layers** panel.

When you first open a PSD or other graphics or photo file in Photoshop Elements, it will likely consist of one layer, labeled "**Background**" on the **Layers** panel. Even if the file does include layers, there may be a **Background** layer at the bottom of the layers stack.

Double-click on the **Background** layer in the **Layers** panel. The **Background** layer will become a layer.

Layered files behave very differently once they have no **Background**. Layers with no background have transparency behind them.

For instance, if you erase or cut an area on a **Background** layer, that area will be replaced by your **Background Color.** However, if you erase or cut an area from a layer, you will cut *through* the layer. What you remove will become transparent!

If you have converted your **Background** into a layer by double-clicking on it, you can remove areas of it by using the **Eraser Tool** or by selecting non-essential areas of the graphic (selecting the white around your logo, for instance, using the **Magic Wand** or the **Quick Selection Tool**) and pressing your **Delete** key.

Double-clicking on a Background layer converts it to a floating layer.

The gray checker pattern behind a layer represents complete transparency through the image file

That light gray checkerboard you see around your graphic (illustrated below) represents alpha. That means there is nothing there. No background. No canvas. Just transparency.

If you'd like to start with a clean slate, you can even remove everything on the layer (press **Ctrl+a** on a PC or ⌘**+a** on a Mac to select all and then press the **Delete** key).

Once you've removed the background, whatever you

draw, write or place on a layer – a graphic, a shape, text, a photo of a person with the background cut from behind him – if it does not cover your entire canvas, will have transparency around it.

And, if you were to save this file without flattening it in a format that supports alpha (ideally a **PSD**), that unused area will remain transparent when you import the file into another Adobe program – such as Premiere Elements.

If you place a graphics file containing transparency on the upper track of a Premiere Elements video project, those transparent areas will also be transparent over your video. Only the graphic itself will show – your video on a lower track will be visible behind and around it.

File formats that support alpha

Although **PSDs** are the ideal (and easiest) format for sending non-square graphics to a Premiere Elements project, there are two other file formats you can export from Photoshop Elements that will include alpha. These are the formats you will use if you are creating non-square graphics for the Web or for a non-Adobe program that doesn't support PSD files.

GIFs were invented by Compuserve (remember them?) in the early days of the Internet, and they remain, along with JPEGs, one of the most common file format used on the web.

But GIFs don't handle color very efficiently. **PNGs** were invented to unite the color qualities of a JPEG with the alpha channel abilities of a GIF.

To export a graphic as a GIF or PNG and maintain transparency around the graphic, go to the Photoshop Elements **File** menu and select **Save for Web**. This will open a workspace for resizing, compressing and optimizing your graphics for export as a JPEG, GIF or PNG (as in the illustration on the right).

Select **GIF** or **PNG-24** from the **Preset** drop-down menu.

Once you've done that, a checkbox will appear offering the option of **Transparency**.

Check this option and your graphic will be exported as a flat graphic, but with the same transparency as your original **PSD** file.

The option to preserve transparency on the Save for Web screen.

The Type Tools

Type Tools Options

Re-Editing Text

Shaping and Distorting Text

Typing on a Path, Selection or Shape

Chapter 10

Create and Edit Text

Typing, sizing, coloring and shaping

The text tools in Photoshop Elements run surprisingly deep.

Not only does the program allow you to work with such basic text attributes as font, style and color, but it also includes a variety of tools for shaping and warping text.

Text sizes and shapes can be edited using the text editor, or a block of text can be sized and shaped as if it were an object – all while remaining editable type.

The Type Tools share the same button in the Toolbox. Three of the tools type text on a shape, selection or path (see page 139).

The Horizontal and Vertical Type Tools type text across or down the page.

Horizontal Type | Vertical Type | Horizontal Mask

Vertical Mask | Text on Selection | Text on Shape

Text on Path

Type Mask tools create a selection in the shape of the typed text.

The Type Tools

The seven **Type Tools** are accessed by clicking the **"T"** button in the **Toolbox** along the left side of the **Editor** workspace, and then selecting the specific **Type Tool** from the **Tool Options Bin**.

Two of these tools add text to your image file as you type.

> The Horizontal Type Tool, as the name implies, types your text from left to right, by default in the **Foreground Color** (see page 57).

> The Vertical Type Tool types your text from top to bottom, by default in the **Foreground Color**. When you press **Enter** as you type, a new column of text is created *to the left* of the first.

 Horizontal text on your image file can be turned into vertical text, and vice versa, by selecting the text and then clicking the **Change the Text Orientation** button in the **Tool Options Bin**.

Two other **Type Tools** create a "mask" or selection in the shape of the text typed.

> The Horizontal Type Mask Tool creates a text-shaped selection mask from left to right as you type.

> The Vertical Type Mask Tool creates a text-shaped selection mask from top to bottom as you type.

Though called **Masks**, these type tools actually create **selections**. (**Layer Masks**, discussed on page 128, are very different and have a very different function in the program.)

As you type with a **Type Mask Tool**, your image file will be temporarily covered by a semi-opaque, red mask. Your text will appear to be cut out of this mask. When you click off of your text or select another tool, your typed text area will become a **selection** (surrounded by "marching ants"). (For more information on making and working with selections, see **Chapter 6, Select and Isolate Areas in Your Photos**.)

The selection created by your **Type Mask Tools** can be manipulated in a number of ways:

> **A selection can be deleted** by pressing the **Delete** key, removing the area you've selected from the layer you've selected it on. Or you can select **Inverse** from the program's **Select** menu and, by pressing the **Delete** key, remove all *except* the text-shaped area.

> **A selection can be cut and pasted** into another image file or onto a new layer in the current file.

> If you switch to the **Move Tool, your selection can be resized or reshaped** by dragging its corner handles.

> **A selection can be colored** using **Stroke** or **Fill.**

> **A selection's lighting and color can be adjusted**, and your adjustments will affect only the selected area.

For the most part, **selections** made using the **Type Mask Tools** are no different than any other **selections** – except that their shape is defined by the shape of the text you type.

Re-edit a text layer

Your text will remain editable as long as it remains a separate text layer in a PSD file. You'll easily recognize a text layer in the **Layers** panel because the layer will appear as a big, gray "**T**", followed by the layer's name (which, by default, will be the text you typed).

Double-clicking the "T" on a text layer makes the text re-editable.

To re-edit a text layer, double-click on the big, gray "**T**" representing the layer on the **Layers** panel. The text layer will be activated and the **Type Tool** will automatically be selected.

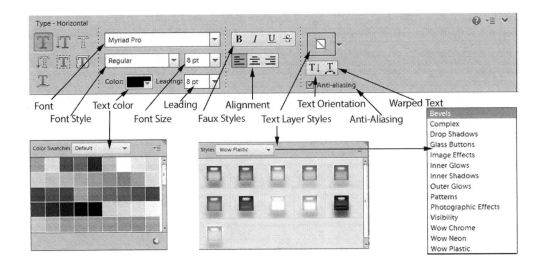

The Type Tool Options Bin

All of the **Type Tools**, whether text tools or mask tools, use a similar **Tool Options Bin**, which runs along the bottom of the **Editor** workspace.

The **Type Tool Options** are primarily used for setting basic fonts, text styles, colors and sizes.

In most cases, the default settings for the **Type Tools** options will be the *last settings you used*. In other words, if you used 8 pt. Myriad Pro Regular to the last time you added text to your image file, the next time you select a **Type Tool**, it will be set to 8 pt. Myriad Pro Regular.

Font. The **Font** drop-down menu lists pretty much every font available on your system. These fonts will vary from computer to computer. Windows includes around 20 basic fonts. Other programs you've installed, including Premiere Elements and Photoshop Elements, may have added a few more.

The symbol to the left of each font in its listing indicates if it is a True Type (**TT**) or an Open Type (**O**) font. Without getting into too deep a discussion of font systems, True Type is the most basic font system. Open Type is the more advanced font system, sometimes including dozens of styles and options within the font. (An Open Type font, for instance, may include the option to use *ligatures* to make an adjacent "f" and "i" into one, combined character with no dot over the "i", as in the word "find.")

A quick way to "call up" a font is to type its name into the **Font** box on the **Tool Options Bin** (without opening the drop-down menu). As you type the name of the font, Photoshop Elements will automatically search and load the font for your **Type Tool**.

Font Style. Most fonts include specific text styles such as **Bold** and **Italic**. Because these styles are designed as part of the font itself, setting them in the **Font Style** drop-down menu is preferred to applying the **Faux Styles** to the right.

Font Size. Measured in "points", font sizes are relative to the pixel density in your image files. In other words, a 14 point font on a low-resolution image will appear much larger than a 14 point font will on a high-resolution image. In addition to setting font sizes numerically, you can size your text as a block, as described in **Shape and Resize Your Text** on page 138.

Leading is the space between lines of text. In most cases, the **Auto** setting will give you the best results. However, for aesthetic reasons, you can manually set your leading tighter or looser. The numerical settings correspond to the font's size.

Text Color. By default, your text will be the **Foreground Color** (see page 57) that was set when you selected the **Type Tool**. You can manually change the **Text Color** by selecting it from this drop-down menu or by clicking on a swatch displayed in the **Color Swatches** panel (available under the program's **Window** menu).

Faux Styles are ways to add styling (bold, italic, etc.) to fonts. They're called "faux styles" because they aren't part of the font's original design, but rather the program's *simulation* of the style. In other words, faux bold merely thickens the font, faux italic slants it to one side, etc.

Paragraph Alignment aligns your text to the left, right or center. **Paragraph Alignment** is important if you plan to create Premiere Elements Movie Menu templates (see **Chapter 13, Advanced Photoshop Elements Tools**) because it will determine the direction your custom text will flow when you type in the names of your scenes or chapters.

Anti-Aliasing. Aliasing has to do with how sharp the edges of a font are. With **Anti-Aliasing** turned off, text can look unnaturally sharp and jagged. You'll probably want to keep the **Anti-Aliasing** checkbox checked then. (For an illustration, see **What is Anti-Aliasing?** on page 65 of **Chapter 5, Get to Know the Photoshop Elements Toolbox**.)

Text Layer Styles. There are dozens of styles which can be applied to your text layer, from bevels to drop-shadows to glows to patterns. Click on the **Text Layer Styles** button, as illustrated on the facing page, to open the option panel. To see the various pages of available styles, click on the pop-up menu at the top of this **Layer Styles** panel.

Warped Text. You can choose a **Warp** style before, after or while you are typing your text. The various warps include arcs, bulges, fish-eyes, waves and twists. And, as you select each, your text will preview the warp for you. Also, once you've selected a warp, you can customize it by adjusting the **Bend, Horizontal Distortion** and **Vertical Distortion** to create pretty much any look you want.

Warp Text options

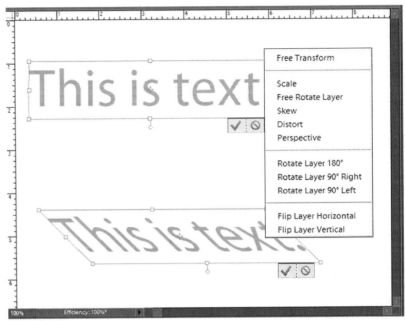

When the Move Tool is selected, text can be resized as if it were vector art by dragging on the corner handles. The right-click (Ctrl-click) option to Skew allows you to angle your text block.

Shape and resize your text

You can resize and reshape a text layer just as you can any other image or shape layer. Because it behaves like vector art, you can enlarge or stretch your text layer without regard to resolution.

 To resize a text layer, select the **Move Tool** in the **Toolbox** and then select the text layer by either clicking directly on it in your image file or clicking on the layer on the **Layers** panel.

Press **Ctrl+t** on a PC or ⌘**+t** on a Mac to put the Editor into **Transform** mode.

The text block will appear with handles on each corner and on the sides. Drag on these corner handles to resize and reposition your text. As long as the **Constrain Proportions** option is selected in the **Tool Options Bin**, the text block will resize proportionately.

Other reshaping options are available by **right-clicking** on the text block . These options are:

Free Transform (default). This option allows for both resizing and rotating of the text block.

Scale. You have the option of resizing the block, but rotation is locked out.

Free Rotate Layer. You will be able to rotate the block, but scaling is locked out.

Skew. By dragging the corner handles, you will slant the text block, as in the illustration above.

Lock in any changes by clicking the green checkmark or by pressing **Enter**. Cancel any changes by clicking the red cancel icon or pressing **ESC**.

Other transform options

The **Distort** and **Perspective** transform options are grayed-out of the text block's **right-click** menu. These options are only available for raster art, but can be applied to text if the text layer has been simplified (converted to pixels).

To simplify a text or shape layer, **right-click** on the text layer in the **Layers** panel and select the **Simplify Layer** option. (Simplifying text turns it into pixels, so it will no longer be editable.)

> **Distort**. By dragging the corner handles of your layer, you will be able to shape it into any four-sided shape you'd like.
>
> **Perspective**. Dragging the corner handles stretches two sides at once – allowing you to stretch and shape your layer so that it appears to have perspective.

For more information on simplifying layers, see **Simplify or Flatten a Layer** on page 126 of **Chapter 9, Work with Photoshop Elements Layers**.

Type on a Selection, Shape or Path

In addition to standard typing tools, Photoshop Elements includes options for typing your text around the outline of a selection or shape or on a path. To select a **Text On** tool, click on the **Type** button on the Premiere Elements **Toolbox** and then select the tool you want from the **Tool Options Bin** that below the **Editor** workspace.

Type Text on a Selection

When **Text on Selection** is selected, your cursor will become a **Quick Selection Tool** (as described on page 55).

1   Drag over your photo to make a **Quick Selection**.

    As you drag, the program will select adjacent areas of similar color. When you are satisfied with your selection, click the green checkmark or press **Enter**.

To Type on a Selection, first use the Quick Selection Tool to create a selected area. Click the check-mark to finalize it.

2   Hover your mouse over the selection path until your cursor indicates you are on the type path.

    Select your font and text characteristics, then click and type. The text will flow around the outside of the selection, beginning at the point on the selection's outline at which you initially clicked.

Hover your mouse over the path created until your cursor displays as the type icon. Click and type.

Tool Options for the Text on Shape Tool include a number of shape options as well as options for setting the color, size, font and style of your text.

Type Text on a Shape

You can create a shape to type along by selecting a shape from the **Tool Options Bin** or by using the **Shape Tool** (see page 76). (The shapes in the **Tool Options Bin** will create a type path only and not an actual shape.)

1   Create a shape.

   To create a shape using the **Text on Shape Tool**, select one of the shape options in the **Tool Options Bin** (as above), then drag to draw the shape on your photo.

2   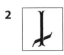 Hover your mouse over the outline of the shape until your cursor indicates you are on the type path.

   Select your font and text characteristics, then click and type. The text will flow around the outside of the shape, beginning at the point on the selection's outline at which you initially clicked.

When you use the Text on Shape Tool, your type will flow around whatever shape you provide for it.

Type Text on a Custom Path

The **Text on Custom Path Tool** will align text along any path you create.

1   Create a path.

   When you select the **Text on Custom Path Tool**, your cursor will become a pencil. Draw the path you would like your text to follow over your photo.

2   Hover your mouse over the path until your cursor indicates you are on the type path.

   Select your font and text characteristics, then click and type. The text will flow around the outside of the selection, beginning at the point on the selection's outline at which you initially clicked.

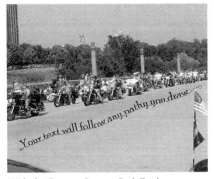

With the Text on Custom Path Tool, your text will follow any path you draw.

Adjustment Filters

The Filter Gallery

The Effects Panel

Effects Filters

Effects Styles

Photo Effects

Chapter 11

Add Photo Effects and Filters

Use Photoshop Elements' special effects

Photoshop Elements includes hundreds of customizable effects and filters that can be applied to your image files.

Filters can add new elements to your image file or they can make your photo look like an artist's sketch or painting.

Effects can be used to add drop shadows and glows around your layers.

Additional effects can make your new photographs look like they were taken a hundred years ago!

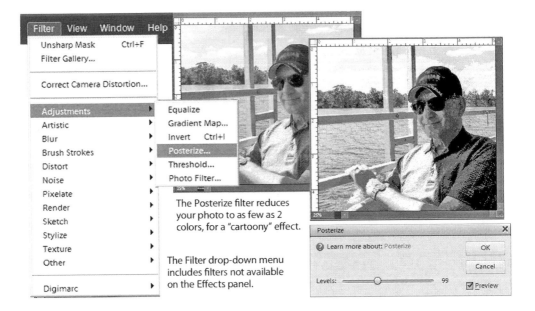

The Posterize filter reduces your photo to as few as 2 colors, for a "cartoony" effect.

The Filter drop-down menu includes filters not available on the Effects panel.

Effects and filters can be used to stylize or create interesting, new looks for your photographs and other image files. You can also just use them to have fun – to make your photo look like a watercolor painting, for instance, or to make a modern photo look like a withered, old snapshot.

Many of Photoshop Elements' filters can be found under the program's **Filter** menu. Except for those listed below, virtually all of these filters can also be found, displayed as intuitive thumbnails, in the **Effects** panel, located by default in the **Panel Bin** to the right of the **Editor** workspace. (If, for some reason, the **Effects** panel has been closed, you can open it by selecting the option under the program's **Window** menu.)

The Adjustments menu

We'll discuss the bulk of the program's **Filters** in our discussion of the **Effects** panel, beginning on page 145.

But there are six filters under the **Filter** menu that are *not* included in the **Effects** panel set. These are the **Adjustment** filters, and they include:

Equalize. This filter interprets the darkest area of your image file as black and your lightest area as white and then it evenly distributes the levels of colors between. The process often softens the contrast in a photo.

Gradient Map. This filter turns your photo into a grayscale image and then it replaces that grayscale with any set of colors, based on the selections you make by clicking on the pop-up menu (as displayed when you click the grayscale area on the option screen).

Invert. Creates a negative of your image file.

Posterize. This filter reduces the number of colors displayed in your image file, based on your settings.

Threshold. Converts your image file into a high-contrast, black & white image, based on the level you set.

Photo Filter. This filter applies one of 20 **photographic filters** to your image file, as if your camera shot your photo through a tinted lens. It can also be used to "warm" or "cool" the colors in a photograph.

Additionally, the **Filter** menu gives you access to an amazing tool for correcting some distortions caused by certain lenses (or, if you're of the mind to, creating some).

Correct Camera Distortion is a filter which reshapes your photo to compensate for rounding or keystoning – unnatural distortion to a photo which can occur because of the use of a wide-angle lens or because it was shot from an unusual angle. Launching the **Correct Camera Distortion** filter opens a workspace in which you can "un-round" or "round" your photo or even reshape it so that it widens at the top, bottom or side, as in the illustration above. This filter works automatically when you combine several shots in a **Photomerge Panorama**, as discussed beginning on page 49 of **Chapter 4, Guided Edits**.

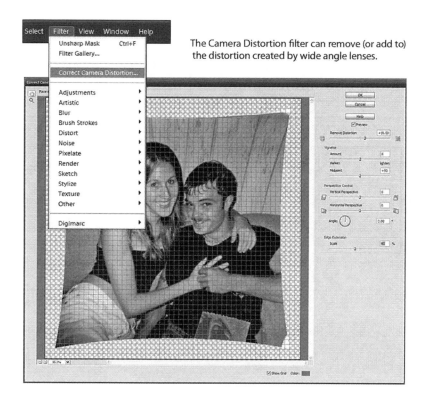

The Camera Distortion filter can remove (or add to) the distortion created by wide angle lenses.

The Filter Gallery

Opened by selecting the option under the **Filter** menu, the **Filter Gallery** is a workspace for applying one or more filters to your image file, setting the filter levels and previewing the results.

It is also a means of quickly browsing a large portion of the **Filter** library, displayed as thumbnails down the center of the panel.

The **Filter Gallery** displays as four panels or work areas.

To the left is the **Preview** window. This window displays your image file as it will appear when the selected filter is applied to it. To the lower left of this display you will find controls for zooming in or out of your image.

The center column of the of the **Filter Gallery** contains a large portion of Photoshop Elements' library of **Filters**, each displayed as a thumbnail representing its effect. These filters are arranged in six categories, which you can open and close by clicking on the little triangles to left of each category's name.

As you click on each filter, a preview of its effect on your image file will be displayed in the **Preview** window. When you select a new filter, the old will automatically be removed when the new is applied.

The Filter Gallery is a workspace for test-driving and multiplying filters applied to an image file.

Zoom level of preview   Preview effects   Filter library   Filter settings   Add new filter layer   Applied filters

The **levels** for each filter are set in the upper right of the **Filter Gallery.** (The drop-down menu above these settings is yet another way to switch from filter to filter.)

In the lower right of the **Filter Gallery** is a **properties** panel, which displays a listing of the filters you have applied to your image.

- You can combine and apply as many filters as you'd like to your image file. To add an additional filter, click on the **New Effect Layer** button at the bottom of this properties listing space.

- Your filters can be turned off and on in this area by clicking the eyeball icon to the left of each effect listing. And filters can be removed completely from this listing by selecting the filter from the list and clicking on the trashcan icon.

The Effects panel

There are nearly 300 effects available on the **Effects** panel, which resides, by default, in the **Panel Bin** to the right of the Photoshop Elements Editor workspace. Some of the tools on this panel are filters. Many more are effects (such as **Drop Shadows** and **Glows**) that can be applied to layers, text or shapes in layered image files or to create a 3D-like photographic special effect.

(If this panel is not visible, click the **Effects** button in the lower right of the **Basic Workspace** interface.)

These effects and filters are available in different categories, which can be accessed by clicking on one of the three category tabs at the top of the panel (**Effects, Filters, Styles**).

You can get a general idea of how each filter or effect will change your image file by looking at the thumbnails displayed in the **Effects** panel.

The size of these thumbnails can be adjusted by selecting one of the **Thumbnail Views** available under the pop-out menu in the upper right of the panel, as illustrated.

145

If your program workspace is in **Custom** rather than **Basic** mode (set under the **More** menu in the lower right of the interface) the **Effects** panel, like all of the panels in the **Panel Bin**, can be undocked, if you'd prefer, and placed anywhere on your computer's desktop. To undock a panel, drag on its tab at the top of the panel.

Once you remove it from the bin, it becomes a "floating" panel and you can position it wherever you'd like in your workspace.

To re-dock the panel, just drag it by its tab back into the **Panel Bin** and release your mouse button. The panel will pop back into the bin.

To return the **Panel Bin** to its original array of panels, go to the **Window** menu and select **Reset Panels**.

Photo Effects

Photo Effects are special effects which can be applied to make your photographs look aged or to divide your photo into separate panels.

All but a few of these **Effects** work by creating a duplicate of the **Background** layer and then applying color or texture effects to it. Because of this, the effects they apply don't change the original artwork. The original photo remains in its unaffected state, hidden behind the layer to which effects have been applied.

The original and the layers to which effects have been applied remain separate as long as you save your file as a layered PSD (Photoshop) file and you do not flatten the layers or save your image file as a format that does not support layers (such as a JPEG or a non-layered TIF).

The layer to which the effect has been applied can then be accepted and kept or deleted (by selecting the layer and clicking on the trashcan icon on the **Layers** panel).

Photoshop Elements includes a number of new categories and very cool photo effects.

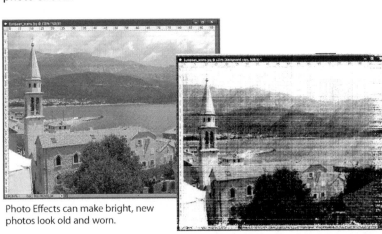

Photo Effects can make bright, new photos look old and worn.

Panels effects divide
your photo into panels
or sections.

The **Photo Effects** include:

Faded Photo creates an old photo effect by fading areas of your
photo from color to black & white.

Glow adds a glossy, foggy effect to the lighter areas of your photo.

Monotone Color reduces your color photo to tints of monochrome
or a single color.

Painting makes your photo look like a fluorescent, oil or watercolor
painting.

Panels divide your photo into four to nine separate panels

Seasons add snow, rain a summery or a wintery look to your photos.

Textures give your photo the look of lizard skin or a rubber stamp.

Vintage effects make your photo look like a faded, tinted
photograph or a pencil sketch.

Filter Effects

Photoshop Elements divides its **Filters** into 12 general categories. These
Filters can be found under the **Filter** menu or accessed by clicking the
Filters tab on the **Effects** panel.

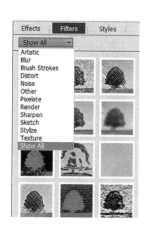

Artistic. These filters give your photo a "painterly" look, as if they
were created by an artist's brush or sketch pencil. It includes
Plastic Wrap, an effect which makes the elements in your photo
look as if they were sealed in Saran Wrap!

Blur. These filters soften or blur an image file or selected area.
Among the blurs are a **Radial Blur**, which gives your photo a
spinning effect, and a **Motion Blur**, which can make your image
file or selected area appear to be zipping by your camera.

Brush Strokes. These filters make your photo look as if it were
painted with fine arts brushes or drawn with ink.

Render Filters, a close-up

The **Render** set of **Filters** deserves a more detailed discussion, because these filters often don't so much change your image file as add new elements to it. They include:

Clouds. When applied to an image file, layer or selection, this filter draws clouds. These clouds will be a combination of the **Foreground Color** and **Background Color** you currently have set (see page 57).

Difference Clouds. This filter draws clouds over your image file or selected area, producing colors that are complementary to the image file's existing colors.

Fibers. This filter draws a fibrous pattern, based on the settings you provide and the **Foreground Color** and **Background Color** you currently have selected. The option panel that opens when you apply this filter allows you to set the **Variance** and **Strength** of the fibers.

Lens Flare. A popular effect, this filter creates the effect of a bright light or sunlight shining back at the camera.

On the option screen, you can set both the brightness and type of light and, by dragging the crosshairs, set where in the photo you'd like the flare to appear.

The Lens Flare filter adds a bright sparkle.

Lighting Effects include a number of presets and custom settings.

Lighting Effects. This filter lets you create the effect of bright light and shadow across your photo, based on a variety of settings.

The circular control allows you to set the angle and intensity of the light, while the various style and slider settings allow you to create dozens of different lighting effects.

Filters available on the Effects panel

Distort. This category includes 3D filters for distorting and reshaping your image files. The **Liquify** filter makes your image file behave as if it were made of smearable paint.

Noise. Filters for softening scratches or flaws in a photo – or creating noise as an effect!

Other. A miscellaneous category of filters, like **High-Pass** and **Offset**, for creating customizable image effects.

Pixelate. Filters which clump pixels, creating mosaic-like versions of your images.

Render. We discuss this unique category of effects in detail in the sidebar on page 148.

Sharpen. The **Unsharp Mask** in this category increases the contrast between pixels to sharpen the look of a photo.

Sketch. These filters give your photos a hand-drawn look, with some filters even simulating the look of various drawing papers. **Photocopy** makes your photo look as if it were run through a Xerox machine. **Chrome** makes it look as if it were formed out of metal.

Stylize. These filters create an impressionistic effect, or they create very unnatural special effects. **Emboss** makes your image file look as it if were pressed into a piece of paper. **Wind** makes the color look as if it was smeared by a blast of air.

Texture. **Texture** filters add a 3D texture to the image, as if it was printed onto a texturized paper. The **Stained Glass** filter adds a mosaic look, which makes your photo look like a stained glass window!

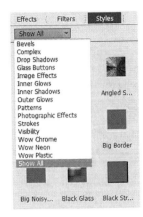

Style Effects

The **Styles** effects are accessed by clicking the **Styles** tab on the **Effects** panel. The styles are displayed as thumbnails representing their effect. Photoshop Elements includes over 175 **Layer Styles** effects in 15 categories.

Layer Styles are, as you might suppose, effects applied to layers in an image file.

In fact, if you try to apply these effects to a flat image file or a **Background** layer, a message will pop up warning you that these effects will only work on layers.

Many of these effects take advantage of the unique nature of layers. The **Drop-Shadows** and **Outer Glows**, for instance, clearly wouldn't show any effect if they were applied to a **Background** layer. Likewise, the **Visibility** effects, which make your layer semi-transparent, by nature deal with the way layers interact.

Styles can be applied to text layers and shape layers as well as image layers. They can even be applied to layered image files with no **Background** layer.

A **Style** is applied by selecting a layer in the **Layers** panel and then either double-clicking on the style or dragging the style onto the layer.

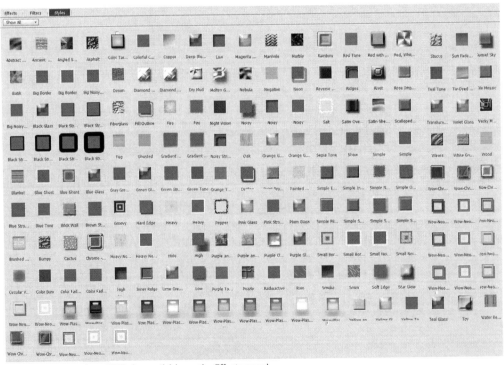

Some of the more than 175 Styles available on the Effects panel

Double-clicking the "fx" button on a layer to which Layer Styles have been added launches the Style Settings screen, where the layer effects can be customized or turned off or on.

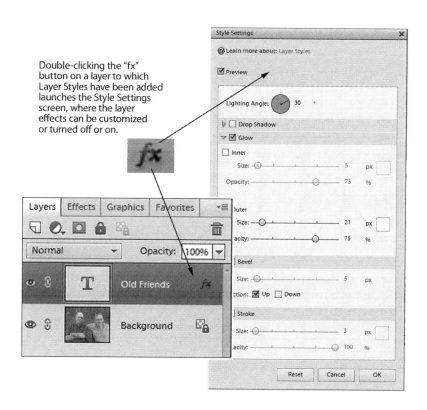

Many **Styles** can be customized on the **Style Settings** screen. To open **Style Settings**, click the cog icon on the top right of the **Effects** panel, or double-click on the "*fx*" indicator on a layer to which **Styles** have been applied, as in the illustration above.

Style Settings for the **Bevel** effect, for instance, include settings for the depth of the bevel and a toggle for setting whether a selected layer bevels up or down. **Glow** settings affect the size, color and opacity of the glow.

Additionally, by checking or unchecking the styles listed on the **Style Settings** screen, you can toggle your **Styles** off and on.

To undo the effect, either click the **Undo** button or press **Ctrl+z** on a PC or ⌘+z on a Mac. To remove all effects from a layer, click the **Style Setting's** panel's Reset button.

The 15 categories of **Styles** are:

Bevels. Bevels create a 3D effect by making your layer look as if it or its frame bulges out of your image file or is impressed into it.

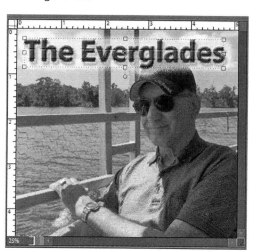

Styles can be added to text layers as well as shape and image layers – and more than one style may be applied to a single layer.

Complex styles combine **Bevel**, **Pattern**, **Texture** and/or **Drop-Shadow** effects to your selected layer.

Drop-Shadow styles cast a shadow from the layer onto lower layers or the **Background**. To change the angle or other characteristics of a **Drop Shadow** once it has been applied, open **Style Settings** by double-clicking on the "*fx*" button on the layer in the **Layers** palette, as discussed on page 151.

Glass Buttons styles turn your selected layer into a beveled, glass-like button.

Image Effects add effects like snow, rain, a jigsaw puzzle texture or a night vision look to your layer.

Inner Glows add a glow color inward from the edge of the layer.

Inner Shadows add a drop shadow inward from the edge of the layer, as if the layer were sunken into the image file.

Outer Glows add a glow outward from the edges of your layer.

Patterns replace your layer with a texture like a brick wall, blanket, stone, etc.

Photographic Effects add a tint to your layer or give it a sepia tone.

Strokes create a frame for your layer in a number of line weights and colors.

Visibility makes your layer semi-opaque, showing the other layers or the **Background** through it.

Wow Chrome replaces your layer with a 3D chrome texture.

Wow Neon replaces your layer with a bright, 3D glowing texture.

Wow Plastic replaces your layer with a shiny, 3D plastic texture.

Adobe Photoshop Elements

Part III
Advanced Photo Editing

Swapping Out a Face

Swapping Out a Background

Healing Blemishes

Removing Things from Photos

Adding Things to Photos

Chapter 12

Photoshop Elements Tricks
Have fun with your photos

Stunt photography – or trick photography – is the fun side of Photoshop Elements.

It's about swapping out elements in your photos – or adding new things or removing things you don't want.

It's about creating situations that didn't really exist.

But there's a "legitimate side" to Photoshop Elements tricks too. They can be very helpful for cleaning up little messes on your photos.

Stunt photography can be a lot of fun. Swapping a friend's face for the Mona Lisa's, for instance. Or making your child look like she's walking on the Moon. It's fun – and surprisingly easy, using just a few basic tools.

But, of course, these tricks can also be functional. Occasionally you've shot a perfect photo – except for a stray wire hanging in the background or an untimely blemish. And sometimes, for a variety of reasons, you just want to place someone in a location other than where he or she was actually photographed.

It's all good. And it's all based on a couple of simple tricks and the basic Photoshop tools described earlier in this book.

Swap out a face

It's about more than just swapping faces, of course. It can be about placing someone into a scene – or even creating a composite of elements from a couple of photos.

I was challenged once with touching up the photo of a person who had a muscle weakness in one eye that caused his left eye to drift. In the photo I had of him, his eyes seemed to be looking in two different directions. By copying his left eye from another photo, I was able to seamlessly replace the drifting eye with one more in line with the right, creating a much more flattering picture.

The process of swapping in an element from one photo to another is best accomplished when you use two key principles:

- Ensuring that the two photo sources have similar resolution, lighting and color; and
- Blending the edges as smoothly as possible between the two photos

In my illustration below, I've gathered two classic Grisetti photos. The first is of me, at age 8, all fully equipped for a day of playing army with my friends. The second, from about 10 years later, is a real-life photo of me from my army days.

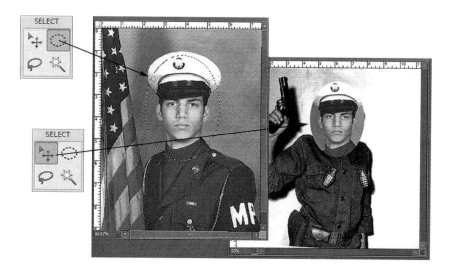

So what would happen if I grafted my somewhat adult face onto my childhood picture?

Well, the resolutions and textures aren't quite the same, and I'm facing a slightly different direction in each photo – but this is just for fun, so let's see how it goes.

1   Dragging the **Elliptical Marquee Selection Tool** over my Basic Training picture, I selected my head (and a little beyond).

   The **Elliptical Selection Tool** is one of the two **Marquee Selection Tools**. If the **Elliptical Tool** doesn't show in your Photoshop Elements **Toolbox**, select the **Rectangular Selection tool** and then switch to the **Elliptical Selection Tool** in the **Tool Options Bin**, as described on page 61.

2   Then, using the **Move Tool**, I (literally) dragged the selected area from my Basic Training photo onto my childhood picture, as illustrated above.

   Although I also could have done this with a cut-and-paste command, dragging from one file to another is the easiest way to copy elements (and even layers) between image files. Because my childhood picture is a black & white photo and my army photo is in color, the area I've copied from one photo to another automatically converts to grayscale.

   Also note that the area I've moved from one photo to the other has become a new layer on the childhood picture.

3   Ensuring that Layer 1 (my face) is selected on the childhood picture, I slid the **Opacity** level on the **Layers** panel to about 60%, as illustrated on page 158. This allowed me to see both the background and layer (as sort of a double-exposure) so that I can scale and position my new face over my old.

4   Dragging the corner handles around my face, I sized and positioned my older face over the younger in the childhood picture, as illustrated on page 158.

   Because I was facing to the right in one picture and a bit more to the left in the other, I flipped the "face" layer horizontally by dragging the side handle for my face completely across and over the to other side, turning it into a mirror image.

I dragged the side corner handle across my face layer to "flip" the image.

With layer opacity set to 50%, I adjusted the placement and scale of my new face over my old.

With opacity back at 100%, I used the Eraser Tool to remove all but my face from the layer.

The final, rather creepy, result

(I could also have done this, by the way, by going to the **Image** menu and selecting **Flip Horizontal** from the **Rotate** sub-menu.)

I knew the two faces weren't going to match up perfectly but, by stretching, scaling and rotating, I am able to line up the eyes and the mouths.

Once the layer was in position, I pressed **Enter** to lock in the scaling. Then I set the **Opacity** for the layer back to 100%.

5   Selecting the **Eraser Tool** and, setting it to a soft-edged 45 px brush in the **Tool Options Bin**, I erased all the unwanted imagery around my "face" layer.

Because the **Eraser Tool** brush setting had a soft edge to it, the line between the erased and unerased areas on the layer were slightly feathered, creating a softer, more natural edge.

Because my face had changed shape over the years, I can't completely replace my young head with my older head – but, when I erase around the sides of my face, my older face blends in pretty well with my younger head.

The result, at left, is just a bit creepy – but it works!

The first step in pasting Sarah into the Monaco scene was using the Magic Wand Tool to select the green background in her photo.

Swap out a background

Swapping in a background uses essentially the same principles as swapping in a head, except that you're trying to create an entire scene from a composite of images.

In the illustration above, I've decided to take Sarah, who was conveniently shot in front of a green screen, and place her in front of the castle wall, overlooking downtown Monaco. (By the way, you can also do this effect using the new **Photomerge Compose** tool, as described on page 45.)

Green screens and blue screens are, of course, great photographic backgrounds for doing this kind of work – as well as for doing Chroma Key and Videomerge, similar background-swapping tricks performed in video.

This is because not only do green and blue screens give you a nice, even color that's easy to select and delete, these bright shades of green and blue don't show up in human skin tones. This makes it easier to separate the human from the background.

1   Using the **Magic Wand Tool**, as illustrated above, I selected the green background, behind Sarah.

The **Magic Wand Tool** is one of the three **Quick Selection Tools**. If the **Magic Wand** doesn't show in your Photoshop Elements **Toolbox**, select the **Quick Selection** or **Selection Brush** and then switch to the **Magic Wand** in the **Tool Options Bin**, as described on page 63.

How much gets selected on a single click of this tool depends on how high the **Tolerance** is set in the **Tool Options**. In order to select the entire green area, I set the **Tolerance** to 25 – and even then needed to hold down the **Shift** key and click on a couple of areas to build the selection until the entire green screen was selected. (At this point, I won't worry about the green showing between her curls.)

Inverse swaps the selection so that Sarah is now selected rather than the background.

2   From the program's **Select** menu, I selected **Inverse**. This swapped the selection area so that now *Sarah* was selected rather than the green screen background.

The Refine Edge tool tightens the edge around the selection and adds some feathering so that the selection blends with its new background. The Overlay View Mode shows unselected areas as overlayed with a red mask.

3   From the **Select** drop-down, I then selected the **Refine Edge** tool. This tool allowed me to tweak the edges of my selected area a bit.

By adjusting the **Shift Edge** slider, I ensured that my selection did not include any of the green screen. I also adjusted the **Feather** slider to 3 px so that the selection edge would be softer and more natural.

4   I then dragged the selected area, Sarah, onto the Monaco photo. Because I had ensured that the photos had similar resolution, Sarah fits nicely onto her new background.

5   Using the 45 px soft-edged brush setting, I dragged the **Eraser Tool** to clean up any stray green left around Sarah. Remember, when you are working with a layer, erasing *cuts transparency through* the layer – revealing the background or layers below.

Using different sized **Eraser Tool** brushes, I removed what I could from between the curls in her hair. Depending on how much detail you're trying to clean up, this part of the process can be the most challenging and time consuming. (I could also have saved myself this clean-up by refining my selection's edge using the **Refine Selection Brush** tool, as described on page 64.)

6   Finally, with **Layer 1** (Sarah) selected, I went to the program's **Enhance** menu, selected the **Adjust Color** sub-menu and then **Adjust Color for Skin Tone**. Using the eye-dropper, I sampled a mid-tone of skin on Sarah's face. Then moving the **Ambient Light** slider (and, to a lesser degree, the **Tan** and **Blush** sliders), I fine-tuned Sarah so that she better matched the color tones of someone standing under the Mediterranean sun.

Finally, using the Adjust Color for Skin Tone tool, Sarah's color temperature is adjusted to more closely match her new background.

Stray green spots, particularly around the hair, are removed with a soft-edge Eraser Tool brush.

Removing blemishes, spots and other embarassments is easy with the Spot Healing Brush.

Remove warts and blemishes

Nobody's perfect. And neither is any scene. Fortunately, Photoshop Elements makes it easy to dab away the occasional blemish.

In the illustration above, we see Sarah posing with her pet budgies. Unfortunately, Sally, the bird on the left, has left an ugly deposit on Sarah's sweater, marring an otherwise very cute picture.

The **Healing Brush Tool** and **Spot Healing Brush** are both very effective for removing these little flaws and spots.

1 With the photo open in the **Editor**, I selected the **Spot Healing Brush** from the **Toolbox** and, in the **Tool Options Bin**, I set the brush size to 34 px (which is just about the size of the spot I wanted to remove).

2 Dragging the mouse over the area, I "painted" the spot with the **Healing Brush**.

When I released the mouse button, Photoshop Elements automatically filled in the area with color and texture information borrowed from surrounding pixels.

And we're done! The **Spot Healing Brush** is a terrific, virtually automatic tool that I find all but indispensable.

With the Spot Healing Brush Tool, you merely "paint" over the area you want to remove and, when you release the mouse button, the program blends color and texture information from the surrounding pixels to fill the area and remove the spot!

The Magnetic Selection Tool makes it easy to follow the color break along Buddy's fur and hat and create a selection isolating the arm area.

Remove big things from your photos

Sometimes you want to remove something larger than a blemish or spot from your photo. Sometimes you may even want to remove an entire person! This is most easily accomplished by "painting" over the object or person with imagery "cloned" from of another area of your photo – using one of the most powerful and popular Photoshop tools in the program's toolkit.

As illustrated above, my friend Ron dressed up and posed his dog, Buddy, for a photo he plans to use for the cover of his Christmas card. Ron, however, prefers that the final photo not include his arm in the shot so that it looks more like Buddy is standing up on his own.

1   Using the **Magnetic Lasso Selection Tool**, I drew a selection lasso along the edge of Buddy's fur and around the area where Ron's arm appears.

The **Magnetic Lasso** is one of the three **Lasso Selection Tools**. If the **Magnetic Lasso** doesn't show in your Photoshop Elements **Toolbox**, select the **Lasso** or **Polygonal Lasso** and then switch to the **Magnetic Lasso** in the **Tool Options Bin**, as described on page 62.

Selecting an area isolates it so that any changes you make will affect only the selected area, and won't affect Buddy).

The Clone Tool uses imagery from the designated area to paint over the brushed area, while the selection restricts changes to the selected area.

The **Magnetic Selection Tool** made it easy to draw my selection because, as I dragged it along Buddy's outline, it followed the color break between Buddy's dark fur and the much lighter background.

2   Switching to the **Clone Stamp Tool,** I **Alt+clicked** to designate the clone source area of my photo – the area of the photo from which I would "borrow" picture information to paint over Ron's arm.

Since I wanted to replace Ron's arm with the color and texture of the painted wall behind it, I held down the **Alt** key (**Option** on a Mac) and clicked to select a spot on the white wall, above Ron's arm. This "source" area is designated with crosshairs, as seen in the illustration on the left.

Once my source spot was selected, I released the **Alt/Option** key.

3   With the **Clone Tool** set to a fairly large brush (200 px in this case) with soft edges (to blend the imagery I'd be adding to the background), I "painted" over Ron's arm, replacing it with the area I'd designated as my clone source.

Because I had created a **selection area**, there was no danger of my accidentally painting the background over Buddy – since he was outside my selection. My painted area was restricted to the area within the "marching ants" dotted lines.

Add things to your photos

Just as the **Clone Tool** can be used to paint over and remove images from your photos, it can also be used to paint new imagery onto a photo – even imagery borrowed from another photo!

For instance, the world may never wonder how I'd look with Jeanne's hair – but it can still be fun to find out.

1   With both photos open (I also ensured both photos were of similar resolution and that our heads were in a similar position), I selected the **Clone Stamp Tool**. I then **Alt+clicked** (**Option+click** on a Mac) on Jeanne's photo to select her hair, at approximately the top center of her scalp. This defined the area of the image I was going to use as my cloning source.

2   I then clicked on the Steve photo (to activate it) and, dragging the **Clone Tool** across it, I painted Jeanne's hair over mine, starting at approximately the same spot on my head as I'd designated for my source on hers.

With the Clone Tool selected, Alt+click to designate the area of your image that is to be used as your source material.

163

Because I was using such a soft, large brush (100 px, in this case) and because Jeanne has such curly hair, I got a lot of the background from her picture along with the hair.

I could also have created a new layer on the Steve picture and painted the hair onto it – and then used the **Eraser Tool** to clean up the layer, removing the background or other unwanted elements that slipped over from Jeanne's picture.

And, okay. I guess I wouldn't make such an attractive blonde.

Though, if I were, I might have a great career as an aging rock star!

As you drag the Clone Tool over your destination image file, the destination is "painted" with imagery from your source.

Chapter 13

Advanced Photo Editing Tools
Photoshop Elements extras

Have you ever scanned in several photos at once and then found yourself cropping and straightening each one individually?

Or have you ever taken several photos of a scene and wondered if there was an easy way to stitch them all together into one big picture?

Photoshop Elements includes tools for doing these things – plus a few more tools worth knowing about, including the ability to interface with a camera or scanner.

In addition to tools for creating and editing graphics and photos, Photoshop Elements includes a number of tools that don't fit into any neat category. These include tools for interfacing with a scanner or camera and tools for processing photo files before you actually bring them into the program. There are also a couple of the program's preferences that are worth knowing about.

Scan your photos

Your scanner's software can be launched and your scanner can be operated and controlled from Photoshop Elements.

On a Mac, this is done through a TWAIN plug-in, which must be installed, as discussed in the sidebar below.

On a Windows PC, your scanner's software is launched through WIA (Windows Image Acquisition).

> To launch your scanner's software from Photoshop Elements on a Windows PC, go to the **File** menu, select **Import**, then either the name of your scanner or the **WIA** support option;

> On a Mac, to go **File/Import/Images from Device**.

> To launch your scanner's software from the Elements Organizer (on Windows PCs only) go to the **File** menu and select **Get Photos and Videos**, or click on the big **Import** button in the upper left of the interface, then select **From Scanner**.

Launching the scanner tool in the Editor.

Whichever you choose, the same scanner software is launched.

As I've said, this software can vary from model to model and from brand to brand of scanner. But the principles are essentially the same:

Many consumer scanners default to an **automatic mode**, which configures the scanner for you and scans your photos at a preset resolution and color setting but which you can customize to some degree. This is the simplest solution – but can produce the most generic results.

Install the scanner plug-in on a Mac

If the scanner attached to your Mac does not appear under **File/Import**, go to APPLICATIONS/ADOBE PHOTOSHOP ELEMENTS 14/SUPPORT FILES/OPTIONAL PLUG-INS/IMPORTMODULES and copy the file **TWAIN.plugin**. Paste this file into APPLICATIONS/ADOBE PHOTOSHOP ELEMENTS 14/PLUG-INS. When you next start Photoshop Elements, your scanner will be accessible from the program's **File** menu.

If your scanner software includes a **professional mode**, it usually includes options for a number of more advanced settings:

Your scanner is controlled by the software that came bundled with it. However, most scanners use similar settings.

- Scan reflective (photo) or transparent (slide)
- Color mode
- Size/resolution
- Unsharp Mask
- Reduce "dotty" look while scanning from newspapers and magazines
- Enrich color on old photos
- Auto light correction
- Soften image to hide dust and scratches
- Preview scan
- Final scan

Reflective vs. Film (or Transparency). If your scanner includes the ability to scan slides and film, this setting controls whether your scanner scans a reflection of the photo or shines light through it.

Photo vs. OCR. Some scanners include the ability to scan documents with **Optical Character Recognition**. This OCR function scans your document in as text, which you can later edit in a word processing program. It's not a flawless system, but it *can* save you a lot of retyping.

Resolution. Remember that the size of the document you will get from your scan is a combination of its size and its resolution. In other words, you may only need a 72 dpi image – but if the photo you're scanning is only the size of a postage stamp, you will need to scan it at a much higher resolution to get enough image data to work with.

My scanner software includes a setting for **Target Size**. If I set this, the software automatically configures the scan to the necessary scan resolution. (Remember, you're always better off having too much resolution and having to rez down than not having enough resolution and needing to force your image larger later.)

Color Mode. There are three main color modes:

24-bit Color is standard **RGB color** – 8-bits per color channel.

Grayscale is monochrome, often called black & white.

But don't confuse it with **Black & White** (also known as **Bitmap**), which reduces all your colors to either 100% black or 100% white. **Black & White** is a color mode that is generally reserved for things like scanning signatures, which generally don't include shades of gray.

Some scanners also include on-the-fly picture adjustments or scan settings. Here are a couple of valuable adjustments.

Unsharp Mask. This will automatically sharpen your scanned images. It's usually best to have it turned on.

Descreening. When scanning photos from newspapers, magazines and low-end print pieces (like high school yearbooks), you may notice your scanned images have a lot of "dotty-ness." Descreening can help soften those low-quality printing artifacts.

Color Restoration. This feature will automatically enrich the color as you scan a faded, old photo.

Dust Removal. This feature adds a slight blur to your scan, sometimes hiding dust or scratches on a photo.

Scanning is usually done in two steps:

1   **Preview Scan. A Preview Scan** gives you a low-resolution preview of everything that's on your scanning table. Your **Preview Scan** will usually include an option for you to define the final scan area by dragging or resizing a marquee, displayed as a moving dotted line outline (the "marching ants").

The area you designate with this outline will be the only area actually included in your final scan.

After a Preview Scan, you will have the option of designating the area of the Final Scan (indicated by a "marching ants" dotted line marquee outline).

2   **Full Scan.** This final scan will be a scan of your *defined area only*, using the color, resolution and adjustment settings you've configured. It will produce an image file that will open in your Photoshop Elements **Editor** for further editing.

A Photoshop Elements feature that is a great supplement to your scanning tools is **Divide Scanned Photos,** discussed on the facing page.

Screen captures

In addition to scanning and downloading photos, you can add images to Photoshop Elements by, essentially, "taking a snapshot" of your computer screen. This can be a very helpful function if you're trying to show someone some strange behavior on your computer or if you, like me, are creating software illustrations for a book. This snapshot is called a **Screen Capture.**

Screen Captures are very easy to do on PCs. To do so, you simply press the **Prt Scr** (short for Print Screen) button on your keyboard. (Holding down the **Alt** key as you press this button captures only the current, active window.) On a Mac, press ⌘+**Ctrl+Shift+3**.

The image will be copied to your operating system's Clipboard. You can then paste this image into virtually any program (including Microsoft Word) by using the **Edit/Paste** option or by pressing **Ctrl+v** (⌘+**v** on a Mac).

You can also open the entire captured image as an image file for editing in Photoshop Elements. To do this, go to the program's **File** menu and select **New,** then **Image from Clipboard**.

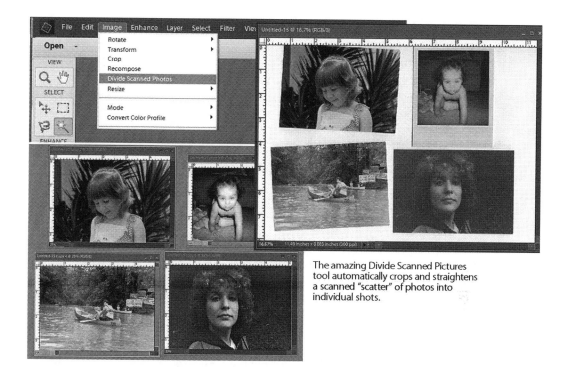

The amazing Divide Scanned Pictures tool automatically crops and straightens a scanned "scatter" of photos into individual shots.

Divide Scanned Photos

If you've ever needed to scan a number of photos in one sitting, you've probably tried to save a little time by scanning several pictures at once. This leaves you with a "scatter" of pictures.

Often, however, it's a such a chore to crop, straighten and save each photo that the time you save scanning several photos at once is traded off in the time it takes to separate and straighten the results!

Thankfully, Photoshop Elements now includes a tool for automatically doing the latter chore for you.

To use it:

1   **Scan a group of photos** at once, as described earlier in this chapter. Although the photos don't need to be straight and aligned, they do need to be far enough from each other that Photoshop Elements sees them as separate image files (as illustrated).

2   In Photoshop Elements, go to the program's **Image** menu and select **Divide Scanned Photos**.

The program will automatically separate each photo into a separate image file, cropping and straightening each as needed.

Download photos from your digital camera

As with the scanner, the software that interfaces with your camera can vary from model to model and brand to brand. And your computer probably includes a number of ways for you to get photos from your camera – all of which will produce editable photo files for Photoshop Elements.

The chief advantage to using Photoshop Elements to interface with your camera and download your photos is that your photos will also be automatically added to your Organizer catalog in the process.

There are two ways to launch the Elements Organizer Photo Downloader for your digital camera:

- Unless you've selected the **Always Do This** option, when you plug your camera into your computer and turn the camera on, **Windows or Finder will launch a pop-up screen** offering a number of optional functions. One of these will be to use the Elements Organizer to download your photos; or

- From the **File** drop-down in the Organizer, select **Get Photos and Videos**, then **From Camera or Card Reader**.

Both methods launch the same **Elements Organizer Photo Downloader**. This option screen allows you to designate where the photos are downloading from, what to name the files and where to save them on your computer.

> **Get Photos From**. From this drop-down menu, select your digital camera, smartphone, iPod or other USB-connected picture-taking device.

Why you should clear your camera's memory regularly

Sometimes, when your camera's storage gets full, you may be tempted to delete just a few photos to make room for a few new ones. There are serious liabilities to doing this.

Your photos are typically stored in your camera or on your camera's storage card as JPEGs. These JPEGs vary slightly in size. Removing a photo or two leaves a "hole" of a certain size on your memory card. When you take a new picture, if it is of a slightly larger than this hole, your camera's storage may corrupt and you could lose several pictures!

For this reason alone, it's good, safe housekeeping to regularly clear off your digital camera's storage completely to "clean" or reformat the memory card.

Connecting your camera to your computer launches an option screen which offers you a selection of all of the photo software installed on your system.

The Adobe Photoshop Elements Photo Downloader includes options for automatically naming your files and for deleting them from your camera after downloading them.

In Advanced Dialog mode, you have the option of selecting which of the photos stored on your camera are downloaded to your computer.

Import Settings/Location. Click the **Browse** button to browse to a location on your hard drive into which you'd like to save your photos.

Create Subfolder. Automatically creates a new photo storage folder on your hard drive for the photo download, according to the specifications you set in the drop-down menu.

Rename Files. Names your downloaded photos according to the specifications you set in the drop-down menu.

Delete Options. Offers the option of deleting your photos from your camera once you've downloaded them to your computer – an easy way to clean up your camera's photo storage.

Advanced Dialog. Clicking this button opens up an option screen which displays all of the photos in your camera's memory. By checking and unchecking the checkboxes, you can select which photos are included in your download and which will remain on your camera.

Edit in Camera RAW

Usually, when you take a snapshot with your camera, your photo is delivered to you as a JPEG. This JPEG has been processed by the camera, automatically adjusting its exposure and white balance, and packaged in a convenient, moderately compressed photo format.

Professional cameras, as well as many of the more advanced consumer cameras today, however, also include the option for you to access the photo data in its **Camera RAW** state.

Camera RAW photos are, as the name implies, raw photo data. The files are uncompressed and none of the usual automatic adjustments have been applied. (Think of them as your photo's "negatives." In fact, RAW files are sometimes even called DNG or "digital negative" files.) They can't be printed or used in their **RAW** state. However, their format gives you much more flexibility, when it comes to making adjustments to your photos. You're working with the raw camera data, not undoing adjustments the camera has already made.

Photoshop Elements includes a surprisingly robust **RAW** photo editor.

Also note that, in Photoshop Elements, you can open *any* photo format in the Camera RAW editor by selecting File/Open in Camera RAW!

This means that, as when you edit RAW photos, your adjustments to any photo will not be permanent – even if you click **Done** and close the photo file – until you click the **Open Image** button and open the photo in the regular Photoshop Elements Editor workspace.

The Photoshop Elements 14 **Camera RAW** adjustments panels, organized under the three tabs to the right of the workspace, include a variety of color correction and sharpening tools.

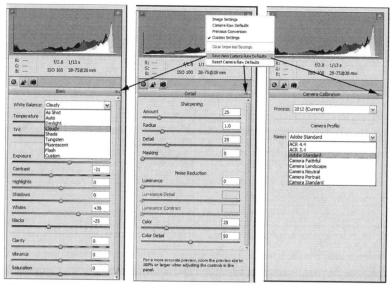

Camera RAW tools for correcting color, sharpening details and selecting a camera profile.

Basic. Under the **Basic** tab are sliders for adjusting your photo's color temperature, white and black balance, brightness, contrast and color saturation. There are also pre-sets for these settings under the **White Balance** drop-down menu at the top of the panel.

Detail. Under the **Detail** tab are adjustments for setting the sharpness and contrast of your individual pixels.

Camera Calibration. Under this tab, you'll find pre-sets that match a number of standard camera settings.

If you click the pop-up menu button in the upper right of any adjustment panel, you'll find the option to save your current settings as your **Camera RAW** default settings, as illustrated above.

Unlike changes you make in the Photoshop Elements Editor, the changes you make to your **RAW** image do not permanently change your file. Even after you've clicked **Done** and closed your **RAW** file, you can re-open it and make further adjustments – or set the adjustments all back to zero.

Once you're satisfied with your adjustments, you can port a copy of the adjusted file to your Photoshop Elements Editor by clicking on the **Open Image** button in the lower right of the **Camera RAW** adjustments panel.

The photo will open in the Editor and you will be able to print it or save it in any of the standard image file formats.

Your original **Camera RAW** image, however, will remain unchanged.

Process Multiple Files

The **Process Multiple Files** feature is a tool for editing or revising a whole batch of photo files in one action. This means that, for instance, you can apply a **Quick Fix** – like **Auto Levels, Auto Contrast, Auto Color** or **Sharpen** – to an entire folder full of photos with just a few clicks! You can also rename an entire batch at once or convert an entire batch to a new file format.

The Process Multiple Files tool (located under the File menu) will process, rename or resize a batch of files in one action.

Creating a separate Destination folder preserves your original files in their original state and size.

A common use of **Process Multiple Files** is to **resize** an entire batch of photos in one action. By properly configuring this tool, you can even send the resized images to another location, preserving your original photos in their original sizes.

1   To launch **Process Multiple Files**, ensure you are in the **Expert** editing workspace and select the option from the Photoshop Elements' **File** menu.

   Process Multiple Files can be applied to a folder or to all of the photo files you have open at the time the tool is launched.

2   Select the appropriate option from the drop-down menu at **Process Files From** and, if appropriate, browse to the photo folder at **Source**.

3   Set the **Destination** if you'd like your changed photo files saved to a new location.

4   If you'd like to rename your photo batch, check the **Rename Files** option and set your desired naming conventions. Generally, a batch of photos uses a similar front name followed by a sequence of alphabetic or numeric suffixes.

5   If you'd like to change the **Image Size** for your batch of photo files, check the **Resize Images** option and then set the **Width** or **Height** and **Resolution**.

As long as **Constrain Proportions** is checked, there's no need to set *both* the **Width** and **Height** for your photos. The tool will resize your photos proportionately, based on the single dimension you define.

For instance, if you are resizing your photos for video, you need only to set the **Width** to 1000 pixels. As long as **Constrain Proportions** is ticked, each photo will be resized to the 1000 pixels wide and whatever height is necessary to keep the photo in its correct proportions.

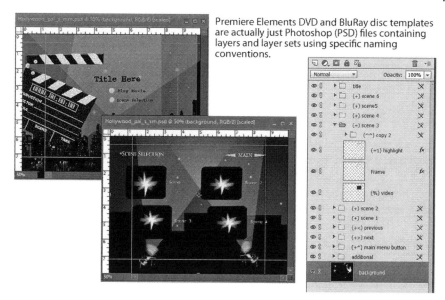

Premiere Elements DVD and BluRay disc templates are actually just Photoshop (PSD) files containing layers and layer sets using specific naming conventions.

Create Premiere Elements Movie Menu templates in Photoshop Elements

You can do a lot of customizing of disc menus right in Premiere Elements (as we discuss in **Chapter 31, Create Movie Menus**). You can customize the text on the buttons, change the fonts, change the locations of the buttons and titles on the menu pages and even swap out an existing template's background.

But, using Photoshop Elements, you can actually *create your own templates* virtually from the ground up! This template can include your own custom background, your custom graphics, your default fonts, your custom buttons and button frames – with each menu page's elements positioned right where you'd like them.

Menu templates are PSD files

Premiere Elements DVD and BluRay disc menu templates are really just PSD (Photoshop) files. They have a specific structure to them – but they are basically PSD files with layers and layer sets laid out in a specific hierarchy.

For a number of reasons, which we'll explain later, we recommend that, when you "create" any new menu template, you begin with an existing menu set.

Just copy and rename **Main Menu** and **Scene Menu** files from an existing template over to a new folder you've created in the DVD TEMPLATES directory.

On a Windows 7, Windows 8 or 10 computer, this directory is located in:

   C:/PROGRAM DATA/ADOBE/PREMIERE ELEMENTS/14.0/ONLINE/DVD TEMPLATES/ALL_LANG

On a Mac, this directory is located in:

LIIBRARY/APPLICATION SUPPORT/ADOBE/PREMIERE ELEMENTS/14.0/ONLINE/DVD TEMPLATES/ALL_LANG

Anatomy of a Movie Menu
Template File Set

HD Movie Menu template

Standard 4:3 Movie Menu

Widescreen Movie Menu

HD Menu Background Video
Widescreen Menu Background Video
Standard 4:3 Menu Background Video
Menu Background Music

Downloaded.txt file

If you see few or no PSD files in these directories, it's because the online content has not been downloaded yet. For more information on downloading additional templates, themes and additional content for Premiere Elements, see the sidebar on page 391.

Studying how these files are named and stored in this folder will help guide you as you create your own.

The illustration above shows the PSD and media files that are combined by Premiere Elements to create a Movie Menu template.

The *names* given to these files are nearly as important as the structure of the files themselves. Each segment of the template file's name has meaning.

In, for instance, **MyTemplate_pal_s_mm.psd**, the "**s**" means that the file is for standard 4:3 video (as opposed to "**w**" for widescreen or "**hd**" for high-definition). The "**mm**" means it is a *main menu* template (as opposed, of course, to an "**sm**" *scene menu* template). So we highly recommend you stick with the standard naming conventions when creating your templates.

The "**pal**" designation in the menu templates used to mean that the template was designed for the PAL video system. However, since version 3 of Premiere Elements, both PAL and NTSC have used the same templates. The "**pal**" designation is just an artifact from the days when there were separate templates. *All* current disc templates are "**pal**" templates.

Template folders also include a number of **PNG** files. These files are the thumbnails that appear when you're browsing the Movie Menu templates in Premiere Elements. We'll show you later how to make them for your template.

Create your new template's folder in the sub-folder that best represents the category you'd like your new template to appear under. (GENERAL, for instance. Or ENTERTAINMENT.) **The name you give your folder will be the name that appears as your template's name in Premiere Elements.**

> **Make sure that any new template folders you create or add to the ONLINE/DVD TEMPLATES directory include a file called DOWNLOADED.TXT,** which you can copy from the folder of another template you've already downloaded. This TXT document tells Premiere Elements not to download a new file to this folder – and, if it's not there, Premiere Elements will *erase your new template* the first time you try to use it!

Naming and storing the files

Whenever you create a disc menu template, **you will need to create both a main menu and a scene menu template** – whether you actually intend to use both menu pages or not. This is because, in order for Premiere Elements to recognize your files as a template, two things are required:

- There must be both an **"mm"** (main menu) and an **"sm"** (scene menu) version of the template files. (The names of both menus must be identical, except for the "mm" or "sm" element, as we'll explain below.)

- Each menu set, as well as any accompanying media files (background music, motion background, etc.), must be in *their own, separate folder* on your hard drive in the DVD TEMPLATES directory. The name you give this folder will become the name Premiere Elements uses for your template.

The basic template file structure

We highly recommend that even if you are "creating your Movie Menu template from scratch," you start with a copy of an existing menu template. There are several good reasons for basing your new template on an existing template set.

Anatomy of a scene button PSD layer set

Layer set folder

Every scene button or menu navigation element has its own sub-menu folder.

Text sub-folder (with multiple language support)

Button highlight

Frame graphic for video thumbnail

Button video Thumbnail

Layer of graphics

Background layer or image set

177

1. Unlike most graphic files you'll create or work with in Photoshop Elements, **disc templates use non-square video pixels**. And, when you work from an existing template, your working files will already be conformed to this video standard.

2. If you use an existing template, **all the necessary layer sets will already be included and named properly**. And it's much easier to discard what you don't want or need (or copy it if you need more) than it is to create a whole tree of layer set folders from scratch.

   And last but not least:

3. **Photoshop Elements can usually *edit* but it can not *create* layer sets!** Layer sets are technically a feature of Photoshop Pro.

Layer sets are sub-folders (and sometimes sub-sub-folders) on the **Layers** panel which contain individual layers, as in the illustration at the bottom of the facing page.

How these sub-folders are set up and how the elements inside each are arranged plays an important role in how your template functions.

If the layer sets aren't set up and named correctly, your template won't work.

Trust us. You'll be way ahead of the game if you start with an existing template set, copied to a new folder.

Replace the background layer of a menu template

Replacing a background of an existing template is relatively easy.

To do this, have both the template you plan to revise and the photo you want to use for your replacement background open.

(If you can not display more than one photo file at once in your Photoshop Elements Editor because they appear as a tabbed set, go to the **Arrange** menu and set it to **All Floating**, as described on page 17.

1. Size your new background photo to around 800x600 pixels. (1920x1080 for a high-definition template.)

   Drag this photo from its existing photo file onto the open menu template file that you want to revise, as illustrated on the next page. Your photo will automatically become a layer in your menu template file!

2. The photo will come in with corner handles, which you can drag to size and position the photo until it fits within the menu template.

   Once it's all in place, press **Enter** to lock in the size.

3. To move this new layer into position as a background layer, grab the layer in the **Layers** panel and drag it down into position right above the layer currently named **Background** (the current background layer for your menu template), as in the illustration.

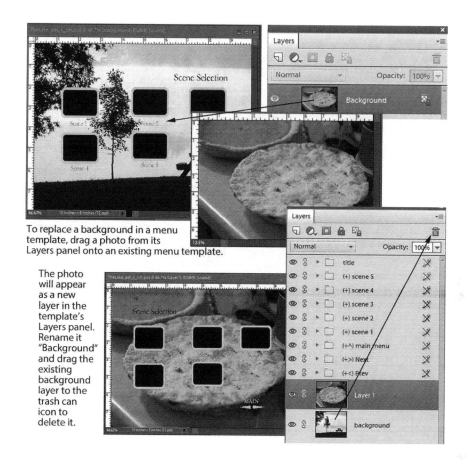

To replace a background in a menu template, drag a photo from its Layers panel onto an existing menu template.

The photo will appear as a new layer in the template's Layers panel. Rename it "Background" and drag the existing background layer to the trash can icon to delete it.

Now drag the old current **Background** to the little trash can icon on the **Layers** panel to get rid of it.

Double-click on the name of the photo layer you have just added so that the name becomes editable and rename it "**Background**".

If there are additional layers or layer sets of graphics, you can delete them also.

Naming this background layer "**Background**" isn't required in order for the template to work, but it is good housekeeping.

It also identifies the layer in the template as a background layer for Premiere Elements – necessary if you decide to replace the background for this template in the **Movie Menus** authoring workspace of Premiere Elements.

Now sit back and admire your work! Even if you do nothing else, you've essentially created your own custom disc menu template!

Scene layer sets

Each of the scene buttons in your disc template file is in a separate folder, or **layer set**, on the **Layers** panel, as illustrated to the right.

Inside each layer set, you'll find graphics for navigation (such as placeholders for the scene menu button thumbnails), a highlight graphic and a sub-folder layer set containing text and named **(^^)**.

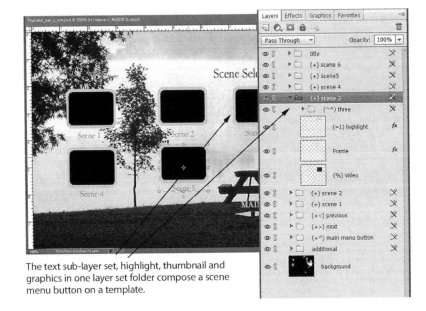

The text sub-layer set, highlight, thumbnail and graphics in one layer set folder compose a scene menu button on a template.

Those little symbols inside parenthesis following a layer's name are key elements in your layer and layer set naming conventions. They identify the function of each layer for Premiere Elements, and it's very important that you use them correctly.

Along with the text **(^^)** sub-layer set, each of these button layer sets also often contains a layer called **(%) video**. This layer includes a graphic (usually a black square but sometimes the Adobe logo) which serves as a placeholder for the disc navigation scene button, corresponding to your Premiere Elements **Menu Marker**. In other words, the **(%)** layer is where the menu button's video thumbnail will display.

There is also a layer called **(=1)**. This is your button highlight. The graphic on this layer will serve as the highlight that appears over your scene menu button when someone watching your disc navigates from scene button to scene button on your menu page.

You can customize these layers any way you want, as long as you keep them in their current layer sets and maintain their names – *as well as their accompanying symbols* – so that Premiere Elements can find them when it turns your template into disc menu pages.

1   Although you cannot create a layer set in Photoshop Elements, you can manipulate the individual layers within each layer set or sub-folder by holding down the **Ctrl** key (the ⌘ key on a Mac) as you click on the layer.

With the **Ctrl** (or ⌘ on a Mac) key held, you can edit, resize and resposition these sub-layers without affecting the other layers in that layer set.

2   You can also swap in any graphic you'd like as your menu highlight, replacing the current one in the layer set. You can even use a hand-drawn image or a photo. Just ensure that it is saved as a layer called **(=1)**.

We do recommend, however, that you never use white as your highlight graphic's color. White often won't appear as a highlight on the final menu.

Additional graphics

Some menu templates also include a layer or two of graphics between the background and the scene layer set folders. The significance of these layers of graphics is that, if you replace the background (by including a media file background or by selecting a custom background in Premiere Elements' menu workspace), these graphics layers will remain.

You can use this to your advantage, if you'd like. You can include still images as a "foreground" layer to your animated background, for instance, or you can use them to create a frame graphic within which to play your background video.

3   You can change the font, size, color or paragraph alignment for any (^^) text layer, as discussed below.

4   You can also add, remove or revise graphics used in these layer sets, such as the frames around the video thumbnail placeholders. And you can even remove the thumbnail placeholder itself, if you'd like your template to have text-only scene buttons.

Text layer sets

Within each layer set folder is a *sub*-layer set called (^^), which includes the text for that button or text block.

Open this layer set folder and you'll find 14 layers of text for this button, each in a different languages. Each language layer is named with an abbreviation identifying the language and the (-) symbol – as in (en_US (-)) Scene 3.

You can change the font, font color, font size and paragraph alignment for any of these layers just by double-clicking on "T" icon on the layer.

If your text layer is disabled or turned off, click the eyeball icon to the left of the layer to turn it on. (Which layers are enabled and which are disabled has nothing to do with how the template ultimately functions.)

As with the graphics layers within the layer sets, you can move the individual layers or the entire (^^) text layer set to a new position on your menu page – independent of the rest of the layer set – by holding down the **Ctrl** (or ⌘) key as you select it.

A text layer set includes support for 14 languages. The text can be edited for content or style by double-clicking on the "T" icon on the layer.

Layer sets are scene buttons

Each layer set (folder) on your **Layers** panel – with its text, highlight, scene thumbnail and possibly thumbnail frame – constitutes one menu button.

And, after you're finished customizing the individual elements for each scene button, you can position and scale each button as a single object. To do this, select the layer set in the **Layers** panel or click on the button on the PSD file in the Editor workspace, then drag it into position or drag the corner handles to resize it.

Adding scene menu buttons to a template

Perhaps you've come upon the perfect Premiere Elements template – only to find that it includes only four scene buttons on a menu page, but you want six. Or you find a template that has no main menu scene buttons when you want three or four.

Fortunately, adding scene menu buttons to a template page is as easy as adding a photo or layer to a PSD file.

1   **To create additional scene buttons** on a current menu page, drag an existing scene layer set folder from its position on the **Layers** panel to the **Add Layer** icon at the top of the **Layers** panel. This creates a duplicate of the entire layer set – and thus creates an additional menu button. Update the text and you're set.

    The duplicate layer set and its contents will have the same names as the original set and its contents – except that the word "copy" will be added to its name. Double-click on the necessary layer names and rename them as appropriate.

2   **To add new scene buttons** to a main menu template that doesn't have any, drag one of the layer set folders from your scene menu template's **Layers** panel, or drag a scene button directly from the scene menu template, and place it onto the main menu image file, as illustrated below.

Scene buttons can be added to a menu page template by dragging their layer sets over from a template with existing scene buttons.

Many buttons and other elements can also be dragged directly from one PSD file to another.

Elements and buttons can be removed by dragging them onto the trash can.

A copy of this layer set will appear in the main menu's **Layers** panel and the scene button will appear on your template file, to be customized and positioned as you'd like.

3   By holding down the **Shift** key, you can select several of these layer set folders at once and drag them all onto your main menu, if you'd like to add several scene buttons in one swoop.

Once there, you can position them and/or their internal elements individually. (Scene Menu buttons link to green **Scene Menu Markers** on your Premiere Elements project timeline. Main Menu buttons link to blue **Main Menu Markers**.)

4   Deleting a scene button from a menu template is as simple as dragging the layer set folder from its position on the **Layers** panel onto the little trashcan icon at the top right of the palette.

Menu buttons can not overlap!

Note that, as you hover your mouse over a scene button on a template file, Photoshop Elements will indicate the "live" area of your button by highlighting it with a blue box outline. This is a very important feature because *one thing Premiere Elements will not tolerate in a disc menu template is overlapping navigation.*

So, as a final test drive once you've finished revising your templates and positioning your buttons, be sure to hover your mouse over each of the buttons on your template page to make sure none of your navigation areas invades another's live space!

Adding background video and audio

In addition to the PSD files that make up a basic DVD or BluRay disc template, Premiere Elements can use audio and video files in the template's directory folder to add motion or music to the disc menu.

Your video background (optionally including audio) can be AVIs, MPEGs or SWFs.

Your audio background can be either an MPs or a WAV file.

The order of the layers in a Disc Menu Template

It is important to note that the *order* of the layer sets in the **Layers** panel – not the *names* of the layer sets – determines the order that Premiere Elements uses them as scene markers. Your first scene, in other words, must be the *bottom*-most scene layer set in the **Layers** panel and the last scene, the top-most.

In other words, even if you call a layer set "Scene Five", if it is stacked below the other layer sets in the **Layers** panel, it will be used for "Scene One" when Premiere Elements uses the template to create its DVD or BluRay disc menu.

To include audio or video backgrounds as part of your templates, you need only *include them in the same directory folder as your disc menu templates* and then name them exactly the same as the template files – except with the letters "**bg**" at the end.

In other words, a video loop background for the main menu

TemplateName_pal_s_mm.psd

would be called

TemplateName_pal_s_mm_bg.avi

A video background file for the scene menu

TemplateName_pal_s_sm.psd

would be called

Template_pal_s_sm_bg.mpg

To apply the same mpeg video to both the main and scene menus, simply omit the "**mm**" or "**sm**" reference in the name as in:

TemplateName_s_pal_bg.mpg

Any AVI, MPG or SWF video file you include in your template folder and name accordingly will automatically replace the background layer in your menu with video when the template is applied in Premiere Elements.

MP3s and WAV files will play audio or music with your menu.

Each of these will, of course, be over-written if you choose to customize the background video or audio for the template in your Premiere Elements' **Add Movie Menu** workspace.

Naming conventions

Though Premiere Elements is surprisingly forgiving about the names used for its DVD and BluRay menu template files, I recommend you stick with the "traditional" names whenever possible.

More than once I've helped troubleshoot a custom menu for a client, only to find that the heart of the problem was his naming one of the layer sets or template files incorrectly. Using standard names made all the difference.

Stick to these basic naming rules and you should be all set:

1 The template set *must* include both a main menu and a scene menu in order to be recognized by Premiere Elements, even if you ultimately plan to use only a main menu for your DVD or BluRay disc.

This set of menu template files should be in its own folder in a category sub-directory of the DVD TEMPLATES folder. The name you give this folder is what Premiere Elements will use as the name of the menu template.

Anatomy of a Movie Menu Template File Set

HD Movie Menu template
Standard 4:3 Movie Menu
Widescreen Movie Menu
HD Menu Background Video
Widescreen Menu Background Video
Standard 4:3 Menu Background Video
Menu Background Music

Downloaded.txt file

2   The main menu and scene menu template must have identical names, save for the "**mm**" and "**sm**" designation.

"**s**" templates are for standard 4:3 video

"**w**" templates are for widescreen 16:9

"**hd**" templates are for high-definition BluRay discs

Since version 3, all Premiere Elements disc menu templates, whether to be used in a PAL or NTSC video project, use the same format – the **pal** designation in their names is merely an "artifact". But it must be included in the template's name in order for the template to work.

That said, the following is the menu template naming convention we recommend you always use, just to stay safe.

TemplateName_pal_s_mm.psd
TemplateName_pal_s_sm.psd

TemplateName_pal_w_mm.psd
TemplateName_pal_w_sm.psd

TemplateName_pal_hd_mm.psd
TemplateName_pal_hd_sm.psd

For background video or audio, tag the letters "**_bg**" onto the ends of the files names.

If the name includes "**sm**" or "**mm**," the media file will function as background for only the scene menu or main menu page, as in:

TemplateName_pal_s_mm_bg.avi
TemplateName_pal_s_mm_bg.mp3

A media file without "**sm**" or "**mm**" in the name will function as background for *both* the main menu and scene menu.

TemplateName_pal_s_bg.avi

Movie Menu Thumbnails

In every Movie Menu template folder included with the program, you will find a number of PNG files. These little files are the thumbnail images that Premiere Elements uses as previews when you select and lay out your **Movie Menus**.

It's not necessary to create a thumbnail for your movie menu – but if you don't, you may see only your template's name and not a thumbnail preview in the **Movie Menus** workspace.

If you browse to the directory folder for a default **Movie Menu** templates with Windows Explorer or Finder, you'll see thumbnail images (PNG files) in several languages. You need only create one each for your scene and main menu in whatever language your program is set up for.

To create English thumbnails:

1   With your main menu template open in the Photoshop Elements Editor, select **Save For Web** from the **File** menu.

   A **Save For Web** option panel will open, as illustrated below.

2   Select the **PNG-24** preset in the upper right of the panel

3   Set the **Image Size/New Size** to 160 px **Width**. (The **Height** will auto-fill.)

4   Click **Save**. A browse screen will open.

5   Browse to the directory folder where your new menu templates are saved.

   Name your file **en_US_TemplateName_pal_s_prv_mm.png**.

Repeat this process for your scene menu template, except replace the "**mm**" in the file's name with "**sm**".

When you next start Premiere Elements, the program should recognize the new template and its thumbnails should appear in your **Movie Menu** workspace.

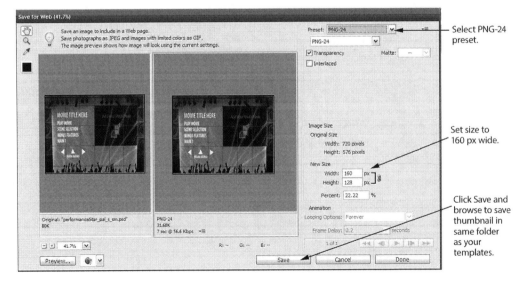

Select PNG-24 preset.

Set size to 160 px wide.

Click Save and browse to save thumbnail in same folder as your templates.

Photoshop Elements Preferences and Presets

The Photoshop Elements **Preferences** are accessed under the program's **Edit** menu (or, on a Mac, under the program's name). Many of these settings are pretty self-explanatory. But here are a few that I think are worth noting:

Saving Files. By default, the program is set to **Always Ask** whenever you try to save or overwrite a file. This drives me crazy! When I want to save my work, *I want to save my work!*

Unless you want to save versions of your photos as you work, I recommend setting **On First Save** to **Save Over Current File**.

File Extensions. For most of your work, it won't matter if your **File Extensions** (.jpg, .gif, .psd) are saved in upper case or lower case. However, in some environments – particularly if you're creating images for the Internet, it can make a big difference. HTML sees upper case letters as different names than lower case. There is no right or wrong setting here, but you do want to be aware of how the program is naming your files so that you can maintain some consistency and control.

File Compatibility. I recommend checking the option to **Prefer Adobe Camera Raw for Supported Raw Files**. RAW is a function of higher-end digital cameras that stores images unprocessed and uncompressed, giving you more control over how the imagery is interpreted and adjusted (as discussed on page 167). If your camera supports it, you'll probably want access to it.

Floating Windows. As discussed on page 16, open files in Photoshop Elements are displayed by default filling the editing workspace. To release your photo files from the interface and have them "float" over the program, check **Enable Floating Documents** checked on the **General preferences** screen.

High-Density Monitor Support. To make Photoshop Elements' menus readable on a wider range of higher density monitor resolutions, the program includes preferences for controlling the size of the text on the program's interface. You'll find these settings (on PCs only) on the **Display & Cursor** page, under **High Density Displays**. In most cases, you can simply leave the **IU Scale Factor** set to **Automatic**. However, it can also be set to manually to **Small (100%)** or, for higher resolution monitors , to **Large (200%).** (You'll need to restart the program in order for the new settings to take effect.)

Transparency. Transparency in an image file is usually represented in Photoshop and Photoshop Elements by a gray and white checkerboard pattern (as seen in **Create non-square graphics** on page 129 of **Chapter 9, Work With Photoshop Elements Layers**). This preference screen allows you to customize the pattern or turn it off completely.

Units & Rulers. This preference screen sets the default measurements that are displayed on your image files in the Editor workspace. For most online work or for editing graphics and photos for video, you may want to set your **Rulers** to **Pixels**, a more relevant measurement than inches or centimeters.

Type. This one is just a personal preference, a peeve left over from my years as a layout artist. If you're planning to work with type in your image files, select the option to use **Smart Quotes**. **Smart Quotes** are the difference between quotation marks and plain old tick marks. The difference, for instance, between " (which are tick marks, used for measurements) and the slightly curved " (true quotation marks). Using true quotation marks can mean the subtle difference between a layout looking "typewritery" and one looking truly designed.

The Organizer has its own set of **Preferences**, also located under the **Edit** menu (on a PC). Among them are settings for configuring how the program interfaces with your scanner and camera.

You'll find information for setting up a **Contact Book** in the Organizer preferences on page 470 and information on setting up **E-mail Sharing** on page 467.

New File presets

Although much of the work you'll be doing in Photoshop Elements will involve working on existing files and photos, occasionally you'll want to create graphics from scratch. To that end, the program comes bundled with a number of New File presets, available under **File/New/Blank File**.

The Preset drop-down menu on the New File panel includes presets for standard paper sizes, web sizes, video graphics and, under **Web, Mobile App Design** or **Iconography** you'll even find a number of presets under the **Size** menu for creating graphics for icons for mobile device and phone apps.

Chapter 14

Learn About Your Photoshop Elements File

Important information on your
Photoshop Elements file window

There is a lot more to a PSD, or an
image file, than meets the eye!

In this chapter, we'll take a close look
at an image file, what Photoshop
Elements has to tell us about it and,
ultimately, what it all means.

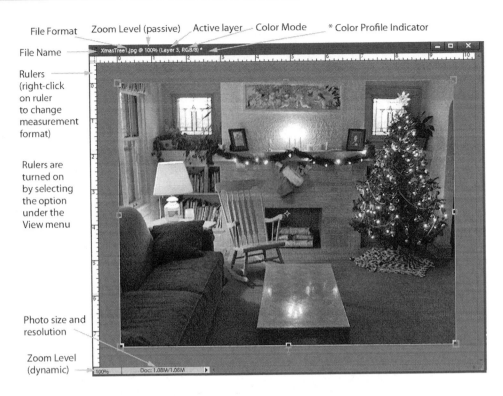

File Format   Zoom Level (passive)   Active layer   Color Mode   * Color Profile Indicator

File Name

Rulers
(right-click
on ruler
to change
measurement
format)

Rulers are
turned on
by selecting
the option
under the
View menu

Photo size and
resolution

Zoom Level
(dynamic)

The Info Bar

Whenever you open a photo or an image file in Photoshop Elements'
Editor workspace, it appears with a frame around it. This frame includes a
lot of useful information about the file.

Along the top of the frame, you'll see:

> **File Name**. This is the name of the file, of course – including the suffix,
> which defines the file's format (PSD, TIF, JPG, etc.).

> **Zoom Level (Passive)**. Displayed both after the **File Name**, at the top
> of the image frame, and in the lower left corner of the image frame,
> this number, a percentage, tells the scale of the image, as currently
> displayed in your Editor workspace. You can zoom in or out by pressing
> **Ctrl++** (the Ctrl and plus key) or **Ctrl+-** (the Ctrl and minus key) on your
> keyboard (or, on a Mac, the ⌘++ or ⌘+-) .

This **Zoom Level** number can be a bit misleading, however. This is because
it is measuring the scale of the picture's size in *pixels* rather than in linear
numbers, such as inches or centimeters.

That means that, if you're looking at an image file with a resolution of
300 ppi at 100% zoom, the picture is going to look about *four times larger* on
your computer monitor than it will when it is printed.

But, for most of the images you're working on for video or for the web, at
100% zoom, your image should appear at just about its actual size.

Layer. If you have a layered PSD file open in your **Editor** workspace, the layer that is currently selected will appear in parentheses, following the **Zoom Level**.

Color Mode. Following the **Layer** notation, or alone in the parenthesis, is the **Color Mode** of your image file. In most cases, this mode will be **RGB/8**. However, if you are editing a monochrome (black & white) photo, this mode will read **Gray/8**.

The **RGB** mode means that the pixels in your image are composed of combinations of red, green and blue. Each of these three colors can be set to any of 256 levels (0-255).

Why 256? Well, this seemingly arbitrary number is actually a very *real* number, with its origins in binary code, the base 2 numbering system that is at the heart of all computer programming. Every instruction written into every computer program is based on some base 2 number.

256 is 2^8 (2 to the 8th power, or 2x2x2x2x2x2x2x2). Hence, the red, green and blue color levels are each 8-bit settings (with 256 possibilities) – which is why the number 8 appears after the RGB **Color Mode** listing.

There are other, by the way, even deeper RGB modes. (16-bit color, for instance.) However, 8-bit color is the standard for video and online graphics, and it is the only RGB color mode that Premiere Elements can work with. Besides, the 256 levels of red, green and blue yields 16,777,216 possible color combinations, which is probably more than enough colors for most photo and video purposes.

Photoshop Elements can work in three additional color modes, which can be selected for your image files under the **Image** drop-down on the Menu Bar.

Grayscale, or black and white, which is actually 256 levels of a single color: black. (White is merely the color black set to the level 0.)

Indexed Color is a system for limiting the number of colors in an image. If you've worked on graphics for the Web, you likely already know how reducing colors on a GIF file can reduce its file size. (Although, because it provides a limited color range, **Indexed Color** is also probably not the best **Color Mode** for working with photos in.)

Bitmap is a **Color Mode** made up of pixels that are only either pure black and pure white – with no shades of gray in between.

Why does a "100% zoom" video fill only part of my computer screen?

Remember, a standard NTSC video frame is only the equivalent of a 640x480 pixel image. Most likely your computer monitor is set to a resolution of between 1024x768 pixels and 1280x1024 pixels. That means that a full-screen video image at 100% zoom may take up only one-fourth of your computer screen! (A high-definition 1920x1080 video, however, will more than likely fill your screen.)

Color Modes and Color Profiles are set under the Image drop-down menu.

A Color Profile is a color management system that determines how your images will display on devices and in programs that also use the same color profile.

The professional version of Photoshop includes additional color modes, which are useful for preparing files, for instance, for production on an offset press. However, for our purposes – and particularly as you produce graphics and imagery for use in Premiere Elements or for the Web – you'll usually be working with **RGB** or **Grayscale** mode only.

> *** (Color Profile)**. An asterisk appearing after the Color Mode listing is an indication that a **Color Profile** has been assigned to the image.

A **Color Profile** is a standardization system for color that can be applied across several programs and hardware devices. This ensures that the image's colors appear the same on every device, and in every application, that's using that same profile. There are two color profiles available in Photoshop Elements: **sRGB** and **Adobe RGB**, both of which are standard enough that either one should produce excellent results.

Many graphics cards and monitors will allow you to set them to a color profile. If it is available on your computer, you'll usually find it listed under **Color Management**, under **Settings/Advanced** for your display. (On a PC you can access these settings in your **Color Management** controls. On a Mac, open your **System Preferences** and click on **Display.**)

Using the same color profile for all of your programs and hardware is the best way to ensure that what you see on your computer is ultimately what you get, image-wise.

To set a precise Zoom Level, type a percentage in this space.

Your file's size and resolution.

Clicking and holding on the size/resolution bar displays a pop-up info panel.

The Status Bar

There's even more information about your file on the **Status Bar,** which appears at the bottom left of your image frame, as illustrated above.

> **Zoom Level (Dynamic).** Although this number, a percentage, is the same as the information displayed at the top of the panel, the **Zoom Level** displayed at the bottom left of an image frame is *dynamic*. In other words, you can click on it and type any number in this space and, when you press **Enter,** Photoshop Elements will jump to that precise zoom view.

> **Size/Resolution.** Along the bottom of your image panel, to the right of the **Dynamic Zoom Level** indicator, is a display listing, by default, your image file's size and resolution. As illustrated above, when you click and hold on this indicator, a pop-up panel will display additional information about your file.

Additionally, as illustrated below, clicking the black arrow button to the right of the **Status Bar** allows you to set this area to display a number of other facts about your image, including the name of the tool that you currently have selected, the size of your image file and even how long it would take your image file to download from a Web site!

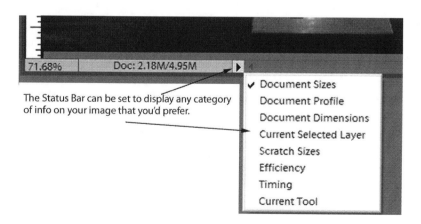

The Status Bar can be set to display any category of info on your image that you'd prefer.

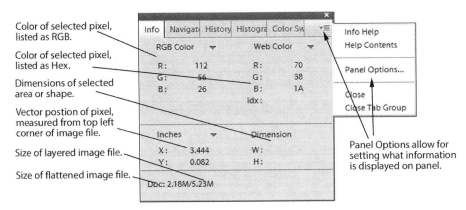

Color of selected pixel, listed as RGB.

Color of selected pixel, listed as Hex.

Dimensions of selected area or shape.

Vector position of pixel, measured from top left corner of image file.

Size of layered image file.

Size of flattened image file.

Panel Options allow for setting what information is displayed on panel.

The Info panel provides a variety of information about your image file.

The Info panel

Another tool for getting information about your image file is the **Info** panel – which is launched from the program's **Window** menu or by clicking the arrow next to the **More** button in the lower right of the program's interface. As illustrated above, this panel displays color and location information about specific pixels you have selected in your image as well as measurements of selected areas.

Color Info. As you hover your mouse over your image, you'll see numbers appearing next to the R, G and B listings in the upper left panel of this palette. These numbers are the color level settings for the individual pixels your cursor is currently over.

The R, G and B listings on the upper right of the panel display as an alpha-numeric combination.

The six number and letter combinations from these three colors are called the pixel color's **Hex** code, a common system for identifying colors on Web files.

In Hex code, for instance:

Black is 000000
White is ffffff
A medium gray is 808080

If you click on the down arrow next to the **RGB** or **Web Color** listing, you can set that panel to display this information using other color definitions, including **HSB** (hue, saturation and brightness).

Vector Position. The current position of your mouse cursor over your image file is listed in the lower left panel of this palette, as measured in pixels from the top left corner of your photo or image file.

By clicking on the down arrow to the right of the *Inches* listing, you can set this information panel – as well as the information panel on the **Dimensions** panel, to the right – to display these measurements as pixels, inches, metric measurements, percentages or even picas.

Dimensions. If you are working with one of the **Marquee Selection Tools** or one of the **Shape** drawing tools (see **Chapter 5, Get to Know the Photoshop Elements Toolbox**), the lower right panel of this palette will display the dimensions of the area you are selecting or drawing. (Professional designers sometimes use this **Info** palette, along with the **Rectangular Marquee** tool, to select and measure areas of their image files.)

Doc Size. The size of the image file you're currently editing is displayed along the bottom of the Info palette.

If you're working on a layered image file, you'll see two numbers listed. The first is the size of the image file once all of the layers in your image file have been flattened; the second is the size of the image file if saved as a layered PSD file.

File Info

New to version 14, Photoshop now includes a detailed **File Information** window which lists an amazing amount of metadata about your photos including data on the lens your photo was shot was, the GPS location of the picture, if a flash was used and detailed RAW data. Additionally, many fields on this panel (on the **Basic** and **DICOM** pages, for instance) are dynamic and can be filled in by you, permanently saving detailed information about the photo file to the file itself.

To access this panel, go the program's **File** menu and select **File Info**.

This metadata, by the way, can be used by the Elements Organizer to catalog and manage your photo. For more information on metadata, see page 438 of **Chapter 34, Manage Your Files with the Organizer**.

Section 2

Adobe
Premiere Elements 14

Get to Know the Premiere Elements Workspaces

Basic Video Editing Moves

What's New in Version 14?

Chapter 15

Get to Know Premiere Elements 14

What's what and what it does

The interface for Premiere Elements has been designed by Adobe to be as simple and as intuitive as possible. It is also remarkably customizable, with a wealth of powerful tools in obvious and, once in a while, not so obvious places.

There have been major changes to the interface in the last few versions of the program. But you'll quickly find that it makes for a mostly improved editing experience all around – for the newbie as well as for the veteran.

Elements Live

The first time you launch any of the Elements programs, the interface will default to **eLive**, a link directly from the programs to an exclusive website full of exciting ideas, tutorials and other content especially for Elements users.

eLive (Elements Live) can be accessed from any computer with a live internet connection by clicking the **eLive** link at the top center of the program's interface.

The Add Media panel   Project Assets   Quick, Guided and Expert View   The Monitor Panel   Export +
(Expert View only)   and eLive link   Share tab

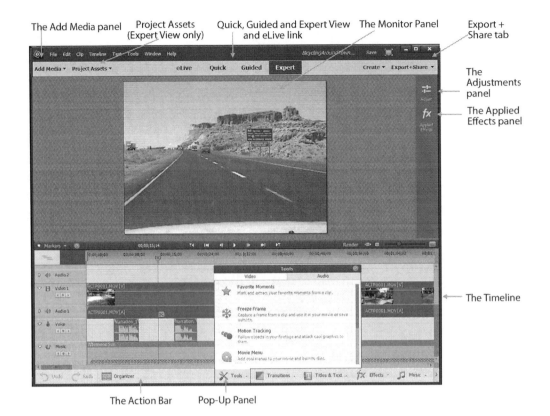

The
Adjustments
panel

The Applied
Effects panel

The Timeline

The Action Bar   Pop-Up Panel

Panels, pop-ups and the Action Bar

The Premiere Elements interface has been designed with efficiency and
readability in mind.

The interface is bright and clean with big, easy-to-find buttons and text
throughout.

Its tools are tucked out-of-the-way – but easily retrievable with just a click or two.

Many of the tools are hidden away in pop-up panels that snap open with just a
click on a tab or button.

The bulk of the tools can be accessed through buttons on the **Action Bar**, which
runs along the bottom of the Premiere Elements interface. (Similar **Action Bars**
run along the bottoms of the Elements Organizer and Photoshop Elements
interfaces.)

The program includes two fully separate (though connected) workspaces: **Quick**
View and **Expert** View – workspaces that allow you to go as deeply into editing
your videos as you'd like. (More on them on page 202.) Additionally, the program
includes a **Guided Edits** View, which function in both Quick and Expert View, and
which take you step-by-step through a number of key editing tasks. (For more
information on **Guided Edits**, see **Chapter 17.**)

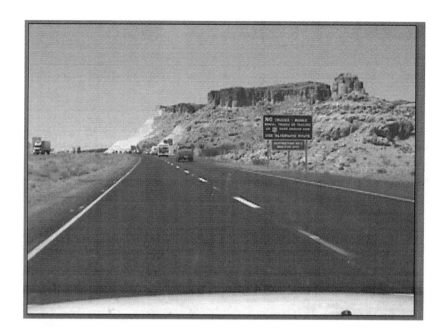

The Monitor panel

The **Monitor** panel is the big center panel on which you'll preview your movie as your work. It usually rests in the top center of the interface – though it can change position to accommodate the **Adjustments** and **Applied Effects** panels when necessary.

If you **right-click** on it, you'll find options for setting its playback quality and magnification.

The Timeline

Both Quick View and Expert View (discussed on the following page) share a similar workspace for assembling your video: The timeline.

Your timeline is really where the bits and pieces become a movie.

The timeline in Expert View.

The timeline in Quick View.

Quick View and Expert View

Premiere Elements offers you two somewhat different workspaces in which to edit your video project: Quick View and Expert View. In both views, you edit on a timeline. However, the timeline, and its features, vary a bit from view to view.

Quick View and Expert View aren't so much totally different interfaces as they are two different ways to approach the same project. In fact, you can switch between them as you work on your project, taking advantage of the best aspects of each.

Quick View	Expert View
Media clips are added directly to the timeline from your computer, camcorder or recording device.	Media clips are gathered into the **Project Assets** panel before they are added to your timeline.
The timeline consists of four tracks: Titles, Video, Narration and Audio.	The timeline can include up to 99 video and 99 audio tracks.
Only the Video track can include video. Only titles and text can be added to the Title track.	Multiple tracks of video can be combined to create effects, including Videomerge, Chroma Key and Picture-in-Picture
Audio levels can be set using tools available in Smart Mix, on the Audio Mixer and on the Adjustments panel.	Audio levels can be controlled at specific points using keyframes created right on the timeline.
A limited number of effects and titles are readily available in Quick View.	The complete set of effects is available.

Customize your workspace

The sizes and the arrangements of the various panels in the interface are easily customizable. Panels can be resized by dragging on the seams between them.

Feel free to experiment and resize the panels by dragging on the borders between them.

Many of the pop-up panels also allow you to stretch them longer so that you can see more of the assets, effects, templates, etc., at once.

To resize your panels, hover your mouse over the seams between the panels until you see the double arrows – then click and drag.

And, if you ever find the program misbehaving or if you just feel like you've lost control of your workspace, you can easily get back to the default look by simply going to the **Window** drop-down menu and selecting **Restore Workspace**.

Minimum screen resolution

Because of the size of the panels and the number of tools that Adobe fits into some rather tight spaces, we recommend that this program not be used on a computer with a monitor with less than 1280x1024 resolution.

There's simply no room for it all to fit otherwise! And, on a smaller screen, you'll spend a lot of time scrolling and resizing panels, trying to get to all the tools.

What's a CTI?

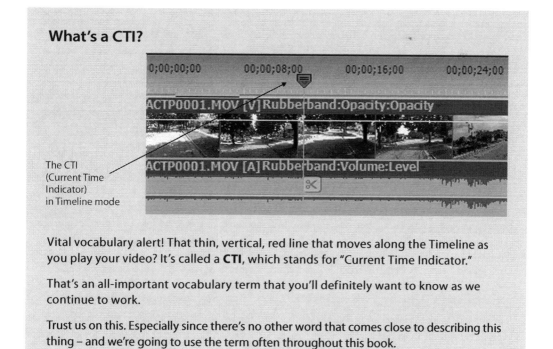

The CTI (Current Time Indicator) in Timeline mode

Vital vocabulary alert! That thin, vertical, red line that moves along the Timeline as you play your video? It's called a **CTI**, which stands for "Current Time Indicator."

That's an all-important vocabulary term that you'll definitely want to know as we continue to work.

Trust us on this. Especially since there's no other word that comes close to describing this thing – and we're going to use the term often throughout this book.

Basic editing moves

No matter what you plan to do with your video and no matter how creatively you plan to do it, the video editing process itself will still fit the same basic structure.

Here's a brief walkthrough of the steps you'll take for creating any video project in Premiere Elements.

1 Gather your media

The assets, or media, you gather to create your movie can come from a variety of sources. It can be video, audio, music, photos or graphics. If you are working in Quick View, any media you gather will go directly to your timeline. If you are working in Expert View, it will go into your **Project Assets** panel.

To import your media into your project, click on the **Add Media** tab on the upper left of the interface.

There are basically three ways to get your media into your project, all accessed by one of the six buttons on the **Add Media** panel (illustrated below). We show you how and when to use each in **Chapter 19, Add Media to Your Project**.

- **Download your video from a hard drive camcorder, flash based camcorder or other video recording device.**

    Hard drive camcorders, including high-definition AVCHD and Flip cam units (the **Flip, AVCHD, Cameras and Phones** button), download their video as files rather than stream it into the program. Media can also be downloaded from other sources, including DVDs (the **DVD Camcorder or PC DVD Drive** button) and **Digital Still Cameras & Phones**.

Add Media options

Launches the Elements Organizer ——— Elements Organizer
Drag videos and photos from Elements Organizer

Opens Explorer or Finder ——— Files and folders
Get videos, photos, and audio files from your computer's hard drive

Launches Photo Downloader ——— Photos from cameras or devices
Get photos from digital cameras, phones, or removable drives

Launches Video Importer ——— Videos from cameras & devices
Get videos from camcorders, phones, or other removable devices

Opens Capture screen ——— Webcam or WDM
Capture video from a webcam or WDM compatible device

Launches Video Importer ——— DVD camera or computer drive
Get video from a DVD based AVCHD camera or your computer's DVD drive

Video streamed from your webcam is captured live through the Premiere Elements Capture workspace.

Video from non-tape-based sources – including hard drive camcorders, Flip and AVCHD camcorders and DVDs – is imported into your Premiere Elements project by the Video Importer, while still photos are downloaded from your digital camera or phone with the Photo Downloader.

When you select the option to Add Media from the Organizer, can locate the photos, video and audio files using the Organizer's management tools.

- **Stream, or capture, your video into your project.**

  If you've got a Webcam or other WDM (Windows Device Model) video or audio device attached to your computer, you can use Premiere Elements to capture the live video directly into your Premiere Elements video project.

  Premiere Elements does not include tools for capturing tape-based video, including video from HDV and miniDV camcorders. However, video from digital tape camcorders *can* be captured as Premiere Elements-compatible video data using various third-party software and then added to your Premiere Elements project. We show you how to capture this type of video in our **Premiere Elements Appendix,** on page 421.

- **Browse to gather media files that are located on your computer's hard drive(s).**

  When you select the **PC Files and Folders** button under **Get Media,** Windows Explorer or the Mac OSX Finder opens, allowing you to browse to video, stills, graphics or music files already on your computer's hard drive. The **Elements Organizer** is a companion file management program that can be used to manage and search media files on your computer. (We explore the Organizer in detail in **Section 3** of this book.)

To add a clip to your timeline in Expert View, simply drag it from the Project Assets panel.

As you add clips, the other clips will "ripple", moving aside if you add the clip in the middle of a project.

To override the ripple effect (as when you're adding music or a video clip to a parallel track) hold down the Ctrl key as you add the clip (or the Command key on a Mac).

Zoom in or out on the timeline by pressing + or - or using the Zoom slider.

2 Assemble the clips on your timeline

Once you've imported your media clips into a project, you can begin the process of assembling your movie. If you are working in Quick View, any media you add to your project will be loaded directly to your timeline. If you are working in Expert View, the clips will be added to your **Project Assets** panel. Editing this video is as simple as dragging these clips from this panel to your timeline.

Once you add your files to your timeline, you'll have a number of options:

- **Trim your clips.** Trimming means removing footage from either the beginning or the end of a clip. To trim a clip, click to select the clip on your timeline and then drag in either the beginning or end to shorten it, as in the illustration on the following page.

- **Split your clips.** Splitting means slicing through your clips so that you can remove footage from the middle or delete one sliced-off segment completely. To split a clip, position the **CTI** (playhead) over your clip at the point at which you'd like the slice to occur and then click on the scissors icon on **CTI**.

- **Place your clip on an upper video or audio track**. An important feature of editing in Expert View is the ability to place your video or audio on tracks other than **Video 1** and **Audio 1**.

  The use of multiple tracks of video is, in fact, key to the creation of many of the more advanced video effects, including **Chroma Key** and **Videomerge**.

To slice a clip in two, click the scissors icon on the CTI playhead.

If a clip is selected on the timeline, only that clip will be split at the position of the CTI; If no clips are selected, all clips on every track on the timeline will be split at the position of the CTI.

◆▶ Trim from Beginning of clip   Trim from End of clip ◆▶

To trim a clip on the timeline, hover your mouse over the beginning or end of a clip until the Trim from Beginning or Trim from End icon appears, then click and drag in or out.

We discuss how to assemble your movie in both Quick View and Expert View in **Chapter 16** and **Chapter 21** respectively. We also show you how to use multi-track editing in order to create a variety of effects and take advantage of several key storytelling techniques.

We'll also show you how to use both automatic and manual tools to work with your audio clips.

3   Add and adjust effects

Premiere Elements comes loaded with dozens of video and audio effects as well as hundreds of preset effects for working magic on your movie.

Adding an effect in Premiere Elements is very easy, as we show you in **Chapter 27, Add Video and Audio Effects**.

1   On the **Action Bar**, click the **Effects** button.

This will open the **Effects** pop-up panel, as illustrated on the following page.

2   Locate an effect.

Go to any category of video or audio effects by clicking the title bar (The bar along the top of the panel) and selecting from the list that appears.

You can also quickly locate any effect by clicking the **Quick Search** magnifying glass button at the top right of the panel and typing in the effect's name.

3 Apply the effect.

To apply the effect, drag it from the **Effects** panel onto a clip on your timeline.

4 Adjust the effect's settings.

Once you've applied your effect, you may or may not see an immediate change in your video clip. To intensify or fine tune your effect, ensure the clip is selected on your timeline, then open the **Applied Effects** panel by clicking the button on the right side of the interface.

To apply an effect to a clip, simply drag it from the Effects panel onto a clip on your timeline.

The **Applied Effects** panel is a tremendously powerful workspace. Not only can you use it to change the settings for individual effects but also as the main workspace for creating and adjusting **keyframes**, Premiere Elements' tool for creating animations, motion paths and effects that change over the course of the clip's playback.

In the **Applied Effects** panel, locate your effect's listing, then click on it to open the effect's settings.

In **Chapter 28**, we'll show you how to customize and fine tune your effects in the **Applied Effects** panel.

Then, in **Chapter 29**, we'll show you how to use keyframes to animate effects and motion paths.

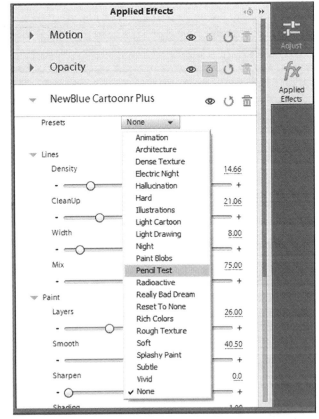

Effects that have been added to a clip appear in that clip's Applied Effects panel, where they can be adjusted and customized.

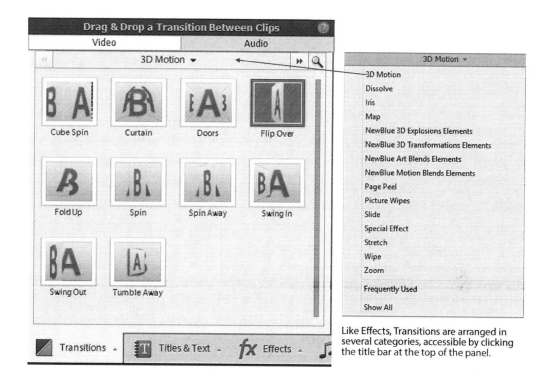

Like Effects, Transitions are arranged in several categories, accessible by clicking the title bar at the top of the panel.

4 Add and adjust transitions

Transitions are the effects or animations that take your movie from one clip to another. Some are gentle and nearly invisible – others are showy and draw attention to themselves. Most transitions are added to your timeline and adjusted similarly to effects:

1 Click on the **Transitions** button on the **Action Bar**.

The **Transitions** panel will open.

2 Locate a transition.

Select any category of video or audio effects by clicking the title bar (The bar along the top of the panel) and selecting from the pop-up list that appears.

You can also quickly locate any effect by clicking the **Quick Search** magnifying glass button at the top right of the panel and typing in the transition's name.

3 Apply the transition.

Apply a transition by dragging it from the **Transitions** panel onto the intersection of two clips on your timeline.

Clicking the More button on the Transition Adjustments panel and scrolling down reveals a number of options for customizing your transition.

Clicking the eyeball button will toggle the panel to display your transition with your actual video clips.

The Custom button will open a screen for customizing the elements of many transitions.

4   Customize your transition.

Nearly all transitions include a number of properties that can be customized, depending on the nature of the transition. Virtually all include options for designating where the transition centers and the duration of the transition as well as an option for setting the transition to reverse its movement (i.e., wiping from right to left rather than left to right).

We'll show you just about everything there is to know about adding and customizing transitions – including why they sometimes seem to behave in very strange ways – in **Chapter 25**. And, as a bonus, we'll even show you how to use the **Gradient Wipe**, a tool for creating your own custom transition effects!

5   Add titles

Titles are text, and sometimes graphics, placed over your clips to provide additional visual information for your video story. Once you've selected a title template, you'll create and customize your titles in Premiere Elements' **Title Adjustments** workspace.

To add a title or text to your movie:

1   Click the **Titles & Text** button on the **Action Bar**.

The **Titles & Text** panel will open.

As with **Effects** and **Transitions**, the panel has several categories of title templates. Among these are text-only stationary titles, titles with graphics and rolling and animated titles

When you drag a title template to the timeline, the Titles & Text Adjustment workspace will automatically open.

In this workspace, you can customize your text's style, color and look as well as add graphics and apply animation.

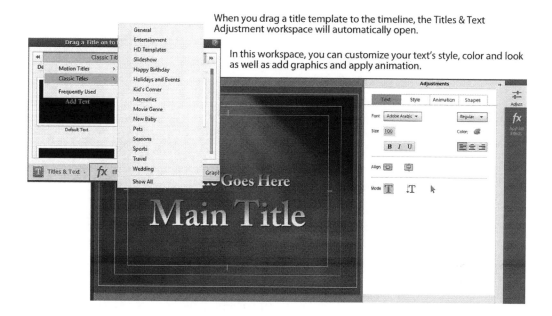

2   Add the title to your timeline.

Drag the title from the **Titles & Templates** panel to your timeline. The **Title Adjustments** workspace will automatically open.

3   Customize the text.

Type your title over the placeholder text.

With your text selected, you can apply text attributes – including setting the font, size, style and alignment. You can also apply a style to your selected text by clicking on one of the **Text Styles** listed on the panel.

4   Customize your title.

The **Title Adjustments** workspace has tools for customizing the look and style of your text, adding and placing graphics and adding very cool text animations. You can also customize your title template and create rolling and crawling titles.

When you want to return to the regular editing workspace, click on the timeline.

We'll show you pretty much everything you could want to know about using Premiere Elements' tools for creating and customizing your text and titles in **Chapter 26**.

Under the Export & Share tab, you'll find several options for outputting your movie.

6 Export & Share your movie

When you're happy with the video project you've created, you'll find a number of options for publishing and sharing it, as we discuss in **Chapter 32**. We'll show you how to publish it to:

- **Devices.** The program will save your finished project as an AVI file, MPEG, QuickTime (MOV) file, AVCHD video, Windows Media (WMV) file or an audio file on your computer's hard drive. Once the output is complete, you can then use these files any number of ways, including posting them online or using them as segments in a larger video project.

- **Disc.** Built into Premiere Elements are tools for creating menus and scene markers so that you can produce great-looking DVDs and BluRay discs.

- **Online.** The program comes complete with facilities for loading your finished video to a social media site like YouTube, Vimeo or Facebook.

- **Audio** or **Image.** Premiere Elements also includes tools for outputting an audio file or a still photo from your movie.

And that's basically it!

You gather your assets; you assemble them on your timeline; you add effects, transitions and titles; then you share your masterpiece with the world.

But between the lines of this simplicity are the countless variations that can elevate your movie project from the realm of a basic structure to something truly amazing!

What's new in version 14?

Adobe has added a couple of interesting new features in its latest version Premiere Elements. It's also done some fine-tuning of the interface to make it easier to locate effects and to focus on the audio aspects of your videos.

Audio view

In its **Expert** view, Premiere Elements now includes an Audio view option, which gives you access to a couple of new audio production tools.

In **Audio View**, the timeline includes a **Master** VU meter, so you can monitor your project's overall audio levels. The timeline headers in **Audio View** also include toggles for muting and soloing audio tracks, so you can focus your audio tuning on one track at a time.

We give you a tour of this new workspace on page 382 of **Chapter 30, Mix Your Audio and Add Music.**

New Guided Edits

Adobe continues to build out the library of **Guided Edits**. In version 14, you'll find new step-by-step guides for adding a **Color Pop** and for building fast and slow motion effects using **Time Remapping**. We look at all of the program's **Guided Edits** in **Chapter 17.**

New right-click Timeline options

Adobe has completely overhauled the context menus available when you **right-click** a clip on your timeline. Rather than having to scroll through a long list of options, the new panels direct you to a tool or feature through easier-to-navigate sub-menus.

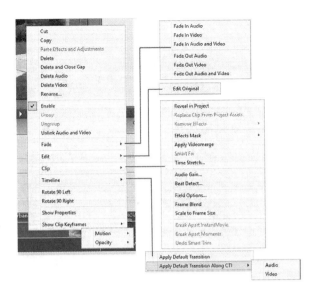

We explain all of these right-click options to you on page 279 of **Chapter 21, Edit Your Video in Expert View.**

Easier to navigate effects, transitions and tools

As they've done with the right-click menus, Adobe has also simplified the navigation in the **Effects, Transitions** and the **Tools** menus.

Effects, Transitions and **Tools** are now divided into separate **Video** and **Audio** listings, making it much simpler to locate exactly the feature you're looking for.

We discuss the **Tools** in **Chapter 23, Use the Premiere Elements Toolkit**, the Transitions in **Chapter 25, Add and Customize Transitions** and we discuss the Effects in **Chapter 27, Add Audio and Video Effects**.

New Motion Titles

Motion Titles are templates that include motion and animation, each element of which can be customized – and your customized title can even be saved as a new template!

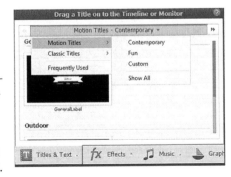

We show you how to use and add **Motion Titles** to your movies on page 342 of **Chapter 26, Add Titles & Text**.

Export & Share

Adobe has completely rethought its output option screen, building it around a more intuitive editors workflow rather than simply offering a list of output options.

Selecting a file output format is as simple as selecting a destination category (**Devices, Disc, Online, Audio** and **Image**) and then selecting a specific spec from that category.

The **Devices** category, for instance, includes options for **Computer, TV** and **Mobile** outputs, while each of these output categories includes presets for 4K, high-definition or standard-definition video. (The panel also includes a **Custom** option, of course, for advanced users and people who prefer to create their own presets.) It's a much more intuitive way to choose an optimized format and resolution of your finished video or audio piece.

We've got a complete tour of this workspace, as well as an explanation of each of its output options, in **Chapter 32, Export & Share Your Video Projects**.

Organizer tune-ups

Finally, Adobe continues to tune up its Organizer, the file management tool bundled with Premiere Elements and Photoshop Elements.

You'll find even more tools for filing and retrieving your photos and video files, including much more advanced tools for categorizing your photos by location and by the faces of people that appear in your pictures.

We discuss this terrific little program and all of its tools in **Section 3 (Chapters 34, 35** and **36)** of this book.

CHAPTER 15

Adobe Premiere Elements

Part IV

Editing in Quick View and Guided Edits

Adding Media to Your Quick View Timeline

Trimming and Slicing Your Video

Adding Transitions

Adding and Adjusting Audio

Adding Titles

Chapter 16

Assemble Your Video in Quick View
The drag-and-drop editing space

Quick View is Premiere Elements' workspace for quickly pulling together a video and applying effects to it.

It combines the simplicity of sceneline editing with the power of a full-fledged Premiere Elements timeline.

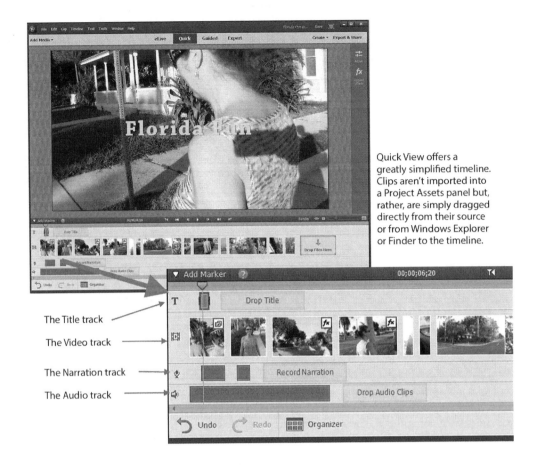

Quick View offers a greatly simplified timeline. Clips aren't imported into a Project Assets panel but, rather, are simply dragged directly from their source or from Windows Explorer or Finder to the timeline.

The Title track

The Video track

The Narration track

The Audio track

Premiere Elements' Quick View timeline makes assembling your movie as fast and easy as possible. It combines the simplicity of the old Sceneline mode with the power of a full-fledged Timeline.

The Quick View timeline includes four tracks in which you can assemble your movie. They are, from top to bottom:

The Title Track. This is where text or titles that will overlay your video is placed. (If you'd prefer your titles with a black background or no background at all, you can also place your titles directly on the **Video Track**. However, only text and titles can be placed on the **Title Track**. Video cannot.) For more information on adding titles to your movie, see **Chapter 26, Add Titles & Text**.

The Video Track. This is the track on which your movie will be assembled. It will also include your video's accompanying audio track.

The Narration Track. Although any audio may be added to this track, this is the track that any recorded narration (see page 295) will appear on by default.

The Audio Track. Music or any other peripheral audio may be added here. For information on adding music to your movie, see **Chapter 30**.

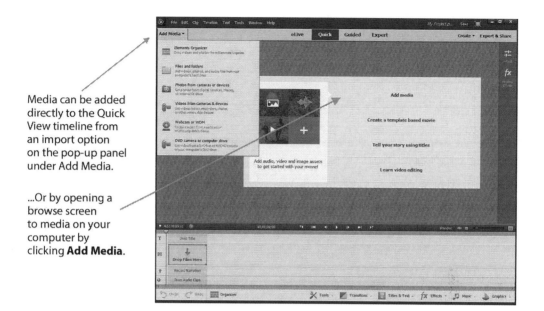

Media can be added directly to the Quick View timeline from an import option on the pop-up panel under Add Media.

...Or by opening a browse screen to media on your computer by clicking **Add Media**.

Add media to your Quick View timeline

Unlike in Expert View (discussed in **Chapter 21**), in Quick View your video and other media isn't imported into a **Project Assets** area before it is added to your timeline. You simply add your media directly to your timeline and start editing! The program will automatically set up your project by matching its settings to the specs of the first video clip you add.

You can add your media to your project in a number of ways:

- Video and other media from Flip, AVCHDs, cameras, phones or removable drive devices are imported to your timeline over a USB connection (as discussed in **Chapter 19**, pages 250-251).

- Live video can be captured from your webcam directly to your timeline (as discussed on page 251).

- Media that's already on your computer can be browsed to by selecting the **Files and Folders** option or located through the Elements Organizer.

The tools for importing your media are accessed through the pop-up menu under the **Add Media** button in the upper left of the program's interface. (For more information on **Add Media**, see **Chapter 19**.) Or, when you first start your project, by clicking the **Add Media** button in the center of the interface, as illustrated above. (Note that the +**Add Media** button will be replaced by the **Monitor** panel, once you begin to assemble clips on your timeline.)

Your media can also be added directly from your computer's Windows Explorer or Mac Finder screens. Simply drag your audio and video clips directly to your Quick View timeline!

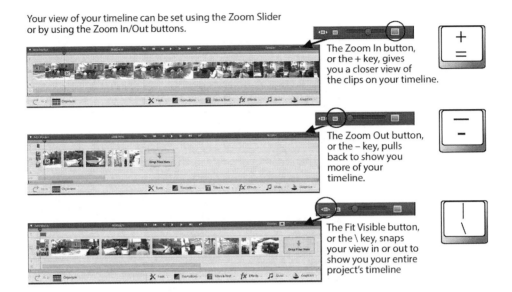

Your view of your timeline can be set using the Zoom Slider or by using the Zoom In/Out buttons.

The Zoom In button, or the + key, gives you a closer view of the clips on your timeline.

The Zoom Out button, or the – key, pulls back to show you more of your timeline.

The Fit Visible button, or the \ key, snaps your view in or out to show you your entire project's timeline

Zoom in or out of your timeline

Once you've added media to your timeline, you may want to zoom out to see the entire movie at once, or zoom in to a single moment or frame to make some fine adjustments.

Along the upper right of the Quick View timeline are controls for zooming in and out your movie. (These controls have the same function on the Expert View timeline.) There are also keyboard shortcuts for settings these views:

The **Zoom In** button incrementally zooms in on your timeline. You can also zoom in by pressing your keyboard's **+** key.

The **Zoom Out** button incrementally zooms out of your timeline. You can also zoom out by pressing your keyboard's **–** key.

The **Fit Visible Timeline** button sets the zoom level so that your entire movie project is visible. You also set this level by pressing the \ key on your keyboard (above the **Enter/Return** key).

The **Slider** can be used to set your zoom level precisely.

Add transitions

A library of transitions can be browsed by clicking on the **Transitions** button on the **Action Bar** along the bottom of the timeline.

In Quick View, you only have access to a handful of transitions. If you'd like to access the full transitions library, switch over to Expert View, where you can access over 100 video transitions in 15 categories plus 2 audio transitions. To learn more about working with transitions in Expert View, see **Chapter 25, Add and Customize Transitions**.

To apply a transition, simply drag it from the Transitions pop-up panel on the Action Bar to the intersection between two clips (indicated in green).

To apply a transition, drag it from the **Transitions** panel to your timeline, as illustrated above. A green highlight will indicate where the transition will be applied.

When you apply a transition, a pop-up menu (illustrated on the right) will prompt you to choose where you'd like the transition applied in relation to the clips. In most cases, you'll choose **Between Clips**.

This menu also allows you to set the **Duration** of the transition, in seconds. This number can be set by clicking on the up and down arrows or by clicking directly on the number and typing in a custom duration. Increments of seconds (such as .5) can be used.

To re-access this panel and revise these properties at any time, **double-click** on the transition on your timeline.

Most transitions also allow for much deeper customization. For more information on customizing your transitions, see page 326.

When you apply your transition (or when you double-click on an existing transition), a pop-up menu will appear offering options for how the transition's duration and how the transition rests between tyour clips.

To replace one transition with another, simply drag the new transition from the **Transitions** panel onto the existing.

To remove a transition, click to select it on the timeline and press **Delete** on your keyboard.

How your transitions behave can be affected by the amount of "head" and "tail" material available on your clips. For more information on this, see **How Transitions Work** on page 330.

Trim or split your video

Video clips, audio clips and even titles can be **Split** or **Trimmed**. To indicate which clips you want to **Split** or **Trim**, click to select the audio or video clip on your timeline so that it is surrounded by a blue highlight, as illustrated on the following page.

Splitting your video means cutting a larger clip on your timeline into smaller clips.

To Split your video:

1   Position the **CTI** playhead so that the frame that displays in you **Monitor** indicates the exact spot you want to slice your video.

2   Click on the scissors icon on the **CTI**.

To split a clip, click on the Scissors icon on the CTI.

Splitting means dividing a clip into smarller clips at the point of the CTI playhead.

Split clips are indicated with ticker markers.

Ticker markers indicated that there is "hidden" video beyond the clip's end points.

Trimming means shortening (or lengthening) a clip on your timeline by adjusting the clip's start and end points.

To trim a clip:

1   Hover your mouse over the beginning or end of a clip on your timeline until the **Trim** indicator appears, as illustrated above.

2   Click and drag to the left or right.

Trim left clip. Trim right clip.

Trimming cuts (or extends) video from the beginning or end of a clip. To trim, hover your mouse over an end of a clip until the trim indicator appears, then click and drag.

A trimmed clip is indicated with a ticker marker.

A clip that has been split or trimmed is indicated with the [E] icon.

Once a clip has been split, it becomes two smaller clips. Each of these clips can also be trimmed.

Add audio to your Quick View timeline

As you add your camcorder video to your **Video Track**, the accompanying audio will be added automatically, as part of an unseen audio track.

The Quick View timeline offers two additional tracks in which you can add audio: the **Narration Track** and the **Audio Track**.

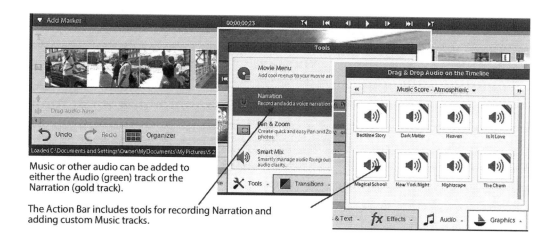

Music or other audio can be added to either the Audio (green) track or the Narration (gold track).

The Action Bar includes tools for recording Narration and adding custom Music tracks.

Although technically you can add audio or music to your movie project on either track, you need to be careful where you place your audio or music if you plan to record narration. Narration gets priority on the **Narration Track**. This means that narration will overwrite any existing audio or music on this track at the position of the **CTI** playhead as your record!

You can place any audio or music clips on the **Audio Track**.

As with your video clips, your audio clips can be **Split** and **Trimmed**, as described on the facing page.

The limitations of Quick View

Although most of the program's features are available in both Quick View and Expert View, a number of features function to a lesser degree or not at all in Quick View. They include:

Multi-track editing. Because the Quick View timeline is limited to one video track, J-Cuts, L-Cuts, split screen and picture-in-picture effects can not be easily created in Quick View.

Chroma Key and Videomerge. Because **keying** effects, including **Videomerge**, require at least two tracks of video in order to create their composite effects, these effects can not be effectively created on the Quick View timeline.

Audio Keyframing. Audio cannot easily be to specific levels at specific points in a clip on the Quick View timeline using keyframes. Audio levels can only be set using the **Smart Mix, Adjustments** and **Audio Mixer** tools.

Fortunately, you can easily switch between Quick View and Expert View as you work on your project so that you can take advantage of the features on each timeline. (However, video and audio added to upper tracks in Expert View will not be visible when you switch to Quick View.)

Adjust your audio levels and mix your audio

The Quick View timeline has a limited number of ways for you to adjust the audio levels or to mix your audio so that one or more audio tracks' levels are lower so that another can dominate.

Smart Mix (discussed on page 298) will automatically mix and adjust your audio levels based on parameters you define.

The Audio Mixer (discussed on page 293) will set audio keyframes for you as you raise and lower levels on the fly as you play your video.

However, each of these methods has its own challenges and limitations. The single best way to precisely control your levels and mix your audio is with audio keyframes (described on page 383), a feature most easily applied on the Expert View timeline.

Add titles

A library of title templates can be browsed by clicking on the **Titles & Text** button on the **Action Bar** along the bottom of the timeline.

The titles library is arranged in categories, and you can browse through the categories of transitions by clicking the backward and forward arrows at the top of the pop-up panel, as illustrated on page 334.

The title templates range from basic text to rolling titles and templates.

Once you've selected a title, drag it to either the **Titles Track** on the Quick View timeline (if you'd like to overlay your video) or to an area on the **Video Track** (if you'd like it to appear with a black or no background).

Once you've placed a title, the **Title Adjustments** workspace will open. In this workspace you'll find options for changing your text's color, style, font or size. You can also add animations and/or graphics to your text.

For more information on working with titles and text, see **Chapter 26, Add Titles & Text.**

Like audio and video clips, titles can be **Split** and **Trimmed**. If your text has animation or a roll or crawl applied to it, the longer you stretch the title on the timeline, the slower the animation and vice versa.

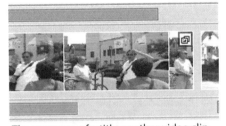

The presence of a title or other video clip on an upper video track is indicated on the Quick Edit timeline with an overlay marker in the upper right corner of the effected clip.

Guided Startup with Premiere Elements

Adding Transitions

Adding Scores

Adjusting Contrast, Brightness and Color

Adding Titles

Recording Narration

Creating Video Effects

Color Pop

Slow Motion

Chapter 17

Use Guided Edits
Simple, step-by-step editing

If you're new to video editing or to Premiere Elements, you might appreciate the program's helpful Guided Edit feature.

Guided Edits walk you through a number of basic editing moves, step by step, explaining how each tool and adjustment works along the way.

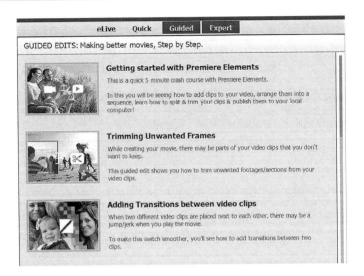

Guided Edits are designed primarily to help you feel comfortable with the program. They'll take you step-by-step through each process, and they'll show you which panels to open and how to use each tool. It's like having your own personal instructor built right into the program!

The **Guided Edits** include:

Getting Started With Premiere Elements shows you how to start a project, gather your media and assemble your media files on your timeline.

Trimming Unwanted Frames demonstrates the basics of trimming and splitting the video clips on your timeline.

Adding Transitions Between Video Clips shows you how to add transitional video effects between the clips on your timeline.

Adding Scores to Your Movie shows you how to add and customize music tracks.

Adjusting Brightness+Contrast & Color shows you how to improve or enhance the color, lighting or contrast in your movie.

Adding a Title to Your Movie shows you how to select, add and modify a title template.

Adding Narration to Your Movie walks you through the process of recording narration into your movie project as your movie is playing.

Creating a Picture-In-Picture walks you through the process of adding a video clip to your movie as a picture-in-picture inset.

Animating Graphics Easily walks you through the process of overlaying a graphic onto your movie and then controlling its movement across your video frame.

Adding Video within a Title walks you through the process of using the Track Matte to create an effect in which your video is seen through your text rather than around it.

Adding an Effects Mask on your Video shows you how to use a mask so that an effect is confined to a designated area of your video.

Making a Black & White Video with Color Pop walks you through the process of stripping all but on color from your movie.

Creating a Slow or Fast Motion Effect shows you how to time shift the playback speed of your movie using the **Time Remapping** tool.

In each case, the program will explain to you which tool to use, then it will highlight on the program's interface the button to click to access or apply the tool or effect.

Guided Edits can be accessed in both the **Quick** and **Expert** view workspaces, though some of these **Edits** will require you to switch over to **Expert** view.

You'll likely outgrow the need for **Guided Edits** fairly quickly, once you learn a few basic moves. However, if you've opened the program for the first time and don't have a clue where to start, **Guided Edits** can help you find your way!

Getting Started With Premiere Elements

This **Guided Edit** will walk you step-by-step through the process of setting up, editing and outputting your movie, including:

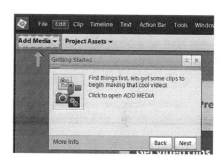

> **Adding Media to Your Project** by either browsing to video files, still photos or audio on your computer or capturing or downloading video from your camcorder.

> **Opening the Project Assets Bin** and showing you how to add your media files form this bin to the timeline.

> **Controlling Timeline Zoom** and the **CTI**.

> **Trimming and Splitting** the clips on your timeline.

> **Adding Transitions** between the clips on your timeline and customizing how the transition positions itself between your clips.

> **Publishing & Sharing** your finished movie.

Trimming Unwanted Frames

This **Guided Edit** will walk you step-by-step through the process of trimming and splitting your movie clips, including:

> **Trimming from the Beginning** of a clip on your timeline.

> **Trimming from the End** of a clip on your timeline.

> **Trimming from the Middle** by splitting a clip in your movie.

Adding Transitions Between Video Clips

This **Guided Edit** is more specific to the process of adding and customizing transitions to your movie. It's steps include:

> **Locating a Transition** and adding it to your movie.

> **Customizing the Transition's position** between your clips.

For more detailed information on using some of the deeper customization tools for creating transitions, see **Chapter 25, Add and Customize Transitions**.

Adding Scores to Your Movie

This **Guided Edit** will walk you step-by-step through the process of adding and customizing Premiere Elements music tracks, including:

> **Working with the Audio Panel** and selecting a **Scores** track.
>
> **Adjusting Intensity** of the Scores track.
>
> **The Fit Entire Video** option.

For more detailed information on using **Scores** to create custom music tracks in your movie, see page 385 of **Chapter 30, Mix Your Audio and Add Music**.

Adjusting Brightness+Contrast & Color

This **Guided Edit**, as you might expect, will walk you through the process of adjusting and enhancing the brightness, contrast and color in a selected video clip. Its step-by-step instructions include:

> **Selecting a video clip** on your timeline and opening the **Adjustments** panel.
>
> **Using the Lighting Quick Fix Preview** tool to set the video clip's brightness and contrast.
>
> **Using the Color Quick Fix Preview** tool to set the video clip's hue, lightness, saturation and brightness.

For more detailed information on using the tools in this panel to correct and enhance your video's color and lighting – as well as the tools for varying these settings using keyframes – see **Chapter 24, Make Adjustments to Your Video and Audio**.

Adding a Title to Your Movie

This **Guided Edit** will walk you step-by-step through the process of adding and customizing a title, including:

> **Working with the Titles Panel** and selecting a title template.
>
> **Changing the Text** in the Title Adjustments workspace.
>
> **Applying Styles to Your Text** to change its look and other characteristics.
>
> **Adjusting Text Properties**, including font, color and alignment.
>
> **Applying Animation to Your Text** using the Titles Animation templates.

For more detailed information on creating and customizing titles and text in your movies, see **Chapter 26, Add Titles & Text**.

Adding Narration to Your Movie

This **Guided Edit** will walk you step-by-step through the process of recording narration to your movie's timeline. It's steps include:

Attaching Your Microphone and making sure it's properly configured in the program's ASIO Settings.

Launching the Narration Tool and starting your recording.

Stopping your recording and reviewing the results.

For more detailed information on configuring your microphone and using the **Narration** tool, see **Add Narration** on page 295 of **Chapter 23, Use the Premiere Elements Toolkit**.

Creating a Picture-in-Picture

This **Guided Edit** will walk you step-by-step through the process of adding a picture-in-picture inset to your movie, including:

Adding Your PiP Video by selecting where you'd like it to appear.

Getting Foreground Video for use as your PiP.

Settings the End Point for the Overlay by trimming your PiP clip.

Adjusting the Position of the Overlay over the main video clip.

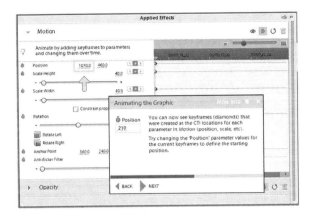

Animating Graphics Easily

This **Guided Edit** will walk you through the process of adding and creating motion paths for a Premiere Elements graphic, including:

> **Adding a Graphic** from the **Graphics** panel.
>
> **Animation Controls** and opening the **Keyframe Controls** on the **Applied Effects** panel.
>
> **Enabling Animation Parameters** and **Adding Keyframes** to create a motion path for your graphic.

For more detailed information on creating your own custom animations with Premiere Elements, see **Chapter 29, Keyframing**.

Adding Video within a Title

This **Guided Edit** shows you how to use the **Track Matte** so that your text becomes a sort of a cookie cutter. The result will be a black video frame with your video only visible through your title's text. The **Guided Edit** will walk you through:

> **Creating a Black Video** clip using the **New Item** feature on the **Project Assets** panel and adding it to the track above your video.
>
> **Adding a Title** to the video track above your black video.
>
> **Adding and Applying the Track Matte Key** effect to create the cookie cutter effect, based on your title, through the black video.

Adding an Effects Mask on your video

This **Guided Edit** shows you how to use the **Effects Mask** to limit the area of your video frame that is affected by a video effect. The **Guided Edit** will walk you through:

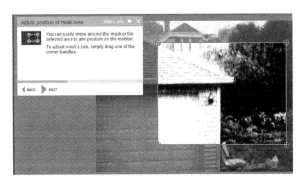

Creating an Effects Masking, which duplicates your video clip and places the duplicate on the video track directly above the original.

Adjusting and Positioning the Mask Area to designate the area that will be affected by your effect.

Selecting and applying an effect. The effect will only be applied to area of your video within the **Effects Mask**.

For more detailed information on creating an Effects Mask, see **Isolate an effect area with the Effects Mask** on page 354 of **Chapter 27, Audio and Video Effects**.

Making a Black & White Video with Color Pop

This **Guided Edit** shows you how to use the **Red Noir Hollywood Look** to strip away all but one color in your video. The **Guided Edit** will walk you through:

Selecting and Applying the Red Noir Hollywood Look, which desaturates most of the colors in your video clip.

Reducing Saturation by designating which color or colors will remain visible and which will be desaturated to black & white.

For more detailed information on the **Red Noir** look, see **Hollywood Looks** on page 352 of **Chapter 27, Audio and Video Effects**.

Creating a Slow or Fast Motion Effect

This **Guided Edit** shows you how to use the **Time Remapping** tool to strip away all but one color in your video. The **Guided Edit** will walk you through:

Opening the Time Remapping Tool, a workspace for controlling the playback speed of your video clip.

Positioning the CTI Playhead to where in your clip you'd like your slow motion effect to begin.

Creating a Time Zone to indicate the area of your clip you'd like the slow motion effect applied to.

Setting playback speed by adjusting the **Time Remapping** slider.

For more detailed information on this tool, see **Create cool Time Remapping effects** on page 301 of **Chapter 23, Use the Premiere Elements Toolkit**.

Adobe Premiere Elements

Part V
Editing in Expert View

Starting a New Project

Selecting Project Settings

Opening an Existing Project

Chapter 18
Start a Premiere Elements Project
Creating and opening your video projects

In early versions of Premiere Elements, setting up your project was a vital, and sometimes challenging, part of the process of making your movie.

Much more happens automatically in Premiere Elements 14 – though there is much to be said for making sure your project gets off to a good start.

When you click on the Video Editor button, you will see the options to start a new project or open an existing one.

The Welcome Screen

When you first start up Premiere Elements, you'll be greeted by the **Welcome Screen**. Very similar to the **Welcome Screen** in Photoshop Elements, it is a launching point for the workspaces of the program.

From this **Welcome Screen** you can start a new Premiere Elements project, open an old one or launch the Elements Organizer. If you have Photoshop Elements installed on your computer, you'll also be able to launch it from this screen.

Bypass the Welcome Screen

If you'd prefer not to be greeted by the **Welcome Screen**, you'll find options for setting how the program

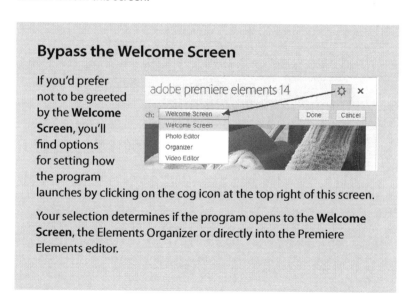

launches by clicking on the cog icon at the top right of this screen.

Your selection determines if the program opens to the **Welcome Screen**, the Elements Organizer or directly into the Premiere Elements editor.

The Elements Organizer

The Elements Organizer is a powerful media file management program that interfaces with both Premiere Elements and Photoshop Elements.

The Organizer allows you to catalog and search your media files based on a wide variety of criteria. Additionally, the Organizer includes a number of tools for creating and sharing your video and photo projects.

The Organizer reads the EXIF data off your digital photos, adds

Keyword Tags (both manually and automatically) to your media clips, gives you the ability to sort your files into **Albums** and serves as a launching point for a number of Photoshop Elements and Premiere Elements functions.

We discuss its features and functions in more detail in **Section 3** of this book.

Start a new project

Selecting the **New Project** option from the **Welcome Screen** takes you to the Quick View or Expert View workspace of Premiere Elements. If you open in the Quick View workspace, you can go to work **Adding Media** and assembling it on your timeline (as described in **Chapter 19**).

By clicking on the Expert button at the top of the interface, you can switch the program to Expert View, with its much more powerful timeline and multi-track capabilities. In Expert View, you gather your media into the **Project Assets** panel before assembling it on the timeline.

Unlike in earlier versions of the program, you usually don't need to worry about selecting settings when starting up a Premiere Elements project. The program will set up your project automatically, based on the *first clip you add to your timeline*. (Though it sometimes has

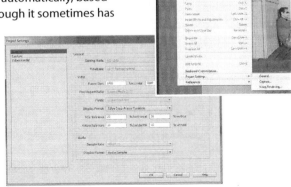

trouble matching settings to still photos and many forms of QuickTime/MOV files – in which case we recommend you **Force Selected Settings** when you start your project, as discussed on the bottom of page 240.)

Meantime, to see which settings your project is currently using, just go to the **Edit** menu and select **Project Properties**.

Starting a new Premiere Elements project

Select the location your project will be saved to.

Name your project.

Most recent project settings.

To start a new Premiere Elements project:

1   Click the **File** menu at the top of the interface and select **New** then, from the submenu, **Project**.

The **New Project** option screen will appear, as illustrated above.

Type the title for your new project in the box displayed at **Name**.

2   Click the **Browse** button to choose a location to save your new project file.

We at Muvipix recommend always selecting the **Browse** option and, wherever you choose to save your file, *creating a new folder* for every new project file.

This little bit of housekeeping keeps all of your new project's files in one neat, little folder. And, when your project is done and you want to clear it from your computer, you can then remove not only the project file but all of the temp, render and scratch disk files Premiere Elements has created for that project simply by deleting that single folder!

This makes post-project cleanup a much easier and neater process.

Manually choosing your Project Settings

In most cases, it's not necessary to manually select your project's settings. Whether you're working in Quick View or Expert View the program will automatically set up your project's settings based on the specs of the first video clip you add to your timeline.

And in most cases, that's good enough.

But there are times when you'll want to impose settings on your project. You may want to set up your project for a specific purpose – creating a project for a DVD, for instance – or if you're mixing different formats of video and you don't want the program to automatically switch project settings on you. Also, at times (particularly when you're editing MOV or MP4 files), the program may have trouble recognizing your video file's specs and matching your project settings to it.

In those cases, you can opt to **Force Selected Settings** on your new project.

3   Click the **Change Settings** button at the bottom of the **New Project** panel.

This will open the **Project Settings** panel, as illustrated on the facing page.

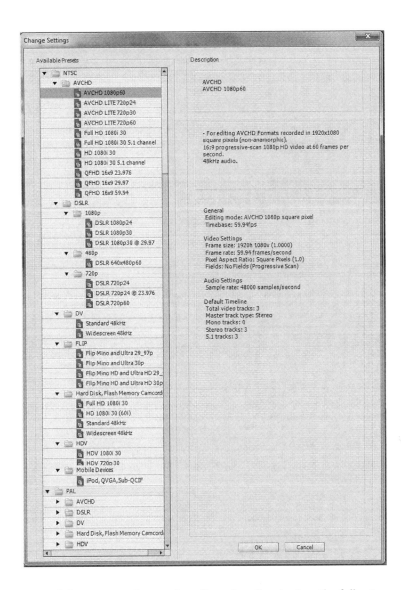

4 Select your project settings (based on the chart on the following pages).

Then click **OK**.

5 Back at the **New Project** panel, check the box **Force Selected Project Setting on This Project**, as illustrated at right.

Your project's settings will not automatically reset when you add a new clip to your timeline.

Premiere Elements 14 project preset options

Premiere Elements includes a wealth of project setting options for editing your video.

In most cases – whenever Premiere Elements recognizes the format of the video – the program will automatically select the appropriate project setting, based on the first video clip you load into your project (though it sometimes has trouble identifying MOV file specs).

AVCHD	AVCHD 1080p60	Full 1920x1080 AVCHD video shooting 60 progressive fps.
	AVCHD Lite 720p24	AVCHD video (1280x720) shooting at 23.976 progressive fps.
	AVCHD Lite 720p30	AVCHD video (1280x720) shooting at 29.97 progressive fps.
	AVCHD Lite 720p60	AVCHD video (1280x720) shooting at progressive 59.94 fps.
	Full HD 1080i 30	AVCHD video (1920x1080 60i/30 fps square pixel, hard drive, high definition) from camcorders that shoot in stereo audio.
	Full HD 1080i 30 5.1 Channel	AVCHD video (1920x1080 60i/30 fps square pixel, hard drive, high-definition) from camcorders that shoot in 5.1 channel audio. *This is the most common format for most newer hard drive, high-definition camcorders.*
	HD 1080 30	AVCHD video (1440x1080 60i/30 fps non-square pixel, hard drive, high definition) from camcorders that shoot in stereo audio.
	HD 1080 30 5.1 Channel	AVCHD video (1440x1080 60i/30 fps non-square pixel, hard drive, high-definition) from camcorders that shoot in 5.1 channel audio. This is the most common format for older hard drive, high-definition camcorders. *Note that, although this format uses less horizontal pixels, it produces the same high-quality, 16:9 image as 1920x1080 video. The pixels are just non-square, or wider than they are tall – as in the traditional television standard.*
	QFHD 16x9 23.976	4K files at 3840x2160 pixel resolution, 23.976 fps.
	QFHD 16x9 29.97	4K files at 3840x2160 pixel resolution, 29.97 fps.
	QFHD 16x9 59.94	4K files at 3840x2160 pixel resolution, 59.94 fps.
DSLR Presets – Use these presets for working with high-quality video from digital still cameras (such as the Canon EOS Movie Full HD series).		
1080p	DSLR 1080p24	1920x1080 16:9 video shooting at 23.976 progressive fps.
	DSLR 1080p30	1920x1080 16:9 video shooting at 30 progressive fps.
	DSLR 1080p30 @29.97	1920x1080 16:9 video shooting at 29.97 progressive fps.
480p	DSLR 640x480p60	640x480 16:9 video shooting at 59.94 progressive fps.
720p	DSLR 720p24	1280x720 16:9 video shooting at 24 progressive fps.
	DSLR 720p24 @23.976	1280x720 16:9 video shooting at 23.976 progressive fps.
	DSLR 720p60	1280x720 16:9 video shooting at 59.94 progressive fps.

continued on facing page

More Premiere Elements project presets

DV	Standard 48 khz	720x480 4:3 video from miniDV tape-based camcorders.
	Widescreen 48 khz	720x480 16:9 video from miniDV tape-based camcorders.
Flip	Flip Mino or Ultra Flip 29.97	Flip standard definition (640x480) video camcorders shooting at 29.97 fps.
	Flip Mino or Ultra Flip 30	Flip standard definition (640x480) video camcorders shooting at 30 fps.
	Flip Mino HD or Ultra HD 29.97	Flip high definition (1280x720) video camcorders shooting at 29.97 fps.
	Flip Mino HD or Ultra HD 30	Flip high definition (1280x720) video camcorders shooting at 30 fps.
Hard Disk, Flash Memory Camcorder	HD 1080i 30	High-definition video (1920x1080) from non-AVCHD hard drive or flash memory camcorders (such as the JVC GZ-HD7).
	HD 1080i 30 (60i)	High-definition video from (1440x1080) from non-AVCHD hard drive or flash memory camcorders that record in 60i format. (The PAL equivalent is, of course, 50i.)
	Standard 48kHz	Standard-definition (720x480) 4:3 video from hard drive camcorders as well as video from DVDs. *It is very important to use this or the following preset with standard-definition MPEG or VOB sources because it will automatically reverse the field dominance in your video, correcting an interlacing issue that can otherwise cause stuttering in your output videos.*
	Widescreen 48 kHz	Video from standard-definition (720x480) 16:9 hard drive camcorders and video from DVDs.
HDV Presets	HDV 1080i 30	Video from tape-based, high-definition HDV camcorders that shoot full HDV at 1440x1080 pixels.
	HDV 720p 30	Video from tape-based, high-definition HDV camcorders that shoot full HDV at 1280x720 pixels (progressive scan at 30 fps).
Mobile Devices	iPods, QVGA, Sub-QCIF	Video from iPods or other mobile devices shooting 640x480 (progressive scan 15 fps).
		Video shot at 1280x720p using iPads, smartphones or other devices will use the Flip HD 30 fps project settings.

PAL presets

The PAL and NTSC options are identical except that the frame rates for PAL presets are 25 fps rather than 30. Additionally, video listed on this chart as shooting at 60i or 60p would appear as 50i and 50p in the PAL system.

There are no Flip presets for PAL. All project presets for Flip cameras are located under NTSC.

The PAL standard definition video frame (the DV and Hard Disk presets for standard and widescreen) would appear as 720x576 rather than 720x480.

Open an old project from the Welcome Screen

Clicking the **Existing Project** button on the **Welcome Screen** will get you access to any work-in-progress or old Premiere Elements projects.

Your most recent projects will appear in the drop-down menu, as illustrated on page 240. Additional Premiere Elements projects on your computer can be accessed by selecting the **Existing Project** option.

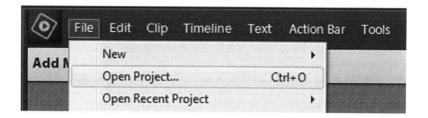

Open a project from within the program

Naturally, you don't have to go all the way out to the **Welcome Screen** to create a new project or to re-open an old one.

Both options are available from the **File** drop-down menu on the top left of the program's interface.

Selecting New **Project** from this menu gives you access to the same **New Project** settings available from the **Welcome Screen**.

Open a project created by a previous version of the program?

Our advice: Don't do it.

It should work. And sometimes it does work. But, for the most part, Premiere Elements goes through such an overhaul from generation to generation, that it usually just leads to trouble. Open only version 14 projects with version 14, version 13 projects with version 13, etc.

Doing otherwise often leads to buggy behavior – audio tracks that mysteriously disappear, clips that behave really strangely, a **Project Assets** panel that seems to have lost its mind.

Your best bet is to finish your Premiere Elements project in the same version of the program you began it in. Trust us on this.

Once it's far enough along that you consider it (or the segment you're working on) to be finished, you can export it from your current project and then import the finished video into a new version 14 project, as described in **Output video for use in another project** on page 405.

But we very much recommend against opening, say, a version 10 project in version 14.

Getting Video from Your Camcorder

Importing Media Already on Your Computer

Working with Photos

Working with Music

Chapter 19

Add Media to Your Project

Capturing video and importing
video, audio and photos into your project

Whether you're working in Expert View
or Quick View, before you can edit your
video, you need to get it (along with
your other source media) into your
Premiere Elements project.

This is a relatively simple process,
but unfortunately one that can
occasionally present some challenges.

Before you can begin editing your Premiere Elements movie, you need to gather your video, still photos, music and audio clips into your project.

The tools for gathering this media can be found by clicking on the **Add Media** tab at the top left of the interface or by using one of the other options listed in the sidebar at the bottom of this page.

The options that appear on this **Add Media** pop-up panel launch any of a number of built-in utilities for gathering your media clips.

Because Premiere Elements does not include capture software for interfacing with miniDV and HDV camcorders, we've included information on getting video from both digital and analog tape-based camcorders using third-party software in our Appendix, starting on page 421.

As the chart on the facing page indicates, there are really only three basic ways to get your media files into a Premier Elements project:

Download your media from a camcorder or other device over a USB connection or rip it from your computer's DVD/CD drive;

Capture live video from your webcam or WDM device; or

Import media that is already on your computer into your project from your hard drive folders or through the Elements Organizer.

Once you've accessed, downloaded or imported your media into your Premiere Elements project, you can either add it directly to your project's timeline (in Quick View) or gather it into your **Project Assets** panel (in Expert View) in preparation for gathering it on your timeline (as we discuss in **Chapter 20**).

In this chapter, we'll look at each of the major media devices and media file sources and show you how to best gather your media from each.

We'll also show you how to work with photos, music and other media.

Four ways to the Add Media option menu

1   Click on the **Add Media** tab; or

2   **Right-click** on a blank area in the **Project Assets** panel and select the **Get Media From** option; or

3   Select **Add Media From** from the **File** drop-down menu; or

4   Drag media to your project directly from the Elements Organizer's **Media Browser** (see **Chapter 34**).

Methods for adding media

There are three basic ways to get media into your Premiere Elements project:

- **Download** your video or other media from a hard drive or SD card-based memory camcorder, camera or other device over a USB connection;
- **Capture** live video from your Webcam or WDM device; or
- **Import** media into your project from your computer's hard drive.

The chart below lists the methods of getting media from a number of sources.

MiniDV tape-based camcorders	Capture video over a FireWire connection using a third-party program like WinDV (see page 421 of the **Appendix**) and then **import** it into your project using **Add Media/Files and Folders**.
HDV tape-based hi-def camcorders	Capture video over a FireWire connection using a third-party program like HDV Split (see page 421 of the **Appendix**) and then **import** it into your project using **Add Media/Files and Folders**.
Webcams	**Capture** video using the Premiere Elements capture interface as discussed on page 251.
AVCHD and other hard drive hi-def camcorders	**Download** video from the camcorder to your computer using the Premiere Elements **Video Importer** over a USB connection as discussed on page 250.
Go Pro, Flip or other sport camcorders or portable devices, like smartphones and iPads	**Download** video from the camcorder or device to your computer using the Premiere Elements **Video Importer** over a USB connection as discussed on page 251.
Flash-based or memory card camcorders, such as the JVC-GZ series	**Download** video from the camcorder to your computer using the Premiere Elements **Video Importer** over a USB connection as discussed on page 250.
DVD camcorders or DVDs	With the finalized disc in your computer's DVD drive, rip and **download** the video files to your computer using the **Video Importer** as discussed on page 252.
Analog video	Capture through a DV bridge or pass-through set-up then **import** it into your project, as discussed on page 422.
Digital still cameras and other portable devices, such as iPads, iPods and phones.	**Download** stills from the camera using the Premiere Elements **Photo Downloader** or video using the **Video Importer** over a USB connection as discussed on page 252.
Music or audio from CDs	Rip the music to your hard drive from the CD and then **import** it into the file(s) using the **Add Media** option **PC Files or Folders** as discussed on page 253.
Video, music or still photos already on your computer's hard drive	**Import** media into your project by browsing to it using the **Add Media** option **PC Files or Folders** as discussed on page 54 or by locating it through the Elements Organizer's **Media Browser** as discussed on page 253.

Add Media options

Launches the Elements Organizer

Opens Explorer or Finder

Launches Photo Downloader

Launches Video Importer

Opens Capture screen

Launches Video Importer

Premiere Elements' Add Media tools

The tools for bringing your media into your project are most simply launched from the **Add Media** pop-up panel, opened by clicking the tab at the top left of the interface.

On this panel, Premiere Elements offers six options for bringing your media into your project (as illustrated above).

- The **Elements Organizer** option will launch the Organizer's **Media Browser** (See **Chapter 34**) within the **Add Media** panel. As discussed on the facing page, the **Elements Organizer** is a companion file management program that can be used to manage and search media files on your computer.

- The **Files and Folders** option will open Windows Explorer or the OSX Finder so that you can browse to your media files (as discussed on page 253).

- The **Photos from Cameras or Devices** option will launch the Adobe **Photo Downloader** (as discussed on page 252), an interface for selecting and downloading still images from a camera or other portable device.

- The **Videos from Cameras & Devices** option will launch the **Video Importer** (see pages 250-251), an interface for selecting and downloading video from a camcorder or other video storage device.

- The **Webcam or WDM** option will launch the program's video capture workspace (see page 251), an interface through which you capture your live Webcam video.

- The **DVD Camera or Computer Drive** option will launch the **Video Importer** (see page 252), which can be used to select and rip the video files your DVD disc.

The Organizer media browser

Media files on your computer can be accessed through the Elements Organizer's Media Browser.

Media in the Organizer can be searched clicking the search button in the upper right corner of the panel or media can be filtered by selecting a media type, or by selecting an Album or or sub-Album.

Add media from the Organizer

The Elements Organizer is a file management program that comes bundled with Premiere Elements and Photoshop Elements.

When you select the **Elements Organizer** option under the **Add Media** tab, the Organizer's **Media Browser** will open within the panel. From this panel, you can access any video, photos or audio files in your Organizer catalog. (For information on creating a catalog and using the Organizer's file management tools, see **Chapter 34**.)

> **To search your media files,** click on the magnifying class at the top right of the panel and type in a search term, as illustrated above.

> **To filter your media files by type**, turn on or off the photo, video and audio filter buttons on the top right of the panel.

> **To see only media files you've assigned to a particular Album,** click on a green **Local Album** along the left side of the panel.

Once you've selected the media files you'd like to add to your project, click the **Add Files** button along the lower right of the panel.

Your video or photo files will be added to your **Project Media** as well as added to the **Video 1/Audio 1** tracks on your timeline at the position of the **CTI** playhead.

If the **CTI** is positioned within rather than at the end of your movie, the new clips will be *inserted* into your movie and all clips to the right on the timeline will ripple further right. For more information on inserting clips into your movies, see **Controlling your timeline's ripple function** on page 269.

Click **Done** to return to the Premiere Elements editing workspace.

The Video Importer

Select the camcorder or device you're connecting to from the drop-down list (such as your computer's DVD drive, if you are "ripping" files from a disk to your computer).

Check the boxes next to the clips you'd like to download to your computer.

Any video clip can be previewed before being selected for download.

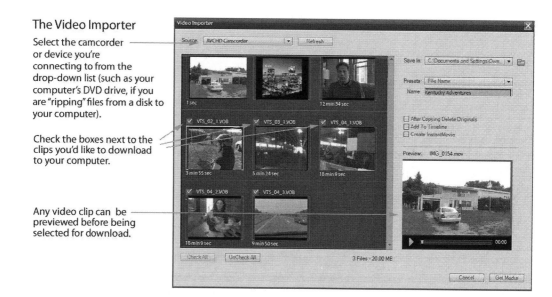

Add video from AVCHD camcorders

As with other hard drive camcorders, the video from AVCHD camcorders is downloaded into Premiere Elements.

1 Connect your AVCHD camcorder to your computer's USB port.

2 Select the **Videos from Cameras & Devices** option from the **Add Media** panel.

 This will launch the **Video Importer,** as illustrated above.

3 Select your camcorder from the **Source** drop-down menu at the top of the **Video Importer,** then browse and select the video clips you'd like to add to your project.

4 Click the **Browse** button to indicate where on your computer you'd like to save the captured files, then click the **Get Media** button at the bottom of the panel to download your video.

Add video from Hard Drive, Flash Drive and SD Card Camcorders

As with AVCHD camcorders, the video from hard drive and flash drive camcorders is downloaded into Premiere Elements.

1 Connect your camcorder to your computer with a USB cable.

2 Select the **Videos from Cameras & Devices** option from the **Add Media** panel.

 This will launch the **Video Importer,** as illustrated on above.

3 Select your camcorder from the **Source** drop-down menu at the top of the **Video Importer,** then browse and select the video clips you'd like to add to your project.

4 Click the **Browse** button to indicate where on your computer you'd like to save the captured files, then click the **Get Media** button at the bottom of the panel to download your video.

Add video from Go Pro, Flip camcorders, iPads, iPods, smartphones and other portable devices

While some devices plug right into your computer, most devices are attached via USB cable. As with hard drive camcorders, the video from Flip camcorders is *downloaded* rather than streamed or captured into Premiere Elements.

1   Connect your sport camcorder, iPad, smartphone or other video device to your computer's USB port.

2   Select the **Videos from Cameras & Devices** option from the **Add Media** panel.

    This will launch the **Video Importer**, as illustrated on page 250.

3   Select your media recording device (Flip, smartphone, iPod, etc.) from the **Source** drop-down menu at the top of the **Video Importer**, then browse and select the video clips you'd like to add to your project.

4   Click the **Browse** button to indicate where on your computer you'd like to save the captured files, then click the **Get Media** button at the bottom of the panel to download your video.

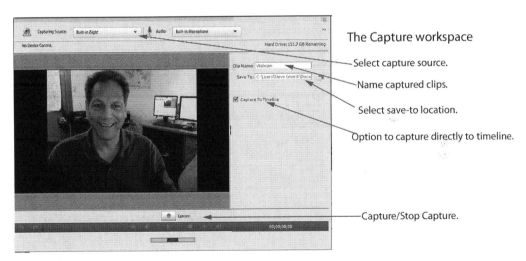

The Capture workspace

Select capture source.

Name captured clips.

Select save-to location.

Option to capture directly to timeline.

Capture/Stop Capture.

Capture video from Webcams or WDM Devices

The **Capture** workspace in Premiere Elements is capable of capturing live video from most Webcams and other Windows Driver Model devices.

To capture webcam video:

1   Select the **Webcam or WDM** option from the **Add Media** panel.

    This will launch the **Capture** workspace, as illustrated above.

2   When you are ready to capture your live video, click the red dot **Capture** button.

    When want to stop your capture, click the **Stop Capture** button.

Add video from DVDs and DVD Camcorders

Video from DVDs or DVD camcorders is downloaded into Premiere Elements using Adobe's **Video Importer** software, as illustrated on page 250.

To get video from a DVD or DVD camcorder:

1 Place the DVD into your computer's DVD drive

Note that discs from DVD camcorders must be *finalized* before Premiere Elements can rip the video from them.

2 Select the **DVD Camera or Computer Drive** option from the **Add Media** panel.

This will launch the **Video Importer**, as illustrated on page 250.

3 Select your computer's DVD drive from the **Source** drop-down menu at the top of the **Video Importer**, then browse and select the video clips you'd like to rip to your project.

4 Click the **Browse** button to indicate where on your computer you'd like to save the DVD's files, then click the **Get Media** button at the bottom of the panel to rip the video files to your hard drive.

Add video from DSLR still cameras and other devices

As with hard drive camcorders, the video from digital cameras and smartphones is *downloaded* rather than streamed or captured into Premiere Elements.

1 Connect your device to your computer's USB port.

2 Select the **Videos from Cameras & Devices** option from the **Add Media** panel.

This will launch the **Video Importer,** illustrated on page 250.

3 Select your USB-connected device from the **Source** drop-down menu at the top of the **Video Importer**, then browse and select the video clips you'd like to add to your project.

4 Click the **Browse** button to indicate where on your computer you'd like to save the captured files, then click the **Get Media** button at the bottom of the panel to download your video.

Add still photos from digital cameras and cell phones

1 Connect your still camera to your computer's USB port.

2 Select the **Photos from Cameras or Devices** option from the **Add Media** panel.

This will launch the **Photo Downloader** as illustrated at the top of page 253.

3 From the **Add Media From** drop-down menu at the top of the **Photo Downloader**, select your camera or other device – then browse and select the photos you'd like to add to your project.

4 Click the **Browse** button to indicate where on your computer you'd like to save the captured files, then click the **Get Media** button at the bottom of the panel to download your video or photos.

As we discuss in **Use photos in your Premiere Elements project** on page 254, for best results your still photos should be resized to an optimal, video resolution size.

The Photo Downloader

Select your camera or other photo device
from the drop-down list at
Get Photos From.

Import photos, video, music and other audio that is already on your computer's hard drive into your project

To load video, audio or stills already on your computer into your Premiere
Elements project:

1   Select the **Files and Folders** option on the **Add Media** panel (or
    select the **Elements Organizer** option to launch the Elements
    Organizer program, as described on page 249).

2   Browse to the file(s) you'd like to import on your hard drive.

    Select the file or files you'd like to add and click **Open**.

You can also quickly open a browse screen from which to import your
media files by **double-clicking** on a blank space (beyond the media
listings) in the **Project Assets** panel.

Music and other audio clips

We've learned from experience that you'll get the best performance from Premiere Elements
if you only use music and other audio files in your projects that are in the **WAV** format – even
if you're using the Mac version of the program. (Most audio formats can be converted to WAVs
using the free PC-based software **Audacity,** as we discuss on page 421 of our **Appendix.**)

Also, note that some commercial DVD and music formats (particularly iTunes) include **digital
rights management,** copy protection software that will prohibit their use in Premiere
Elements. Adding protected music to your project will often trigger an error message.

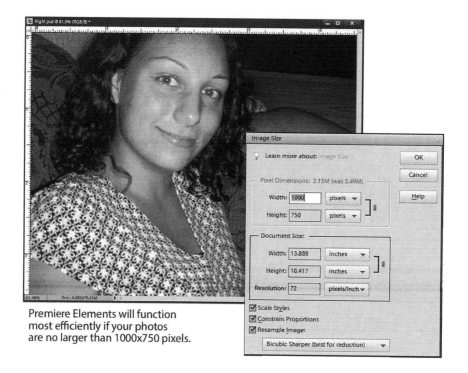

Premiere Elements will function
most efficiently if your photos
are no larger than 1000x750 pixels.

Use photos in Premiere Elements

Premiere Elements can work with virtually any of the major photo or
graphics formats, including JPEGs, GIFs, TIFs and PSDs (native Photoshop
and Photoshop Elements files).

The exceptions are images using the CMYK color mode or RGB photo files
using other than standard 8-bit color. But, if you are creating your graphics
or using photos from a consumer graphics program (such as Photoshop
Elements) or from a digital camera, scanner or other device, then you don't
need to worry about these exceptions. Virtually all photo and graphics files
from these sources are compatible with the program.

Premiere Elements will also support transparency (alpha channels) so
that file formats like GIF, PNG and PSD files with transparent areas will
display, when used in a video project, with these areas transparent.

This is particularly useful if you're using one of these graphics file types
on an upper video track with a video layer behind it (see **Use L-cuts, J-
cuts and multiple tracks** on page 272 of **Chapter 21, Edit Your Movie
in Timeline Mode**) or as a graphic added to a title (see **Add a graphic to
your title** on page 341 of **Chapter 26, Add Titles & Text**).

Photos make great source files for a Premiere Elements project, but
you'll find the highest quality results and the best performance from the
program if the sizes of your photos are properly optimized before you
bring them into your project.

We urge you to make sure that any photo you use (especially if you use several in a slideshow) has been resized to no larger than 1000x750 pixels (2000x1500 for a high-definition video project) before you bring it into your Premiere Elements project. This will ensure the best quality and optimal program performance. (Photos taken directly from digital cameras can be 20 to 25 times that size!)

At first this may seem to go contrary to common wisdom.

Traditionally, the higher the resolution of your photo, the better the quality of the output. But remember that Premiere Elements is a *video* editing program, and video is a relatively low resolution medium (essentially the equivalent of 640x480 pixels). And, to a point, reducing the resolution of a photo or graphic to be used in a video actually *improves* the quality of the video output. (1000x750 pixels and 2000x1500 pixels seem to be that point for standard definition and high-def video, respectively.)

The reason for this has to do with a process called downsampling, the system a video program uses to bring high-resolution photos down to video size. Premiere Elements does a fair job of this – but, as any pro knows, nothing that happens automatically will be as clean or as efficient as what you do manually. "Down-rezzing" is definitely one of those things.

But there's also a more pressing reason for downsampling your photos yourself. The process of "down-rezzing," like the process of assimilating non-DV-AVI files into a video project, is a very intensive process. So intensive, in fact, that it is *the single biggest reason Premiere Elements crashes*, particularly during the rendering or disc burning process.

It also takes a lot longer for the program to down-rez, for instance, a 4000x3000 pixel photo than it does a 1000x750 pixel photo.

Much, much longer. And would you rather wait an hour or two for the program to create your DVD or 10 hours for a process that might end up with the program choking and dying anyway?

Graphics and photo formats for Premiere Elements projects

For photos, the most size-efficient file format is the JPEG. As an alternative, PSD files and TIFs use less compression and, though larger, also produce excellent results.

However, because JPEGs are highly compressed, they do not make the best format for graphics that include clean, distinct edges, such as logos or graphics that include text. In these cases, PSDs, TIFs and even PNGs produce the crispest lines.

Trust us on this. Optimize your photo sizes to 1000x750 pixels for standard definition video and DVDs and 2000x1500 pixels for a high-definition video project before you import them into Premiere Elements. It can save you hours of anguish and misery in the end.

Photoshop Elements, by the way, has a very nice batch resizing feature that can resize a whole folder full of photos in just a few clicks. This feature is called **Process Multiple Files**, and it is located under the Photoshop Elements **File** menu.

Also, *before* you do bring those photos into your video project, go to Premiere Elements' **Preferences/General** (under the **Edit** menu on a PC) and uncheck **Default Scale to Frame Size**.

Left checked, **Scale to Frame Size** automatically sizes your photo to fill your video frame, giving a false representation of your photo in the video frame in addition to really getting in the way when you're trying to add motion paths to your photos.

In the event this option was checked when you imported your photos into your project, you can also turn it off for each photos individually by **right-clicking** on each photo on the timeline and unchecking the **Scale to Frame Size** option on its pop-up menu.

For information on applying flicker removal to the photos and still graphics in your Premiere Elements project, see **Add still photos to your project** on page 274 of **Chapter 21, Edit Your Project in Expert View**.

The Project Assets Panel

Color Bars and Countdown Leaders

The Clip Monitor

The Create Slideshow Tool

Chapter 20

Explore the Project Assets Panel

The parts that will form your movie

In Expert view, Project Assets is the panel into which you will gather the video, still photos, music and audio that you will use to create your movie.

In the Project Assets panel, you can arrange and categorize your project's media files and then pre-trim them prior to adding them to your timeline.

Open panel by clicking on tab.

Filter views
Video
Still Image
Audio

Clips in use on your timeline are indicated with a green dot.

Panel Options

Pin View*

Remove clip

Move up a Folder level

Quick search for clip

*Pin view keeps the Project Assets panel open while you open other panels.

Only available in Expert view, the **Project Assets** panel is the area where you gather the media you've captured, downloaded or imported into your project.

The **Project Assets** panel is opened by clicking on the **Project Assets** button on the upper left of the program's interface.

But in addition to serving as a holding area for your video project's media, this panel includes a number of great tools for managing, ordering and preparing your clips for your movie's timeline.

Where are my Project Assets in Quick view?

Quick View does not include a **Project Assets** panel.

In Quick View, any media files you add to your project are added directly to your timeline.

However, Expert and Quick View are actually just two views of the same project. Media files added directly to your timeline in Quick View are added to the Project Assets panel automatically.

So, if you switch from Quick view to Expert view while working on your project, you will find that any media you've added to your Quick View timeline has automatically been added to that project's Expert View **Project Assets** also.

Project Asset views

By default, the media clips in your **Project Assets** panel are displayed in **Grid View** – video and stills displaying as thumbnails and music and other audio displaying as speaker icons. Below the title for each clip is an indicator of the clip's duration (measured in hours, minutes, seconds and frames). Clips used in your movie project are indicated with a little green dot.

To switch your **Project Assets** to **List View**, click on the **Panel Options** button in the upper right of the panel and select **View**, as illustrated to the right.

The Panel Options menu on the top right of the panel allows you to switch views for your assets.

Filters can set to display only video, stills and/or audio.

In **List View**, your media clips appear in a list with columns listing their **Media Type, Frame Rate** and **Duration**. In the **Used** column, a little blue dot indicates that your clip is in use on your timeline and the **Video Usage** column indicates how many times your clip appears in your movie.

The clip listing can be re-ordered by clicking on the column header for any column. For instance, clicking on the **Media Duration** column header will list your clips according to the length of each clip. Clicking on a column header a second time will reverse the order for that column's listing.

In the upper left of the panel are three buttons for toggling on and off which media are displayed in the panel. If you toggle on the **Video** button, for instance, and you toggle off the **Still Image** and **Audio** buttons, you will set the panel to display *only* the video in your project and hide the other two types of media files.

Organize your media files with folders

This is one of my favorite Premiere Elements features, extremely valuable when you're trying to sort through a large number of media files.

Folders allow you to sort the clips in your **Project Assets** panel into little bundles, like directories on your computer, making it easier to keep all the clips you'll need for a given segment of your project in one neat little place.

To create a folder, select the **New Folder** option under the **Panel Options** menu at the upper right of the panel. (You can also select the option from a context menu when you **right-click** on an empty area of the **Project Asset** panel.)

Folders can be used in either List view or Grid view.

In List view, you can toggle open a folder to see its contents or, in either view, double-click to enter the folder.

To leave a folder, click the Up Folder Level button.

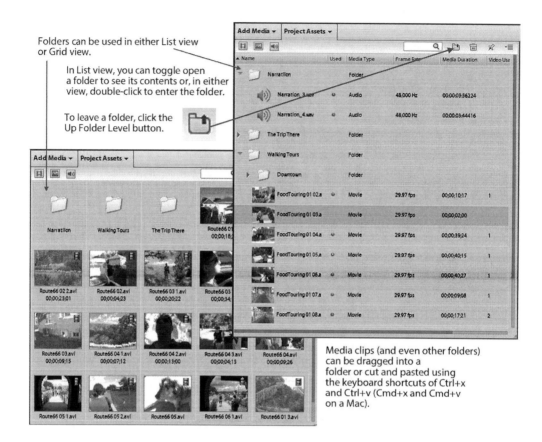

Media clips (and even other folders) can be dragged into a folder or cut and pasted using the keyboard shortcuts of Ctrl+x and Ctrl+v (Cmd+x and Cmd+v on a Mac).

Once you have a folder created, you can drag your media files into it – sorting your clips so that all of your files for a particular sequence of your project are in the same folder, for instance.

You can even create sub-folders within your folders – and even sub-sub-folders! – so that it becomes very easy to manage and locate the files you need without having to scroll through a long list of clips.

Even as you're editing, you can drag your media clips around, and in and out, of folders to get them out of your way without affecting their positions or function on your timeline.

Delete clips from your Project Assets panel

There are two ways to remove a clip from your project:

Right-click on the clip in **Project Assets** and select **Clear**; or

Select a clip in **Project Assets** and press your keyboard's **Delete** key.

Either way, the media clip will be removed from your project – though it will *not* be deleted from your computer's hard drive.

Create color mattes, bars and tone and countdown leaders

Among the custom clips available under the New Item button are Bars and Tone, a Countdown Leader and a color clip (Color Matte) of any color you want.

A host of very cool tools for creating special clips are available under the **New Item** sub-menu on the **Panel Options** menu on the upper right of the panel.

These special clips include:

Adjustment Layer creates a layer from which you can make non-permanent adjustments to your video. We discuss this feature in more detail on page 320.

Title launches the Premiere Elements **Titles & Text** workspace. We explore this tool in much greater detail in **Chapter 26, Add Titles & Text.**

Bars and Tone creates a clip of bars and audio tone, which broadcasters often require at the beginning of every video in order to calibrate their equipment to your movie's sound levels and color profile.

Black Video and **Color Matte** create blank clips of whatever color you designate. These clips can then be used behind titles or as blank spaces in your video.

Universal Countdown Leader (not available on the Mac version) creates a customizable countdown sequence (including an audio "blip" at two seconds) that can be placed at the beginning of your video – another feature broadcasters often require so that they can cue up the beginning of your movie.

Pre-trim your clips in the Clip Monitor

The **Clip Monitor** is a pop-up screen for previewing playback of a clip. It's also a work area in which you can pre-trim a clip prior to adding it to your project's timeline by setting **In** and/or **Out** markers.

The **Clip Monitor** can be used to trim clips in the **Project Assets** panel or clips that have already been added to your timeline.

A clip's **Clip Monitor** is launched either by **right-clicking** on the clip and selecting the **Open in Clip Monitor** option – or by simply **double-clicking** on the clip.

Running along the bottom of the **Clip Monitor** is a little timeline representing the duration of the clip.

As illustrated on the facing page, when you set **In** or **Out** markers in your **Clip Monitor**, only the segment of the clip between those markers will be displayed during the clip's playback in your movie.

In other words, if you have a 5-minute clip, you can set the **In** and **Out** markers so that only a 30-second segment of the clip is actually displayed in your movie – rendering the clip essentially a 30-second clip.

In the **Clip Monitor,** the "live" segment of the clip is indicated with a lighter, blue segment area on the **Clip Monitor's** mini-timeline. You can adjust this live area's length by either dragging the end points in or out, or by playing the clip using the playback controls at the bottom of the **Clip Monitor** and clicking on the **Set In** or **Set Out** buttons to isolate the segment you want to use.

The **In** and **Out** markers in the **Clip Monitor** can be used to isolate segments in audio clips as well as video.

You can not set **In** and **Out** markers on titles and still images, however, because they are stationary elements.

Take a shortcut to "Add Media"

If you want to import additional media from your computer into your Premiere Elements project, or if you want to launch a video capture without leaving the **Project Assets** panel, there is a shortcut to the **Add Media** option menu built right into the panel.

As illustrated at the top of page 264, if you **right-click** on a *blank* area of the **Project Assets** panel, beyond your media listings, you will have access to the same **Add Media** options as are available on the **Add Media** panel.

Additionally, you can quickly open a browse screen so that you can import media already on your computer by simply **double-clicking** on a blank area after your **Project Assets** panel's listings.

The Clip Monitor launches when you double-click on any clip on the timeline or in the Project Assets panel.

Clips can be trimmed in the Clip Monitor either by dragging the in and out points on the mini-timeline or by playing the clip and clicking the Set In and Set Out buttons.

Although the original clip remains its original length, only the "trimmed" segment (the blue highlighted segment in Premiere Elements) will display when the clip is placed on the timeline.

Once the **Clip Monitor** has been launched, it will stay open as long as you keep your project open or until you manually close it.

Because this panel tends to pop up in the middle of the workspace whenever it launches, I usually launch it as soon as I open a project. Then I position it off to the side, out of the way, and leave it open. That way, if I later need to open a clip in this panel for previewing or trimming, the **Clip Monitor** will play this clip where I've positioned it instead of in the middle of my work.

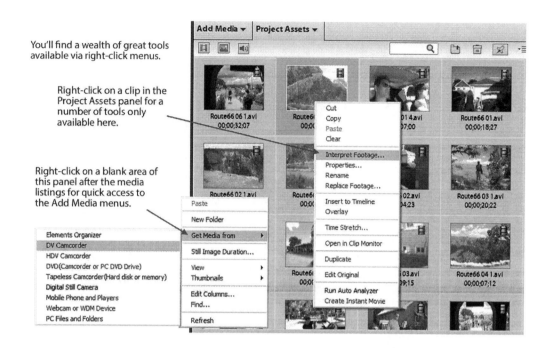

You'll find a wealth of great tools available via right-click menus.

Right-click on a clip in the Project Assets panel for a number of tools only available here.

Right-click on a blank area of this panel after the media listings for quick access to the Add Media menus.

Valuable Project Assets panel right-click tools

There are a number of great tools available throughout Premiere Elements that can be (and sometimes can *only* be) accessed by **right-clicking** on clips or in panels.

I do a thorough discussion of these tools in my *Steve's Tips* article "Powerful Tools in Premiere Elements' Right-Click Menus," available on the Muvipix.com product pages.

Here are a couple of my favorite right-click tools available exclusively in the **Project Assets** panel.

Interpret Footage – Believe it or not, 4:3 standard definition video and widescreen 16:9 standard definition video use exactly the same number of pixels to create a video frame. The difference is that the pixels (the tiny squares of color that combine to create every frame of video) are shaped differently. Widescreen 16:9 pixels are much wider than standard 4:3 video pixels.

Right-clicking on a clip and selecting **Interpret Footage** gives you access to options for conforming a widescreen clip to fit in a standard video or vice versa.

This tool is invaluable if, for some reason, you find yourself with a clip that looks strangely squished, stretched or distorted (as when you add a 16:9 video to a 4:3 project).

Duplicate – This selection makes a duplicate of the clip you've right-clicked on. This is very helpful, for instance, if you've created a title slide with a style you'd like to re-use. You merely **duplicate** it and then revise the duplicate as needed. (Also see **Duplicate a title** on page 346.)

Rename – You can rename a clip by selecting this **right-click** option or by simply double-clicking slowly on the name of the file in the **Project Assets** panel listing so that the name becomes highlighted. Renaming a clip doesn't change the name of the file on your hard drive, by the way. Nor does it affect the clip's position or function on the timeline. But it can make it easier for you to identify the file later.

Create a slideshow in the Project Assets panel

One of my favorite "hidden" features in the Premiere Elements **Project Assets** panel is the **Create Slideshow** tool.

To access this great little tool, select a number of clips or stills from the **Project Assets** panel (by holding down the **Ctrl** or ⌘ key or the **Shift** key as you select) and then **right-click** on the selected clips and select **Create Slideshow**.

As you can see below, in the illustration of the **Create Slideshow** option screen, you can set the **Ordering** of your slides in a couple of ways.

Sort Order. In **Sort Order**, the **Slideshow Creator** places your slides in the same order as they appear listed in the **Project Assets** panel.

Selection Order. In **Selection Order**, the **Slideshow Creator** places your slides according to the order you click-selected them in the **Project Assets** panel.

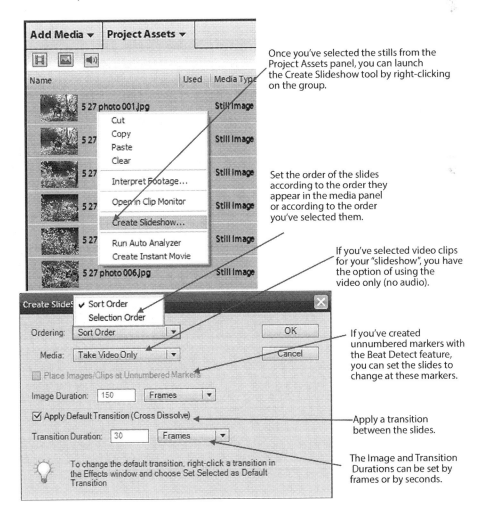

Once you've selected the stills from the Project Assets panel, you can launch the Create Slideshow tool by right-clicking on the group.

Set the order of the slides according to the order they appear in the media panel or according to the order you've selected them.

If you've selected video clips for your "slideshow", you have the option of using the video only (no audio).

If you've created unnumbered markers with the Beat Detect feature, you can set the slides to change at these markers.

Apply a transition between the slides.

The Image and Transition Durations can be set by frames or by seconds.

On the **Create Slideshow** option screen, you also have a number of ways to set the duration of your slides:

Image Duration. You can set your slides to change after a designated interval of time.

Unnumbered Markers. You can set them to change at **Unnumbered Markers** on the **Timeline** (For more information on **Unnumbered Markers**, see **Detect beats in your music** on page 387 of **Chapter 30, Mix Your Audio and Add Music**).

You can use either video or still clips in your slideshow – although only stills can be set to change at a given duration or at the unnumbered markers created by the **Detect Beats** tool.

If you use video clips in your slideshow, the **Create Slideshow** panel includes the option to remove the audio from the clips, as illustrated on the previous page.

You can also select the option to apply a **Default Transition** between your slides. (For information on designating the **Default Transition**, see page 328 of **Chapter 25, Add and Customize Transitions**.)

For information on how to optimize your stills for a slideshow, see **Use photos in Premiere Elements** on page 254 of **Chapter 19, Add Media to Your Project**.

There are actually a number of different ways to create a slideshow in Premiere Elements, including a **Slide Show Creator** tool built into the Elements Organizer (see page 461) and **InstantMovie** slideshow themes. (For more information on creating **InstantMovies**, see **Chapter 22**.)

Adding Clips to Your Timeline

Auto Enhancing Your Clips

Splitting and Trimming Your Clips

Working with Multiple Tracks of Video

Rendering Your Timeline

Chapter 21

Edit Your Video in Expert View

Where your movie comes together

The Expert View timeline is where your clips are gathered, ordered, trimmed, split, rearranged, and where effects are applied. It's where your movie finally comes together – just as in Quick View.

But Expert View gives you a much more powerful timeline, greater access to your clips and more professional-level tools for working with them.

In Expert View, your clips are dragged from the Project Assets panel to any of up to 99 audio and/or video tracks. Transitions are added to points at which clips meet.

Expert View in Premiere Elements is the more professional-style workspace.

There are three main differences between the Quick View and the Expert View timelines:

In Expert View, media is added to the **Project Assets** panel before it is brought to the timeline. In the **Project Assets** panel, your media can be more easily managed and even pre-trimmed before it is added to the timeline. (For more information on the **Project Assets** panel, see **Chapter 20**.)

While Quick View is limited to four tracks, the Expert View timeline includes the option for up to 99 tracks of video and up to 99 tracks of audio. Multi-track editing allows for some effects that are virtually impossible in Quick View.

In Expert View, video and audio clips can be manipulated at specific points using keyframing right on the timeline, allowing you to create and control fade ins or outs and, more importantly, allowing you to control and mix audio levels at specific points using keyframing (see page 383).

Nonetheless, Quick View and Expert View are still just two faces of the same project. In other words, you can switch between the two views as needed as you develop your timeline, taking advantage of the benefits of each view as you work.

Expert View allows for multiple tracks of audio and video and gives you greater access to each clip's levels.

Controlling the timeline's "ripple" function

Video 1 and Audio 1 on your timeline in Premiere Elements are set, by default, to **"ripple"** as you add, remove and trim clips on the timeline.

In other words, by default:

When you Insert a clip into an assemblage of clips, the clips on all tracks on the timeline will **split** and/or ripple to the right to accommodate the new clip.

When you trim or extend a clip on Video 1 or Audio 1, the rest of the clips on the timeline will ripple, or move right, to accommodate this change.

When you add audio to your Narration or Soundtrack, the timeline will *not* ripple.

When you Delete a clip from Video 1/Audio 1 on your timeline, the clips on all tracks will ripple to the left to fill in the gap, unless there is a clip filling this gap on a parallel audio or video track.

When you Delete a clip from a track *other than Video 1 or Audio 1*, the timeline will not ripple. To ripple the timeline left to fill this gap, **double-click** to select the gap and press the **Delete** key on your keyboard or **right-click** and select **Delete and Close Gap.**

In most cases, rippling will work to your advantage. If you've got an assemblage of audio and video clips in your movie and you decide to reorder them or add a clip to the middle of your project, you'll want the rest of the clips in your movie to stay in relative position, moving as a group to allow for the inserted or removed clip.

But there may also be times when you'll want to override this ripple function. To override the ripple function:

Hold down the Ctrl key on a PC or the ⌘ key on a Mac as you add your new clip(s) to your timeline. When you override the ripple function, the rest of your clips will remain locked in their positions on your timeline as you add or remove a clip, and you'll be able to place your music on an audio track – or any clip on any other audio or video track – without disturbing the rest of your movie.

Hold down the Alt/Option key as you insert a clip to your timeline to limit the timeline's rippling to the track you're adding your clip to. The rest of your movie's video and audio clips will remain in place.

Smart Fix your clips

When your clips have been Auto-Analyzed and Smart Tagged, the program will offer to apply a Smart Fix Auto Enhance when you place the clip on your timeline – correcting the contrast and brightness and, if necessary, stabilizing the camera movement.

Premiere Elements includes the option to have the program automatically apply a **Smart Fix** to your clips as you add them to your timeline or sceneline.

When this tool is enabled in the program's **Preferences** (under the **Edit** menu on a PC, as discussed below), an option panel will appear each time you add a new clip to your timeline or your sceneline, asking if you would like the program to **"Fix quality problems in your clips?"** (This option panel will only appear if your clips have been **Smart Tagged** prior to your adding them to your project, as discussed on the facing page.)

If you select **Yes**, Premiere Elements will automatically apply the necessary contrast levels to the clip and, if it judges the clip as too shaky, will apply automatic image stabilization!

If the clip is very long and has inconsistent quality issues, the program will even keyframe variations of contrast! (There is no way to set this feature to correct only contrast *or* only stabilization, by the way. Your options are only to have both applied or neither.)

In our experience, the results are usually very good (even if the applied effects mean that the program must then render the clips before they play back smoothly).

This feature can be turned off at any time by checking the **Do Not Show Again** box in the **Smart Fix** pop-up panel, as illustrated above.

To re-activate this feature later, go to the **Edit** drop-down on the Menu Bar and select **Preferences**. On the preferences **General** page, check the box that says **Show All Do Not Show Again Messages**.

Smart Fix can also be applied manually to clips that are already on your timeline using the **Smart Fix** tool located on the **Adjustments** panel, as discussed on page 313).

As discussed in the sidebar on the facing page, the automatic **Smart Fix** tool will only be available for clips that have been previously **Auto-Analyzed**.

Timeline views

Premiere Elements includes a number of features for viewing your timeline, depending on how closely you want to look at your movie.

Using the zoom tool, for instance, you can zoom out to view your entire movie at once – or you can zoom in close enough to see your video's individual frames.

To zoom in or out on your timeline, drag the slider (on the upper right of the **Timeline** panel) left or right – or use the following keyboard shortcuts:

Using the Timeline zoom slider (or your +, – and \ keys) you can zoom out to see your whole project or or zoom in close enough to see individual frames.

Pressing the – key on your keyboard zooms out.

Pressing the + key zooms in.

Pressing the \ key (above the **Enter/Return** key) automatically zooms out to display your entire movie.

To make more efficient use of the panel's vertical space, individual tracks on the Timeline can be toggled between a compressed and an open view.

Open or closed video and audio tracks

In Premiere Elements, you can also toggle the views of the individual tracks on your timeline to display as either open – which allows you to view your video clips as thumbnails and your audio clips as waveforms – or closed, reducing the amount of vertical space the **Timeline** panel requires when you are using multiple tracks of video and audio, as illustrated on the right.

Clips must be Auto Analyzed in order to be Smart Fixed

The **Smart Fix** option panel, discussed on the facing page, will appear as you add your clips to your timeline only *if* these clips have been previously **Auto Analyzed**. This is because the **Smart Fix** tool takes its cue from information gathered by the **Media Analyzer/Auto-Analyzer,** an Elements Organizer feature that automatically analyzes and records metadata to your clips based on content and quality issues.

The **Media Analyzer** is set up in the Elements Organizer's **Preferences**, located under its **Edit** drop-down menu on a PC. In this preference panel, you have the option of setting the **Media Analyzer** to automatically **Auto Analyze** every clip in your Organizer catalog, or to only analyze clips meeting specific criteria (for more information, see page 440). On most faster computers, the **Media Analyzer** will work unobtrusively in the background, without interfering with your other editing work, running when you are not working on your computer.

You may, as an alternative to this automatic function, manually prep your clips for **Smart Fix** (or the other Premiere Elements tools that require **Auto Analyzing**) by selecting clips in the Elements Organizer **Media Browser** or the Premiere Elements **Project Assets** panel, either one at a time or several at once, **right-clicking** and selecting the option to **Run Auto Analyzer** from the context menu.

To add a clip to your timeline, simply drag it from the Project Assets panel.

As you add new clips, the other clips will "ripple", moving aside if you add the clip in the middle of a project.

To override the ripple effect (as when you're adding music or a video clip to a parallel track) hold down the Ctrl key (or the Cmd key on a Mac) as you add the clip to your timeline.

Zoom in or out on the timeline by pressing + or - or using the Zoom slider.

Add clips to your timeline

Adding clips to your project's timeline in Expert View is about as intuitive as it can be. You simply drag the clips from the **Project Assets** panel to a video or audio track.

You can reorder the clips on the timeline by dragging them around. Placing a clip to the left of another clip will cause it to slide it aside ("ripple" it) to accommodate the move. (See page 269 for information on overriding the ripple feature on your timeline.)

To delete a clip from your timeline, click to select it and press the **Delete** button on your keyboard or **right-click** on it and select **Delete and Close Gap**. Unless there are clips on parallel video or audio tracks, the timeline will ripple to fill in the gap.

To remove a clip *without* causing the other clips to ripple or fill in the gap, **right-click** on the clip and select **Delete** instead.

Once your clips are assembled, you can apply transitions between them. More information on this feature can be found in **Chapter 25, Add and Customize Transitions**.

Trim or split your clips

Once a clip is on your timeline, you can edit it to remove unwanted portions by **trimming** and/or **splitting** it.

Trimming removes footage from the beginning or end of a clip.

Splitting divides your clip into smaller segments, which you can then remove or rearrange.

To slice a clip in two, click the scissors icon on the CTI playhead.

If a clip is selected on the timeline, only that clip will be split at the position of the CTI; If no clips are selected, all clips on every track on the timeline will be split at the position of the CTI.

◄┇ Trim from Beginning of clip

Trim from End of clip ┇►

To trim a clip on the timeline, hover your mouse over the beginning or end of a clip until the Trim from Beginning or Trim from End icon appears, then click and drag in or out.

Trim a clip on your timeline

To **trim a clip**, click to select the clip on your timeline and hover your mouse over the clip's beginning or end.

As you hover your mouse over either end of a clip, it will switch to trim mode (becoming a ┇► or a ◄┇ cursor). Click and drag the end of the clip to trim it – removing footage from or adding footage to the clip's beginning or end.

The **Monitor** will preview the new in or out point as you drag. (For information on pre-trimming your clip before you drag it to the timeline, see **Pre-trim your clips in the Clip Monitor** on page 262 of **Chapter 20, Explore the Project Assets Panel**.)

If you find, after removing a segment, that you've removed too much of a clip – or not enough – you can simply re-drag the end of the clip to replace or remove the extra frames. (In non-linear editing, nothing is ever permanently removed from a clip.)

Split a clip on your timeline

To **split a clip** – either to remove a portion of it or to isolate a segment so that you can move, or add an effect to, it – position the **CTI** (Current Time Indicator) at the point on your timeline you'd like to slice and then click the **Split Clip** (scissors icon) button on the **CTI**, as illustrated above.

If you have a clip *selected* on your timeline, this tool will slice only that clip; if you have no clips selected, this tool will slice through *all* of the clips on all tracks at the **CTI's** current position except the **Narration** and **Soundtrack** tracks.

If you then want to delete the segment you've sliced (or sliced on either side of), click to select the segment, **right-click** and choose **Delete** or **Delete and Close Gap**, depending on whether or not you'd like the timeline to ripple to fill the gap.

Remove audio or video from your clip

As you can see on page 279, **right-clicking** on a clip on your timeline gives you access to a number of helpful features, tools and options.

> To make a clip on your timeline video only, **right-click** on the clip and select **Delete Audio**.

> To make a clip on your timeline audio only, **right-click** on the clip and select **Delete Video**.

Fade in and out of your clip

The simplest way to fade into or out of a clip on your timeline is to **right-click** on it and, from the **Fade** sub-menu, select **Fade In, Fade Out** or **Fade In and Out.** (In Expert view, separate options are offered for fading in or out of your video, your audio or both, if your clip includes both, as illustrated on page 279.)

By default, your fades will last one second. You can, however, adjust the keyframe positions to lengthen or shorten that time.

To do this, look for the white dots that Premiere Elements has placed to create the fade on the thin, horizontal, yellow **Rubber Bands** (representing the video's **Opacity** or the audio's **Volume**) that run through your clips.

Add still photos to your project

Still photos are dragged to the timeline just as video clips are. By default, the duration of a still photo in a Premiere Elements project is **five seconds**. (This default can be changed under **Edit/Preferences** – although changing it will only affect photos brought into the program *after* the preference has been changed.)

You can increase or decrease how long the photo displays on the timeline by dragging to trim or extend it, just as you would to trim or extend any video clip, as described in **Trimming and Splitting** on page 272.

As explained in **Use Photos in Premiere Elements** (page 254) in **Chapter 19, Add Media to Your Project**, you'll get the best performance from stills in a standard video project if they are sized to no larger than 1000x750 pixels (or 2000x1500 pixels for a high-def project).

Additionally, once you've placed a photo on your timeline, you can eliminate a somewhat common problem (related to interlacing) by **right-clicking** on the still on the timeline and selecting **Field Options** and then selecting the **Flicker Removal** option.

Applying this setting will preempt a fluttering problem that sometimes manifests itself in video outputs when highly detailed or high contrast photos are used in Premiere Elements projects.

These dots are called **keyframes**, and we discuss them in much greater detail in **Chapter 29, Keyframing**.

By default, this yellow **Rubber Band** represents the **Opacity** (or transparency) of your video clip. On an audio clip, the **Rubber Band**, by default, represents its **Volume** level.

See how the line slants down before or after that keyframe? That's your fade in or fade out of the clip's **Opacity** or **Volume** levels.

Adjusting those dots' positions relative to the end of the clip, by clicking on them and dragging them to new positions, extends or shortens the duration of your fade in or fade out.

To find out more about adjusting your audio's volume and how to control it at specific points in your movie, see **Adjust audio levels at specific points on your timeline** on page 383.

Fade ins and fade outs are really just keyframed Opacity and Volume properties. You can change the length of the fade by changing the positions of the keyframe points on the timeline.

Output a segment of your video using the Work Area Bar

The Work Area Bar can be set to designate only a portion of your video project. Most Export + Share options allow you to output the Work Area Bar segment only.

The **Work Area Bar** is the lighter gray area that runs along the ticker at the top of the timeline, defined by a silver marker on either end. By default, this bar covers your entire video project and grows and shrinks automatically with your project as you edit.

But, by dragging its beginning and end handles, you can manually set the **Work Area Bar** to cover only a portion of your video editing project, as illustrated above. In this way, you can designate only a portion of your project for output.

Nearly all of the output options under the **Export & Share** tab include a checkbox option for **Export Work Area Bar Only**, as in the illustration above. Checking this option directs the program to output *only* the segment of your project you've defined with the **Work Area Bar**. For more information on this function, see the discussions under each output option in **Chapter 32, Export & Share Your Video Projects**.

To reset the **Work Area Bar** to cover your entire project, **double-click** on its top edge.

Use L-cuts, J-cuts and multiple tracks

The ability to compose your video using several audio and video tracks greatly expands your ability to use interesting and professional-style editing techniques in your video projects.

Multiple tracks of audio, of course, merely mix into a single soundtrack for your movie. (See **Mix Audio** in **Chapter 30, Mix Your Audio and Add Music**.)

But, with multiple tracks of video you can combine elements from several video clips at once to create a number of interesting visual effects.

Think of multiple tracks of video as a stack, like a stack of photos. In most cases, only the uppermost photo in the stack will be visible.

However, if you change the size and position of the photos on the top of the stack, you can see several photos at once. (One example of this, the **Picture-in-Picture** effect, can be achieved using **Presets**, as discussed on page 359 of **Chapter 27, Add Video and Audio Effects**, or by adjusting their **Scale** and **Position**.)

You can also reveal portions of clips on lower tracks by using effects such as **Chroma Key** (as discussed on page 356 of **Chapter 27, Add Video and Audio Effects**), any of the **Matte** effects or even the **Crop** effect to make areas of some clips transparent.

By keyframing the effects in the **Applied Effects** panel, you can also make these positions, sizings or other settings change over the duration of the clip, creating an animated effect. (For more information, see **Chapter 29, Keyframing**.)

Using multiple tracks of video and then scaling and positioning your clips on each, you can have any number of video images in your video frame at the same time. (Think of the grid of faces in the opening credits of *The Brady Bunch* – or see my multiple-panel illustration below.) The products page at Muvipix.com offers a wealth of tutorials describing techniques for achieving these effects using a number of video tracks and effects.

Additionally, two popular techniques that use multiple tracks of video are the **L-cut** and the **J-cut** – so named because, back in the days of single-track editing, when a segment of video had to be removed and the audio left in place to allow for the placement of alternate video, the primary video and audio clip resembled an "L" or a "J" (depending on which segment was removed).

Using Scaling and Position settings with multiple tracks of video allows for Picture-in-Picture effects as well as the opportunity to do split screens, showing several video clips on screen at once

L-Cut
Main video starts
on top, then goes
under "B roll"

J-Cut
"B roll" starts on top,
then cuts to reveal
main video

As audio from main clip continues, video cuts to or from "B roll" footage.

Imagine a TV news report that features video of a reporter standing in front of a burned-out building, describing the fire that destroyed it.

As he continues speaking, the video cuts away to footage shot earlier of the fire itself. That's an **L-cut**. (A **J-cut**, on the other hand, begins with the cut-away video and the reporter's voice, then cuts to the video of the reporter finishing his report.)

Creating an **L-cut** is easy with multi-track editing.

1   Put the main video, the clip of the reporter speaking to the camera (we'll call it **Clip A**), on Video track 1.

2   Holding the **Ctrl** key (to override the timeline's ripple function), place the second video – the footage of the fire (**Clip B**) – on Video track 2.

3   Overlap the latter part of **Clip A** with **Clip B**, as seen in the illustration on the previous page.

4   **Right-click** on **Clip B** and select **Delete Audio**, if you need to remove its audio track.

Voila! Tweak **Clip B**'s position for maximum effect and you're done! We begin with the reporter speaking to the camera and, as he continues to speak, we cut away to the footage of the fire.

L-cuts and **J-cuts** are very effective for news-style reports as well as for interviews, in which you cut away from the person speaking to separately shot footage of what he or she is describing. It's a great way to reinforce, with images, what's being presented verbally.

By the way, here's some professional vocabulary to impress your friends with. That secondary footage that plays as the main video's audio continues? It's commonly called **"B-roll footage"**, a relic from the days when this kind of editing actually did involve pasting in footage from a separate roll of film or video.

Render your timeline

When you are working in Expert View, as you add effects and transitions or other video sources to your project (including photos), you will see orange lines appear above the clips, as illustrated on the right.

These orange lines are indications that these segments of your timeline need to be rendered – converted to the workflow video format. As more and more of your project requires rendering, your computer will begin to operate more sluggishly and the program may even notify you that your system is running low on memory. Your preview video will also suffer a reduction in quality.

An orange line just below the ticker along the top of the timeline indicates a segment that requires rendering.

You can render your timeline by pressing Enter or clicking the Render button.

Once the sequence is rendered, the orange line will turn green.

This is because, until you manually render these segments, the program is continually creating "soft renders" of them –"on the fly" previews of your unrendered files. And that puts a lot of strain on your system.

In Quick View, there is no orange line on the timeline to indicate the need to render. The only indication will be little pop-ups suggesting that it might be a good idea to render to improve your performance.

To **Render** your video projects' timeline, click the **Render** button on the top right of the timeline.

Alternatively, you can just press the **Enter/Return** key on your keyboard – or select **Render Work Area** from the **Timeline** drop-down at the top of the interface. (Note that only the area of your timeline covered by the **Work Area Bar** – see the sidebar on page 275 – will be rendered.)

Manually rendering your project will create temporary video segments that the program can use to create a clean, clear preview playback of your project – while greatly reducing the strain on your system's resources.

Once your clip has been rendered, the orange lines above the clip will turn green and your playback will be much cleaner and smoother.

You can render your clips continually as you're working. Or you can wait until your playback performance starts to lag. It's up to you.

But do be aware that, if you're having playback problems and your timeline has a lot of orange lines running across the top, a few seconds of rendering can usually do a lot to improve the program's performance.

Setting your Timeline Render quality

The quality of your **Timeline Rendering** has nothing to do with how your final video output will look. **Timeline Rendering** is purely for your own personal preview as you edit.

In the program's **Preferences/General** (under the **Edit** menu on a PC), you have the option of selecting either **High Quality Timeline Render** (which is slower but prettier) or **Draft Quality** (which is faster but uglier). Choose whichever best fits your priorities.

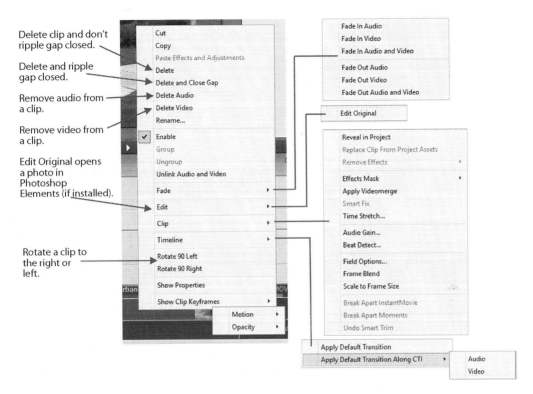

Delete clip and don't ripple gap closed.

Delete and ripple gap closed.

Remove audio from a clip.

Remove video from a clip.

Edit Original opens a photo in Photoshop Elements (if installed).

Rotate a clip to the right or left.

Valuable right-click tools on the timeline

Right-clicking on a clip on your timeline gives you access to a number of valuable tools. To simplify navigation, Adobe has placed many of these right-click options in sub-categories.

To delete a clip without changing the position of any other clip on your timeline, select **Delete**.

To delete a clip and "ripple" the timeline to fill in the gap, select **Delete and Close Gap**. (The gap will only close, however, if there are no clips on parallel video or audio tracks preventing it from being a true gap!)

To remove the audio or video portion of a clip, select **Delete Audio** or **Delete Video**, as discussed on page 274.

To remove all effects and adjustments applied to a clip, select **Clip/ Remove Effects**.

To break apart the audio and video tracks of a clip so that each can be positioned separately, select **Unlink Audio and Video**.

To **Fade In** or **Fade Out** the audio, video or both, select a **Fade** option, as discussed on page 274.

To change the gain level of an audio clip, select **Clip/Audio Gain**, as discussed on page 384.

Selecting an InstantMovie Theme

Customizing Your Theme's Elements

Creating a Video Story

Chapter 22

Create an InstantMovie
or a Video Story
Quick and easy ways to create movies

InstantMovies, as the name implies,
are easy, automatic ways to assemble
movies from your video clips – complete with
titles, special effects and music.

Video Stories give your more control in the
process. You select and arrange the clips, and
the Video Story tool will provide the magic!

Additional content

You may notice a little blue flag over the upper
right corner of a number of InstantMovie
themes and Movie Menu templates.

This blue flag indicates that the template or
theme is available but has not yet been installed on your computer. When you
select this template or theme, the program will automatically download it for
you from the Adobe site – a process that should only take a moment or two.

If you'd like to download all of these themes or templates at once, right-click
on any one and select the Download All option.

Make an InstantMovie

InstantMovie Themes are packets of effects, transitions and music which can be applied to your raw footage to create an exciting movie automatically. To create an **InstantMovie**, you merely provide the raw footage and select a **Theme**, and Premiere Elements does the rest!

To create an **InstantMovie:**

1 Gather your clips on the timeline.

InstantMovies can be used in either Quick View or Expert View.

In Quick View, use **Add Media** to bring your video or still photos to your project's timeline. In Expert View, gather your video or stills from your **Project Assets** panel and drag them to your timeline.

Ideally you'll want at least 2-3 minutes of footage. Place the clips on the timeline in the order you'd like them to appear in your **InstantMovie**.

InstantMovie will use – *and then replace* – all of the footage on this video track.

2 Click the **Create** button in the upper right of the interface and select **InstantMovie**.

The pop-up panel will display a library of movie **Themes**, as illustrated above.

The title bar at the top of the panel is set to **Show All** by default. To filter your view of these **Themes**, click on this title bar and select from the **InstantMovie** categories.

You can see an animated preview of any **Theme** by selecting its thumbnail and then clicking on the play button that appears.

3 Once you've selected a **Theme** for your **InstantMovie**, click the **Next** button in the lower right of the panel.

4 The panel will display a list of the optional elements that make up your **Theme's** template, as illustrated on the right.

Type the titles you'd like included in the boxes provided, then select or deselect the elements you'd like applied to your movie.

You can even swap out music by selecting the **My Music** option and browsing to a music file on your computer.

(You may need to scroll down to see the entire list of optional elements, then click on the little triangles to the left of the listed categories of options to see the entire options list.)

Once you've selected and customized the elements you'd like included, click the **Apply** button in the lower-right corner of the panel.

Premiere Elements will **Auto-Analyze** the clips on your timeline (see page 440), process all of the options and then apply the **Theme** elements you've selected.

After your automatically-generated movie appears on your timeline, the program will offer to render it for you.

Once you've selected a Theme, you can customize it by including your own text and selecting which elements will be applied.

It's a good idea to accept this offer, as your movie will likely need to be rendered before it will play at full quality. The rendered video will provide you with a much cleaner representation of what your final video output will look like.

For more information on the rendering process, see **Render your timeline** on page 278 of **Chapter 21, Edit Your Video in Expert View**.

Instant Movie Themes include sliders for setting the speed of the cuts and the intensity of the effects.

Once you've created your **InstantMovie**, you have the option of using **Export & Share** to output it as is – or you can break it apart in Premiere Elements and continue to edit and customize it.

To break apart an **InstantMovie**, select and right-click the InstantMovie clip on your timeline and select the option to **Break Apart InstantMovie**.

The **InstantMovie** will be broken into its individual video and audio clips, titles and effects.

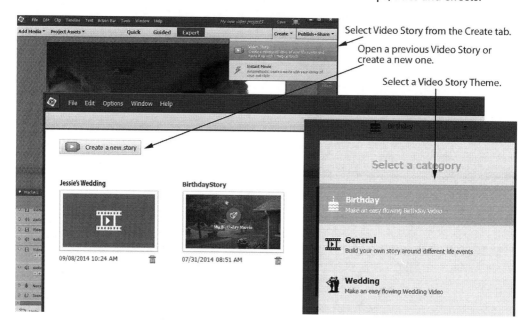

Select Video Story from the Create tab.

Open a previous Video Story or create a new one.

Select a Video Story Theme.

Create a Video Story

Video Story is a wizard-like tool for building stories out of your raw video footage.

A little more hands-on than **InstantMoviemaking**, **Video Story** walks you through the process, step by step, providing simple drop-in templates along the way and yet still leaving plenty of room for customization.

1   Click the **Create** button in the upper right of the interface and select **Video Story**.

   A panel will open which displays your previously created **Video Stories**. To start a new story, click the **Create a New Story** button as illustrated above.

   A **Video Story** introduction screen may display. You can view it, **Exit** it or select the **Skip** option to go directly to the **Video Story Theme** panel in the future.

2   Select a **Video Story Theme**.

   Click to select a theme or category for your **Video Story**.

   A preview panel will open. On this preview panel, you can see a sample of what your **Video Story** theme in action.

   If you want to return to the **Video Story Theme** panel, click the name of your theme at the top of the panel. Otherwise, click **Get Started**.

If the video that you want to use in your **Video Story** is already on your timeline, check the **Use Media From My Timeline** box.

3   Add media to your project.

On the **Get Media for Your Story** screen (illustrated above), select a video source from the left panel. You can add your video by browsing the Elements Organizer, get video from your camcorder or portable device (see pages 250-251), get photos from your still camera (see page 252) or import video or photos from your computer's **Files and Folders** (see page 253).

Drag your media from the **Add Media** panel onto the **Story Assets** panel or, if you are browsing files and folders on your computer, select the files you'd like to add and click the **Open** button.

Your video or photos will be added to your **Story Assets**.

Click **Next**.

4   Add media to your project's chapters.

Drag your media clips from the **Story Assets** panel, on the left, to the placeholder boxes in the **Story Overview** panel. These placeholder boxes represent the chapters in your **Video Story**, so you can add several clips to a single placeholder. (**Title** placeholders can include only one clip each).

To remove a chapter from your movie, click the trashcan icon at the bottom of a placeholder box.

To gather additional media for your project, click the **Add Media** button in the upper right of the **Story Assets** panel.

You'll be returned to the **Get Media** panel, as in **Step 3.**

Click **Next**. The tool will **Auto Analyze** your media clips and assemble your movie into a thumbnail preview.

5   Arrange and customize your **Video Story.**

The panel along the left side of the **Detail View** window lists your **Video Story's** chapters, as illustrated below. Select a chapter to customize and edit its elements.

When a chapter is selected, you have the options of dragging the clips in that chapter into a new order and customizing the chapter's title.

To change the name of a chapter, click on the chapter's name in the box at the top left of the panel and overwrite it.

To set the overall mood of your **Video Story**, select from the **Chapter Mood** drop-down menu at the top right of the **Detail View** panel.

To do more in-depth customization, click the **cog** to the right of the **Chapter Mood** drop-down, as illustrated below. This will open a settings panel in which you can select your own custom music track, apply or remove a video filter to your clips and/or change your movie's pace (**Edit Speed**).

To **Add a Chapter** or to **Add a Caption** or **Add Narration** to the current chapter, click a button along the bottom of the workspace panel.

To see your entire **Video Story** displayed, click the **Overview** button at the top of the **Detail View** panel. All of your **Video Story's** chapters and

In each chapter's Detail View, you can add or rename a chapter, select a mood, add your own music, add a chapter, add a caption or record narration.

media clips will be displayed at once. In this view, you can arrange or customize the individual elements and even drag the chapters themselves into a new order.

Hover and click on the star to open the clip in the Favorite Moments workspace.

6   Edit the individual clips.

To edit an individual clip in any chapter, ensure you are in **Detail View** and hover your mouse over the clip. Click the white star that appears, as in the illustration above. Your clip will open in the **Favorite Moments** workspace (see page 304). In the **Favorite Moments** workspace, you can select the segment(s) from the clip you'd like included in your final movie.

7   Publish your movie.

Click **Preview Story** in the lower right of the panel to play a preview of your **Video Story**.

Click **Save to Timeline** to return to the editing workspace.

Click **Export & Share** to output your finished movie. (**Export & Share** options are discussed in **Chapter 32**.)

Click **Exit** to cancel the project.

Adobe Premiere Elements

Part VI

The Premiere Elements Action Bar

Mixing Your Audio

Grabbing a Freeze Frame

Recording Narration

Creating Pans & Zooms

Smart Mixing and Smart Trimming

Time Remapping and Time Stretching

Selecting Favorite Moments

Motion Tracking an Object in Your Video

Adding Graphics

Chapter 23
Access the Premiere Elements Toolkit
Powerful tools on the Action Bar

The Action Bar that runs along the bottom of the Premiere Elements interface offers quick access to dozens of tools for applying transitions and effects, making titles, adding clip art, adding music and narration and creating menus for your DVDs and BluRay discs.

Through the Action Bar, most of the program's coolest tools are only a few clicks away!

The Premiere Elements Toolkit is divided by tabs into Audio and Video Tools.

The Audio Mixer is only available in Expert View.

Running along the bottom of the program's interface is the **Action Bar.** From this **Action Bar,** you have easy access to dozens of tools, effects, transitions and graphics.

Clicking the **Tools** button launches a pop-up menu with several very cool tools, listed under a **Video** and an **Audio** tab.

Video tools include:

Favorite Moments, a tool for selecting the best segments of a video clip and compiling a new sequence from them.

Freeze Frame, a tool for saving a still photo of a frame of your movie.

Motion Tracking, a cool tool that allows you to link a graphic to an object or person in a clip so that it will automatically follow this object or person around your video frame.

Movie Menu, which opens a workspace for building a menu system for your DVDs, AVCHD or BluRay discs. (We discuss this feature in detail in **Chapter 31.**)

Pan & Zoom, which opens a very intuitive workspace for creating pan and zoom motion paths for your slideshows.

Smart Trim, a tool for automatically removing poor quality video from your project.

Time Remapping, an amazing new workspace for creating fast-motion and slow-motion segments in your movie.

Audio tools include:

Audio Mixer (available only in Expert View), a tool for monitoring and setting the volume levels of your movie's audio.

Narration, a tool for recording a live narration track as your movie plays.

Smart Mix, a tool which automatically mixes the audio levels for your movie, based on criteria you define.

Mix and monitor your audio levels

The **Audio Mixer** can be used to monitor as well as adjust the audio levels on specific tracks.

The Audio Mixer will display separate controls for each audio track. If adjustments are made while playback is stopped, adjustments will affect the entire clip. If made during playback, audio keyframes will be created.

To open this tool, click on the **Tools** button on the **Action Bar** and select **Audio Mixer**. (Note that this tool is available in Expert View only.)

The **Audio Mixer** displays the audio levels for each of your active audio tracks and offers controls for raising and lowering these audio volume levels.

The **Audio Mixer** is a great panel to keep open as much as possible while you work so that you can monitor your movie's audio levels, particularly as you begin the final phases of editing your project. For best results, never let your audio levels peak in the red. Overmodulated audio can sound distorted and fuzzy.

The **Audio Mixer** can also be used to adjust the levels for your individual audio clips:

- When you're not playing your video project, click to select a clip on the timeline at the position of the **CTI** (Current Time Indicator). Raising or lowering the **Audio Mixer** slider for that track will raise and lower the volume level for that entire clip.

- If you adjust the sliders as your video is playing, on the other hand, keyframe points will be added to your clips so that the audio is raised or lowered in real time at the points at which you adjusted the sliders.

As you play your project, watch the meters for each track, adjusting the sound levels as necessary to keep these levels as much as possible in the green, with the bulk of the audio peaking at zero.

In our opinion, this tool serves much more effectively as an audio meter than an audio level adjustment tool.

If used to adjust volume levels while the video is playing, it simply places too many hard-to-adjust audio keyframes on the timeline. You'll get much neater and much more effective results if you use the technique we describe in **Adjust audio levels at specific points in your video** on page 383.

Freeze Frame options

Duration of still if added
directly to timeline.

Option to launch in
Photoshop Elements editor.

Option to export as
a BMP picture file.

Option to insert still directly
to movie's timeline.

Grab a Freeze Frame

Freeze Frame is found on the **Tools** panel, launched by clicking the **Tools** button on the **Action Bar.** (Although it might more accurately be called a "frame grab" tool, since it doesn't so much *freeze* a frame of your movie as much as it *grabs* a frame from it and saves it as a photo file.)

Selecting this tool brings up an option screen which displays the grabbed frame from your video (based on the position of the **CTI** on your timeline) as well as a number of options for saving it, as illustrated above.

- You can choose to simply **insert** the still in your movie. The inserted still will display in your video project at whatever duration you've indicated in **Freeze Frame Duration**.

- Selecting the option to **Edit In Photoshop Elements After Inserting** loads the still into your movie and simultaneously launches it in the edit space of Photoshop Elements.

  Once you've made any adjustments to the photo in Photoshop Elements and saved the file, the updates will automatically appear in the photo in Premiere Elements.

- Whether or not you choose to insert the still into your movie, your **Freeze Frame** will be saved to your hard drive as a Bitmap (BMP) file and will appear in your current **Project Assets** panel.

One thing to note is that many video formats (DV-AVIs, for instance) store picture data in non-square pixels. So, if your video is, for instance, 720x480 anamorphic pixels in size, your **Freeze Frame** may look a bit squished or stretched when you print it or open it in Photoshop Elements.

If you'd prefer to save a **Freeze Frame** of your movie as a JPEG or TIF for use in either another video, Web or print project, you may prefer to use the **Still Image Share** output option that we discuss on page 414 of **Chapter 32, Export & Share Your Video Projects.**

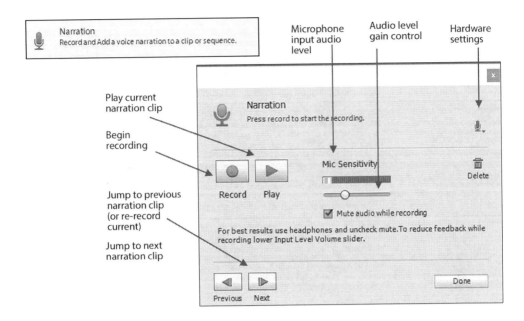

Add Narration

With this tool, you can add narration to your project – and even record it as you watch your video playing.

1   To launch the **Record Voice Narration** tool, click on the **Tools** button on the **Action Bar** and select **Narration**. (In **Audio View**, as discussed on page 382, you can also select which audio track you'll record your narration to.)

The **Record Voice Narration** panel will open.

If your microphone is properly configured, you should see the audio input level displayed on the **Mic Sensitivity** meter in the center of the panel as you speak.

Adjusting your ASIO settings

If the **Narration Tool** isn't recognizing your microphone at all (and you'll know, because your voice won't register on the **Narration** panel's input level meter), it could be that your microphone needs to be set up in the program's **ASIO Settings**.

- Go to Premiere Elements' **Preferences** (under the **Edit** menu on a PC) and select the **Audio Hardware** page. Click the **ASIO Settings** button.
- On the **Input** tab, ensure your microphone is checked.

If your microphone is still not detected (or it isn't listed in the **ASIO Settings**) on your PC, you may need to go into the **Sound** settings in the Windows **Control Panel** and ensure that your microphone is set as the default input under the **Recording** tab.

You'll want to keep your microphone input level green and full, adjusting the slider as necessary for optimal sound.

Turn down your computer's speakers. Wear headphones or select the option to **Mute Audio While Recording** so that you don't get feedback from your speakers as you record.

2 To record your narration, click the red **Record** button.

The panel will display a three-second countdown and then will begin recording as your movie plays.

Click the same button again to stop the recording.

The program will place the narration clip that you've recorded on the **Narration** audio track.

3 Note that, when you've finished recording, the **CTI** will jump back to the beginning of your narration clip.

This is so that, if you're unhappy with the results, you can immediately re-record your narration clip. Your new narration will automatically replace your old.

The two shortcut buttons on the panel will jump you back to the beginning of the clip you've just recorded (or to the next or previous narration clip). You can then click the play button to hear the results.

A good microphone and good, quality sound card are essential to getting a good strong narration recording.

If Premiere Elements isn't recognizing your microphone, click the **Hardware Settings** button (the little microphone icon) on the upper right corner of the **Narration** panel) and ensure your microphone input is properly configured.

Create a Pan & Zoom motion path

The **Pan & Zoom Tool** allows you to create motion paths – pans and zooms across your photos – using a very intuitive interface. (It's, of course, not the only way to create motion paths. For more information on using keyframes to create custom motion paths, see **Chapter 29, Keyframing**.)

Although this tool can also be used on video, the effect will create the best results when used on photos that have a slightly higher resolution than the video project. As we explain in **Use photos in Premiere Elements** on page 254, you'll get the best balance of photo quality and system performance if your photos are no larger than 1000x750 pixels in size. (For high-definition video, you can go as large as 2000x1500 pixels.)

To demonstrate this tool, we'll create a simple motion path over a photo.

With the CTI at the beginning of the timeline, drag the corner handles to size and position Frame 1 to create the initial composition for your motion path.

Move the CTI to the end of the timeline and then drag the corner handles of Frame 2 to create the composition you'd like your motion path to end on.

Place the CTI at other positions on the timeline and click the New Frame button to create as many additional motion path keyframes as you need (including hold motion frames) to build your motion path.

1   Click to select a still photo on your timeline.

2   Click on the **Tools** button on the **Action Bar** and select **Pan & Zoom.**

The **Pan & Zoom** workspace will open, as above.

The concept behind this workspace is a simple one: You indicate the views you'd like for the beginning and end of your motion path and Premiere Elements will create the path of motion between them.

3   Create an initial motion path keyframe.

Ensure that the **CTI** is at the beginning of the timeline that runs along the bottom of the workspace. (You should see a little, diamond-shaped keyframe on the timeline at the **CTI's** position.)

Drag on **Frame 1** (the green box) and on its corner handles to size and position the frame to create the initial composition you'd like for your motion path. (To quickly build a motion path to the faces in your picture, click the **Face Frames** button in the upper left of the workspace.)

4   Move the **CTI** to the end of the timeline.

There will be another diamond-shaped keyframe at this position on the timeline. When you move the **CTI** over this keyframe, **Frame 2** (a second green box) will become highlighted.

Size and position **Frame 2** to create the composition you'd like to end your motion path with. (A little blue line will indicate the duration (in seconds) of your motion.)

Click the **Preview** button along the bottom right of the panel to preview your motion path.

You may add additional keyframes to create additional movements if you'd like. To do this, move the **CTI** to other positions on the timeline and click the **New Frame** button in the upper left of the workspace, as illustrated above.

5   When you are finished, click **Done** to return to the regular editing workspace.

If you'd like to further customize this motion path, you can do so by opening the clip's **Motion** properties, as described in **Chapter 29, Keyframing.**

Smart Mix your audio

Premiere Elements' **Smart Mix** tool will automatically adjust the levels of several audio tracks to allow one track to dominate over the others.

In other words, if you've got a sequence that includes music, narration and the original audio from a video clip, **Smart Mix** can be set to automatically lower the music and other audio levels whenever there is a narration clip.

1   To set the criteria for your audio clip adjustments, click the **Tools** button on the **Action Bar** and select **Smart Mix** from the pop-up menu.

The **Smart Mixer Options** panel displays each audio track in your Premiere Elements project and allows you to indicate, with drop-down menus, which tracks will serve as your audio **Foreground**, which will serve as **Background** and which will be **Disabled** completely. (As illustrated below.)

2   Once you've set your preferences for the tool, activate the **Smart Mix** feature by clicking on the **Apply** button.

In the SmartMixer, you designate which audio tracks will dominate and which will be lowered or eliminated completely.

When applied, Smart Trim automatically creates the necessary keyframes to lower the audio on the tracks you've designated as Background.

The **Smart Mixer** will create the necessary audio keyframes – which appear as little white dots on your audio clip(s) (as seen above) – to lower the volume of the audio clip(s) that you've designated as **Background** audio.

Further, if you move or change a clip you've indicated as your **Foreground** and re-apply **Smart Mix**, the **Smart Mixer** will automatically remove or revise the audio keyframes!

To set preferences for the **Smart Mixer** – including how much the **Background** audio is reduced in volume and if the **Foreground** audio is automatically **Normalized** – go to the Premiere Elements **Preferences** panel (under **Edit**) and select the **Audio** page.

Smart Trim your video

Smart Trim
Let Premiere Elements edit your footage for a crisper video.

The **Smart Trim** tool analyzes clips you've added to your movie's timeline, indicating which sequences do not meet quality standards, then recommends trims to remove segments from your clips (or automatically trims the sequences for you).

1 To **Smart Trim** your video, click the **Tools** button on the **Action Bar** and select **Smart Trim** from the pop-up menu.

If your video has not already been analyzed in the Element Organizer, the **Auto-Analyzer** will automatically search all of the videos on your timeline and indicate in which segments the lighting is bad, the picture is blurry or the camcorder was not held steady.

These indicated areas – called **Suggested Trimmings** – will appear with blue diagonal lines over them, as illustrated on the following page.

If you hover your mouse over these areas, the program will indicate why it recommends they be removed.

If you hover your mouse over a Smart Trim Suggested Trimmimg, Premiere Elements will explain why the segment should be removed.

You may then opt to either remove any or all of the **Suggested Trimming** segments or to override the program's suggestion.

2 Click on a **Suggested Trimming** to select it.

The diagonal shading will highlight in light blue.

By dragging on either end of this selected segment, you can trim or extend the length of this **Suggested Trimming** area.

3 Once you've tweaked your **Suggested Trimming** area, **right-click** on this area and select the option to:

Trim, or remove the **Suggested Trimming** segment from your video.

Keep, or opt not to remove the **Suggested Trimming** segment.

Select All of the **Suggested Trimmings** and remove them.

Right-click on a selected Suggested Trimming area to select whether to cut it or to override the recommendation.

Additionally, this context menu includes access to the **Smart Trim Options** panel.

A pair of sliders on the **Smart Trim Options** panel allows you to set a **Quality Level** and an **Interest Level** for any new clips you add.

Quality automatically checks your clips for issues like blurriness, shakiness, brightness and contrast.

Interest examines the segments recommended for deletion based on your **Quality** setting and re-evaluates their content to see if they're actually worth saving, based on your **Interest** level.

In other words, the **Interest Level** and **Quality Level** balance each other out, according to the levels you set.

On this **Options** panel, you can also set **Smart Trim** to **Automatic** mode, in which case it will automatically remove any **Suggested Trimming** areas from your video timeline as it detects them.

Create cool Time Remapping effects

Time Remapping is one of the newest and most sophisticated tools in the Premiere Elements toolkit.

With **Time Remapping**, you designate a section of a clip on your timeline and the tool will suddenly speed it up or slow it to a crawl – then just as suddenly, bring it back to real time – like it's some Guy Ritchie film.

You can slow you video to nearly a standstill with this tool, by the way. The **Remapping** feature of this tool does an excellent job of blending the motion in between frames so that your slowed action (up to one-eighth speed) looks smooth and even.

The workspace for this effect is very simple, yet also surprisingly powerful.

1   Click to select a clip on your timeline.

2   Click the **Tools** button on the **Action Bar** and select **Time Remapping** from the pop-up menu.

The **Time Remapping** workspace will open. Your clip will be displayed on a timeline along the bottom of the interface.

3   Create a **Time Zone** by moving the **CTI** to the approximate location of the clip you'd like to remap and either clicking the **Add Time Zone** button in the lower left of the interface or clicking the **+** sign on the **CTI**.

A yellow-green box will indicate the location of the designated **Time Zone** on your clip. The speed of your playback for this **Time Zone** is indicated by a number in the upper left of this box– which by default reads 1.0x (normal speed).

Clicking on the + on the CTI or clicking the Add Time Zone button...

...creates a Time Zone on your timeline which you can lengthen, shorten or slide to a new position.

4   Tweak your **Time Zone's** location or size by dragging on either end of this green box. The duration of your **Time Zone** segment is indicated in the lower right of the workspace interface.

5   Select a **Time Remapping** speed using the big slider.

The **X** indicator on the upper left of the green box will indicate the new playback speed of your **Time Zone**, while the **Duration** indicator will list its adjusting playback time. In other words, a 10-second **Time Zone** set to play at 2.0x will have a duration of 5 seconds. Pretty simple, right?

Your **Time Zone** can be remapped to play in forward or reverse, by clicking on either button above the slider.

You can add several **Time Zones** of varying speeds to a single clip, by the way. Although they can't overlap or double-up on each other.

Your audio will be sped up or slowed down right along with your video. If the sped-up/slowed-down audio doesn't fit with your vision, you can remove the audio by clicking the **Remove Audio** button in the lower left of the interface. This will, however, remove the audio from the entire clip, not just the **Time Zone** segment. So if that's not your intention, you may want to leave the audio alone at this point and keyframe it to no volume during the **Time Remapping** segment (as we show you on page 383).

Finally, if the shift to high or low speed and back again seems too abrupt, you can select the option to **Ease In** or **Ease Out** of the **Time Remapping** segment.

Time Stretch your scenes

Time Stretch (available only in Expert View) isn't nearly as sophisticated a tool as **Time Remapping** – but it gets the job done.

Unlike **Time Remapping, Time Stretch** is applied to an entire clip on your timeline at once rather than applied to a designated segment.

To **Time Stretch** a clip:

1   Click to select a clip on your timeline.

2   **Right-click** on your clip and select **Clip** then, from the sub-menu, select **Time Stretch**.

The **Time Stretch** option screen will open, as illustrated below.

3   Set the amount your clip will be **Time Stretched** by either designating the percentage of playback **Speed** or by setting the **Duration** you'd like the clip to extend or contract to. (The shorter the **Duration**, the faster the **Speed**, and vice versa.)

To play a clip in reverse, check the **Reverse** option box.

Auto Select Favorite Moments

Favorite Moments Settings   Trim Favorite Moment segment   Start/End Favorite Moment

Select Favorite Moments from your video clip

Favorite Moments is a cool workspace for locating and creating a compilation of your favorite segments from a longer video clip.

Like the **Clip Monitor** (see page 262), the **Favorite Moments** workspace is a tool for previewing and trimming your video clips. But, with the **Favorite Moments** tool, you can select and fine tune several segments of your video clip. The program will then add a simple **Default Transition** between your selected segments.

1   Open the **Favorite Moments** workspace.

Select a clip on your timeline, then click on the **Tools** button on the **Action Bar** and select **Favorite Moments**.

The **Favorite Moments** workspace will open, as illustrated above.

Your clip will be displayed on the workspace's timeline.

To preview your clip, click on the playback button along the bottom of the **Monitor** window or start and stop playback using your keyboard's spacebar. You can also manually place the **CTI** playhead dragging it to any spot.

2   Start a **Favorite Moments** selection.

There are two ways to create a **Favorite Moments** selection:

Click the **+** sign on the **CTI** playhead. An orange, one-second overlay will appear on your clip.

Stretch or trim this overlay by dragging on either end of it until your "favorite moment" is selected.

Alternatively, you can simply play your video through and click the **Star** button (at the bottom center of the workspace) to mark the beginnings and ends of your "favorite moment" selections.

Clicking the **Star** button starts a selection and clicking it again ends it. Using the same process, you can create as many selected segments on your clip as you'd like.

Clicking the **Auto Mark Moments** button will launch the **Auto Analyzer** (page 440), and the tool will then automatically select **Favorite Moments** based on the visual quality of the video in your clip.

3   Adjust and customize your selection.

Drag either end of an orange selection overlay to trim, extend or move it. The **Monitor** panel will display your selection's new beginning or end point.

4   Customize your **Favorite Moments** Settings.

To control how the tool processes your selections, click the **Settings** button in the lower left of the tool's interface.

When the **Favorite Moments** tool generates your finished compilation, the tool will automatically add a **Default Transition** between your selections. By default, this transition is a **Cross-Dissolve** – however, you can set any transition as your **Default Transition**, as we discuss on page 328.

To turn off the option to add a transition between your selected segments, uncheck the **Apply Default Transition** option on the **Settings** panel.

The **Mark Moments Settings** will optionally add a pre- or post-duration to your selections. This adds a few extra frames to the beginning or end of each selection so that a vital part of your selected segment doesn't get lost during the transition between segments.

Finally, the **Exit Settings** allow you to set whether your finished **Favorite Moments** compilation appears as a single clip on your timeline or if the tool creates a separate short clip of each selected segment.

Click Select Object, then drag corner handles of the Selection Box to define the object or person to track.

Click Track Object. The tool will automatically follow your object with a yellow box.

Follow an object or person with Motion Tracking

Premiere Elements' **Motion Tracking** tool will lock onto an object or person you indicate in a clip and follow it, him or her around your video frame.

You can then link a graphic to that object or person and the program will automatically create a motion path so that the graphic moves around the video frame along with the tracked person or object!

You can, for instance, link to someone running across your frame with clip art of a hat or a cartoon talk bubble, and that hat or bubble will stay with that person throughout the clip.

To use the **Motion Tracking** tool:

1 Click to select a video clip on your timeline. For best results, make sure the **CTI** playhead is positioned at the point in your clip at which you'd like your **Motion Tracking** to begin.

2 Click on the **Tools** button on the **Action Bar** and select **Motion Tracking.**

The **Motion Tracking** workspace will open in the **Monitor** panel, as illustrated above.

3 Click the **Select Object** button.

A selection box will appear on your video. Drag on the box's corner handles to position this box or the person or object in your video that you'd like to track. (The more distinct in color your selected object is from your video's background, the better the tool will work.)

4 Once you've framed the object or person to be tracked, click on the **Track Object** button.

The program will analyze the clip and automatically create the motion keyframes necessary to follow your indicated person or object around your video frame.

When it has finished, if you play or scrub the clip (by dragging the **CTI** back and forth), a yellow box should follow the indicated object or person around your video frame.

To link a graphic to your **Motion Track**:

Click on the **Graphics** button on the right end of the **Action Bar**, as discussed in **Add a Graphic to your movie** on page 309.

Select a graphic from one of the 13 **Graphics** categories. Drag the graphic onto the **Motion Tracking** yellow rectangle (which will turn temporarily blue) on your **Monitor** panel, at the point in your video in which you'd like this graphic to first appear.

You can size or position this graphic by dragging on its corner handles or dragging it around.

The graphics clip will be added to a video track above your current video. When you leave the **Motion Tracking** workspace (by clicking on the timeline, for instance), the tool will create the necessary motion keyframes so that the graphic will follow your object or person.

When a graphic is linked to the Motion Tracked object, the program creates keyframes so that the clip follows the object across the video frame.

Premiere Elements includes a set of animated clips that move or change shape as they follow your Motion Track across your video frame.

You can lengthen the duration of most graphics by dragging on one end to extend it on the timeline. However, animated graphics have a fixed duration and can not be extended.

Similarly, you can link a picture-in-picture video or previously-created title to your **Motion Track**:

Click on the **Project Assets** button (which, in Expert View, will now have moved to the upper *right* of the program's interface, as illustrated below).

Select a video clip from the **Project Assets** panel and drag it onto the **Motion Tracking** yellow rectangle (which will turn temporarily blue), at the point in your video in which you'd like this graphic to appear.

You can size or position this clip by dragging on its corner handles or dragging it around.

The clip will be added to a video track above your current video. When you leave the **Motion Tracking** workspace (by clicking on the timeline, for instance), the tool will create the necessary motion keyframes so that the graphic will follow your object or person.

Thought and Speech Bubbles are some of the most fun graphics to follow people in your videos with. Like titles, these graphics clips can be opened and customized.

Cartoon Thought or Speech Bubbles graphics can be used to follow a person in your video.

1   Add a graphic from the **Thought and Speech Bubbles** category, as described in **Step 5** above.

2   A pop-up panel will appear. Type in your custom text. (You can modify it, as well as the text's style and font, later.) Click **OK**.

You can size or position this clip by dragging on the corner handles or dragging it around. The **Thought or Speech Bubble** clip will be added to a video track above your current video. When you leave the **Motion Tracking** workspace (by clicking on the timeline, for instance), the tool will create the necessary motion keyframes so that the graphic will follow your object or person.

Once the program has finished creating the **Motion Track** so that the **Thought or Speech Bubble** follows your selected object or person around your video frame, you can open the **Bubble** and customize it.

3   Select the **Thought or Speech Bubble** clip on your timeline and click the **Adjust** button on the right side of the interface.

The **Thought or Speech Bubble** will open in the **Title Adjustments** workspace, where you can change the text, the text's style, color, position and color, as described in **Chapter 26, Add Titles & Text**.

Don't worry that, when you open the **Thought or Speech Bubble** in the **Title Adjustments** workspace, it enlarges to fill your **Monitor** panel, as on the facing page. It does this for editing purposes only. When you close the **Adjustments** panel or click on the timeline to return to the regular editing workspace, the **Thought or Speech Bubble** will revert to the size and position you set for it when you created your **Motion Tracking** graphic.

If you reopen the **Motion Tracking** tool a number of times for the same clip, you may find yourself with several yellow rectangles following your object(s) or person(s) around. To remove the extra rectangles, click to select each, then **right-click** and select **Delete Selected Object**.

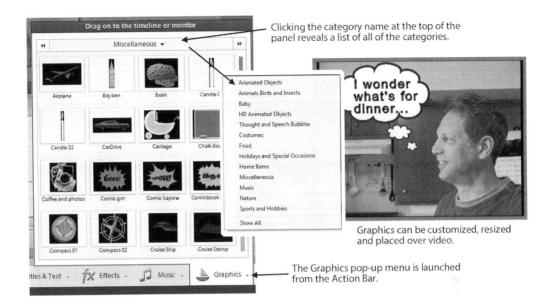

Clicking the category name at the top of the panel reveals a list of all of the categories.

Graphics can be customized, resized and placed over video.

The Graphics pop-up menu is launched from the Action Bar.

Add a graphic to your movie

A cool little extra feature that Adobe includes with Premiere Elements is a library of over 350 video graphics in 13 categories, including cartoon characters, food, musical instruments, wigs and costumes and themed graphics for birthdays and holidays, new babies and sports.

And most interesting of all, a number of these graphics are even animated!

These animated graphics include cartoon faces that move, a fluttering butterfly, a storm cloud, fire, steam and a circle of stars.

These graphics are transparent, so you can place them right over your video.

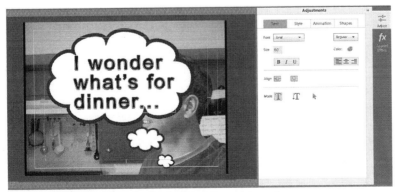

Graphics, like titles, can be edited in the Title Adjustments workspace.

To access the Premiere Elements **Graphics** library, click on the **Graphics** button at the far right of the **Action Bar**. To add a graphic to your movie, simply drag it to your timeline – or directly onto your **Monitor**.

Among my favorite graphics are the **Thought and Speech Bubbles**.

Functioning essentially like title templates, a thought bubble or speech bubble is dragged to your timeline on a video track above existing video or directly onto the clip in the **Monitor** panel. You can then size it by selecting the clip in your **Monitor** and dragging in or out on its corner handles.

To edit and customize the text, just **double-click** on the graphic clip on your timeline. The graphic and text will open in the **Title Adjustments** workspace, as described in **Chapter 26, Add Titles & Text**.

Smart Fixing Your Video

Color, Gamma and Lighting Adjustments

Adjusting Color Temperature and Tint

Adjusting Volume, Balance, Bass and Treble

Keyframing Adjustments

Adjustment Layers

Chapter 24

Make Adjustments to Your Video and Audio

Correct and customize your clips' levels

Premiere Elements includes a whole panel of adjustment tools for correcting your videos' colors, lighting and color temperature and for setting your audio's volume and balance.

Even better, thanks to Adobe's simple Quick Fix interface, making these adjustments couldn't be more intuitive!

The Adjustments pop-up is opened by clicking the Adjust button along the upper right side of the program's interface.

Adjustments can be made by selecting a variation in the Quick Fix interface.

Your current adjustment setting is represented by the center thumbnail.

The More button opens up a more traditional slider interface.

Reset removes all adjustments made in this panel.

A green dot indicates an adjustment that has been applied.

The **Adjustments** panel includes eight powerful video tools and five helpful audio tools for fine tuning the color, lighting, sound and balance levels of your video and audio clips. Which adjustment tools are available depends, of course, on whether the clip you've selected on your timeline includes audio, video or both.

The **Adjustments** pop-up panel is launched by clicking the **Adjust** button in the upper right of the Premiere Elements interface.

Applying an **Adjustment** to a clip is as simple as selecting an audio or video clip on your timeline and selecting an option from the listing in the pop-up menu.

Each video **Adjustment** tool (except **Smart Fix** and the **Shake Stabilizer**) includes an intuitive, picture-based interface as well as a slider-based adjustment tool set (opened by clicking the **More** button, as illustrated above).

In the picture-based Tic Tac Toe-style adjustment tool (called the **Quick Fix** interface), your un-adjusted image is represented by the center square thumbnail. Adjustments are applied to your video as you click on one of the surrounding squares. To reset your image's look, click the center square.

Any adjustments can also be undone by clicking the **Reset** button in the lower left of the tool panel (or by, of course, pressing **Ctrl+z** on your keyboard (⌘+z on a Mac) to undo the last adjustment applied).

Most of the video **Adjustment** tools include options also for adjusting several individual lighting and color elements. For instance, the **Color Adjustment** tool includes options for fine-tuning **Hue, Lightness, Saturation** and **Vibrance** (as discussed below).

A number of tools also include the option to apply **Auto Levels** or **Auto Fixes**. Once you've applied an **Auto Fix**, you can, of course, further tweak your levels using the **Quick Fix** interface or sliders.

Once any **Adjustments** have been applied to a clip, a green dot will appear on the right end of the **Adjustments** panel next to the applied effect's listing, as illustrated on the facing page.

Smart Fix

Smart Fix is a tool which automatically adjusts the lighting and color in your video and, if necessary, adds the **Shake Stabilizer** effect (see below) to reduce movement in handheld shots.

(Note that, if your clip has not yet been analyzed and **Smart Tagged** by the Elements Organizer's **Media Analyzer** (see page 440), the program may need to **Auto-Analyze** the clip before a **Smart Fix** adjustment can be applied.)

When a simple tweak is needed, **Smart Fix** often does a very good job.

The Shake Stabilizer

The Shake Stabilizer locks onto the content in the center of your video and then adds several adjustment keyframes to the position of your video to keep that content in the frame's center. It can be a great tool for taking some of the shake out of your handheld camera shots.

It's not magic – and it can't take the shake completely out of every video – but it is remarkably effective and it can certainly smooth out most of the bumpier bumps.

To use it, simply select the clip you want to stabilize on your timeline, click the **Adjust** button to open the **Adjustments** panel, click on **Shake Stabilizer** and then click the **Quick** or, for more challenging video, the **Detailed** button. The program will analyze the content of your clip, apply the **Shake Stabilizer** effect and make the necessary adjustments.

If you need to, you can further tweak the effect in the **Applied Effects** panel.

Auto Smart Tone

Like the new similarly-named feature in Photoshop Elements, **Auto Smart Tone** allows you to adjust your video clip's color tone levels by intuitively moving a control dot toward previews of various tone variations. (Tone is similar to brightness and contrast, but is somewhat more sophisticated, usually based on the range of individual red, green and blue levels in your video.)

The tool also includes an automatic **Smart Tone** feature, which can be activated by simply clicking the **Apply** button on the **Auto Smart Tone** panel.

To manually adjust your video's color tone:

1   Select **Auto Smart Tone** from the program's **Adjustments** menu, then click **Custom**.

The **Smart Tone** workspace will open.

A grid with a control dot in the center will appear over your video. On each of the four corners of the workspace will appear thumbnails representing tone level variations.

2   Adjust your video's tone.

To adjust your video's tone, drag the control dot toward the corner thumbnail that best represents the tone you'd like your photo to have.

Smart Tone adjustments are made by dragging the control dot toward the variation that best represents the adjustment you want.

If you check the option to **Learn From This Correction** in the lower left of the workspace, the next time you apply **Auto Smart Tone**, the tool's default setting will be based on the tone levels you've set in the past.

Color

The **Color Adjustments** tool has separate adjustment panels for **Hue, Lightness, Saturation** and **Vibrance**.

Hue is the color mix itself, as imagined on a color wheel with violet in the upper left, magenta in the upper right, cyan in the lower right and green in the lower left. Changing this effect will shift the color hue values of all of the colors in your clip.

Lightness is the amount of white or black mixed with the color.

Saturation is the amount of hue applied (more blue or less blue, for instance).

Vibrance, similar to saturation, is the overall richness or intensity of the colors.

The panel includes an **Auto Color** button for a quick color correction.

Color (RGB)

In contrast to the **Color Adjustments**, the **Color (RGB) Adjustments** are concerned only with the levels of **Red**, **Green** and **Blue**, the three primary colors of video.

Selecting one of the squares on each of the color's **Quick Fix** interfaces, or adjusting the corresponding slider, sets an intensity level for that particular color only (on a scale of 0% to 200%) without affecting either of the other two colors' levels.

Gamma

Gamma is basically how bright or dark a picture is. Unlike **Lighting** (below), which bases its changes on the whitest white point and the blackest black point in an image, **Gamma** brightens

or darkens an image based on its mid-tones. In other words, **Brightness** and **Contrast** deal with how white or black an image is, while changing the **Gamma** level brightens or dims the image.

It's a subtle difference, to be sure. But the important thing to understand is that sometimes a video needs its **Lightness** adjusted – and sometimes it needs its **Gamma** adjusted. So, if one doesn't work, try the other. Eventually, you'll come to recognize the difference.

Lighting

Lighting sets the level of the whitest white and the blackest black in your video and/or adjusts the contrast between them. This **Adjustment** includes five separate adjustment panels: **Brightness, Contrast, Exposure, Black** and **White**.

Brightness sets the levels for the blackest black or whitest white point in your video image. The higher the black level, the darker your image will look; the higher the white level, the lighter.

Contrast increases or reduces the difference between the lighter and darker elements in your image.

Exposure simulates lighting adjustments usually made automatically in your camera or camcorder as it takes a picture or shoots your video. This can be a great tool for fixing a picture shot, for instance, in shade with a brighter background, in which your subject came out too dark.

Black increases or decreases the amount of black in your video image.

White increases or decreases the amount of white in your video image.

(If the **Black** and **White** options aren't visible on your panel, you can scroll to see them by clicking the arrow to the right of the **Exposure** tab along the top of the panel.)

In addition to the **Auto Levels** and **Auto Contrast** buttons, this **Adjustment** tool includes an **Auto Fix** checkbox along the top right of the panel. Checking this box applies a **Lighting Auto Fix** to your video image – however, it also locks out the other tools on this panel from further adjustment.

Temperature and Tint

Temperature and **Tint** are color correction tools for compensating for video shot in less-than-ideal lighting conditions – or, of course, for intentionally applying a cooling or warming effect.

Color Temperature refers to the frequency or temperature of light applied to a given scene. Sunlight and outdoor lighting, for instance, has a color temperature of about 6,500 K, which gives pictures shot outdoors a slightly blue tone. Indoor incandescent lights are around 3,000 K, giving your pictures a redder or yellower tone.

In most cases, you don't notice the difference in color temperatures because your eyes – and camcorders – automatically adjust for it.

Color temp set too low.

However, if you've ever shot a video or taken a picture in which a person is lit by indoor lighting while standing in front of a window or an open door, you've seen the difference. The camera adjusts to one or the other color temperature, and you end up with either the person looking orange or the outdoor background looking blue.

Proper color temp setting.

This can also happen if you've been shooting indoors and then run outdoors and start shooting before your camcorder has a chance to reset. The leaves on the trees come out all green-blue!

Color temp set too high.

Temperature adjusts the color temperature of your video image so that the unwanted blue or red/yellow tones are corrected.

Tint, a more primitive way of correcting color, shifts the hue of your video to various levels of red, green and blue.

You can also use these **Adjustments** to intentionally change the tint of your video to create, for instance, a spookier, gloomier tone.

However, to achieve these visual effects, you may find Premiere Elements' **Hollywood Looks** much more effective. For more information on these **Effects**, see page 352.

Volume

Pretty simply, **Volume** increases or decreases the loudness of your audio clips. This adjustment, by the way, can also be made by raising and lowering the yellow horizontal line running through the audio clips on the Expert

View timeline. These levels can also be adjusted higher or lower at specific points on your timeline using keyframing, as we discuss on page 318.

Balance

Balance adjusts the levels of your right and left stereo audio channels with respect to each other.

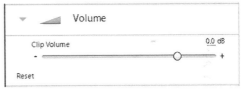

By the way, if you've recorded with a monaural device and you have audio on only one channel, you spread it across both channels equally using the **Fill Left from Right** or **Fill Right from Left Audio Effects**, as discussed on page 362.

Treble and Bass

These **Adjustment** tools decrease or increase the levels of specific frequencies on your audio clips.

Treble adjusts the levels of the higher frequency sounds in your audio.

Bass adjusts the levels of the lower frequency sounds.

Audio Gain

While the **Volume** sets how loudly your audio clip plays, **Audio Gain** increases or decreases the loudness of the *original audio* on the clip. The difference is subtle but worth knowing.

When I've got audio that I've recorded at too low a level and I want to make it louder, **Audio Gain** is my preferred tool for doing so. Increasing the gain tends to make the audio sound richer and fuller in addition to simply louder. At least to my ears.

When you click the **Apply** button on this tool panel, the **Audio Gain** tool launches. For more information on using this tool, see page 384.

Keyframe your Adjustments

By default, changes made in the **Adjustments** panel are applied to your entire clip. In other words, if you change the **Temperature** of a clip, you change it for the entire clip. If you raise the **Volume**, you raise the volume level overall for the entire clip.

Click the stopwatch icon at the top of the panel to open the keyframing workspace.

However, sometimes you want these **Adjustments** to vary over the course of a clip – if, for instance, your clip includes both video that needs color correction and video that does not, or your audio includes both loud and quiet moments that you want to even out.

To set up your **Adjustments** to vary their levels over the course of a clip, you use a process called **keyframing. (Adjustments keyframing** is only available in Expert View.)

To create keyframes that vary the levels of your **Adjustments:**

1 Open the keyframing workspace.

 With the panel open for the **Adjustments** tool you want to keyframe, click the stopwatch icon at the top right of the **Adjustments** panel.

 The **Adjustments** panel will stretch wide – sliding your **Monitor** way off to the left of the interface – and a mini-timeline will appear to the right of your selected **Adjustments** tool. (By nature of their effects, **Smart Fix** and **Audio Gain** do not have keyframing workspaces.)

The mini-timeline in this keyframing workspace represents the duration of the clip you have selected on your timeline.

Once you've created your initial settings, click the stopwatch icon next to the slider to start keyframing and make your initial keyframe.

When you change the position of the CTI and change your settings, new keyframes are automatically created, and Premiere Elements builds the transition or animation between them.

2 Set your adjustment level.

Drag the **CTI** in the keyframe workspace to the point on your clip's mini-timeline that you'd like your first setting to be applied.

Click the **More** button at the bottom right of your **Adjustment** tool's panel to open the slider interface and make your adjustment. (Although you can make your adjustments using the sliders or the **Quick Fix** interface, you'll need to have the sliders visible to create your initial keyframe.)

3 Create an initial keyframe.

Click the stopwatch icon to the left of the slider or the sliders you've adjusted (as illustrated above) to begin keyframing.

A horizontal line will appear to the right of your adjustment, and a little diamond keyframe at the **CTI's** position will indicate your current adjustment setting.

4 Create a second keyframe.

Move the **CTI** in the keyframe workspace to a new position and change your adjustment(s) setting.

A new keyframe will automatically be created, and the program will automatically create the animation or transition between the two.

You can create as many keyframes as you need to create the effect you want. And you can change, move and remove your keyframes as needed. (Or, by clicking the stopwatch again, remove all keyframes completely.)

Keyframes have many applications in Premiere Elements, from creating motion paths over photos and creating animations and special effects to precisely mixing audio tracks. For more information on this powerful tool, see **Chapter 29, Keyframing.**

For information on using keyframes to precisely control the Volume levels on your audio clips, see **Adjust your audio levels at specific points in your video** on page 383.

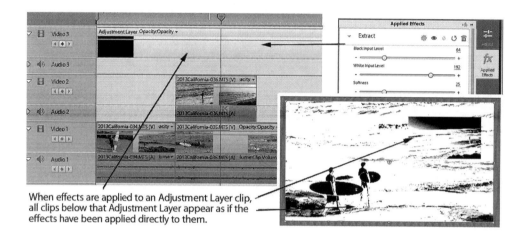

When effects are applied to an Adjustment Layer clip, all clips below that Adjustment Layer appear as if the effects have been applied directly to them.

Add Effects and Adjustments to your movie with Adjustment Layers

Adjustment Layers are a feature that allows you to add all of your effects and adjustments to a null video track, affecting the look of all of the video on tracks below it.

An **Adjustment Layer**, then, can be used to apply an effects or adjustments to an entire sequence or to your entire movie at once.

The effects you add or adjustments you make are made to the **Adjustment Layer** clip rather than directly to your individual video clips.

This could come in handy if, for instance, you wanted to apply the **Old Film** effect or the **Animated FilmLook** overall to your whole, finished movie instead of adding the effect one clip at a time.

Adjustment Layers can be added in both Quick View and Expert View.

To add an **Adjustment Layer** to your movie project:

1   Select an **Effect**.

     Click on the **Effects** button and the **Action Bar** that runs along the bottom of the program.

Making Adjustments to Your Video and Audio

The Adjustment Layer clip will appear, by default, on an upper video track, over your entire movie. (This track will not be visible in Quick View.)

Apply Effects or Adjustments to the Adjustment Layer rather than directly to the video clips on your timeline.

Select an effect as described in **Chapter 27, Add Audio and Video Effects**. (You can add more effects or adjustments after you create the initial **Adjustment Layer.**)

2   Create an **Adjustment Layer**.

Drag your selected effect onto the **Monitor** panel.

A pop-up panel will ask, **Do you want to apply this effect to your entire movie?** Click **Yes**.

An **Adjustment Layer** clip will be added to your timeline.

In Expert View, this **Adjustment Layer** will appear as a clip on an upper video track. This **Adjustment Layer** clip will be, by default, the same length as your movie and will appear over your entire movie.

In Quick View, you will not see the **Adjustment Layer** on your timeline. However, its effect will be seen throughout your movie.

3   Customize your effect.

Your effect can be customized using the same tools described in **Chapter 28, Adjust Applied Effects**. However, any adjustments or changes in effects' settings will be made to the **Adjustment Layer** clip rather than the individual clips in your movie.

Effects settings or video adjustments will be applied to the entire area covered by the Adjustment Layer.

4   Apply additional effects or adjustments.

With the **Adjustment Layer** clip selected on the your timeline, you can add, remove or customize as many effects or video adjustments as you'd like. Any effects you add or adjustments you make will affect all of the video clips under the **Adjustment Layer.**

5   Trim and position the **Adjustment Layer.**

If you'd like your **Adjustment Layer's** effects to only apply to a segment of your timeline rather than to your entire movie, you can trim and position the **Adjustment Layer** clip as you would any other video clip on your timeline.

To temporarily turn off the effects added and adjustments made to your **Adjustment Layer,** right-click on the **Adjustment Layer** clip on your timeline and uncheck **Enable.**

To permanently remove the effects you've added overall to your movie, simply select and delete the **Adjustment Layer** clip.

Customizing Your Transitions

Transitions Defined

How Transitions Work

The Gradient Wipe

Chapter 25

Add and Customize Transitions

Cool ways to get from one scene to the next

Transitions in Premiere Elements
are very easy to use.

However, as with most of
Premiere Elements' features,
there is also a surprising amount
you can do to customize them, if
you know how.

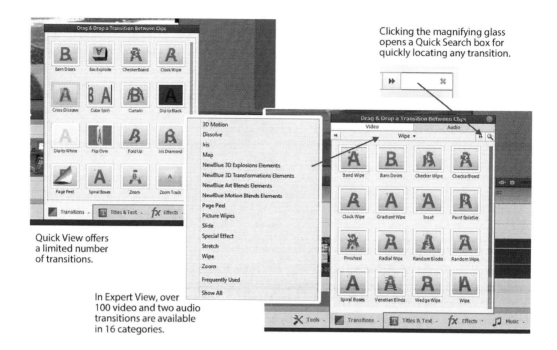

Clicking the magnifying glass opens a Quick Search box for quickly locating any transition.

Quick View offers a limited number of transitions.

In Expert View, over 100 video and two audio transitions are available in 16 categories.

Transitions are added between clips from the **Transitions** pop-up panel, launched from the **Action Bar** along the bottom of the interface.

Whether you're working in Quick View or Expert View, transitions are added to your project essentially the same way. However, Expert View offers a much wider selection of transitions and transition categories.

To apply a transition:

1   Click the **Transitions** button on the **Action Bar** along the bottom of the interface.

The **Transitions** pop-up panel will open.

Once the panel is open, you can enlarge it by dragging on the black bar at the top of the panel.

2   Browse to a transition.

In Quick View, Premiere Elements offers you about a dozen basic video transitions.

In Expert View, you will find over 100 video transitions in 15 categories, plus 2 audio transitions. To select a category and browse to a transition, either:

• Click on the category title bar at the top of the panel, as illustrated above. A complete list of transition categories will appear, and you can click to select and jump to the category; or

In Quick View, a transition appears as a link between two clips.

In Expert View, a transition overlaps a portion of each clip.

- Click on the black double-arrow to the right or left of the category title bar to scroll through the various categories.

You can also **Quick Search** directly to any transition by clicking on the magnifying glass in the upper right of the **Transitions** pop-up panel (as illustrated on the facing page) and then typing in the transition's name.

3   Apply the transition.

Drag your selected transition onto the intersection of two clips.

A **Transition Adjustments** option panel will open.

4   Set your transition's **Duration** and **Alignment**.

Your transition will last 1 second by default. You can change the duration by clicking the up or down arrows to the right of the current **Duration** length or you can simply type over the current **Duration**. To set your transition's **Duration** to fractions of a second, use decimal points. For instance, a transition will last two and one-half seconds if you set its **Duration** to 2.5 sec.

Your transition's **Alignment** is, by default, centered between your two clips. However, if you'd prefer (or if you lack adequate "head" or "tail" material [see page 330] on one or the other clip) you can manually set its **Alignment** over the left or the right clip.

Mac transitions: A limited edition

The Mac version of Premiere Elements 14 does not include all of the transitions available in the PC version. For a list of the omitted effects, see page 420 in the **Appendix**.

The **Transitions** panel includes a **Default Transition**, which is used to transition between clips when you use the **Project Assets' Slideshow Creator** (page 265) as well as by the **Add Transition Along the CTI** tool (see **Apply a transition to several clips at once** on page 329).

By default, the **Default Transition** is the **Cross-Dissolve**. However, you can manually set any transition as your **Default Transition**, as discussed on page 328.

Customize your transition

Most transitions include a number of options for customizing their look, animation, borders, colors and other transitional elements.

These options are set in the **Transition Adjustments** panel that appears when you first add the transition to your timeline – or whenever you **double-click** on an existing transition. Click the **More** button on the lower right corner of this panel to access the deeper transitions properties settings, as illustrated below.

At the very least, you'll have a couple of basic customization options available to customize, depending on the complexity of the transition itself. Some transitions have several customizable features. You may need to scroll down in the panel to see all of the options available.

An option available for nearly every transition is **Reverse.** Reversing changes the direction of a transition so that, for instance, it replaces the old clip with the new in a movement from left to right, rather than from right to left.

When you have finished customizing your transition, click **Done**.

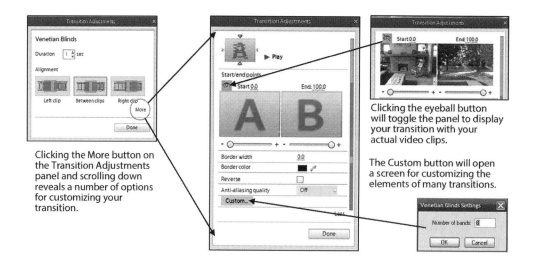

Clicking the More button on the Transition Adjustments panel and scrolling down reveals a number of options for customizing your transition.

Clicking the eyeball button will toggle the panel to display your transition with your actual video clips.

The Custom button will open a screen for customizing the elements of many transitions.

Fade in or out of a clip

Fades, in and out of a clip, are most easily achieved by **right-clicking** on a clip on your timeline and, from the **Fade** submenu, selecting **Fade In, Fade Out** or **Fade In and Out.**

If you've selected a clip that includes both audio and video in Expert View, you'll find separate fade options for the audio and the video. In Quick View, the fade in or fade out is always applied to the both the audio and video on a clip.

Video transitions

Video Transitions are displayed in the **Transitions** panel as thumbnails representing their effect. If you click or hover your mouse over any thumbnail, you will see an animated representation of the **Transition** in action.

The categories of **Video Transitions** are:

3-D Motion. These transitions give the illusion that your video clips are transitioning by turning around or flipping over in three-dimensional space.

Dissolve. Cross-Dissolve is the most basic transition, a dissolve from one clip to the next.

The **Dip to Black** transition fades the first clip to black before fading the next clip in from black.

Iris. Iris transitions change from one clip to another through a shape.

Map. These transitions map their transitional phase to your clip's luminance values.

NewBlue 3D Explosions, NewBlue 3D Transformations, NewBlue Art Blends, NewBlue Motion Blends. These categories contain very cool effects created by NewBlue, one of the world's top video effects companies.

Page Peel. These transitions give the illusion of a page peeling or rolling away between clips.

Picture Wipes. These transitions use graphics (such as stars, travel signs or wedding dress lace) to transition from one clip to another.

Slide. Slide transitions push one clip out of the way so that another is revealed or they transition between clips through sliding boxes or swirls.

Special Effects. A hodgepodge of very showy transitions.

Stretch. These transitions seem to twist or stretch one clip away to reveal another.

Wipe. A variety of transitions that replace one clip with another with a clear line of movement. (See **Create custom transitions with the Gradient Wipe** on page 331 for information on the unique features of this transition.)

Zoom. A collection of high energy transitions that suddenly shrink or enlarge one clip to reveal another.

Audio transitions

To access the **Audio Transitions**, open the **Transitions** panel, click on the **Audio** tab. (Audio transitions are only available in Expert View.)

There are only two **Audio Transitions** – **Constant Gain** and **Constant Power** – both variations of an audio cross-fade.

The difference between the two is minor, having to do with whether the effect transitions from one audio clip to another in a linear fashion or by varying the audio levels as they crossfade.

Of the two, **Constant Power** is generally considered to provide the smoother transitional sound – though, in reality, most people can't really tell the difference.

Set the Default Transition

If you use the **Create Slideshow** feature in Premiere Elements (see page 265), create a compilation of **Favorite Moments** (see page 304) or you **Add a transition to several clips at once**, as discussed on the facing page, the program will place the **Default Transition** between your slides or video clips.

By default, that transition is a **Cross-Dissolve**. However, you can designate any transition in the **Transitions** panel as your **Default Transition**.

To designate a transition as your default, **right-click** on the selected transition in the **Transitions** panel and select the **Set Selected as Default Transition** option.

Push   Slash Slide   Slide

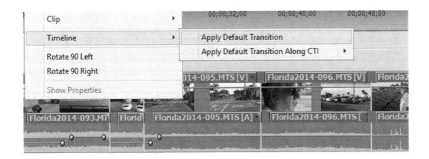

Apply a transition to several clips at once

In Premiere Elements you can add a transition between several clips in one move.

To apply the **Default Transition** to several clips at once:

1   Select your clips, either by holding the **Shift** or **Ctrl** key (⌘ key on a Mac) as you click to select clips on your timeline, or by dragging across your timeline from beyond your clips to "lasso" the clips you would like to select. (You can also use **Ctrl+a** – ⌘+a on a Mac – to select all of the clips on the timeline.)

2   Once the clips are selected, **right-click** on the group and select **Timeline,** then **Apply Default Transition** from the context menu.

You may get a warning that your selected clips include "Insufficient media. This transition will contain repeated frames."

This means that one or more of your clips lacks enough "head" or "tail" material and that, if you proceed, some of your transitions will be composed of freeze frames. (For more information on why this happens and what you can do about it, see the discussion of **How transitions work** on page 330.) The only alternative to letting the program generate freeze frames is to trim back your clips so that at least one second of transitional material exists beyond the in and out points on each clip.

There is currently no way to add a transition other than the **Default Transition** (or to add random transitions) to multiple clips in one move.

Add a transition automatically

You can quickly apply the **Default Transition** at the position of the **CTI**. To do so, position the **CTI** playhead over the intersection of two clips, **right-click** and select the option to **Add Default Transition Along the CTI.**

Using the **Page Up** and **Page Down** keys on your keyboard, you can quickly jump from intersection to intersection of clips on your timeline, adding transitions along the way.

How transitions work

To create the transitional sequence, the transition must "borrow" extra footage – from beyond the out point of clip 1 and from beyond the in point of clip 2, sometimes resulting in the transition showing frames you've trimmed away.

Out point of clip 1

"Head material" beyond the in point of clip 1

Transitional segment

"Tail material" beyond the out point of clip 2

In point of clip 2

Sometimes transitions seem to behave in mysterious ways. They may show frames of video you've trimmed away – or they may show a freeze frame of your video during the transition. However, once you understand what's actually going on, you may find it easier to work with the process to resolve these issues.

1 In order to create the transitional segment – the segment during which both clips are displayed – the transition that you've added needs *a few extra frames*, beyond one clip's end and the next clip's beginning, as illustrated above.

Officially these extra frames are called "**head**" and "**tail**" material.

Unfortunately, this sometimes means that frames you've trimmed away from the end or beginning of a clip will appear during this transitional segment!

If this happens, you may need to trim a few more frames from the beginning or end of the clip so that, even amidst the transition, these unwanted frames are not displayed.

2 If there are no extra frames beyond the beginning or end of your clips for the program to use to create its transition, the program will create a **freeze frame** of the last available video frame for the clip and use that for the transitional material.

This, too, can be a bit annoying if you're not aware of why it's happening. Once again, the solution is to trim back the clip so that the transition has at least a second of "head" or "tail" material to work with.

3 You may also find, sometimes, that the transition will not sit evenly between two clips on your timeline but, rather, seems to be entirely over one or the other clip.

This is because the transition was not able to find the necessary head or tail material on at least one of the clips – so it has positioned itself over the clip that offers the most available transitional footage.

If this is not what you want, you can go to **Transition Adjustments**, as described on page 325, and set the transition's **Alignment** so that it sits evenly over both clips. However, you may find that this also creates an undesirable effect (such as a freeze frame in the head or tail material of one clip).

So weigh your options carefully. The default point at which the transition lands is usually the best available position for it.

4 If you're using transitions between several photos (as in a slideshow) or even titles, you may find that the transition regularly rests over one or the other clip entirely. In this case, it's best not to bother to tweak its position since, with a still image, head, tail and freeze frames all look the same.

The Gradient Wipe transition creates a wipe based on a pattern from black to white.

Click the More button on the Transitions Adjustments panel to view the transition's properties.

To load a custom pattern, click the Custom button in the Transition Properties panel, then click Select Image in the Gradient Wipe Settings and browse to your image.

Create custom transitions with the Gradient Wipe

One of the most versatile **Video Transitions** available in Premiere Elements is the **Gradient Wipe** (available in the **Wipe** category).

The **Gradient Wipe** will create a *custom pattern* wipe from one clip to another based on any gradient (black to gray to white) pattern you provide!

When you first drag the **Gradient Wipe** transition onto a point between two clips, the **Gradient Wipe** Settings panel will open.

You can also re-open this panel at any time by **double-clicking** on the transition on your timeline, selecting **More** and then again clicking on the **Custom** button on the **Transitions Adjustments** panel, as illustrated above.

The **Gradient Wipe Settings** panel will display a default gradient pattern along with a slider to adjust its level of softness.

To use any black and white pattern to create your custom wipe, click on the **Select Image** button. A browse screen will open allowing you to locate and apply any image file on your computer.

The **Gradient Wipe** will base its wipe shape and animation on a movement from the blackest area to the whitest area in the graphics file or pattern you've provided.

In other words, by using a grayscale image you've created in Photoshop Elements, you can design virtually any transitional wipe pattern you can imagine!

For more information on the **Gradient Wipe** and how to use it – plus a free pack of several gradient patterns – just search for my *Steve's Tips* article "The Gradient Wipe" and the free "Gradient Wipe Pack" on the products page at Muvipix.com.

Titles and Title Templates

Editing Your Titles

Applying Styles, Graphics and Animations

Rolling/Crawling Options

Adding Graphics to Your Titles

Chapter 26

Add Titles & Text

Using title templates and text

With Titles, you can create opening or closing credits for your movie.

Or you can use them to add subtitles or captions to your videos.

Additional content

You may notice a little blue flag over the upper right corner of a number of title templates.

art-in-motion_title

This blue flag indicates that the template or theme is available but has not yet been installed on your computer. When you select this template or theme, the program will automatically download it for you from the Adobe site – a process that should only take a moment or two.

If you'd like to download all of these templates at once, right-click on any one and select the Download All option.

You can browse through the categories of available
Titles & Text templates by clicking the arrows at the top
of the panel...

...or, if you click the title bar at the top of the panel, all
of the categories will be displayed.

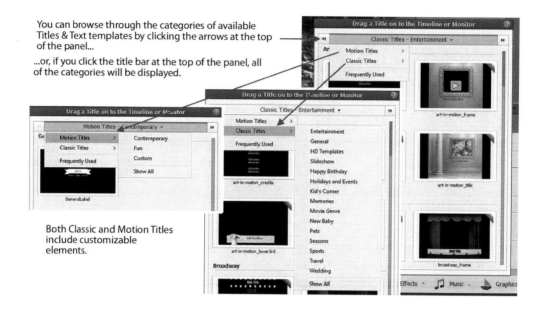

Both Classic and Motion Titles
include customizable
elements.

Titles and other text can be used to help tell your video's story – or to give credit
where credit is due.

Premiere Elements comes loaded with hundreds of title templates in several different
categories. And, new to version 14, the program also includes **Motion Titles**, animated
templates with easily customizable elements. (We show you how to use them on
page 342.)

Within each category of **Classic Titles** are sets or themes. Each theme includes at least
four template styles:

A still title, usually with stylized text and often accompanied by theme graphics.

A rolling title with a template for a list of names.

A crawling title (which moves left to right or right to left across the screen).

A lower third title, in which the text is positioned in the lower one-third of the
video frame.

Many of these templates include custom graphics – which you can reposition or
remove in the **Title Adjustments** workspace. And most of the templates that include
graphics also include transparent areas (which appear as black on the thumbnails in
the **Titles & Text** panel) through which any video placed on a video track below the
title will show through.

To add any title or text template to your movie:

1   Click on the **Titles & Text** button on the **Action Bar** that runs along the bottom
of the program's interface.

The **Titles & Text** pop-up panel will open.

Once the panel is open, you can enlarge it by dragging on the black bar at the
top of the panel.

2   Browse to a title.

To browse through the title template theme sets.

- Click on the category title bar (which displays the name of the title category at the top of the panel, as illustrated on the facing page) and select either the **Classic Title** or **Motion Title** (see page 342) category. A complete list of title template categories will appear. Click to select a specific sub-category; or

- Click on the black double-arrow to the right and left of the category title bar to scroll through the various categories.

Once you've selected a category, scroll down the panel to select a title theme and a specific title.

3   Add your title.

Drag your selected title template onto your timeline.

You can add your template to the **Video 1** track, in which case any transparent areas will appear as black in your video, or you can add it to an upper video track, in which case any transparent areas in the title template will show the video on the track or tracks below it.

Once you've placed your title, the program will open up in the **Title Adjustments** workspace, where you can further customize the look and content of your text and accompanying graphics.

Safe Margins

When your title opens in the **Title Adjustments** workspace, you'll notice two concentric rectangles overlaying the **Monitor** panel. These rectangular overlays are called **Safe Margins** – and they are guides for placing important information in your video frame so that they don't become victim's of overscan, television's terrible habit of cutting off up to 10% of the area around the edge of a video frame.

The inner rectangle is called the **Title Safe Margin.**

Keeping all of your onscreen text within the bounds of this inner **Title Safe Margin** ensures that it will always be displayed completely, with no chance of any accidental cut-off.

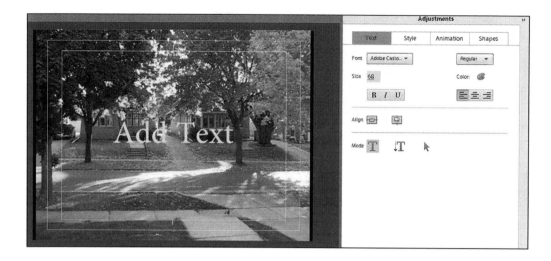

Customize your title in Title Adjustments

When you first add a title or template to your timeline – or any time you **double-click** on an existing title – the program will open into the **Title Adjustments** workspace.

In this workspace, you can customize and color your text, add additional text, draw, add and remove graphics and add a variety of animations.

The **Adjustments** panel in this workspace (illustrated above) is your toolkit for creating and customizing your titles. Its tools are organized under four tabs, as detailed on the next pages:

> **Text**, where you'll find tools for setting your text's font, style and color.

> **Style**, a catalog of more than 80 text styles that automatically apply fonts, colors, strokes and drop-shadows to your text and graphics.

> **Animation**, a catalog of nearly 50 pre-created text animations.

> **Shapes**, a toolkit for creating and coloring basic shapes and selecting and positioning text boxes and graphics in your video frame.

Create a quick title

If you want to just add a plain vanilla text title to your movie – or maybe a basic roll or crawl – without rooting through dozens of templates, you can do so simply by selecting the **New Text** option under Premiere Elements' **Text** menu.

A title, in the default color and font, will be added to your project at the position of the **CTI** and you'll be launched into the **Title Adjustments** workspace, where you can customize your text's font, size and color and/or add animation and graphics.

Edit your title's Text

The **Text** panel contains tools for creating, customizing and positioning your text.

The top half of this panel includes tools for setting your text's **Font, Size, Style, Color** and **Left, Center** and **Right** paragraph alignment within its text box. (For more information on coloring your text, see **Color your shape or text** on page 339.)

The **Align** tools will automatically center any selected text boxes or graphics horizontally or vertically in your video frame.

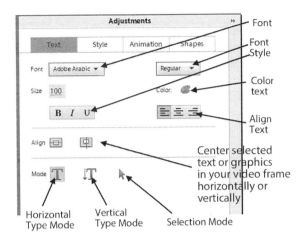

The three **Mode** buttons determine the mode of your cursor.

> In the default **Horizontal Type** mode, you can edit existing text or create a new text box by clicking and typing outside of an existing text box.

> In **Vertical Type** mode, any text you type will be written down rather than across.

> In **Selection mode**, you can use your cursor to select a text box or a graphic, resize it by dragging on its corner handles or drag it to a new position on your title area.

Give your text a Style

Under the **Styles** tab in the **Title Adjustments** workspace, you'll find over 100 **Text Styles** – combinations of fonts, font styles, colors and, in some cases, drop shadows and glows that can be applied to selected text simply by clicking on it.

If you **right-click** on any of these **Text Styles**, you will find the option to set that particular style as your **Default Style**. This style will then automatically be applied whenever you open a new title.

One other thing worth noting: In order for you to color your text's stroke (its outline) using the **Color Properties** tool on either the **Text** or **Shapes** tab, *you must first have a* **Text Style** *applied to the text or graphic that includes a stroke or outline.* Otherwise, the **Stroke** color option will not be available.

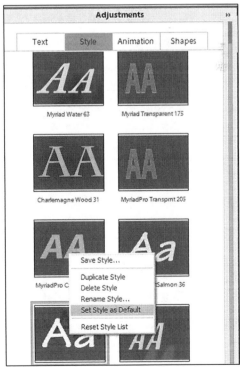

Add a Text Animation

Under the **Animation** tab in the **Title Adjustments** workspace, you'll find over three dozen **Text Animations** – very cool pre-programmed movements for getting your text on and off screen. Some juggle entire words, others dance your titles around one letter at a time.

These **Text Animations** are in several categories, and you can browse the various categories by clicking the title bar at the top of the panel or by using the arrow buttons on either side of the title bar.

> **Fades** bring your text in or out with a fade to or from transparency.
>
> **Move In and Out** animate your text one letter at a time.
>
> **Pan and Zoom** animations reveal your text through a slow zoom in or out.
>
> **Slide animations** slide your text in from off-screen all at once or one letter at a time.

Special Effect is a collection of very interesting ways to reveal your text.

Twist and Turn animations spin and twist in or out your text or individual letters.

To see a preview of how an animation looks when applied, hover your mouse over the animation thumbnail until a **Play** button appears, then click on this **Play** button.

To apply a **Text Animation** to your title:

- Your text or text block must be selected on the **Monitor**;
- Your text block must *not* be more than one line long; and
- A **Text Animation** must be selected.

To apply a **Text Animation** to your text:

1 Select your text on the **Monitor** in the **Title Adjustments** workspace.

2 Click to select a **Text Animation**.

3 Click the **Apply** button at the bottom of the **Animation** panel.

4 To undo a **Text Animation**, select the text again and click the **Remove** button.

The speed of your animation is based on the length of your title. To slow your title's animation, stretch the title longer on your timeline. To speed it up, trim it shorter.

Animations are applied, by the way, to individual text boxes – not to entire titles (which can include several text boxes). So a single title could conceivably include several animated blocks of text!

Add Shapes to your title

The tools under the **Shapes** tab in the **Title Adjustments** workspace are similar to those under the **Text** tab – except, of course, that the tools under this tab are for drawing basic shapes onto your title.

As on the **Text** tab, the three **Mode** buttons determine the mode of your cursor.

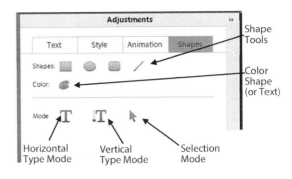

- In the default **Horizontal Type** mode, you can edit existing text – or create a new text box by clicking and typing outside an existing box.

- In **Vertical Type** mode, any text you type will be written down rather than across.

- In **Selection mode**, you can use your cursor to select a text box or a graphic, resize it by dragging on its corner handles or drag it to a new position on your title area.

Color your shape or text

Clicking the **Color** button (the painter's palette) on either the **Text** or **Shapes** tabs opens a **Color Properties** panel for setting the color of whatever text or graphic you have selected.

To color your selected graphic or text, click the **Fill** button on the panel and then select a color using the **Color Mixer** at the top of the panel.

A **Stroke** is an outline around your text or graphic. A strange quirk in the program is that you *cannot* add or color your text's **Stroke** in this panel unless a **Text Style** has first been applied to it that includes a stroke (see page 337). Even stranger, this applies to shapes as well as text: To color a stroke around a shape, you must first apply a **Text Style** that includes a stroke to your shape!

The **Gradient** drop-down menu allows you to color your **Fill** or **Stroke** with either a solid color or any of a number of gradient mixes. (Or, using the **Ghost** option, to make your text or graphic invisible except for its **Stroke** or **Drop Shadow**.)

A **Drop Shadow** can be added to any text or graphic.

Crawls move horizontally across the screen;
Rolls move up from the bottom of the screen.

Options for starting or ending the title
off the screen.

Ease In and Ease Out slow the title at the
beginning or end of the roll or crawl.

Create rolling or crawling titles

In addition to **Text Animations**, you can use more traditional ways to move
your titles on and off the screen. Premiere Elements includes a tool for
making any title you create **roll** (move up over a video frame) or **crawl** (move
left to right, or right to left) across your video frame.

The **Roll/Crawl Options** panel is launched from the Premiere Elements
Text menu (as illustrated above) – and, of course, it's only available while
you're in the **Title Adjustments** workspace.

The options you select in this panel will apply to the entire title you are
currently editing. In other words, whatever else you've got on your title –
text animations, graphics, etc. – setting options in the **Roll/Crawl** panel
will make it all roll or crawl across your screen. (If you've selected a title
template that is already set to roll or crawl, you'll find that, when you open
this panel, some of the options on this panel have already been set.)

The settings on the **Roll/Crawl Options** panel are fairly intuitive. If you
select **Crawl**, for instance, you have the option of setting it to either **Crawl
Left** or **Crawl Right** across the video frame.

The **Timing** options allow you to set if and how your roll or crawl starts
and/or ends off screen.

- You have the options of setting your title to **Start Off Screen** and/or
  End Off Screen. Alternatively, you can manually set the **Preroll** or
  Postroll time for how long the title is off the screen before or after it
  rolls or crawls.

- The **Ease In** and **Ease Out** options allow you to change the rolling or
  crawling movement from a steady speed to one that begins slowly
  and then speeds up (**Ease In**), or vice versa (**Ease Out**).

The speed at which the title rolls or crawls is determined by how long the
title is on your timeline. Extending (by dragging one end to lengthen) the

title on your timeline will **increase its duration and thus slow the speed** of the roll or crawl; dragging in one end of the title to **decrease its duration will increase the speed** of the roll or crawl.

As an alternative to using these automatic roll and crawl options, you can manually keyframe the movement of your title so that it is revealed through any movement, effect or animation you can imagine. To learn more about using keyframing to create animations, see **Chapter 29.**

Add a graphic to your title

To add a graphic, photo or any image on your computer to your title, select the option to add an **Add Image** from the Premiere Elements **Text** menu or **right-click** on the **Monitor** and select the **Image** option there. (This option is only available while you're in the **Title Adjustments** workspace.)

Once you've added the graphic, use the **Selection Tool** to size and position it in your video frame (as discussed in **Add Shapes to your title** on page 339).

You can grab an image from the Premiere Elements **Graphics** collection (see page 309) by browsing to C:/Program Files/Adobe/Premiere Elements 14/Clip Arts/Common on a PC – or, on a Mac, by browsing to Library/Application Support/Adobe/Premiere Elements/14.0/Online/Clip Arts/All_Lang.

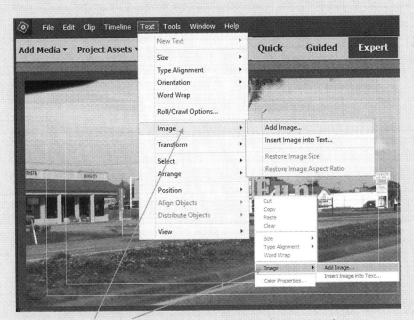

To add a graphic, photo or image to your title in the Title Adjustments workspace, select the option from under the Text menu or right-click on the Monitor and select the option from the context menu.

Add a Motion Title to your movie

New to version 14, **Motion Titles** are animated title templates that include text motion and animated graphics – each of which is easily customizable.

And, if you're happy with your custom elements, you can even save your new title as a template in your own personal library!

Adding a **Motion Title** is similar to adding a **Classic Title**:

1   Click on the **Titles & Text** button on the **Action Bar** that runs along the bottom of the program's interface.

The **Titles & Text** pop-up panel will open.

Once the panel is open, you can enlarge it by dragging on the black bar at the top of the panel.

2   Browse to a title.

To browse through the title template theme sets.

- Click on the category title bar (which displays the name of the title category at the top of the panel, as illustrated above) and select the **Motion Title** category. A complete list of title template categories will appear. Click to select a specific sub-category; or
- Click on the black double-arrow to the right and left of the category title bar to scroll through the various categories.

Once you've selected a category, scroll down the panel to select a title theme and a specific title.

3   Add your title.

Drag your selected title template onto your timeline.

You can add your template to the **Video 1** track, in which case any transparent areas will appear as black in your video, or you can add it to an upper video track, in which case any transparent areas in the title template will show the video on the track or tracks below it.

Once you've placed your title, the program will open up in the **Motion Titles Adjustments** workspace, where you can further customize the look and content of your text and accompanying graphics.

Motion Titles include built-in animation for both the text and graphics. You can preview the title's animation at any point by playing your video's timeline. However, because these animation's animation can challenge even the most powerful personal computers, you may want to **Render** the timeline (Press **Enter**, as on page 278) to create a hard render preview before you preview the playback.

You can return to the **Motion Titles Adjustments** workspace at any time by double-clicking on the title on the timeline.

The animation in each **Motion Title** is programmed into the template itself. This means that, even if you customize the text or replace the graphics, the original animation will remain intact.

4   Customize your title's text.

As illustrated below , when you select any block of text in your title, the **Motion Titles Adjustments** panel will display a **Text** option panel, in which you can type in your custom text. The panel will also offers you the option to customize your text's font and color (as on page 337), add a text style (as on page 337) or add a text animation (as on page 338).

You can also change the location of the text block in your title by dragging it into a new position in the **Preview** window.

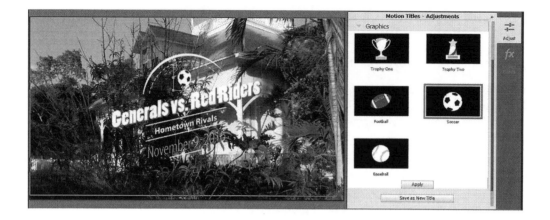

5 Customize your title's graphics.

As illustrated above, when you select a graphic or graphical element on your title, the **Motion Titles Adjustments** panel will display alternative graphics.

To apply the new graphic, **double-click** on it or select the graphic and click the **Apply** button at the bottom of the panel.

The graphic you use to replace the original graphic will display with the original **Motion Title's** animation.

6 Customize your titles background.

When you click on the background of the title displayed in the **Preview** window, the **Motion Titles Adjustments** panel will display a **Background** options drop-down menu. By default this menu is set to **Transparent**, displaying the video, if any, below the title on the timeline.

If you select the **Color Matte** option from this drop-down menu, the **Color Picker** will open, from which you can set the color of your title's background. Once you select a color and close the **Color Picker**, the

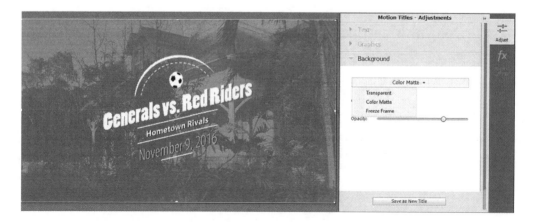

Motion Titles Adjustments panel will display an **Opacity** slider. The higher the Opacity setting, the more this color background will obscure the video, if any, below the title on your timeline.

If you select the **Freeze Frame** option from this drop-down menu, the title will use the current video frame displayed in the **Preview** window as a background. The higher the **Opacity** setting, the more this freeze frame will obscure the moving video below the title on your timeline.

When you're done editing your title, click the **Adjustments** button on the right side of the interface to close the **Motion Titles Adjustments** workspace, or simply click on the timeline.

Be sure to render your timeline (press **Enter**) before playing back your **Motion Title** sequence.

To re-edit the title, simply **double-click** on the title clip on your timeline.

7   Optionally save your title as a new template.

Once you've customized your **Motion Title**, you can save it as a new template. To do so, simply click the **Save as New Title** button on the **Motion Titles Adjustments** panel and name your title.

This new template will then be available on the **Titles & Text** panel for any future project under the **Motion Titles/Custom** category.

Finish your title

Once you've completed your title, click on the timeline to leave the **Title Adjustments** workspace and return to regular video editing mode. Your new title will appear as a clip on your timeline.

Re-edit a title

If, after you've created a title, you'd like to re-edit it, you can re-open it in the **Title Adjustments** workspace by **double-clicking** it on your project's timeline or by simply clicking to select the title on your timeline and then clicking the **Adjustments** tab on the right side of the interface.

Duplicate a title

If you like how your title looks and you want to re-use the look and style for another title, you can duplicate it and then edit the duplicate.

To duplicate a title, **right-click** on it in the **Project Assets** panel and select **Duplicate**. You can then drag the duplicate title to your timeline and **double-click** on it to re-open its **Title Adjustments** workspace for editing.

It's important that you *duplicate* your title in the **Project Assets** panel rather than merely copying it or doing a copy-and-paste on the timeline.

If you create a *copy* of your title rather than make a duplicate, you've merely created a "clone" – and any changes you make to one title *will be made to both*.

Duplicating a title creates a copy of it, which you can use as a template for a new title. Copying a title, on the other hand, creates a "clone" of your title, such that any changes you make to the original are made to both titles.

And that's likely not how you intend to use the title's copy.

Duplicating creates an *independent* and editable copy of your title.

Render your title

Your title will likely look a bit rough when you first play it back from your timeline. To see a cleaner playback of your title sequence, press **Enter** on your keyboard or click on the **Render** button along the top right of the timeline. Rendering creates a preview video of the segment that smooths your playback and gives you a much better idea of what your final video output will look like. (For more information, see **Render your timeline** on page 278.)

Video Effects

Color Correction Tools

Chroma Key

Videomerge

Preset Video Effects

Audio Effects

Chapter 27

Add Audio and Video Effects
Bringing excitement to your movie

There is an amazing number of effects
available in Premiere Elements –
too many, in fact, to display on a
single panel.

The program includes nearly 90 video
and 20 audio effects as well as nearly 275
automatic, or "Preset" effects, that include
applied effects as well as keyframed
animations – all of which are infinitely
customizable.

Adjustment Layers

In addition to applying effects to individual clips, you can also add
effects overall to change the look of a whole sequence in your movie
or to your entire movie at once using Adjustment Layers.

For more information on using and adding Adjustment Layer clips to
your timeline, see page 320.

You can browse through the categories of available Effects and Presets by clicking the arrows at the top of the panel...

...or, if you click the title bar at the top of the panel, a list of all of the categories will be displayed.

Each category includes a number of effects.

Clicking the magnifying glass button opens a Quick Search tool that quickly locates any effect as you type its name in the box.

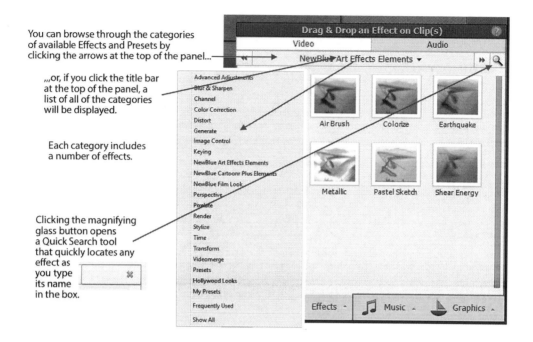

Premiere Elements' **Video Effects** and **Audio Effects** libraries are accessed by clicking the **Effects** button on the **Action Bar**, along the bottom of the interface.

In addition to its huge catalog of **Video Effects** and **Audio Effects**, the **Effects** panel includes **Presets**, pre-programmed effects (many of them animated), and a **My Presets** folder where you keep your own custom-created effects and animations.

Presets and **Video Effects** display in the panel as thumbnails, demonstrating their effect. Animated **Preset** effects can be previewed by clicking on the thumbnail image. **Audio Effects** appear as speaker thumbnails.

As indicated in the illustration above, you can also quickly call up an effect simply by clicking on the magnifying glass button on the upper right of the panel and typing its name in the search box. As you type, the program will search in real time.

Applying an effect or preset is as simple as dragging the effect from this panel onto a clip on your timeline.

Once an effect has been added to a clip, its settings can be modified, customized and even be animated. (In fact, some effects won't even change your clip much at the default settings.) For more information on customizing these settings – or removing an applied effect completely – see **Chapter 28, Adjust Applied Effects**.

You can apply any number of effects to a clip. In fact, you can even double-up the same effect on the same clip (such as **Channel Volume** on an audio clip) to increase its intensity. Sometimes the way effects interact with each other on a clip can create a new effect all its own.

Video effects can also be applied to an **Adjustment Layer** rather than directly to a clip, as discussed on page 320.

Apply an effect to several clips at once

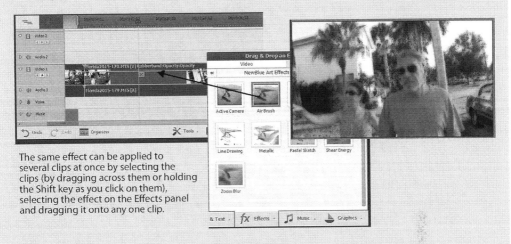

The same effect can be applied to several clips at once by selecting the clips (by dragging across them or holding the Shift key as you click on them), selecting the effect on the Effects panel and dragging it onto any one clip.

Premiere Elements includes the ability to apply an effect to several clips at once.

To apply an effect to several clips in one move:

1   Select your clips, either by holding the **Shift** or **Ctrl** key (⌘ key on a Mac) as you click to select clips on your timeline or by dragging across your timeline from beyond your clips to "lasso" the clips you'd like to apply the effect to. (You can also use **Ctrl+a** on a PC or **⌘+a** on a Mac to select all of the clips on the timeline.)

2   Once several clips are selected, go to the **Effects** panel and locate the effect you want to apply.

Drag the effect onto any one of your selected clips.

The effect will be applied to all of your selected clips.

You can fine-tune the effects in the **Applied Effects** panel (one clip at a time). For more information on adjusting effects settings, see **Chapter 28, Adjust Applied Effects.**

To create and customize an effect on one clip and then apply the same effect and settings to several other clips, use the **Paste Effects and Adjustments** feature, as we also discuss on page 372.

Mac video effects: A limited edition

The Mac version of Premiere Elements 14 does not include all of the effects available in the PC version. For a list of the omitted effects, see page 420 in the **Appendix**.

Premiere Elements' video effects

Premiere Elements' video effects are arranged in categories. To jump to a category, click on the category title bar at the top of the panel, as illustrated on page 348, and select your category from the drop-down menu. To browse the categories, use the arrow buttons to the right and left of the category title bar.

Here are the various categories as well as brief descriptions of how some of the key effects in that category work.

Advanced Adjustments. The **Advanced Adjustment** effects work primarily with color. These are the effects you'll use if you want to change or correct color in your clip.

Additionally, **Lighting Effects** imposes a spotlight-like effect on your clip.

Posterize reduces the number of colors in your clip, making it appear more cartoon-like.

And the **Shadow/Highlight** effect is a great way to decrease contrast in a clip (e.g., the sky is too bright and the shade is too dark). Also available in Photoshop Elements is **Shadow/Highlight,** one of my personal favorite picture-saving effects!

New in this category is the **Vignetting** effect, illustrated below, which makes your video lighter toward the center and darker around the sides.

Blur & Sharpen. These effects soften or sharpen your picture.

The **Ghosting** effects leaves a very cool trail behind objects that are moving in your clip.

Channel. Invert, the single **Channel** effect, turns your video's picture into its negative.

Color Correction. The effects in this set – **HSL Tuner, Split Tone** and the **Three-Way Color Corrector** – are advanced tools for enhancing and correcting the color in your video. We take a close-up look at the **Three-Way Color Corrector** on page 355.

Distort. The **Distort** effects warp, twist and/or bend your video image.

Generate. The **Lens Flare** effect in this category adds a bright, white flare to a spot on your video picture, as if a light is being shone back at the camcorder.

Image Control. These effects offer tools for color, contrast and light adjustments. Among this set are tools for tinting, replacing and even removing the color completely from your video.

Keying. Keying effects remove or make transparent a portion of your video's picture.

A powerful tool in this category is the **Chroma Key** effect, which we discuss in detail on page 356. Other effects in this category are essentially the **Chroma Key** preset applied to certain colors (**Green Screen Key, Blue Screen Key**).

Others, like the **Garbage Mattes**, create transparent areas in a clip that can be shaped with user-defined corner handles.

The Vignette effect.

The very cool, new NewBlue Cartoonr effect.

Note that the Chroma Key, Green Screen Key and Blue Screen Key effects are not available on the Mac version of Premiere Elements. On a Mac, the alternative keying effect is Videomerge, as discussed on page 358.

NewBlue Art Effects, NewBlue Film Look, NewBlue Motion Effects. These effects categories include high-level image effects created by NewBlue, one of the world's top video effects companies.

One of the most popular of these is the **Old Film** effect, a highly customizable effect which makes your video look like a damaged, worn, old movie.

NewBlue Cartoonr Plus Elements. This effect makes your videos look cartoon-like, as in the illustration above right!

Perspective. These effects can be used to make your video image look as if it is floating or rotating into space.

Pixelate. The **Facet** effect in this category reduces your video picture to a group of large color blocks.

Render. The **Lightning** effect is great fun, although it takes a lot of computer power to create and customize it!

The **Ramp** effect fades your video out across the screen in a gradiated pattern.

Stylize. The effects in this category, as the category name implies, can be used to create a highly stylized video.

Time. Effects in this category change how your video displays motion by reducing or affecting the look of the frame rate.

Note that this is *not* the place to go if you want to slow down or speed up a clip. That's the **Time Stretch** effect (see page 303), available in the toolkit launched from the **Tools** button on the **Action Bar.**

Transform. A real hodgepodge of effects, this category includes some stylized effects, some 3D transformations and, for some reason, **Clip** and **Crop**, two effects for trimming off the sides of your video picture.

(For the record, **Clip** trims away the sides of your video and replaces them with color while **Crop** trims away the sides and replaces them with transparency – a significant difference, if you're using your cropped clip on an upper video track with another clip on a track below it).

To learn more about using the **Crop** tool (or **Clip** tool, since you use the same method to adjust both) see **Types of effects settings** on page 370 of **Chapter 28, Adjust Applied Effects.**

Videomerge. This effect is essentially a more automatic version of the **Chroma Key** effect. When applied to a clip, it removes what it interprets to be the background in a single step. We take a **Close-Up** look at how to use it on page 358.

For information on changing settings for effects, see **Adjust settings for effects and properties** in **Chapter 28, Adjust Applied Effects.** For information on animating effects to change over time, see **Chapter 29, Keyframing.**

Apply a Hollywood Look to your video

Relatively new to Premiere Elements are **Hollywood Looks**, a collection of 16 very cool color presets that automatically give your video the moody look of an artsy Hollywood production (or of a cheap home movie).

Included in this set are effects for shifting colors, tinting your videos, brightening them or making your videos look dark and creepy.

The **Hollywood Looks** included with Premiere Elements 14 are:

Comic uses the **NewBlue Cartoonr Plus** effect to make your movie look like an animated cartoon.

Cross Process desaturates the color in your video, reducing it to shades of gray, blue and yellow.

Crushed Color washes out the color in your video. Great for doing *Cold Case*-style flashbacks.

Deep Copper makes your video black & white with a cold, coppery tone.

Dreamy applies an ethereal **Gaussian Blur** effect.

Hollywood Movie increases the blue levels of your video to give it a more filmic look.

Horror desaturates the color to give your video a dull, deadly look.

Newsreel and **Old Film** lower or remove your color levels and "damage" the video to make it look older and worn.

Pandora turns everyone's skin blue (like the Na'vi characters in *Avatar*).

Hollywood Looks change the visual tone of your movie by applying preset effects and adjustments in a single move.

Comic	Cross Process	Crushed Color	Deep Copper
Dreamy	Hollywood Movie	Horror	News Reel
Old Film	Pandora	Red Noir	Sparta
Summer Day	Trinity	Vintage	Yesteryear

Red Noir desaturates all of the colors except for a few spots of red.

Sparta gives your video a surreal, golden look.

Summer Day washes out your video's color with yellow "sunshine".

Trinity shifts your video's tint to mystical green shades.

Vintage makes your video look like an old home movie.

Yesteryear shifts the tint of your video toward orange and green to create the mood of a faded memory.

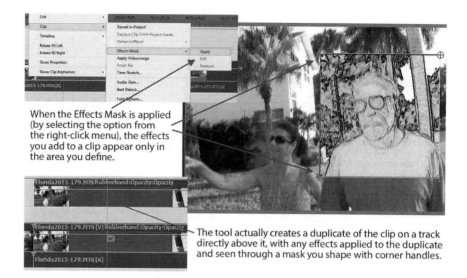

When the Effects Mask is applied (by selecting the option from the right-click menu), the effects you add to a clip appear only in the area you define.

The tool actually creates a duplicate of the clip on a track directly above it, with any effects applied to the duplicate and seen through a mask you shape with corner handles.

Isolate an effect area with the Effects Mask

The **Effects Mask** enables you to isolate an area of your video and apply an effect to it without affecting the other areas of the clip. (This effect is only available in Expert View.)

For example, with the **Effects Mask**, you can define a rectangular area any place in your video frame and apply the **Black & White** effect to it. The area within the defined rectangle will be black & white while everything in the video frame outside this rectangle will remain in color.

To create an **Effects Mask**:

1   **Right-click** on a clip on your timeline and, from the **Clip** sub-menu, select **Effects Mask** and then **Apply**, as illustrated above.

    A duplicate of your clip will appear on the Video 2 track and a rectangle, with four active corner handles, will appear in your **Monitor.**

2   Click and drag the corner handles to define the mask area.

    This area can be moved and re-shaped later, if you'd like.

3   Click on the **Effects** button on the **Action Bar,** then select and apply an effect to the clip on Video 2 (or simply drag it onto the **Monitor**).

    The effect will be applied only to the area defined by the rectangular mask.

To fine tune the effect, select the clip(s) (they'll be grouped, and when you select one, you'll select both) and open the **Applied Properties** panel, as described in **Chapter 28, Adjust Applied Effects**.

Adjust your added effect as described in **Adjust an effect or property** on page 368.

- To re-edit the position and shape of the **Effects Mask**, **right-click** again on the clip on your timeline and select **Effects Mask** then **Edit** from the context menu. The corner handles will again become active and you will be able to drag them, or the mask box, to any new position on the **Monitor** display.

- To remove the **Effects Mask**, **right-click** on the clip on your timeline and select **Effects Mask** then **Remove**. The duplicate clip will be removed from the Video 2 track and any effects you've added will be applied to the entire original clip.

   The effect(s) can then be removed from the original clip by **right-clicking** on the clip and selecting the **Remove Effects** option.

Close Up: The Three-Way Color Corrector

Premiere Elements includes exciting, professional-style effects for correcting and enhancing the colors in your videos (located in the **Color Correction** category of **Effects**).

One of the most advanced is the **Three-Way Color Corrector**. Modeled after color correctors in professional video editing software, this effect allows you to adjust the hue, saturation and lightness for your video's individual **Shadows (Blacks)**, **Midtones (Grays)** and **Highlights (Whites)**.

To adjust the effect's levels, open the **Applied Effects** panel (as discussed in **Chapter 28**).

Locate the **Color Corrector** listing on the **Applied Effects** panel. Under each of the effect's three tonal levels, you will find a color wheel.

To adjust that tonal level's hue and lightness, drag the center circle point around within the color wheel. To adjust the hue's saturation, move the slider below the wheel.

To see which areas of your video image are being affected with each adjustment, check the **Preview Impact Area** checkbox.

For best results, we recommend you adjust **Shadows (Blacks)** first, then **Highlights (Whites)**, then **Midtones (Grays)**.

Close-Up: Chroma Key

Whether you're aware of it or not, you've encountered **Chroma Key** (and its variations in **Green Screen** and **Blue Screen**) countless times.

Every time you've watched a televised weather report – the weather person apparently standing in front of satellite video and moving maps – you've actually seen a **Chroma Key** effect. That weather person is, in reality, standing in front of a plain green screen, electronics removing this green background and replacing it with the weather graphics for the broadcast.

Place your foreground clip on the Video 2.

Place your new background on the Video 1 track, directly below the Video 2 clip.

Chroma Key

Apply the Chroma Key effect to the clip on Video 2.

Virtually every movie that includes scenes of live actors interacting with special effects is using some form of **Chroma Key** – as those actors, like the weather person, perform in front of a green or blue background, which is later swapped out with some new background or effect.

Creating the effect is fairly simple. And once you understand how it works (and maybe how to combine it with keyframed motion), you'll be able to create many of these same big-screen Hollywood effects at home. **(Sadly, this effect is not available on the Mac version of the program. However, the Videomerge effect [page 358] serves nearly the same function.)**

Here's how it works: You shoot your subject standing in front of an evenly-colored screen – usually bright green or blue (colors that are not present in human skin tones). This clip is placed on an upper video track. Your new background is placed on a lower video track, directly below it on your timeline.

The **Chroma Key** effect is then applied to the clip on the upper track and its "key" color is set to the color of the background. **Chroma Key** then renders that "key" color transparent, revealing through it the video on the track below – making it appear that your subject is standing in front of whatever video you've placed on the lower video track!

The **Chroma Key** effect actually appears in a couple of forms in the **Keying** category of Premiere Elements' **Effects**. Also known as the **Blue Screen Key** and the **Green Screen Key**, though the function of the effect is essentially the same – a designated color, or range of colors, on a clip is made transparent. The **Green Screen** and **Blue Screen Keys** are merely preset to the two most commonly used "key" colors.

To create a **Chroma Key** effect, you'll need two things: A video clip that has been shot with a subject standing in front of an evenly-colored, evenly-lit green or blue background and a second clip with a background you'd like to swap in.

By the way, you can only effectively do a **Chroma Key** effect in Expert View, because it requires two video tracks, as shown in the illustration.

Continued on facing page

Chroma Key (continued)

1   Place the video you shot in front of a green or blue screen (we'll call it your **Key Clip**) on the Video 2 track, as illustrated on the facing page.

Place the video or still of the background you want to swap in on the Video 1 track, directly below the **Key Clip**.

2   Apply the **Chroma Key** effect to your **Key Clip.**

3   With the **Key Clip** selected on your timeline, click the **Applied Effects** button to open the **Applied Effects** panel.

4   In the **Applied Effects** panel, click the **Chroma Key** listing to open its properties, as illustrated.

5   On the **Applied Effects** panel, click to select the little **eye dropper** icon next to the color swatch (technically called the **Color Sampler**). Your cursor will become an **eye dropper.**

Use this eyedropper to click on the green or blue colored background in your **Key Clip** in the **Monitor**.

On the Applied Effects panel, locate the Chroma Key effect listing. Click to select the Sampler (eye dropper) and use it to sample the green background on the clip in your Monitor. It will become transparent – revealing the new background on Video 1.

6   Once you've selected your **key color**, most of the **Key Clip**'s background will become transparent, revealing the background clip you've placed on Video 1.

You'll likely need to do some fine-tuning with the sliders in the **Chroma Key** properties to remove the **Key Clip**'s background completely and smooth the edges between the keyed area and the subject in the foreground.

One very effective way to fine-tune your **Chroma Key** is to check the **Mask Only** option in the **Chroma Key** properties.

This will display your keyed foreground as a white silhouette so that you can focus on removing the keyed area while maintaining the integrity of your foreground subject.

It's usually best to adjust only the **Similarity** and **Blend** levels in **Mask Only** mode. Once you've got these properties adjusted as well as possible, uncheck the **Mask Only** box to return to regular view before adjusting the other properties.

You may also find that the **Green Screen Key, Blue Screen Key** or even **Videomerge** (page 358) will work more effectively for your particular needs or situation than the **Chroma Key** effect.

Don't be afraid to experiment and see which **Keying** effect works best for your situation!

Close-up: Videomerge

As with **Chroma Key**, **Videomerge** works by making areas on a clip transparent – and it tends to do this fairly automatically.

You'll find access to the **Videomerge** effect in several places throughout the program:

Videomerge can be applied by right-clicking on the clip on your timeline.

- **When you drag a potential "key" clip to your timeline** – If you drag to your timeline a clip that includes a flat, evenly-colored background, the program will launch a pop-up panel asking if you'd like **Videomerge** to be applied to the clip.

- **On the Effects panel** – Like **Chroma Key**, **Videomerge** can be applied to a clip by dragging the effect from the **Effects** panel (from the **Videomerge** category) onto a clip.

- **Right-click on a clip** – **Right-click** on any clip on the timeline, in the **Clip** sub-menu, you'll find the option to **Apply Videomerge**.

- **On the Monitor** – If you drag a clip onto the **Monitor** while holding down the **Shift** key, the pop-up menu will offer you the option of adding the clip to the track directly above the currently-displayed video clip and applying the **Videomerge** effect to it.

The settings for Videomerge are much simpler than those for Chroma Key.

Once applied to a clip, the **Videomerge** effect has a greatly simplified "key" adjustment tool.

Click the **Applied Effects** tab on the right side of the interface to open the **Applied Effects** panel for the clip. Click on the **Videomerge** listing to open its settings control panel.

The **Videomerge** effect's control panel includes only a few simple adjustments:

- An **eyedropper** for designating the color to be keyed. (Check the **Select Color** box to use the eyedropper to sample your clip's background color on the **Monitor**.)

- A **drop-down Preset list** for controlling how detailed the **Videomerge** key is.

- A **Tolerance** slider for setting the range of colors to be keyed.

- The option to **Invert Selection**, which makes the clip transparent *except for* the designated key area.

In our experience, **Videomerge** is easy to use and surprisingly effective. In many situations, it's a great alternative to the **Chroma Key, Blue Screen** and **Green Screen Key** effects.

And, as the Mac version of the program does not include **Chroma Key, Green Screen Key** or **Blue Screen Key**, it is the only way to create this type of effect on the OSX platform.

Preset Effects

Although they appear as a separate category of effects on the **Effects** panel, **Presets** are, actually, effects to which settings have already been applied. Some of these presets change the size or texture of your video clip, or create a **Picture-in-Picture** effect. Others include animated effects so that your video image moves or changes size or an effect's settings change over the course of the clip. (For more information on motion paths and animated effects, see the **Chapter 29, Keyframing**.)

Presets are represented as thumbnails on the panel and, if you hover your mouse over those that are animated, a preview of the animation will play.

Once you apply a **Preset** to a video clip, you can open the clip's **Applied Effects** panel and customize the settings or animations. (For information on making these adjustments, see **Adjust an effects or property** on page 368.)

The Preset category includes hundreds of pre-set up effects and effect animations in a dozen sub-categories.

To apply a preset effect to a clip, just drag the preset from the **Presets** panel to your clip on the timeline or onto the **Monitor** panel.

The nearly 275 **Presets** fall into a number of categories.

Bevel Edges. These presets create the illusion of a raised edge along the sides of your video clip.

Blurs. Animated **Blur** presets go from blurry to clear or clear to blurry, and can be applied to the beginning or end of a clip.

When using multi-track editing (See **Use L-Cuts, J-Cuts and multiple tracks** on page 276 of **Chapter 21, Edit Your Video in Expert View**), you can use these keyframed blurs as transitions between video tracks.

Color Effects. These presets can be used to tint your clip or to increase the color saturation.

Presets are pre-set Effects, often with keyframed motion.

Applying a Picture-In-Picture preset to a clip on Video 2 is a quick and easy way to create a Picture-in-Picture composite of the clips on Video 1 and Video 2.

Drop Shadows. These presets reduce your clip's scale and create a shadow effect so that your clip appears to be floating – an effect that's most effective when applied to a clip on the Video 2 track, casting a shadow over a clip on the Video 1 track.

Some of these presets use motion paths so that the shadow moves around over the course of your clip.

Horizontal Image Pans, Horizontal Image Zooms, Vertical Image Pans, Vertical Image Zooms. These presets are pre-programmed motion paths for panning and zooming around your photos – their names describe which size photo they are preset to pan or zoom across.

They'll do the job in a pinch, but you'll have much more control over the process if you use keyframing to create your own motion paths, as explained in **Chapter 29, Keyframing**.

The biggest challenge to using these preset pans and zooms is that they are designed for specific sizes of photos (as indicated in each preset's name). If the photo you are panning and zooming around is smaller than the effect, for instance, the effect may pan right off the edge of your photo!

With **keyframing** – and even the **Pan & Zoom Tool** (page 296) – you have the ability to control *precisely* how your motion path behaves.

Mosaics. These animated presets go to or from a mosaic pattern and can be applied to the beginning or end of your clip.

Picture-in-Picture (PiP). The PiP presets, when applied to a clip on the Video 2 track with another clip on the Video 1 track under it, automatically reduce the scale of the clip on the Video 2 track and reposition it in the video frame, such that both it and the clip under it are on screen at the same time (as illustrated above).

Create a custom preset

You can easily create your own presets, saving your custom effects settings, animations or motion paths for future use.

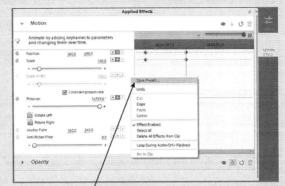

To create a custom preset, **right-click** on the effect it represents in your clip's **Applied Effects** panel and select the **Save Preset** option, as illustrated above.

Once you've created settings for an effect or created a keyframed effect or motion path, you can save it as a custom preset effect by right-clicking on it (Ctrl-clicking on a Mac) in the Applied Effects panel and selecting the option to Save Preset.

Once you have saved the preset, it will be available in the **My Presets** category on the **Effects** panel.

When you Save Preset, you can name it, set it to apply to the beginning or end of a clip and give it a description.

Applying a custom preset to a clip is just like applying a default preset.

Click to select the clip on your timeline and then drag the preset onto it from the **My Presets** category on the **Effects** panel.

Once saved, your preset will appear in My Presets in the Effects panel for all of your Premiere Elements projects.

Some **Picture-in-picture** presets will even add motion, changing the scale or position of **PiP** over the course of the clip – sometimes even incorporating an elaborate animation effect, such as spinning.

Solarizes. These animated presets go to or from a bright **Solarize** effect, and can be applied to the beginning or end of a clip.

Twirls. These animated twirling effects can be applied to the beginning or end of a clip.

Audio effects

Premiere Elements includes 19 effects in its **Audio Effects** category. (The Mac version includes a slightly reduced set, as discussed on page 420.)

These effects are designed for adding special effects to your audio files or for filtering the sounds in your movie. (More basic audio effects, such as **Channel Volume**, **Bass** and **Treble** are found on the **Adjustments** panel, as described on page 317.)

A number of these effects (**DeNoiser, Highpass, Lowpass** and **Notch**) are filters for removing sounds at certain frequencies.

The **DeNoiser** effect reduces noise in your audio clip. The **DeNoiser** is primarily designed to clean up tape hiss that may have crept into your audio.

Dynamics is a processor for cleaning and "sweetening" your movie's sound.

The **Dynamics** effect can be used to compress the sound of your audio by reducing the difference between the highest and lowest levels in a clip. **Dynamics** also lets you "sweeten" the sound by removing some background noise, reducing distortion or otherwise balancing the dynamic range. Well tuned dynamics can give your video a richer, more professional, more big-screen movie-like sound. Premiere Elements also includes six audio enhancement effects from NewBlue – high-end, professional-style tools for reducing noise and sweetening your audio: **NewBlue Audio Polish, NewBlue Auto Mute, NewBlue Cleaner, NewBlue Hum Remover, NewBlue Noise Fader** and **NewBlue Noise Reducer**.

Fill Left with Right and **Fill Right with Left** are very helpful effects for those times when you have an audio clip with audio on only one of your stereo channels (as when you record with a monaural microphone). Applying **Fill Right with Left** or **Fill Left with Right** to the clip takes the mono audio from one channel and uses it for both the right and left stereo channels.

Delay and **Reverb** create echo effects.

And just for fun, there's the **PitchShifter**, which changes the pitch of an audio track, usually in very unnatural and often comic ways, as indicated by some of the names of some of its presets: **Female Becomes Secret Agent, Cartoon Mouse, Boo!, Sore Throat, A Third Higher, Breathless, Slightly Detuned, A Quint Up** and **A Quint Down.**

As with video effects, the intensity or other settings for your audio effects can be applied constantly, over the entire duration of a clip, or variably, using keyframes – adding an echo to one portion of a clip but not another, for instance.

For more information on changing settings for effects, see **Adjust an effect or property** on page 368 of **Chapter 28, Adjust Applied Effects.**

For information on keyframing effects to specific settings at specific points in your movie, see **Chapter 29, Keyframing.**

Many effects can be set using adjustment controls or by selecting a preset from the drop-down menu

Cool Tricks & Hot Tips for Adobe Premiere Elements

There is practically no limit to the special video and audio effects you can create with Premiere Elements.

If you'd like to learn some advanced tricks – like creating explosions in the sky or making a person appear to confront his identical twin, making your photos look three-dimensional or creating amazing titling effects – check out our *Cool Tricks & Hot Tips for Adobe Premiere Elements 11*. (And, yes, it also works with versions 12, 13 and 14, of course).

Our *Cool Tricks & Hot Tips for Adobe Premiere Elements 14* is in production now and should be available in February of 2016.

Full of bright, colorful illustrations and step-by-step instructions for creating 50 very cool special effects, with dozens of helpful "Hot Tips" thrown in for good measure, it's a book that will show you the amazing potential of this simple, inexpensive program.

The book is available through major online bookstores, like Amazon.com, as well as at the Muvipix.com store.

For more information as well as examples of some of the effects you'll learn to create, see Muvipix.com/cooltricks11.php.

Opening the Applied Effects Panel

Default Clip Properties

Adjusting Effects

Copying Effect Attributes

Chapter 28

Adjust Applied Effects

Customizing your effects' settings

The Applied Effects panel is second
only to the timeline as the most
powerful and important workspace
in Premiere Elements.

The timeline may be where you
assemble, trim and order your clips,
but the Applied Effects panel is
where you make the movie magic
happen!

It's where the effects are customized
and sometimes even animated.
It's where motion paths and many
special effects are created.

Once an effect has been applied to a clip on your timeline, the settings for that effect can be adjusted in the Applied Effects panel.

After you've applied a video or audio effect to a clip on your timeline, you'll want to tweak its settings to customize how it affects your clip.

This customization is done in the **Applied Effects** panel.

The **Applied Effects** panel will list all of the effects added to your clips (as well as a couple of default properties, as discussed on the facing page). These effects and properties each include individual settings for customizing the way the effect behaves.

These custom settings can be made overall, affecting the look or sound of an entire clip, or they can be keyframed, creating an animated effect.

Keyframing is the process of creating motion paths or effects that change settings over time (such as a **Crop** effect in which the cropped area changes shape or a **Ripple** effect that shows actual, moving ripples across your clip). For a more detailed discussion of created animated effects, see **Chapter 29, Keyframing**.

Open the Applied Effects panel

Click to select a clip on your timeline and then click on the **Applied Effects** tab on the right side of the program's interface, as illustrated above.

The **Applied Effects** panel will display a list of any effects applied to your selected clip as well as a couple of default video properties, as illustrated at the top of the facing page.

To access the individual settings for any applied effect, click on that effect's listing.

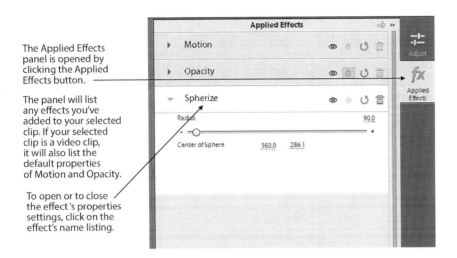

The Applied Effects panel is opened by clicking the Applied Effects button.

The panel will list any effects you've added to your selected clip. If your selected clip is a video clip, it will also list the default properties of Motion and Opacity.

To open or to close the effect's properties settings, click on the effect's name listing.

Clip effects and properties

The **Applied Effects** panel lists any effects you've added to a selected audio or video clip.

In addition, there are two default properties that will appear on this panel for every video clip – **Motion** and **Opacity**.

Click on the **Motion** or **Opacity** listing to open that property's individual settings, illustrated below right.

> **Motion.** Includes individual settings for **Position, Scale** and **Rotation** – the settings used to keyframe pan & zoom motion paths over photos. (See **Chapter 29, Keyframing** for detailed information on how to create motion paths using these properties.)
>
> > **Position** is the location of a clip in your video frame, based on its center point, measured in pixels. For a 720x480 video frame, default center is 360, 240. For a 1920x1080 frame, default center is 960, 540.
> >
> > **Scale** is the size of your clip, listed as a percentage, 100 being default.
> >
> > **Rotation** is a measure of degrees of angle imposed on your video image.
> >
> > The settings for a clip's **Motion** properties can be changed in this panel or, more intuitively, by clicking on the video image in the **Monitor** panel and dragging it or its corner angles to change its position, resize the clip or rotate it (as discussed on page 368).

Opacity. Opacity is the transparency level of a clip. (Well, technically "opacity" is the *non*-transparency level of a clip.)

A **Fade In** or **Fade Out** transition is, technically, a function of the clip's **Opacity** property. Because of that, a **Fade In** or **Fade Out** can be added to a selected video clip by selecting the option here in the panel as well as by selecting the option from the **right-click** menu, as discussed on page 274. (A **Fade In** or **Fade Out** uses **Opacity** keyframed animation to bring the clip from transparency/black to 100% opaque or vice versa.)

The **Opacity** property settings also include an option for setting the clip's **Blend Mode. Blend Modes** are a bit beyond the scope of this book, but basically they're a high-level way of setting how a selected clip reacts with the video tracks below it on your timeline. In the vast majority of your work, you'll likely leave it set to **Normal**. But if you'd like to explore this advanced "bonus" tool Adobe has included, you can place a video on a track below your selected video and experiment with the interesting effects the different **Blend Modes** produce.

Many effects can be added to a single clip, and you can even add multiple instances of the *same* effect to increase its intensity. For instance, several **Channel Volume** effects can be added to the same clip, each adjusted to full volume, to raise the sound level of a clip several times.

Adjust an effect or property

Once you've opened the **Applied Effects** panel for a clip, you'll see a list of all of the effects added to that clip as well as the default properties of **Motion** and **Opacity,** as applicable.

To open up the individual settings for an effect listed in the panel, click on the effect's listing.

A few effects, such as the **Black & White** effect, have no settings at all. They are either on or off.

Some effects (such as **Lightning**) offer dozens of settings for customizing the effect. Others (such as **Posterize**) may offer only a few – or even a single "intensity adjustment" slider.

A number of effects (**Spherize**, for instance), when first applied to a clip, may not show a significant change at their default settings. You need to adjust the effect's settings in the **Applied Effects** panel to see any real change.

There are always several ways to adjust the settings for an effect.

Numbers – The numbers that represent an effect can, depending on the effect, represent the effect's **Position** (measured in pixels across the frame), percentage (as in **Opacity**) or intensity. To change a number, click on it and type in a new amount.

Adjusting Applied Effects

Effects settings can be adjusted by moving the sliders or by typing over the numbers.

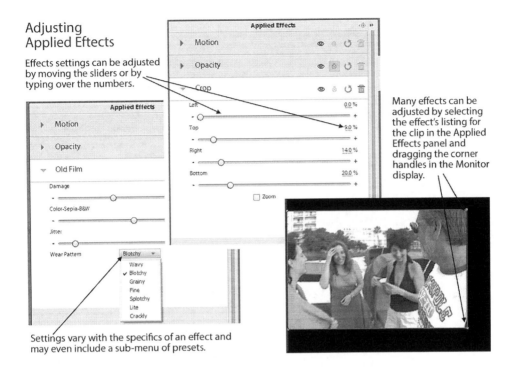

Many effects can be adjusted by selecting the effect's listing for the clip in the Applied Effects panel and dragging the corner handles in the Monitor display.

Settings vary with the specifics of an effect and may even include a sub-menu of presets.

Alternatively, you can click and drag right and left over a number ("scrubbing" its value) to increase or decrease its level.

Sliders – The intensity or percentage settings for a large number of effects settings can be increased and decreased by moving its sliders back and forth.

On the Monitor – For a number of effects, the most intuitive way to change the effect's settings is to click and drag right on the video displayed in the **Monitor**.

When the effect's listing is selected in the **Applied Effects** panel, a position marker or corner handles will appear on the clip in the **Monitor**, as illustrated above. You can then click on this marker or corner handle and drag them into your desired positions.

For effects that involve motion (such as repositioning, rotating or resizing the video image) dragging a corner handle in the **Monitor** will move, rotate or resize the image.

For effects that involve shaping or sizing (such as scaling, cropping or using one of the garbage mattes) dragging the corner handles will reshape the image or affected area.

Once you change your effect's settings, the changes will be immediately displayed in your **Monitor** panel. (If they're not, it's because the **CTI** playhead isn't positioned over the clip you're adjusting on your timeline.)

Disable or remove an effect

Once you've adjusted the settings for an effect, you can do a before-and-after comparison by temporarily turning off – or disabling – the effect.

Effect enabled

Effect disabled

To temporarily turn off the effect, click on the eyeball icon to the right of the effect listing in the **Applied Effects** panel.

When you disable the effect, the eyeball icon will appear with a slash through it, and the effect's change on your video image will disappear.

To re-enable the effect, click on the same spot. The eyeball icon will return and the effect will once again be applied to your clip.

To remove an effect from a clip, click on the trashcan icon on the right end of the effect's listing. (The **Motion** and **Opacity** properties can not be removed.)

To remove all effects and adjustments from a clip, **right-click** on the clip on your timeline and select **Remove Effects/All Effects**.

The exception is the **Lightning** effect, which is so intensive and erratic that you'll need to play back the clip to see how your adjusted settings have affected the clip.

Types of effects settings

Because effects change your clips in different ways (some that shift colors, some that create transparency [see **Chroma Key** and **Videomerge** in **Chapter 27, Add Audio and Video Effects**], some that reshape or distort your video image), each effect has its own unique settings.

Some settings increase the intensity of an effect. Some add optional elements to the effect. Other settings, depending on the effect, may shift color or define which areas on your video image are affected.

The **Crop** effect is an example. The settings for the crop effect define the percentage of the video image that will be cropped from each side. Dragging a slider representing any side will crop away that side of the clip.

Additionally, an effect's settings can be set to vary as the clip plays, creating an animated change, as illustrated on page 379.

- The **Basic 3D** effect, for instance, can be keyframed to create the illusion that your video image is tumbling back into space.
- The **Crop** effect can be animated using keyframes so that the amount of the video image that is cut away changes, opening or closing the cropped area over the course of the clip.

- **Fast Blur** and **Gaussian Blur** can be set to blur and then come back into focus.

For more information on how to create these types of motion paths and animated effects, see **Chapter 29, Keyframing** .

Save a custom Preset

Once you've adjusted, or even keyframed an effect or property, you can save its custom settings as a **Preset** so that you can use it on another clip at any time, even in another project.

To save your customized effect or keyframed animation as a **Preset**, **right-click** on the effect's listing in the **Applied Effects** panel and select **Save Preset...**

An option screen will then prompt you to name your preset, as illustrated below.

If your effect includes an animation, the screen will ask you if you'd like to set this animation to be applied to the beginning or end of the clip it is applied to.

You can also include a description of the effect, if you'd like.

Click **OK** to save the **Preset**.

The new **Preset** will be available in the **My Presets** category on the **Effects** panel. You can then apply this preset to a clip just as you would apply any effects, by selecting the clip on your timeline and dragging your **Preset** onto it.

When a **Preset** is applied to a clip, it adds the effect, your settings and any animations you included with it.

Once you've created settings for an effect or created a keyframed effect or motion path, you can save it as a custom preset effect by right-clicking on it in the Applied Effects panel and selecting the option to Save Preset.

Once saved, your preset will appear in My Presets in the Effects panel for all of your Premiere Elements projects.

When you Save Preset, you can name it, set it to apply to the beginning or end of a clip and give it a description.

Paste Effects and Adjustments

If you've customized the settings for an effect – or created a keyframed animation – for one clip, you can easily apply it to another or even several other clips with just a few clicks using the **Paste Effects and Adjustments** feature.

Right-click on a clip on your timeline to which you've added your effect or keyframes and select **Copy** from the context menu.

Then select another clip – or even a group of clips – **right-click** on this group of clips and select **Paste Effects and Adjustments**.

All of the original clip's effects, adjustments and keyframed actions will automatically be applied to your selected clips!

Chapter 29

Keyframing
Animating effects and creating motion paths

Keyframing is the system that Premiere Elements uses to create motion paths, and to create and control effects that animate or change their settings over time.

With keyframing, you can control the level of an effect or the scale and/or position of a clip at precise points throughout the duration of the clip.

You can raise and lower the audio level at precise points; you can create panning and zooming around a photo; you can even animate, at precise points in any clip, the intensity or movement of a video or audio effect.

The principle is a simple one: You indicate which two or more points (**keyframes**) on your clip represent settings for a position, scale, effect or level of an effect and the program automatically generates the transitional animation between them. (Note that keyframing in the **Applied Effects** panel is only available in Expert View.)

You can, for instance, set **Scale** and **Position** settings in the **Motion** property to create one keyframe point displaying a close-up of one corner of a still photo, and then set the **Scale** and **Position** settings of a second keyframe point so that the entire photo is displayed. Premiere Elements will automatically create the smooth animation between those two positions, seeming to zoom out from the corner to a view of the entire picture.

With Premiere Elements, you can add any number of keyframes to a clip, creating as much motion or as many variations in your effects' settings as you'd like.

But the real power of this tool is in how easy it is to revise and adjust those positions and settings, giving you, the user, the ability to fine tune your motion path or animation until it is precisely the effect you want to achieve.

Although there are other workspaces in which you can create and edit keyframes (See **Adjust the audio levels at specific points in your video**, on page 383), most of your high level keyframing animation will likely be done on the **Applied Effects** or the **Adjustments** panel.

The Pan and Zoom Tool

In addition to its traditional keyframing workspace, Premiere Elements includes a very intuitive workspace for creating pan and zoom motion paths over your photos, accessible by way of the **Tools** button on the **Action Bar**.

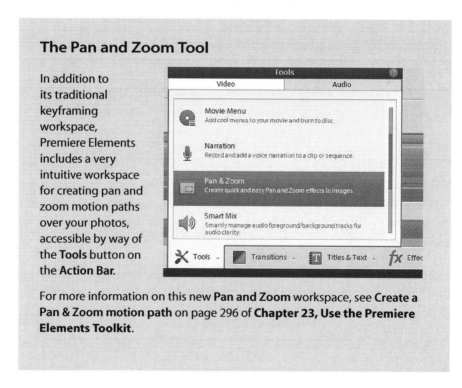

For more information on this new **Pan and Zoom** workspace, see **Create a Pan & Zoom motion path** on page 296 of **Chapter 23, Use the Premiere Elements Toolkit.**

Keyframing is about creating animated effects or motion paths using points representing different position or effect settings.

Premiere Elements creates a smooth, animated transition between these "keyframes."

A motion path between Position and Scale settings on a photograph is called a motion path or a Pan & Zoom – or, commonly, a Ken Burns effect.

Keyframing vs. adjusting an effect's settings overall

Until you begin a keyframing session (by clicking the **Toggle Animation** button, as described below), any positioning, scaling or settings you make for an effect or property in the **Applied Effects** panel will apply to your *entire* clip.

In other words, if you change the **Scale** to 50% in the **Motion** properties, your entire clip will appear at 50% of its size.

 However, once you click **Toggle Animation** (the little stopwatch icon) and turn on keyframing, every change to the effect or property you make will generate a **keyframe point** at the position of the **CTI** (Current Time Indicator) on your timeline.

It becomes a sort of "waypoint" for your effect or motion path.

When you create another keyframe point later in the clip and apply new settings to the effect or property, the program will create a path of motion, animation or transition between the two points.

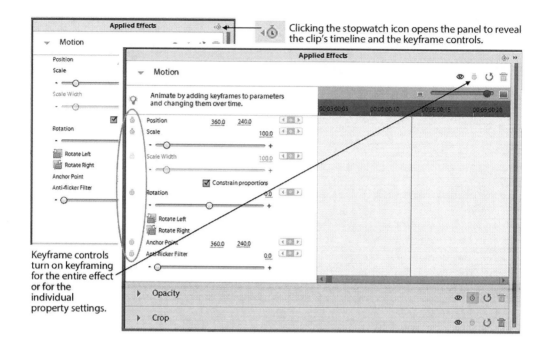

Clicking the stopwatch icon opens the panel to reveal the clip's timeline and the keyframe controls.

Keyframe controls turn on keyframing for the entire effect or for the individual property settings.

Open a keyframing session

When you first open the **Applied Effects** panel for a clip, the keyframing workspace is hidden.

To reveal this workspace (the **keyframing timeline**), click on the **Show Keyframes** button (the stopwatch icon with the arrow pointing left) in the upper right of the panel, as illustrated above. (Expert View only.)

The **keyframing timeline**, which appears to the right of your settings, is your workspace for creating, adjusting and editing your keyframes.

The time positions on this timeline represent positions, in time, on the clip itself. In fact, if you're editing in timeline mode, you'll notice that, as you move the **CTI** on the **keyframing timeline,** the **CTI** on your project's main timeline will move in sync with it.

Create a simple motion path using keyframes

To demonstrate how to use keyframes, we'll create a simple motion path – a pan and zoom across a photo.

1   With the **Applied Effects** panel open and a still photo clip selected on your timeline, click on the **Motion** property listing to reveal the settings for **Motion – Position, Scale, Rotation** and **Anchor Point.**

Click the stopwatch to toggle animation and begin keyframing.

Keyframes will automatically be created when you toggle the animation on.

Change the position of the CTI on the timeline and then change the settings for your effect. New keyframes will automatically be created representing these new settings.

CTI (Current Time Indicator).

Keyframes.

Toggle Animation (turns keyframing on and off).

2   Turn on keyframing for the **Motion** property by clicking on the **Toggle Animation** button (the stopwatch at the top right end of the **Motion** property listing, as illustrated above).

When you click the **Toggle Animation** button, a keyframe point – or set of keyframe points – will automatically be created at the position of the **CTI** representing the current settings for that effect.

3   Move the **CTI** to a new position, a few seconds to the right, on the clip's **keyframing timeline.** Then change the **Position** and **Scale** settings, by changing the setting numbers or by clicking on the clip in the **Monitor** panel and either dragging the screen image to a new position or dragging on its corner handles to resize it.

As you change the settings at this new **CTI** position, new keyframe points will automatically be generated on the **keyframing timeline.** (You can also manually create new keyframes by clicking on the diamond-shaped **Make Keyframe** buttons to the right of each effect's setting, as detailed on the following page.)

You have just created a simple motion path!

If you play back the clip, you will see how the program creates an animated movement between your two sets of keyframe points, using your keyframed settings to define the path.

A Simple Motion Path Created with Keyframes

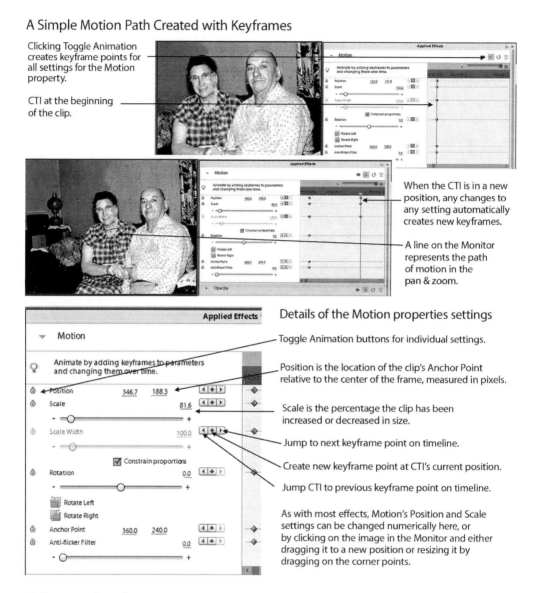

Clicking Toggle Animation creates keyframe points for all settings for the Motion property.

CTI at the beginning of the clip.

When the CTI is in a new position, any changes to any setting automatically creates new keyframes.

A line on the Monitor represents the path of motion in the pan & zoom.

Details of the Motion properties settings

Toggle Animation buttons for individual settings.

Position is the location of the clip's Anchor Point relative to the center of the frame, measured in pixels.

Scale is the percentage the clip has been increased or decreased in size.

Jump to next keyframe point on timeline.

Create new keyframe point at CTI's current position.

Jump CTI to previous keyframe point on timeline.

As with most effects, Motion's Position and Scale settings can be changed numerically here, or by clicking on the image in the Monitor and either dragging it to a new position or resizing it by dragging on the corner points.

Edit your keyframes

The beauty of the keyframing tool is that any motion path or effects animation you create with it is infinitely adjustable.

By dragging the keyframe points closer together or further apart on the **keyframing timeline**, you can control the speed at which the motion occurs. (The closer the keyframes are to each other, the faster the animation.)

You can add more keyframe points and/or delete the ones you don't want. And, if you really want to go deep, **right-clicking** on any keyframe point accesses you the option to **interpolate** the animation movement or use **Bezier** control handles to change the shape of the motion path or vary the speed of the motion.

Many applications for keyframing

Keyframing has many applications in Premiere Elements. (It's also a feature of Premiere Pro, After Effects and virtually every professional video editing system.) It can turn pretty much any effect into an animation. And it can be used to vary audio effects and levels as well as video.

Using Keyframes to create animated effects

Using the Basic 3D effect with keyframes to animate screen image to spin in 3D.

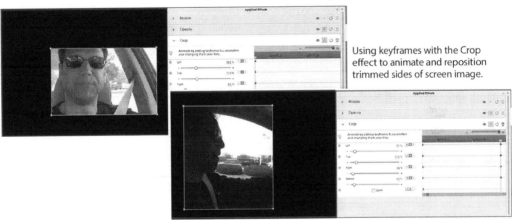

Using keyframes with the Crop effect to animate and reposition trimmed sides of screen image.

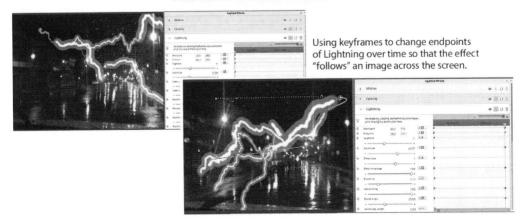

Using keyframes to change endpoints of Lightning over time so that the effect "follows" an image across the screen.

The Adjustment panel (Chapter 10) also includes a keyframe control timeline so you can, for instance, keyframe your Saturation level to make your video shift from color to black & white.

Keyframing can be used to control audio volume levels at precise points in your video project. (For more on controlling audio levels with keyframes, see **Adjust the audio levels at specific points in your video** on page 383 of **Chapter 30, Mix Your Audio and Add Music**.) You can also keyframe audio and video **Adjustments**, as we show you on page 318.

With keyframing, you can control effects, such as **Crop**, so that the area of your image that's cropped widens, narrows or changes position as the clip plays, as illustrated on page 379.

Or you can very precisely increase or decrease the intensity of an effect on a clip or animate a **Picture-in-Picture** effect. (See **Use L-cuts, J-cuts and multiple tracks** on page 276.)

You can even use keyframes to create an animated 3D movement for your video image using the **Camera View** or **Basic 3D** effect so that your video images seems to tumble head over heels in space.

Indeed, mastering the keyframing tool is the key to getting to the deeper aspects of Premiere Elements (or Adobe After Effects, Premiere Pro and even Apple's Final Cut programs).

It may not seem intuitive at first. But, once you develop a feel for how it works, you'll soon find yourself able to see all kinds of applications for it in creating and refining all manner of visual and audio effects.

For more information on some of the deeper aspects of keyframing and their applications, see my *Steve's Tips* articles "Advanced Keyframing: Editing on the Properties Panel Timeline" and "Advanced Keyframing 2: Keyframing Effects," available for our subscribers on the products page at Muvipix.com.

There is practically no limit to the special video and audio effects you can create with Premiere Elements.

Adjusting Audio Levels with Keyframes

Normalizing Your Audio Gain

Creating Custom Music Tracks with Adobe Scores

The Premiere Elements Sound Effects Library

Detecting Beats in Your Music

Chapter 30

Mix Your Audio and Add Music
Working with sounds and music

Great sound is as important as great visuals in your video project. And Premiere Elements includes a number of tools for adding and enhancing your audio and music files.

Premiere Elements even includes Scores, an amazing tool for creating musical tracks – based on your custom specifications – for your movies!

Additional content

You may notice a little blue flag over the upper right corner of a number of music Scores.

This blue flag indicates that the template or theme is available but has not yet been installed on your computer. When you select this template or theme, the program will automatically download it for you from the Adobe site – a process that should only take a moment or two.

Drama

If you'd like to download all of these templates or Scores at once, right-click on any one and select the Download All option.

Audio View switch.

Tracks can be toggled
open or collapsed for space.   Mute a track.   Solo a track.

Monitor and control master
audio levels.

Your audio is as at least as important to your movie as your video. And Premiere Elements includes a number of powerful tools for creating custom music tracks, monitoring and adjusting your audio levels and mixing the levels of your various audio sources.

Audio View

New to version 14, Premiere Elements includes an **Audio View** workspace, where you can focus on the audio aspects of your production. To switch between **Classic View** and **Audio View**, click the toggle at the top left of the timeline, as illustrated above.

When you're in **Audio View**, you'll be able to monitor the overall audio level for your movie using a **Master** VU meter to the right of the timeline. (To monitor and adjust the audio levels for specific tracks, we recommend you use the **Audio Mixer**, as discussed on page 293.)

It is very important that your audio levels do not peak in the red on your VU meter! Overmodulation can result in poor and distorted audio for your movie.

Collapsed view full view

By default, your audio tracks are collapsed in order to conserve vertical space. To toggle open a track, click the little white triangle on the left side of the track.

In the fully open view, you'll be able to see the waveforms for your clips' audio and adjust the audio levels for each track (as discussed on the facing page).

Solo and Mute an audio track

Muting a track means to temporarily disable its audio. Soloing a track means muting all other tracks so that only the selected "solo" track can be heard.

To **Mute a track,** click on the audio icon on the track header.

To **Solo a track**, click on the headphones button on the audio track.

Clicking the red button on any track allows you to record narration to that track. For more information, see **Add Narration** on page 295 of **Chapter 23, Use the Premiere Elements Toolkit**.

Adjust your audio levels at specific points in your video

In Expert View, with your audio tracks toggled open (see page 271), yellow lines (officially called **Rubber Bands**) running horizontally through your clips represent the clips' volume levels, as illustrated below. Raising or lowering a clip's volume level is as easy as dragging this yellow line up or down. (Also see **Monitor and mix your audio levels** on page 293.)

But what about if you want to raise and lower the audio levels for a clip at specific points?

Say you want to fade your music down for a few seconds so that your narration track can dominate? Or you have a conversation recorded in which one person speaks very quietly and you need to raise the audio level for his part of your clip, while leaving the audio level for the rest of the clip as is?

That's when you use audio keyframes.

Create audio volume keyframes on your timeline

To create **keyframes** for your audio clips:

1   Click to select an audio or audio/video clip on your Expert View timeline and position the **CTI** (Current Time Indicator) over the approximate spot where you want to add a keyframe.

     (A clip must be selected and the **CTI** positioned over it in order to create a keyframe on the timeline.)

2   Click on the little, diamond-shaped **Make Keyframe** button on the track header, left of the video or audio track, as illustrated.

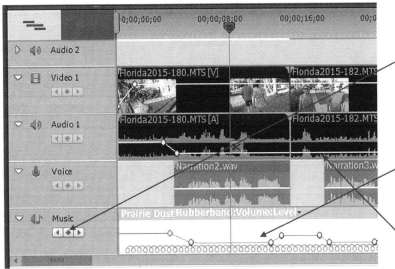

Audio keyframes adjust audio levels at specific points

When a clip is selected (clicked on), audio keyframes can be added with the timeline's Add/Remove Keyframe button.

Keyframes are added at the position of the CTI, but can be dragged to any position.

Dragging the keyframes higher raises the clip's audio level; dragging them lower reduces the audio level.

Dragging the yellow line with no keyframes applied raises or lowers the audio level for the entire clip.

This will create a keyframe point, which will appear as a white dot on your audio clip's **Rubber Band** at the position of the **CTI**.

You can drag this dot to any position on the clip, or change or delete it at any time.

3   Adjust the keyframe point's position to adjust the clip's volume levels.

- Positioning the keyframe higher on the clip increases the audio volume level at that point.
- Lowering it decreases the audio volume level.

In the illustration, the music on the Soundtrack has been temporarily lowered so that the narration can be heard.

You can create as many keyframes as you need, using several to set the audio levels higher for some segments, and lower for other segments, on your clips.

To delete an audio keyframe, **right-click** on the white diamond keyframe point and select **Delete** from the context menu.

Audio **Volume** keyframes can also be created and adjusted in the **Adjustments** panel (as discussed on page 318 of **Chapter 24**).

Normalizing and raising your audio's gain

There's a slight but significant difference between raising your audio's volume and raising it's gain. Volume is the amplification applied to your clip's audio. It makes whatever sound is on the clip louder.

Gain, on the other hand, refers to the level of audio on the clip itself. Raising a clip's gain makes its waveform on your timeline bigger and thicker. And increasing the gain can add a richness and fullness to the increased sound level that raising the volume doesn't. Well, at least to my ears anyway.

The **Normalize** tool is designed to automatically raise whatever sound is on your clip to a good, full level.

To use the **Normalizer, right-click** on your audio clip, select **Clip/Audio Gain** from the right-click menu. On the **Clip Gain** panel that opens, click the **Normalize** button.

If the **Normalize** tool doesn't automatically raise your clip's gain level enough, you can also manually raise the sound level yourself by typing a **db** number in the **Gain** box. I've rescued some very low level audio by applying a **Gain** of 10 db or more to it.

Audio Gain adjusts the strength of the original audio on your clip.

Create custom music clips with Scores

Replacing the old **SmartSound Express Tracks** plug-in, **Scores** is Premiere Elements' built-in tool for creating and customizing your movie's music.

The **Scores tool** creates royalty-free music tracks. That means you can use the music this tool generates in any project – even a professional or work-for-hire project – without concern for rights management. **Scores** are yours to use any way you'd like (short of re-selling the music tracks as your own compositions, of course).

Scores are found under the **Audio** button on the **Action Bar** that runs along the bottom of the program. It includes over 50 musical clips in 7 categories:

Content with a blue banner over the upper right corner will be downloaded when and as you use it.

- **Ambient** – Gentle, subtle music scores that set the mood of a scene by playing quietly in the background.

- **Atmospheric** – Scores designed to less subtly set a scene's mood, from dark to magical.

- **Blues** – Cool, bluesy musical scores.

- **Country** – Rural scores, representing everything from mountain music to traditional country to rockabilly.

- **Rock-Pop** – Upbeat brassy or guitar-based rockers.

- **Urban** – R&B scores with strong rhythms and funky tones.

- **Weddings** – Traditional wedding scores, including the *Canon in D* and *Wedding March*.

You can sample any **Score** by hovering your mouse over the thumbnail on the **Audio** panel until a **Play** button appears, then clicking on it.

Like most additional content in the program, **Scores** are downloaded to the program when you use them in a Premiere Elements project. Scores that have not yet been downloaded to your computer are indicated with a blue banner over the upper right corner, as in the illustration above.

Although the program comes with a wide selection of musical options, the real beauty of **Scores** is that it will generate custom music to fit your specific needs.

In other words, once you've placed a **Score** on your timeline and you've trimmed it to whatever length you need, the program will *re-generate* the **Score** so that, at your custom length, the clip has a natural beginning, middle and end.

When you first add a **Score** to your timeline (and once it's been downloaded to your computer, if necessary), a **Score Property** panel will offer you the option of setting the **Score's** intensity (which you can preview before finalizing) and for automatically setting your clip to trim itself to the length of your movie.

When you add a Score to your timeline, you'll have the options of setting and testing its intensity and of setting it to automatically extend itself to the length of your movie.

Your Score will automatically generate a natural beginning, middle and end for the clip based on the settings you've selected.

When you click **Done**, the program will generate your custom musical track and add it to your timeline. Even after you've created your musical track, you have the option of manually trimming or extending the length of your **Score** clip. The program will automatically re-generate the musical clip based on the length and properties you've selected.

The **Score Properties** panel can be re-opened at any time by **double-clicking** on the music clip on your timeline.

Add Sound Effects to your movie

As a very cool added-value bonus, Premiere Elements comes bundled with a library of over 260 sound effects in 13 categories. These range from ambient sounds, like a **Basketball Game** or **Auto Shop** to weather to science fiction to animal sounds.

It's really a terrific library of high-quality sounds!

You'll find them under the **Audio** button on the **Action Bar.**

The Beat Detect Tool

Adjust settings as needed for your music.

Click to select your musical clip on the timeline, then select Beat Detect from the right-click menu (or the Tools menu at the top of the interface).

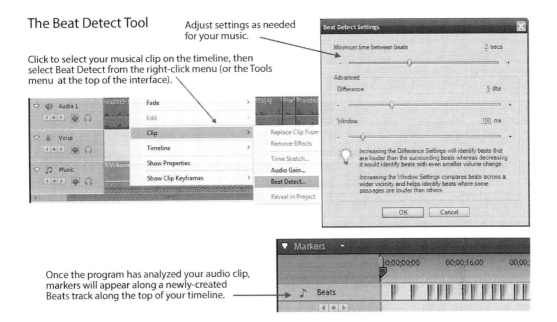

Once the program has analyzed your audio clip, markers will appear along a newly-created Beats track along the top of your timeline.

Detect beats in your music

This cool tool can be used as part of the process of creating a slideshow so that your slides change in rhythm with your music. (Note that the **Beat Detect** tool is only available in Expert View.)

To use the **Beat Detect** tool:

1. Click to select a music clip on your timeline or sceneline.

    When a clip is detected on your timeline, it will be highlighted.

2. Click on the **Tools** menu at the top of the program's interface or **right-click** on the clip and select **Clip**, then **Beat Detect**.

    The **Beat Detect Settings** option screen will open, as illustrated above.

3. Set the sensitivity and limitations of your beat detection.

4. Click **OK**.

The tool will then analyze your music clip and create a series of markers, representing your music clip's rhythm, on a newly-created **Beats** track along the top of the timeline.

Once these markers have been created, you can use them as indicators for the **Create Slideshow** tool in the **Project Assets** panel so that your slides will change in rhythm with the music.

For information on using the **Create Slideshow** tool, see page 265 of **Chapter 20, Explore the Project Assets Panel**.

Additional Audio Tools

Premiere Elements offers several other tools for adding to and mixing your movie's audio, some of which are discussed in greater detail in **Chapter 9, Use the Premiere Elements Toolkit**:

The **Audio Mixer** is a tool for monitoring your movie's audio levels and for mixing your volume levels on the fly, as your movie timeline plays. For more information on using it, see **Mix and monitor your audio levels** on page 293.

Smart Mix will automatically mix your movie's audio, based on the criteria you select. In other words, you can set **Smart Mix** to make narration your foreground audio and your music your background. The program will automatically set the music on your timeline to play at regular volume, then lower the music's volume automatically whenever it encounters a narration clip. For more information on this tool, see **Smart Mix your audio** on page 298.

The **Narration** tool lets you record a narration track right into your movie, even while watching the movie play! For more information on this tool, see **Narration** on page 295.

The **Adjustments** panel includes tools for raising and lowering your clips' **Volume**, adjusting the **Balance** of your stereo channels and raising and lowering the levels of **Bass** and **Treble**. For more information on these tools, see page 317 of **Chapter 24, Make Adjustments to Your Video**.

And, finally, the program includes several great **Audio Effects** for sweetening your audio, reducing noise, adding echo effects and filtering certain frequencies to clean your audio or creating special audio effects. You'll find out all about them on page 362 of **Chapter 27, Add Audio and Video Effects**.

Adobe Premiere Elements

Part VII

Export & Share
Your Videos

Chapter 31

Create Movie Menus
Authoring your DVDs and BluRay discs

Once you've finished your Premiere Elements video project, you'll want to share it in the most attractive package possible.

Premiere Elements includes over 70 templates for creating DVD and BluRay disc menus for your videos. And it includes tools for customizing them in a variety of ways!

Additional content

You may notice a little blue flag over the upper right corner of a number of Movie Menu templates.

This blue flag indicates that the template or theme is available but has not yet been installed on your computer. When you select this template or theme, the program will automatically download it for you from the Adobe site – a process that should only take a moment or two.

If you'd like to download all of these templates at once, right-click on any one and select the Download All option.

Although the DVD and BluRay menu authoring system in Premiere Elements isn't as advanced as it is in many standalone disc menu authoring programs, you can do a surprising amount to personalize your disc menus just by using Premiere Elements' library of disc menu templates and its fairly powerful menu customization features.

Once you've applied and customized your disc menus, you can then create a DVD, AVCHD or BluRay disc using the options under the **Export & Share** tab, as described in **Chapter 32, Export & Share Your Video Projects.**

Add Menu Markers to your movie project

The **Set Menu Marker** tool is a very important part of the DVD and BluRay disc authoring process in Premiere Elements.

The **Menu Markers** you place on your timeline will link to buttons on your disc's main menu and scene menu pages.

To create a **Menu Marker,** position the **CTI** (Current Time Indicator) on your timeline at the approximate position you'd like your marker to appear. (You don't have to be precise. You can drag the marker to a new position later.) Then click **Markers** at the top left of the timeline and, from the drop-down menu, select **Menu Marker**, then **Set Menu Marker**, as illustrated above.

When you select this option, a **Menu Marker** option panel will open. (You can reopen this panel at any time by **double-clicking** on an existing menu marker on your timeline.) This panel allows you to name your marker as well as determine the role the marker will play in your disc.

As indicated by the **Marker Type** drop-down menu (and detailed along the bottom of the panel), there are three different types of **Menu Markers:**

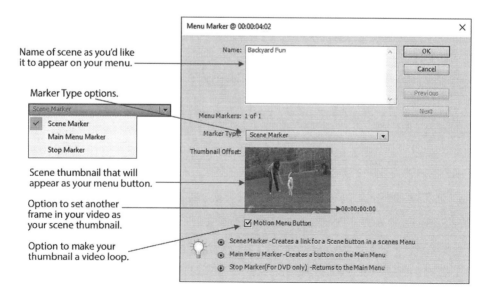

Name of scene as you'd like it to appear on your menu.

Marker Type options.

Scene thumbnail that will appear as your menu button.

Option to set another frame in your video as your scene thumbnail.

Option to make your thumbnail a video loop.

Green **Scene Menu Markers** will be linked to scene buttons on your DVD or BluRay disc's **Scene Menu** page(s).

Blue **Main Menu Markers** will be linked to scene buttons on your DVD or BluRay disc's **Main Menu** page(s).

Red **Stop Markers** stop your movie's playback and return your viewer to your disc's **Main Menu** page. By using these **Stop Markers**, you can create a disc with a number of short movies on it, your viewer returning to the main menu at the end of each.

1   Type a name for your marker in the space provided. This name will automatically appear as the name of the linked button on your disc's main or scene menu.

2   The image from your movie displayed in the **Thumbnail Offset** window is what will appear as your menu button thumbnail on your menu page.

Changing the timecode that appears to the right of this thumbnail – either by typing in new numbers or by clicking and dragging across the numbers – will change which frame from your video is displayed as the button link. (Although changing this thumbnail image will *not* affect the location of the marker itself on your project's timeline.)

3   Checking the **Motion Menu Button** checkbox will cause your button to appear as a short video loop rather than a freeze frame from your video.

Clicking and dragging over the timecode for the Thumbnail Offset numbers changes the thumbnail image that is displayed for the Menu Marker on your disc menu without changing the marker's position.

For more information on how to create and use **Menu Markers**, see my *Steve's Tips* article "DVD Markers," available on the products page at Muvipix.com.

Add Menu Markers automatically

When you select the **Movie Menu** option on the **Tools** pop-up panel on the **Action Bar**, you'll find an additional option, in the lower left corner of the panel, for adding menu markers automatically to your timeline.

If you check this option and click **Settings**, you'll find options to:

- Add menu markers at each scene.
- Designate regular time intervals at which markers will be added; or
- Designate the total number of markers you'd like added to your movie and let the program set them at even paces throughout your movie.

Categories of menus can be browsed through or you can jump to one particular category by clicking the category title bar.

The Movie Menu template panel is launched by selecting the option under the Tools button on the Action Bar.

Once you've selected a template, click Continue.

Add a Movie Menu

After you've added menu markers to your timeline, your next step is to apply a **Movie Menu** template to your movie.

Premiere Elements comes bundled with over 70 standard and hi-def disc templates, in 14 categories, ranging from Entertainment to Travel to Sports to Kids to Birthdays and Weddings – from playful to serious to silly to artistic.

Many of these templates come complete with audio and/or video background loops that add life to your menu pages. These animated templates are indicated with a little media icon on the upper right corner.

Also, many of these templates include a "drop zone," a designated area on the menu page into which you can place a video clip or still. (More about that on page 399.)

Apply a DVD or BluRay movie menu template

To add a Movie Menu template to your project:

1   Click the **Tools** button on the **Action Bar** along the bottom of the interface and select **Movie Menus**.

    The **Movie Menus** templates option panel will open.

2   Select a template.

    The templates are in 14 different categories. You can browse each category by clicking the forward and backward arrows on either side of the **Category** title bar at the top of the panel (which opens to "Entertainment"). Alternatively, you can click on the **Category** title bar and a pop-up menu will list all of the templates categories. Click to select the category you'd like to jump to.

    When you've selected a template, click the **Continue** button at the lower right corner of the panel, as illustrated above.

In the Movie Menus Adjustments workspace, you can customize the way your menu pages and scene buttons look and function.

Click Preview Disc to test drive your menus.

Add a different disc template.

The **Movie Menus Adjustments** workspace will open. The **Main Menu** page of your movie's disc menu will be displayed in the big **Movie Menus Layout** window, and thumbnails of each page of your **Main** and **Scene Menus** will appear along the bottom.

Your movie will always have a **Main Menu**. If you've added scene menu markers, it will also include a **Scene Menu**. The program will add as many extra pages as necessary to accommodate all of your scene and main menu markers.

Clicking on any of the thumbnail menu pages along the bottom of the preview window will bring that menu page up in the **Movie Menus Layout** window so that you can customize its individual elements.

As mentioned in **Add Menu Markers**, on page 392, the names you give to your main and scene menu markers will appear as the names of the scene menu links and main menu links on your disc menus. (To change these names, **double-click** on a scene button, as described at the bottom of page 397.)

To see your menu system in action and test drive the links embedded in it, click the **Preview Disc** button at the top right of the workspace.

An important note about **Preview Disc**: The purpose of the preview is to allow you to see a *representation* of how your menu elements will come together and to allow you to test the navigation buttons.

*It is not meant to be a representation of the **quality** of your final menu template.* And, in fact, you'll probably be a bit disappointed with the quality of the picture onscreen. **Preview** is merely an opportunity for you test your navigation buttons.

So don't panic. Once your project is rendered and encoded as a disc, the quality will be up to DVD or BluRay standards.

Click on the background in Movie Menus Layout window to open the background replacement options.

Click to replace background of menu with your own still or video loop.

Set at which point in the clip to begin video loop.

Click to replace or add your own audio loop.

Set at which point in the clip to begin audio loop.

Menu previews.

Set the duration for your video/audio loop (max of 30 seconds).

Customize your menus

Adobe has made it very easy to customize your menu pages right in this **Movie Menus** workspace. As a matter of fact, once you've applied a template, as described on the previous pages, the **Adjustments** panel will open to the right of the **Movie Menus Layout** panel and will display options for customizing your menu pages and scene buttons, as illustrated above.

Which customization options are available in this panel depends on which elements you have selected on the **Movie Menus Layout** window.

- **If you have the menu background selected** in the **Movie Menus Layout** panel, the **Adjustments** panel will display options for replacing the menu background with a still, video and/or audio clip, as discussed in **Customize a menu background** below.

- **If you have a block of text selected** in the **Movie Menus Layout** panel, the **Adjustments** panel will display options for customizing the text's font, style and color, as discussed on page 398.

- **If you have a menu button selected** in the **Movie Menus Layout** window that includes a thumbnail image, the **Adjustments** panel will display options for replacing or customizing the thumbnail image as well as options for customizing the accompanying text's font, style and color, as discussed on page 397.

Customize a menu background

When you have the menu page background selected in the **Movie Menus Layout** window, the **Adjustments** panel will display options for replacing the background with a still or video, and/or replacing or adding a music or audio clip, as illustrated above.

Some **Movie Menu** templates allow you to replace the entire background of the menu page. (The **Elegant** template, illustrated above, in the **Wedding** category is an example.)

If your template has a **Drop Zone** in it – indicated with an **Add Media Here** emblem – replacing the background will add your video or photo in a way that integrates it with the menu template, as discussed on page 399.

If you're using a video clip as your menu background:

- You can use the **In Point** timecode (either by dragging your mouse across the numbers or by playing to a particular point and then pausing) to set your video loop to begin at a specific point in the clip.

- You can set the **Duration** of the video loop for any length up to 30 seconds.

You can also add or swap in audio or music loops that play as your menus are displayed. Additionally, you can set the **In Point** for your audio clip such that the audio loop begins playing at any point in the song or clip.

To revert back to your menu's default background, music or sound, click on the corresponding **Reset** button.

Above is the same menu seen on the facing page, but with a new background image swapped in.

When a text block is selected in the Layout window, the Adjustment displays options for changing the font, style and text color. (Double-click on a text block to change its content.)

Customize your text

Double-click on a text block or menu button to edit or replace the text.

When you double-click on a text block, you will access an option screen for customizing the text.

When you double-click on a scene link on a menu page, you will re-open the Menu Marker workspace in which you can customize the text, thumbnail or other attributes of the link on the page.

When a scene button or text block is selected, the Adjustments panel will display
options for customizing the text font, style and color as well as for customizing
the button thumbnail with a still or video loop (motion menu).

Customize your text styles

When you click to select a text block in the **Movie Menus Layout** window,
the text customization workspace will display in the **Adjustments** panel.

Using this menu, you can change the font, font size and even color of the
text.

The **Apply to All Text Items** button will apply your current font and text
style to all of the text that appears on this menu page.

Once you've customized the look of your text, you can also customize its
position on the menu page.

Click on the text block or button on the **Movie Menus Layout** window and
drag it to where you'd like it to appear.

Two Main Menu pages customized from the same Movie Menu template.

To add a still or video to a template's Drop Zone, click to select the Drop Zone or background of the template, then click the Video or Still Browse button and browse to your still or video clip.

Drop Zone.

The still or video will be integrated into the menu page's existing graphics.

Add a photo or video clip to a menu page "Drop Zone"

A number of **Movie Menu** templates include a **"Drop Zone"** – a designated area on the template into which you can place your own pictures or videos.

Templates that include **Drop Zones** (and most of them do) will be indicated with the **Add Media Here** graphic.

Adding a still or video file to a **Drop Zone** is essentially the same process as replacing a menu background with a still or video: You select the **Drop Zone** or background in the **Movie Menu** Layout window and then click the **Video or Still Replace** button on the **Adjustments** panel and browse to your clip.

The difference is that, rather than replacing the entire background, your photo or video will be integrated into the existing design of the menu page's graphics, as illustrated above.

A number of templates (the **Entertainment** category's **Art-in-Motion**, and the **Memories** category's **Yearbook** and **Family Memories**, for instance) will drop your still or photos into an existing design so that it appears to be a painting on the wall or a photo in a photo album.

Overlapping scene buttons

If, in the process of arranging your scene buttons on your menu (or, occasionally, if you've added lots of text), your buttons display with a red frame around them, this is an indication that you have two buttons sharing the same space or overlapping.

If you move the buttons apart (or even resize the buttons by dragging in on their corner handles), the red frames should disappear.

Overlapping buttons are not a big deal, if you're playing your disc on a DVD or BluRay player. The player reads each button individually. But, if you play your disc on a computer, overlapping buttons can makes it difficult to select one button or the other since their hyperlinks share the same space. Because of this, **the program will not let you create a DVD, AVCHD or BluRay disc if any scene buttons are overlapping.**

Sharing Your Movie as a Computer File
Sharing Your Movie to a Portable Device
Sharing to a DVD or BluRay Disc
Sharing Your Movie Online

Chapter 32
Export & Share Your Video Projects
Outputting from Premiere Elements 14

Once you've finished your video masterpiece, you're ready to output your video and share it with the world.

There are many ways to output from Premiere Elements, and a surprisingly large number of formats you can output to.

Adobe has completely rethought the output interface in Premiere Elements 14. The new **Export & Share** panel is designed to be more workflow-based.

You choose the destination, and Premiere Elements will provide you the most optimized format.

The **Export & Share** categories include:

Quick Export – A quick, general-purpose video output.

Devices – Share your finished video as a computer file or as an optimized file for viewing on a TV or mobile device (as discussed on page 403). This destination also saves video that can be used in another project or which can be ported to a third-party DVD or BluRay authoring program like Adobe Encore or Sony DVD Architect (see the sidebar on page 408).

Disc – Burn DVD, BluRay and AVCHD discs (as discussed on page 409).

Online – Upload your video to Facebook, Vimeo or YouTube (as discussed on pages 412).

Audio – Output the audio only from your movie. Output options are available in standard Windows format (WAV), Mac format (AIFF) and compressed AACs and MP3s.

Image – Output a frame of your video as a picture file (as discussed on page 414).

The **Computer** category also includes options for creating your own custom output presets.

Quick Export

Although Premiere Elements offers you options to create specific video formats, optimized for specific situations, sometimes you just want to output a quick, simple, general-purpose movie.

The **Quick Export** share option creates a video that you can display on your computer, watch on a mobile device or upload to a website like YouTube, Vimeo or Facebook. In a pinch, you can even use it as source video in another video project.

The video produced by **Quick Export** is a 1280x720 30 progressive frames per second MP4 with an 8 Kbps variable bit rate and compressed AAC audio. Although not optimized for every situation, these specs produce a nice-looking, compact, general purpose movie.

Scroll to see all Resolution options.

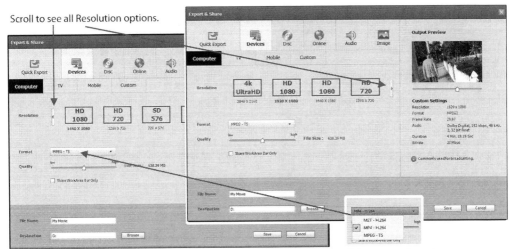

Select option to output Work Area Only.

Select export format.

Output your movie for playback on a computer, for posting online or for use in another project

The **Export & Share** to **Devices/Computer** output category is far and away the most powerful. Under this tab you'll find options for saving your videos to your computer and for creating optimized files for TV players and mobile devices. Selecting the proper output is as easy as just selecting your destination or device and the resolution you want your video file to be.

Export & Share a computer file

Under **Export & Share/Devices/Computer**, you'll find the greatest number of movie output options.

Files output to **Computer** can, of course, be played on your computer's media player – but they can also be used as source media in another editing project.

This is where you'll find the option to output a **DV-AVI** (full quality video) file (on PCs) and **DV-MOV** (on Macs), as explained in **Output video to be used in another video project** on page 405. This is also where you'll find the option to output **4K UHD** (Ultra High Definition XAVC-S), a format with four times the resolution of high-definition TV (3840x2160 pixels). (As illustrated above, you may need to use the left and right arrows to scroll through all of the **Resolution** options.)

Some **Resolutions** can output in more than one format. **HD 1080**, for instance, can be output as an M2T, MOV, MP4 or MPEG-TS file.

The chart on page 404 indicates the best use for each output, resolution and format. Descriptions of each video format can be found on page 416.

Computer Output Formats

4K UltraHD 3840x2160	MP4-XAVC	3840x2160 29.97p fps ultra high-definition video, ideal for UHD display or uploading to video sharing sites like YouTube.
HD 1080 1920x1080	M2T-H.264	Ideal format for saving video for use in a 1920x1080 AVCHD project or for outputting video for a BluRay disc authoring project in a program like Adobe Encore or Sony DVD Architect.
	MOV-H.264	Ideal QuickTime 1920x1080 30p fps video for Mac playback and uploading to sites like YouTube or Vimeo.
	MP4-H.264	Ideal MP4 1920x1080 29.97p fps video for uploading to sites like YouTube.
	MPEG-TS	1920x1080 29.97p fps high-definition saved in MPEG format.
HD 1080 1440x1080	M2T-H.264	Ideal format for saving video for use in a 1440x1080 (non-square pixels) AVCHD project.
	MP4-H.264	Ideal 1440x1080 29.97p fps (non-square pixels) video for uploading to sites like YouTube or Vimeo.
	MPEG-TS	1440x1080 29.97 fps (non-square pixels) high-definition saved in MPEG format.
HD 720 1280x720	M2T-H.264	1280x720 30p fps video, ideal for uploading to video sharing sites like YouTube.
	MOV-H.264	1280x720 30p fps QuickTime video, ideal for Mac playback or uploading to video sharing sites like YouTube or Vimeo.
	MP4-H.264	1280x720 30p video, ideal for uploading to video sharing sites like YouTube or Vimeo.
	MPEG-PS	1280x720 29.97p fps video, a good format for using in a 1280x720 video project.
SD 576 720x576	AVI-DV	The PC-based PAL format for standard definition TV. Ideal for use in a PAL standard def video project.
	MOV-DV	The Mac version of the PAL format for standard definition TV. Virtually identical to the AVI-DV and, for the most part, can be used interchangeably with DV-AVIs in a Premiere Elements project.
	MP4-H.264	25p fps optimized for 720x576 onscreen or online viewing.
	MPEG-PS	Ideal format for outputting video to be used in a PAL DVD authoring project in a program like Adobe Encore or Sony DVD Architect.
	WMV-VC1	Standard definition PAL file in the Windows Media format. (Not available on a Mac.)
SD 480 720x480	AVI-DV	The PC-based NTSC format for standard definition TV. Ideal for use in a NTSC standard def video project.
	MOV-DV	The Mac version of the NTSC format for standard definition TV. Virtually identical to the AVI-DV and, for the most part, can be used interchangeably in Premiere Elements project.
	MP4-H.264	30p fps optimized for 720x480 onscreen or online viewing.
	MPEG-PS	Ideal format for outputting video to be used in a NTSC DVD authoring project in a program like Adobe Encore or Sony DVD Architect.
	WMV-VC1	Standard definition NTSC file in the Windows Media format. (Not available on a Mac.)

Some HD formats are available to output as 1920x1080 or 1440x1080. 1440x1080 is an older high-definition format that uses non-square pixels while the more standard 1920x1080 uses square pixels. The video in either pixel format is virtually identical – both produce high-definition 16:9 video frames. But, for the most part, 1440x1080 is considered somewhat obsolete (relatively speaking) while 1920x1080 is considered the current HD standard.

To export only a segment of your project, indicate that segment with the **Work Area Bar** and check the **Share Work Area Bar Only** option. (For more information, see **Output a segment of your video using the Work Area Bar** on page 275 of **Chapter 21, Edit Your Video in Expert View**.)

Output your video for use in another video project

Working on a long project in short pieces

You'll often find a longer project much easier to work with if you work on it in shorter pieces. Doing this can minimize system lugging and maximize program responsiveness as well as reduce the likelihood that you'll run into problems when you try to output your finished movie. Once each segment is finished and output, open a new project and combine the segments into a final mix.

In order to do this with minimal loss of quality and maximum performance, you'll want to output each segment in its ideal video format – a format that the program is designed to work with natively and won't have to re-render. Instructions for outputting each of these ideal video formats is found below.

For standard definition video

If you'd like to export your video project – or even a portion of your project – so that you can import it into a standard definition Premiere Elements video project on a Windows computer, use **Export & Share/Computer/SD 480** (or SD 576 for PAL) in the **AVI-DV** format. The file you output will have an **.avi** suffix.

The Macintosh equivalent to the **DV-AVI** file is the **DV-MOV**. To output a **DV-MOV** file from your project, use **Export & Share/Computer/SD 480** (or SD 576 for PAL) in the **MOV-DV** format. The file you output will have a **.mov** suffix.

For high-definition video

If you'd like to export your video project – or a portion of your project – from an HDV (tape-based high-definition) project for use in another HDV project, use **Export & Share/Devices/Computer/HD 1920x1080** in the **MPEG-TS** format.

If you're working on an Full AVCHD project, output your video by clicking use **Export & Share/Devices/Computer/HD 1920x1080** in the **M2T-H.264** format.

Both forms of high-definition video will output with the **.m2t** suffix.

Output your movie for playback on a TV

The outputs available under **Export & Share/Devices/TV** are optimized for playback on an HDTV.

This video is saved in the MPEG format, and the outputs can also be used as source media if you are porting your video over to a BluRay authoring program like Adobe Encore or Sony DVD Architect.

TV Output Formats		
4K UltraHD	MP4	3840x2160 video optimized for viewing on a 4K UltraHD TV.
HD 1080 **1920x1080**	MP4	1920x1080 30p MP4 for viewing on HDTV.
	MPEG	1920x1080 30p MPEG video optimized for playing on an HDTV or outputting for BluRay disc authoring.
HD 720	MP4	1280x720 30p MP4 for viewing on HDTV.
	MPEG	1280x720 30p MPEG for viewing on HDTV.

To export only a segment of your project, indicate that segment with the **Work Area Bar** and check the **Share Work Area Bar Only** option. (For more information, see **Output a segment of your video using the Work Area Bar** on page 275 of **Chapter 21, Edit Your Video in Expert View**.)

Output your movie for a mobile phone or portable device

The outputs available under **Export & Share/Devices/Mobile** are optimized for playback on smartphones and other portable devices – from iPods, iPads and iPhones to Android phones and tablets.

This video is saved in the H.264 (MP4) format, a high-quality compressed video format that is playable on virtually any portable device, smartphone or tablet.

Mobile Output Formats		
HD 1080 1920x1080	MP4-H.264	1920x1080 30p fps format optimized for smartphones and mobile devices.
HD 800 1280x800	MP4-H.264	1280x800 30p fps format optimized for smartphones and mobile devices. Unlike most HD formats, this outputs 4:3 rather than 16:9 widescreen video.
HD 720 1280x720	MP4-H.264	1280x720 30p fps format optimized for smartphones and mobile devices.

To export only a segment of your project, indicate that segment with the **Work Area Bar** and check the **Share Work Area Bar Only** option. (For more information, see **Output a segment of your video using the Work Area Bar** on page 275 of **Chapter 21, Edit Your Video in Expert View.**)

Create a custom output preset

If none of the standard video formats or codecs meets your needs, Premiere Elements offers you the option of creating your own custom output preset under **Export & Share/Devices/Custom.**

When you click the **Advanced Settings** button on this panel, you'll access a panel from which you can choose any of a dozen video, three still photo or four audio **Formats** in a wide variety of codecs (including an uncompressed video file and an animated gif).

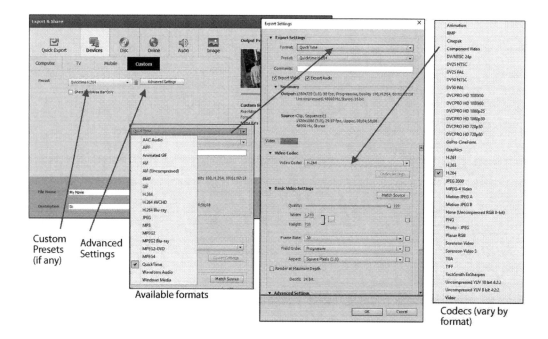

Custom Presets (if any)   Advanced Settings

Available formats

Codecs (vary by format)

You'll also find options for setting your own resolution, quality level and bitrate and frame rate as well as if this frame rate is interlaced or progressive.

The **Match Source** button will create an output that matches the specs of your original video.

Once you've set up your preset and you click **OK**, you'll be prompted to name your preset. This preset will then be available for any future project.

Output your video for use in a third-party disc authoring program

Premiere Elements is designed to be a total package video editor, taking you all the way from capturing your video to outputting a finished DVD or BluRay disc, complete with menus and scene markers.

But some find the disc authoring tools in Premiere elements a bit limiting. And if you count yourselves among those, you can still use Premiere Elements to edit your videos – and then use a third-party disc authoring program like Adobe Encore or Sony DVD Architect to create your menus and discs.

As indicated in the chart on page 404, to output the ideal of video for these programs, use the following **Export & Share** options:

For a DVD project, use **Export & Share/Devices/Computer/SD 480** (or SD 576 for PAL) and the MPEG-PS format with the **Quality** slider pushed all the way to High.

For a BluRay project, use **Export & Share/Devices/Computer/HD 1080** (1920x1080) and the M2T-H.264 format with the **Quality** slider pushed all the way to High.

Burn your movie to a DVD or BluRay Disc

One of the most popular ways to share movies from your Premiere Elements projects is to burn them as a DVDs or high-definition BluRay discs.

Premiere Elements will burn to both single-layer and dual-layer discs and to both DVD and BluRay formats. (The program automatically scans your system to see which disc burner hardware you have and if you have a disc in the drive.)

Disc Output Formats		
DVD	SD 576	Burns your video as a standard definition disc in the PAL format.
	SD 480	Burns your video as a standard definition disc in the NTSC format.
Blu-Ray	HD 1080 1920x1080	Burns your video as a high-definition BluRay disc in standard 1920x1080 HD.
	HD 1080 1440x1080	Burns your video as a high-definition disc in less standard 1440x1080 HD.
AVCHD	HD 1080 1920x1080	Burns your video as a high-definition disc in standard 1920x1080 HD.
	HD 1080 1440x1080	Burns your video as a high-definition disc in less standard 1440x1080 HD.

DVDs are standard definition video discs and can be played in both DVD and BluRay disc players. As a rule of thumb, you can fit about 70 minutes of full-quality video onto a standard (4.7 gigabyte) DVD at full video quality and about double that on a dual layer disc.

BluRays are high definition video discs that can only be played in BluRay disc players. A BluRay disc (which can store 25 gigabytes of data) can hold about two hours of high-definition video, while a dual-layer BluRay disc can hold about twice that.

AVCHD discs are essentially BluRay video files burned to a DVD disc. Since BluRay discs cost a bit more than DVDs, this can save you some money – although the storage capacity of a DVD limits you to about 20-30 minutes of high-def video.

Note that AVCHD discs, despite using DVD disc media, can *not* be played in DVD players! Since their data is essentially BluRay, AVCHD discs can only be played in BluRay disc players.

If you put more than these recommended capacities on a disc, Premiere Elements will automatically reduce the quality of the video as needed if you have the **Fit Contents** option checked. (This reduced quality may not be noticeable unless you try to squeeze considerably more content onto the disc than the optimal capacity.)

1   Under the **Export & Share** tab, select **Disc.** On the **Disc** option screen, select the type of disc you want to burn.

2   Although DVDs can only be output from Premiere Elements at standard interlaced frame rates, BluRays and AVCHD discs can be set to output video at either NTSC (29.97), PAL (25) or 23.976 frames rates. Many people feel that the 23.976 (24p) frame rate provides a much more cinematic viewing experience.

In addition to providing the option to burn your video directly to a disc, the **Type** menu at the bottom of the panel also gives you the option to burn your disc files to an ISO image file, as discussed in page 411.

If you select the option to save your disc files to an ISO file, you will be able to browse to the location you'd like your files saved in the **Destination** field.

Note that the folder you save your ISO file to must have no other files in it!

The challenge with home-burned DVDs and BluRays

Although this is becoming less of an issue as home-burned DVDs and BluRay discs have grown in popularity, it's important to realize that not all DVD and BluRay players can play home-burned discs. This is because the process used to create commercial discs (pressing) is very different than the process you use to create discs on your computer (a chemical process).

Manufacturers have recognized the growing popularity of creating home-burned DVDs and BluRay discs and have been making their players more and more compatible with them. But be prepared for the occasional friend or client who simply can't play a disc you've created!

Disc files saved as an **ISO file** can be archived to your hard drive. A third-party program like ImgBurn (a free download) or your operating system's disk utilities can then used to output copies of your DVD or BluRay from this image file as needed, as discussed on page 423.

3 Click the **Burn** button.

Burn your disc files to an ISO image file

In addition to the option to burn your video files directly to a disc, Premiere Elements offers you the options to save your disc files as an **ISO** image file on your hard drive. An ISO file is a package that includes all of the video and menus for your DVD or BluRay disc in a single file.

To access this option, click the **Type** drop-down menu for your DVD, BluRay or AVCHD.

Once a DVD or BluRay image file is created, you can use your computer's disc burning software (Nero, ImgBurn, etc.) or your computer's disk utilities to burn a DVD or BluRay disc from this ISO file. We show you how to do this in **Burn a DVD or BluRay disc from an image file** on page 423 of the **Appendix**.

Why save your disc files as an ISO?

At first, the idea of burning your DVD, BluRay or AVCHD disc to a file on your computer rather than directly to a disc may seem like an unnecessary workaround. After all, if you're eventually going to burn these files to a disc, doesn't burning them to a file just take more time and add extra steps to the process?

But there are a couple of advantages to burning your files to your hard drive:

Burning your DVD, BluRay or AVCHD disc files to a file on your computer archives your finished disc. In other words, it saves a library of your work. Disc files are relatively small compared to raw footage and, should you need to grab footage from one of your finished projects, it will be readily available on your hard drive.

It makes outputting several copies of your discs very easy. The least preferred way to make several copies of a DVD or BluRay disc is to burn one master and then make several copies of it. It usually works okay, since it's a digital copy – but it's a sketchy way of doing things. Like typing onto carbon paper. When you've stored your disc files on your computer's hard drive, on the other hand, every disc you output from these files is essentially an *original*!

It can save you a world of heartache. The process of burning a DVD or BluRay directly to a disc sometimes fails. And the point at which is most often fails is during the during disc burn. In other words, if something goes wrong at the point the computer is transferring your transcoded files from the temp storage to your disc, you lose everything. Saving your DVD, BluRay or AVCHD disc files to your hard drive dodges that risk. You know your disc files are safe and complete. All that's left to do is write them to a disc.

By the way, the process of saving your files to your computer and then writing them to a disc takes virtually no more time than burning your Premiere Elements project directly to a disc. So there's no cost whatsoever.

Which is why writing your DVD, BluRay and AVCHD disc files to your hard drive rather than burning directly to a disc is pretty much standard operating procedure for most video editors I know.

Labeling discs

At Muvipix, we recommend that you *never* stick a label onto your DVD or BluRay disc.

Labels can throw the spin and balance off when the discs are loaded into a player and the glue and label can damage the media itself. If you'd like to customize your discs, we recommend that you buy printable discs and use a good inkjet printer with disc printing capabilities. Epson and HP make very nice printers with this feature for under $100.

Upload your video to Facebook, Vimeo or YouTube

To upload your video to directly to a social media site:

1   On the **Export & Share** tab, select **Online**, then select the site you'd like to upload your video to.

2   Select a resolution and quality.

In most cases, you'll probably want to select the highest resolution available. For Facebook and Vimeo, this will be 1280x720. Files destined for YouTube can be as large as 1920x1080.

Likewise, in most cases you'll choose the **High** quality option. However, particularly if you've got a longer movie, reducing the quality to Standard can reduce your upload time.

3   Click the **Begin Share** button.

If this is the first time uploading to Facebook, Vimeo or YouTube from the program, an option screen will ask you to **Authorize** the upload.

Click the **Authorize** button. Your web browser will open to the Facebook, Vimeo or YouTube authorization page.

If you are already logged into the site, you're done with the authorization. You can close your web browser and return to the program to finish the authorization.

Otherwise, log in to the site and, when prompted, close your browser and return to Premiere Elements.

4   Give your video a title and description. If you are uploading to Vimeo YouTube, you will also have the option of adding search word tags.

5   If you are uploading your video to Vimeo or YouTube, click **Next** and then select a category for your video and set whether it is for public or private viewing.

Click **Upload**. Your video will be rendered and uploaded to the site.

Output a still image of your current video frame

The **Export & Share/Image** screen give you the option to output **a frame of** your video as a **JPEG Image**. This **Image** can be saved as high-definition 1920x1080, 1440x1080 or 1280x720 or as standard definition 720x480.

The **JPEG** output option here makes this a great alternative to the **Freeze Frame** option available in the program's **Tools** (discussed on page 294 of **Chapter 23, Use the Premiere Elements Toolkit**) since this tool includes more options for customizing the settings of your output.

The 1920x1080 and 1280x720 resolutions create still photos with square pixels from your high-definition videos. The 1440x1080 and 720x480 resolutions will produce still photos with non-square pixels, which can look a bit oddly stretched in some applications. We show you how to create your own custom 640x480 square pixel preset for outputting still photos from 4:3 standard definition video in the sidebar on the facing page.

Non-square pixels

Pixels are the tiny blocks of color that make up your digital photos and video.

For reasons that date back to the early days of television, the vast majority of television video is made up of **non-square pixels.** This is true for PAL as well as NTSC video.

In standard NTSC video, these pixels are approximately 90% as wide as they are tall. Thus a 720x480 pixel video image becomes a 4:3 aspect ratio video (the equivalent of a 640x480 *square-pixel* video). A widescreen video is made up of the *same number of pixels* – however, because these pixels are 120% as wide as they are tall, a 720x480 pixel widescreen video has a 16:9 aspect ratio.

Some high-definition camcorders shoot their video in 1440x1080 *non-square* pixels. This produces exactly the same size video as a camera that shoots in 1920x1080 *square* pixels.

Create a custom JPEG output preset

Custom Presets
(if any)

Advanced Settings

Uncheck the Constrain lock and type in the width and height (640 and 480). Make sure the Aspect is set to Square Pixels (1.0).

The **Image** output presets included with Premiere Elements are designed to produce a still photo that can be used in a video. Because of this, the standard definition options (**JPEG - NTSC SD** and **JPEG - PAL SD**) will produce a still that is composed of anamorphic – or *non-square* – video pixels. This means that, if you use one of these stills on a Website or in a print project, your photo will be oddly distorted.

For this reason, we recommend that, in addition to the pre-loaded presets, you create an additional, *square pixel* output preset for your general-purpose JPEG frame grabs.

1   Go to the **Export & Share** tab and select the **Image** destination option.

Select the **Custom** tab.

2   Click the **Advanced Settings** button.

The **Export Settings** panel will open.

3   On the **Export Settings** options panel, under the **Video** tab, set the **Aspect** drop-down to **Square Pixels (1.0)**.

Click the chain link button to turn off **Constrain Proportions** and then set the **Width** to 640 and the **Height** to 480. (For widescreen video, use a **Width** of 854.)

Click **OK**.

4   In the **Choose Name** screen, type the name **"Square Pixels,"** then click **OK** to save it.

This **Square Pixels** option will now be available on the **Presets** drop-down menu whenever you use **Export & Share** to create a JPEG still of your current video frame.

Video output formats

The majority of video output formats available under **Export & Share** tab are **DV-AVI**s (Windows only), **MPEG**s, **WMV**s (Windows Media Video – available on Windows computers only), **MOV**s (QuickTime video – including **DV-MOV** files) and **MP4**s. You'll find at least one of these options offered under each of the **Export & Share** output destinations.

Here is a brief discussion of each major format and its best use:

DV-AVIs. At one time the ideal video format for editing on a personal computer, **DV-AVIs**, the format produced when standard definition video is captured from a miniDV camcorder, are still the easiest format to edit with both the Windows and Mac versions of Premiere Elements. Although affordable high-definition camcorders have pretty much made this format obsolete, it can still be found in many standard definition workflows, including DVD production. To output a **DV-AVI** from your project, select **Export & Share/Device/ Computer/SD 480** (or **SD 576** for PAL video) with the **AVI-DV** preset. (This option is not available in the Macintosh version of Premiere Elements. However, the **MOV-DV**, discussed below, is virtually identical.)

DV-MOVs are the Macintosh equivalent of **DV-AVIs**. It is the format that is created when miniDV footage is captured to a Macintosh computer. To output a **DV-MOV** from a Premiere Elements project, select **Export & Share/Device/Computer/SD 480** (or **SD 576** for PAL video) with the **MOV-DV** preset.

MPEGs are a high quality video delivery format that comes in a number of forms. A form of **MPEG**, called a VOB file, is the format used to store the video on DVDs. To output a DVD-quality MPEG from your project, select **Export & Share/Device/Computer/SD 480** (or **SD 576** for PAL video) with the **MPEG-PS** preset.

Most consumer high-definition camcorder video is saved as a form of high-def **MPEG** called an **M2T**.

M2T videos are high-quality, high-definition MPEG files. This is the format that is created when you capture video from an HDV camcorder or download video from an AVCHD camcorder, as discussed in **Chapter 19, Add Media to Your Project**.

To output an editable high-definition **M2T** video from Premiere Elements, select **Export & Share/Device/Computer/HD 1080 (1920x1080)** with the **MPEG-TS** preset.

To output an editable AVCHD **M2T** video from Premiere Elements, select **Export & Share/Device/Computer/HD 1080 (1920x1080)** with the **M2T-H.264** preset. These are the ideal formats to output if you plan to use your output video in another high-def project, as discussed on page 405.

AVCHD is an advanced format for outputting your video. Its H.264 codec delivers high-quality video in a highly-compressed file. As noted under the **M2T** file description at the bottom of the previous page, at its highest quality **M2T** file, the AVC codec can produce good, editable high-def video. At higher compressions, however, the **AVC/H.264** codec can be used to create video for display on mobile device (see page 406-407) or to create a high-quality file for upload to YouTube, Facebook or Vimeo.

In fact, if you are having problems uploading directly to a **YouTube** or **Facebook,** or if you're unhappy with the results using the **Export & Share/Online** tools in Premiere Elements, you can manually produce your own high-quality videos and then manually upload them using the To output an AVC file, select **Export & Share/Device/Computer/ HD 1080 (1920x1080)** with the **MP4-H.264** or **MOV-H.264** preset. (Either preset will do. They each produce about the same quality video at approximately the same file size.)

Windows Media (WMVs) were once considered the Internet standard for web-based video. This is because Microsoft's ubiquitous presence meant that virtually every computer in the world had the necessary software to play them. However, in more recent years, **AVCHD/ MP4** video, which produces a smaller file at a higher quality, has challenged its popularity.

WMVs can be created in the Windows version of Premiere Elements only by selecting a **Export & Share/Device/Computer/SD 480** option (or **SD 576** for PAL video) with the **WMV-VC1** preset.

QuickTime (MOVs) are the standard file type for video edited, stored and delivered by MacIntosh computer programs. Since the **MOV** file is more of an envelope than a specific format, **MOVs** can be anything from highly compressed online video to video created for mobile devices to high-quality editable video to uncompressed video, depending on the codec, resolution and compression level of the file. You'll find a number of **MOV** output variations represented in **Export & Share/Device/Computer** (see page 404) as well as in **Export & Share/Device/Mobile** (see page 406).

XAVC/MP4 video is a Sony-created consumer version of **4K**, also known as **UltraHD** – a format with nearly four times the resolution of 1920x1080 high-definition. **XAVC** uses AVC/H264 compression to create an MP4 which, though highly compressed, can be used to create some amazingly sharp and detailed videos (from 4K source video, of course).

To output a 4K MP4 video from Premiere Elements, select **Export & Share/Device/Computer/4K UltraHD**.

"Real World" System Requirements

Features not included in the Mac version

FTP Utilities

MiniDV and HDV Video Capture

Burn a Disc from a DVD or BluRay Image File

Premiere Elements Keyboard Shortcuts

Chapter 33

A Premiere Elements Appendix
More things worth knowing

Recommended "Real World" computer specs

Most current off-the-shelf computers are capable of running Premiere Elements and editing standard consumer video (miniDV, AVCHD and video from smartphones and GoPro-type "action cams") with little or no modification.

The program does not use GPU acceleration, so there is little benefit to an advanced graphics card. (Even an onboard Intel graphics system will work fine.) Though, for best performance, we recommend a decent load of RAM (4-8 gigabytes minimum on a 64-bit operating system) and a current processor.

We've found the benchmark charts put together (and continually updated) by PassMark to be tremendously helpful in choosing and evaluating a processor. Any processor that rates a 5,000 or better should be able to handle Premiere Elements and most standard video formats with ease.

PassMark's benchmarks can be found at http://www.cpubenchmark.net/high_end_cpus.html and its linked pages.

The addition of a second hard drive (either internal or external) – one dedicated to your video projects and source files – can give your workflow a tremendous boost.

Not only does it often make the process go more smoothly, since it keeps the video data flow and scratch disk files separate from your operating system's paging files, but it also reduces fragmentation of your video files.

If you install an internal second hard drive for video editing, make sure to set it up in your BIOS (the set-up that displays before the operating system launches, when you first start up your computer) as well as in your operating system.

And, if you're working in Windows, whether you use an internal or external drive, make sure that the drive is formatted NTFS rather than FAT32 (which all drives are factory formatted as by default) in order to avoid FAT32's file size limitations.

Converting a drive from FAT32 to NTFS is easy and you won't lose any data already on the drive in the process. The instructions for doing so are available all over the Web, including on the Microsoft site.

Features not included in the Mac version

Although the Mac and the Window versions of Premiere Elements function virtually identically, there are a number of features available on the PC that are not available on the Mac.

The Windows version includes 87 video effects and 19 audio effects. The Mac version includes 72 video effects and 15 audio effects. The following **Video Effects** are not included in the Mac version:

Blur & Sharpen: Anti-Alias, Ghosting

Distort: Bend, Lens Distortion

Image Control: Color Pass, Color Replace

Keying: Blue Screen Key, Green Screen Key, Chroma Key, RGB Difference Key

Transform: Camera View, Clip, Horizontal Hold, Vertical Hold

The following **Audio Effects** are not included in the Mac version:

Denoiser, Dynamics, Pitch Shifter, Reverb

The Windows version of Premiere Elements includes 107 video transitions. The Mac version includes 50 video transitions.

The following **Video Transitions** are not included in the Mac version:

3D Motion: Curtain, Doors, Fold-Up, Spin, Spin Away, Swing In, Swing Out, Tumble Away

Dissolve: Dither Dissolve, Non-Additive Dissolve, Random Invert

Iris: Iris Points, Iris Shapes, Iris Star

Map: Channel Map, Luminance Map

Page Peel: Center Peel, Peel Back, Roll Away

Slide: Band Slide, Center Merge, MultiSpin, Slash Slide, Sliding Bands, Sliding Boxes, Swap, Swirl

Special Effect: Direct, Displace, Image Mask, Take, Texturize, Three-D

Stretch: Cross Stretch, Funnel, Stretch, Stretch In, Stretch Over

Wipe: Band Wipe, Checker Wipe, CheckerBoard, Clock Wipe, Paint Splatter, Pinwheel, Radial Wipe, Random Blocks, Random Wipe, Spiral Boxes, Venetian Blinds, Wedge Wipe, Zig Zag Blocks

Zoom: Cross Zoom, Zoom, Zoom Boxes, Zoom Trails

Valuable free or low cost tools and utilities for Windows

Audacity (audacity.sourceforge.net) is, hands down, the best *free* audio editing software you'll find anywhere. Easy to use, loaded with preset audio filters and yet extremely versatile.

Audacity can convert audio formats as well as adjust audio levels and "sweeten" your audio's sound. You can also record into it from a microphone or external audio device and edit audio with it. A real must-have freebie that you'll find yourself going to regularly!

FTP software

FTP software uploads files from your computer to a website and downloads files from a site to your computer. There are many great applications out there.

Here are a couple of personal favorites.

FileZilla Client is the current favorite FTP utility of a number of Muvipixers. Efficient, dependable and easy-to-use, sending files to a Website with **FileZilla** is as simple as dragging and dropping.

FileZilla Client is available free from filezilla-project.org.

Easy FTP (free from www.download.com and other sources) – Free and nearly as intuitive as **FileZilla**.

Disc burning software

Our favorite disc-burning software is, nicely enough, absolutely free!

ImgBurn is available at imgburn.com, and it's a great tool to use to burn your DVD or BluRay files to a disc as described in **Burn a disc from a DVD or BluRay image file** on page 422.

MiniDV and HDV video capture

Premiere Elements no longer includes a built-in tool for capturing video from a tape-based camcorder. The program still supports and edits miniDV and HDV footage. However, it no longer includes a video capture tool.

Here are our favorite third-party programs for capturing tape-based miniDV and HDV footage on a Windows PC. All are designed to work with camcorders that are connected to your computer via a FireWire or IEEE-1394 connection (also known as iLink).

Once captured with this software, your video should load and edit perfectly in Premiere Elements using the method described in **Import photos, video, music and other audio that is already on your computer's hard drive into your project** on page 253.

WinDV (free from windv.mourek.cz/) – A great DV capture utility with a simple interface.

HDVSplit (free from http://www.videohelp.com/software/HDVSplit – A great capture utility for HDV video. Though technically discontinued, the software still works great at capturing video from high-definition tape-based camcorders.

On a Mac, video captured from a tape-based camcorder via a FireWire connection using **iMovie** is perfectly compatible with Premiere Elements. An excellent third-party program for capturing miniDV video to a Mac is **LifeFlix**, available for $9.95 from the App Store.

Capture analog video through DV bridges and pass-throughs

There's a difference between a DV bridge and a plain old capture device or capture card. Capture devices merely digitize your video input to any of a number of video formats. DV bridges, on the other hand, are specifically designed to **convert any video and audio input into DV-AVI files,** the preferred video format for PC-based video editors. (Macs also prefer DV video, although they are saved as DV QuickTime files [MOVs] rather than AVIs. The video data content, however, is identical.)

DV bridges range from relatively inexpensive to high-end professional devices with time base correction and other video optimizers. The best value on the market in DV bridges and a Muvipix recommended "best buy" is the **Canopus/Grass Valley ADVC Converter,** a favorite of many videographers.

(Another great DV bridge device that, technically, has been discontinued but can still be found on the web is the **ADS Pyro AV Link.** Because this device is discontinued, it can be often found for as little as $100 on sites like eBay.)

The **Grass Valley ADVC** will take any AV input (a camcorder, a DVD player, a VCR or virtually any other video source, including live video) and port it into your computer as a high-quality DV-AVI or, on a Mac, DV-MOV file. This great device can be had for a street price of under $200, a great value if you plan to edit a lot of video from non-DV sources.

Capturing video from a DV bridge is easy. Just plug your camcorder's, DVD player's or VCR's AV cables (RCA jacks) into the DV bridge's inputs and plug the bridge (connected by FireWire) into your computer.

Your computer will recognize the device just as it would a miniDV camcorder connection. You can then use a program like the excellent WinDV (discussed in **MiniDV and HDV video capture** on the facing page) to capture the video.

The capture process itself is essentially the same as capture from a miniDV camcorder. The only difference is, since there's no direct connection between your video source device and the computer, you won't be able to control the device with your capture software or break scenes by timecode.

But, once you've got the device cued up to the segment you want to capture, just click the **Capture** button and you're good to go!

By the way, the **Canopus ADVC** can also be used with DVD camcorders and hard drive camcorders, so it's a great way to make any non-miniDV video 100% Premiere Elements compatible.

An alternative to a DV bridge is a set-up called a **pass-through,** which essentially uses a miniDV camcorder as a makeshift DV bridge.

To set up a pass-through connection, attach your non-DV camcorder to your miniDV camcorder via its AV input cables, then link the miniDV to your computer via FireWire.

With the miniDV camcorder in play mode (but without a tape inside) the non-DV camcorder's video flows through the miniDV and into the computer, where it's captured as DV-AVIs.

A DV bridge downloads DV video from a VHS camcorder over a FireWire connection.

The biggest challenge to using this method is that fewer and fewer new miniDV camcorders support a pass-through connection. And it's very difficult to glean, from most spec sheets, which camcorders do before you buy one.

But, if your miniDV camcorder is pass-through capable, this is a simple and effective method of digitizing almost any analog video input.

Burn a DVD or BluRay disc from an image file

For a number of reasons, you may want to save you finished DVD or BluRay disc as an ISO image file on your hard drive rather than burn them directly to a disc.

Sometimes it's out of necessity. Sometimes your computer operating system is configured in such a way that Premiere Elements isn't able to burn your DVDs or BluRays directly to a disc.

Other times it's by choice. I often *prefer* to "burn" my disc files to my hard drive for archiving, and then use a program like ImgBurn to burn copies from this ISO file to a disc as needed.

That way I've always got a finished copy of my disc files available, and every "copy" I burn off is actually an original disc, based on the original Premiere Elements disc encoding.

Whatever your reason, it's fairly easy to burn your disc files to your hard drive and then use a third-part program (like ImgBurn) to produce DVDs and BluRay discs from these files.

1   Go to **Export & Share/Disc,** select the **DVD, BluRay** or **AVCHD** option and set the **Type** to **ISO Image,** as discussed on page 411 of **Chapter 32**.

The program will go through the process of encoding and creating your disc files.

2 Once the disc files are created and saved to your hard drive, you can use your computer's burner software, third-party burner software like Nero or our recommended free disc burner utility **ImgBurn** (see **Disc Burning software** on page 421) to burn the image file as a DVD or BluRay disc.

Select the option to Write Files/Folders to Disc from main ImgBurn page.

Browse to select your ISO file as your Source, then click Burn.

To burn a DVD, AVCHD disc or BluRay from an **ISO** file, select **Write Image File to Disc** from the ImgBurn main menu. When the software opens, click the **Source** button and browse to and select the **ISO** file, then click the **Burn** button.

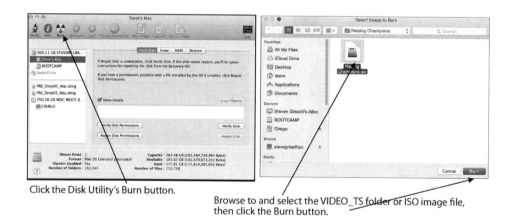

Click the Disk Utility's Burn button.

Browse to and select the VIDEO_TS folder or ISO image file, then click the Burn button.

On a Mac, the built-in **Disk Utility** tool can be used to burn your files to a disc.

To open the **Disk Utility**, go to the **Finder** menu and select **Go**, then **Utilities**. **Double-click** to open the **Disk Utility** tool.

1 Click the **Burn** button at the top of the tool.

A browse window will open.

2   Locate and select the ISO file created by Premiere Elements.

Click **Burn**.

Unpack your ISO

If you'd prefer to store your DVD or BluRay as a folder of individual files rather than an ISO image, you can unpack the image file using your computer's operating system.

On Windows:

1   **Right-click** on the ISO and select **Open with/Windows Explorer**. The browser window will reveal the disc's **OpenDVD** and **VIDEO_TS** folders.

2   Select the folders, **right-click** and select **Copy** and then **Paste** these folders to a new location on your hard drive.

On a Mac:

1   **Right-click** on the ISO and select **Open**. The browser window will reveal the disc's **OpenDVD** and **VIDEO_TS** folders.

2   Select the folders, right-click and select **Copy** and then **Paste** these folders to a new folder on your hard drive.

To use ImgBurn to burn a DVD or BluRay disc from these files, select **Write**

Select the option to Write Files/Folders to Disc from main ImgBurn page.

Select a folder as your source and then browse to and select your DVD's VIDEO_TS folder. Click Burn.

Files/Folders to Disc from the ImgBurn main menu. When the software opens, click the **Source/Folder** button and browse to and select the **VIDEO_TS** folder that was created when you burned your DVD or AVCHD files to a folder, then click the **Burn** button.

On a Mac, use the same process as you would for burning a disc from an ISO file to burn the **VIDEO_TS** folder to a disc, as described on the facing page.

Keyboard shortcuts for Premiere Elements

These key strokes and key combinations are great, quick ways to launch features or use the program's tools without having to poke around the interface.

In virtually every workspace the arrow keys (Down, Up, Left, Right) will move the selected object in that direction. Shift+Arrow will move it several steps in one nudge.

Many of these shortcuts are slightly different on a Macintosh computer. Usually the **Command**(⌘) key is used in place of the **Ctrl** key – although a number of keyboard shortcuts may not work at all.

Program Controls

Ctrl O	Open project	Ctrl X	Cut
Ctrl W	Close project	Ctrl C	Copy
Ctrl S	Save project	Ctrl V	Paste
Ctrl Shift S	Save project as...	Tab	Close floating windows
Ctrl Alt S	Save a copy	Ctrl Q	Quit program
Ctrl Z	Undo	F1	Help
Ctrl Shift Z	Redo		

Import/Export

F5	Capture	Ctrl Shift M	Export Frame
Ctrl I	Add Media	Ctrl Alt Shift M	Export Audio
Ctrl M	Export Movie	Ctrl Shift H	Get properties for selection

Media and Trimming

I	Set in point	Page Up	Go to previous edit point
O	Set out point	G	Clear all in/out points
Q	Go to in point	D	Clear selected in point
Page Down	Go to next edit point	F	Clear selected out point
W	Go to out point	Ctrl E	Edit original
		Ctrl H	Rename

Play/Scrub Controls

Space bar	Play/stop	Shift Right	Step forward five frames
J	Shuttle left	Home	Go to beginning of timeline
L	Shuttle right	End	Go to end of timeline
Shift J	Slow shuttle left	Q	Go to in point
Shift L	Slow shuttle right	W	Go to out point
K	Shuttle stop	Page Down	Go to next edit point
Arrow Left	One frame back	Page Up	Go to previous edit point
Arrow Right	One frame forward	Ctrl Alt Space	Play in point to out point with preroll/postroll
Shift Left	Step back five frames		

Timeline Controls

Enter	Render work area
Ctrl K	Razor cut at CTI
+	Zoom in
-	Zoom out
\	Zoom to work area
Ctrl A	Select all
Ctrl Shift A	Deselect all
, (comma)	Insert
. (period)	Overlay
Ctrl Shift V	Insert Clip
Alt [video clip]	Unlink audio/video
Ctrl G	Group
Ctrl Shift G	Ungroup
X	Time stretch
Del	Clear clip (non-ripple)
Backspace	Ripple delete (fill gap)
S	Toggle snap
C	Razor tool

V	Selection tool
Alt [	Set Work Area Bar In Point
Alt]	Set Work Area Bar Out Point
Ctrl Alt C	Copy attributes
Ctrl Alt V	Paste Effects and Adjustments
Ctrl Shift /	Duplicate
Shift * (Num pad)	Set next unnumbered marker
* (Num pad)	Set unnumbered marker
Ctrl Shift Right	Go to next clip marker
Ctrl Shift Left	Go to previous clip marker
Ctrl Shift 0	Clear current marker
Alt Shift 0	Clear all clip markers
Ctrl Right	Go to next timeline marker
Ctrl Left	Go to previous timeline marker
Ctrl 0	Clear current timeline marker
Alt 0	Clear all timeline markers

Title Window Controls

Ctrl Shift L	Title type align left
Ctrl Shift R	Title type align right
Ctrl Shift C	Title type align center
Ctrl Shift T	Set title type tab
Ctrl Shift D	Position object bottom safe margin
Ctrl Shift F	Position object left safe margin
Ctrl Shift O	Position object top safe margin
Ctrl Alt Shift C	Insert copyright symbol
Ctrl Alt Shift R	Insert registered symbol
Ctrl J	Open title templates
Ctrl Alt]	Select object above
Ctrl Alt [	Select object below
Ctrl Shift]	Bring object to front
Ctrl [	Bring object forward
Ctrl Shift [	Send object to back
Ctrl [	Send object backward

Alt Shift Left	Decrease kerning five units
Alt Shift Right	Increase kerning five units
Alt Left	Decrease kerning one unit
Alt Right	Increase kerning one unit
Alt Shift Up	Decrease leading five units
Alt Shift Down	Increase leading five units
Alt Up	Decrease leading one unit
Alt Down	Increase leading one unit
Ctrl Up	Decrease text size five points
Ctrl Down	Increase text size five points
Shift Up	Decrease text size one point
Shift Down	Increase text size one point

Media Window

Ctrl Delete	Delete selection with options	End	Move selection to last clip
Shift Down	Extend selection down	Page Down	Move selection page down
Shift Left	Extend selection left	Page Up	Move selection page up
Shift Up	Extend selection up	Right	Move selection right
Down	Move selection to next clip	Shift]	Thumbnail size next
Up	Move selection to previous clip	Shift [	Thumbnail size previous
Home	Move selection to first clip	Shift \	Toggle view

Capture Monitor Panel

F	Fast forward	Left	Step back
G	Get frame	Right	Step forward
R	Rewind	S	Stop

Properties Panel

Backspace	Delete selected effect

Narration Panel

Delete	Delete present narration clip	Space	Play present narration clip
Right Arrow	Go to next narration clip	G	Start/Stop recording
Left Arrow	Go to previous narration clip		

Note that Premiere Elements also allows you to modify any of these keyboard shortcuts and to create your own shortcuts for dozens of other tasks. You'll find the option to do so under the Edit drop-down menu.

Need some Basic Training?

Want some help with the basics of Premiere Elements?

Want some free hands-on training?

Check out my free tutorial series **Basic Training with Premiere Elements** at Muvipix.com.

This simple, eight-part series will show you how to set up a project, how to import media into it, basic editing moves, adding transitions and effects, how to create titles, how to add and customize your DVD and BluRay disc menu navigation markers and how to export your finished video.

And did I mention that it's free?

To see the series, just go to http://Muvipix.com and type "Premiere Elements Basic Training" in the product search box.

And while you're there, why not drop by the Community forum and say hi! We'd love to have you become a part of our growing city. Happy moviemaking!

Steve, Chuck, Ron and the whole Muvipix team

Section 3

The
Elements Organizer

File Management with the Organizer

The Media Browser

Keyword Tags and Metadata

Smart Tags and the Media Analyzer

Storing Your Media in Albums

Identifying People, Places and Events

Chapter 34
Manage Your Files with the Organizer
Getting to Know the Media Browser

The Elements Organizer, which comes bundled with both Photoshop Elements and Premiere Elements, is Adobe's media file management tool.

It's a way to organize, to search and to create search criteria for your audio, video and photo files.

It also includes a number of great tools for creating everything from slideshows to DVD case covers from your media files!

A companion program to both Premiere Elements and Photoshop Elements, the Elements Organizer is a media file management system. It includes several interesting ways for you to organize and search your still photo, video, music and audio files

Additionally, the Organizer includes a number of tools for working with your media files to create photo projects, like calendars, scrap books and slideshows, as we discuss in **Chapter 35, Create Fun Pieces** and **Chapter 36, Share Your Photos and Videos**.

The Elements Organizer links directly to both Premiere Elements and Photoshop Elements and it can be launched from the **Welcome Screen** of either program – or by clicking the **Organizer** button on the **Action Bar** along the bottom left of either program's interface.

Think of your Elements Organizer as a giant search engine that can be programmed to store and retrieve the audio, video and still photo files on your computer, based on a wide variety of criteria – some of which you assign, some of which are assigned automatically and some of which are inherently a part of your photo, sound and video files when they're created.

Adaptive Grid vs. Details View

The **Media Browser** in the Organizer displays your files by default in **Adaptive Grid View**, an efficient way to view and browse the media files on your system. Unfortunately, it doesn't give you easy access to information about your media files or even display the file names.

To display more detailed information about your media files, go to the program's View menu and select **Details**.

You can also toggle between these **Details View** and **Adaptive Grid View** by pressing **Ctrl+d** on your keyboard (⌘**+d** on a Mac).

These search criteria aren't limited to obvious details – such as the type of media or the date it was saved to your computer.

Search criteria can include **Keyword Tags** – or it can be minute technical details, such as the type of camera that was used to shoot a photo or whether the photo was shot with a flash or natural light.

Additionally, the Organizer includes features that support other tools and functions in both Premiere Elements and Photoshop Elements. The **Media Analyzer/Auto Analyzer**, discussed on page 440, for instance, prepares your video files for use with the **Smart Fix** and **Smart Mix** tools in Premiere Elements.

Your Elements Organizer's media files can also be assigned **Tags**, categorized according to the **People** in them or the **Places** they were shot, or identified by the **Events** they represent.

The Media Browser area

The main area of the Organizer's interface, in which your media files are displayed as thumbnails and which dominates the Organizer workspace, is called the **Media Browser.**

There are several types of media files, and they are each represented by slightly different thumbnail images in the **Media Browser,** as illustrated to the right:

Video file

Video files are represented as image thumbnails with a filmstrip icon on the upper right corner.

Photo files are represented by a plain thumbnails of the image files.

Audio files are represented by gray thumbnails with a speaker icons on them.

The size of these thumbnail images in the **Media Browser** is controlled by the slider at the bottom right of the interface.

Photo file

Under the **View** drop-down on the Organizer menu bar, in the **Media Types** sub-menu, you can filter which file types are displayed in the **Media Browser.**

Using the tabs along the top of the interface, you can set whether the **Media Browser** displays your files as categories of **People, Places** or **Events** – categories we'll show you how to build later in this chapter.

Audio 1_2.wav

Audio file

The Back or All Media buttons

Whatever tags or filters you've applied, you can always work your way back to a display of all the media in your **Catalog** by clicking the **Back** or **All Media** button in the upper left of the **Media Browser**.

In **Detail View** (see page 433) media file **Details** (such as the date the file was created or its **Star Rating**) as well as its **File Name** can be displayed under its thumbnail in the **Media Browser**

Although by default the files are listed according the date they were created – most recent to oldest – you can display them in a couple of different orders. To change the order your files are displayed in, select an option from the **Sort** menu at the top left of the **Media Browser**.

Oldest or **Newest** lists your files according to the date they were saved to your computer, either most recent first or least.

Name lists your files alpha-numerically, according to their names.

Import Batch lists only the files which have been added recently to your Elements Organizer **Catalog**.

The Organizer Catalog

The media files that the Organizer manages and displays, as well as the metadata that defines them, are said to be in the Organizer's **Catalog**. Some files and information are added to this **Catalog** automatically, while others may be added to the **Catalog** manually.

The Elements Organizer's **Catalog** is a file that includes data and metadata on all of the video clips, audio clips and photo files in your computer's **managed** folders (see page 438) as well as any media files that you've edited with Premiere Elements or Photoshop Elements.

If you download or capture video or photos to your computer using any of the tools in Premiere Elements or Photoshop Elements, they too are automatically added to your Organizer's **Catalog**.

Manually add to and update your Organizer Catalog

The first time you launch the Elements Organizer, it will offer to search your computer for media files in order create to your initial **Catalog**. (If you've had a previous version of the Organizer installed, the program will offer to simply update your existing **Catalog**.) If you're running the program on a Mac, it may even offer to build its initial **Catalog** from the data in your iPhoto catalog.

Import media files into your Catalog

You can manually add files to your **Catalog** by clicking the **Import** button in the upper left of the interface.

- To manually add files, and folders full of files, to your Organizer's **Catalog**, select **From Files and Folders**. Browse to the folder or files you would like to add and then click **Get Media**.

- To download media **From a Camera or Card Reader** or (on a Windows PC) to add images **From a Scanner**, select the respective option.

- To *automatically* add media files to your **Catalog**, select **By Searching**. The program will automatically search your entire computer (or specified folders) and add any media files it locates automatically.

Your **Catalog**, by the way, does not actually *contain* your media files. It's merely a data file with links to and metadata for your media files. A **Catalog** file is actually a relatively small file – and, in fact, you can create several catalogs and manage them under the program's **File** menu.

Resync an out-of-sync Catalog

If you move, delete or change files using Windows Explorer, Finder or a program other than one of the Elements programs, you may find your Organizer's **Media Browser** will indicate some thumbnails as broken or outdated links.

To update these connections manually or to remove the thumbnail of a deleted file from the Organizer **Catalog**, go to the **File** menu and select the option to **Reconnect/All Missing Files**.

The Organizer will update your links and indicate for you all of the thumbnails in the **Media Browser** that do not have files linked to them, offering you the options of re-connecting the links or of deleting these dead thumbnails.

To avoid the program losing track of the links to your media, it's best to use the Elements Organizer to move or remove files from your computer:

- To delete a file using the Organizer, **right-click** on the file(s) and select **Delete from Catalog**. You will then be given the option of merely removing the file from the **Catalog** or removing it completely from your hard drive.

- To move a file to a new location on your computer using the Organizer, click to select the file(s) in the **Media Browser** and, from the **File** drop-down, select the option to **Move,** then browse to the new location.

Switch between Album and Folder Views

By default, the **Media Browser** displays your files according to the dates they were saved, from most recent to oldest.

The panel along the left side of the interface displays a list of the **Albums** you've created, (if any). If you click on an **Album**, the **Media Browser** will display only the media in that **Album**. (For more information on creating and managing **Albums**, see page 443.)

If you click on the **Folders** tab at the top of this panel, the panel will display a list of the "**managed**" folders on your computer's hard drive(s). (For information on managing your computer's folders, see page 438.)

The **Folders** panel will display your managed folders as a **List** or, if you select the **Tree** option, it will display your computer's entire file directory.

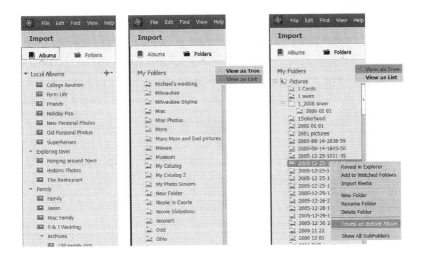

Managed, Unmanaged and Watched Folders

As far as your Organizer's **Catalog** is concerned, there are three types of folders on your hard drive. These folders are listed when the left side panel is in **Folder** view (see the bottom of page 437).

Unmanaged Folders are folders whose contents do not have any links to the Organizer. The folder either does not contain any media files or the media files have not yet been added to the **Catalog**.

Unmanaged Folder

Managed Folders are folders whose contents have been added to the **Catalog** and whose media files can be viewed and searched by the Organizer.

Managed Folder

Watched Folders have a dynamic link to the Organizer's **Catalog**. As media files are added to a **Watched Folder**, they are automatically added to the **Catalog**.

Watched Folder

(Note that any media files which are used in a Premiere Elements project or are edited and saved in Photoshop Elements are *automatically* added to the **Catalog**, regardless of where they are stored.)

The very first time you launch the Organizer, it will search your computer for media files and automatically convert a number of folders into **Managed Folders**.

You can also manually designate a folder as a **Managed Folder** or a **Watched Folder** by setting the left side panel to **Folder** view (see the bottom of page 437) and selecting the **Tree** display option (to view your computer's entire file directory). **Right-click** on any folder you'd like to manage and select either **Import Media** (which will convert the folder into a **Managed Folder**) or **Add to Watched Folders**.

What is metadata?

Metadata is the hidden information embedded into virtually every computer file, including when the file was saved, who modified it last, what program created the file, etc.

The Elements Organizer uses metadata to manage, order and search your media files.

All of your media files carry some metadata. By default, your files are displayed in the Organizer's **Media Browser** according to the date created – most recent first. (To see the file's title, created date, etc., go to the **View** menu and select **Details**.)

"**Date saved**" is the simplest display of metadata and the most basic way to manage your media files – but it's far from the only way. Virtually any metadata can be used to search, organize or gather your media.

You might be surprised to learn how much metadata is added to your photos and video files by your camera or camcorder automatically.

If the **Keyword Tags/Information** panel isn't displayed to the right of the **Media Browser,** click the **Tags/Info** button in the lower-right corner of the interface. Select the **Information** tab at the top of the panel and select a photo that you've downloaded from a digital camera in the **Media Browser.**

If you open the **Metadata** section of this panel, as illustrated on the right, and then click on the button in the upper right of this panel to display the **Complete** metadata, you'll see an amazing amount of information – from the date and time the photo was shot to the photo dimensions, the make, model and serial number of camera that was used to take the photo, the shutter speed, if a flash was used, what settings and F-stop setting was used, if it was shot with manual or automatic focus and so on.

All of this is metadata. And it can be used – along with any additional metadata you assign to your photos and video manually – as search and sort criteria in the Elements Organizer.

To search by metadata, go to the **Find** drop-down on the Organizer Menu Bar and select the option to search **By Details (Metadata)** as illustrated below.

In the option screen that opens, you can set up a search to find, for instance, all photos shot on a specific date or at a specific time, at certain camera settings – in fact, you can search by pretty much any of the metadata attached to your photo or other media file!

Also under this **Find** drop-down menu, you'll find many more search methods for your files. One of the most amazing search functions, in my opinion, is the Organizer's ability to locate files that contain **Visual Similarity with Selected Photo(s) and Video(s)** (under **Visual Searches**).

That's right: If you have a picture of the beach or the mountains or even of an individual, the Organizer will find for you all of the other photos in your collection that have similar color schemes and visual details!

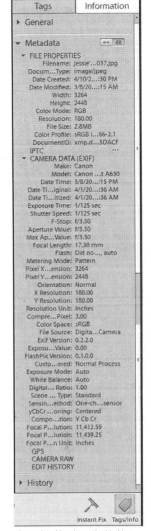

Some of the Metadata embedded in a typical digital photo.

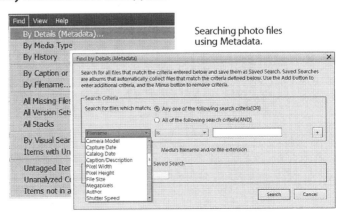

Searching photo files using Metadata.

Add your own Metadata

There are a number of ways to add searchable metadata to your media files. You can, for instance:

Your media files can be categorized by keyword, date, people, place or event.

> Place your media in an **Album** (as discussed on page 443).
>
> Add **Keyword Tags** (as discussed on page 444).
>
> Apply one to five **star ratings** to your clips by dragging across the stars that appear under the thumbnail in the **Media Browser.** (If you don't see stars under your clips, go under the **View** menu and select **Details** and/or zoom into the displayed thumbnail using the slider in the program's lower right.)
>
> Identify your photos by the **People** in them (a process the program does semi-automatically, as discussed on page 445).
>
> Tag your photos and videos with the **Place** they were shot (as discussed on page 447).
>
> Associate your media with a **Date** or an **Event** (as discussed on page 449).

Using both metadata that you supply and metadata supplied automatically by the camera or other device you've recorded your media with, the Organizer provides you with a wide variety of ways to organize and search your media files.

Auto Analyze your media

The **Media Analyzer** (also called the **Auto Analyzer**) is a key feature of the Organizer that works silently in the background, analyzing and logging information about your photos, video and audio files.

As it analyzes your media files, it records metadata about a number of your media files' qualities, including information on the content of your video or photos (for instance, if there are close-ups, if your photos or video includes faces) as well as information on flaws or visual quality in your media files (for instance, if your picture is too dark or too light or if your video includes a lot of jiggle).

This information will then be used by various "**Smart**" tools in Premiere Elements to make automatic corrections to your video or photos:

> Premiere Elements' **Smart Fix** tool (see page 270) uses data gathered by the **Media Analyzer** to make automatic adjustments to your video's brightness or contrast or to automatically apply video stabilization.

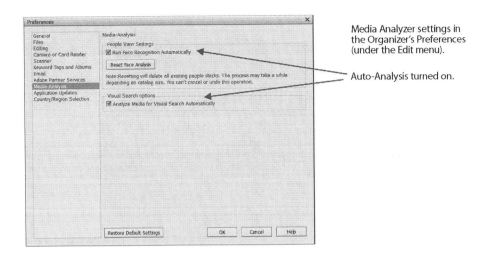

Media Analyzer settings in the Organizer's Preferences (under the Edit menu).

Auto-Analysis turned on.

The **Smart Trim** tool (see page 299) uses data gathered by the **Media Analyzer** to recommend cuts to remove poorer quality sequences.

The **Motion Tracking** tool (see page 306) uses data gathered by the **Media Analyzer** to build motion tracks based on objects in your video.

The **InstantMovie** tool (see page 282), **Video Story** tool (see page 284) and the **Auto Mark Moments** feature in the **Favorite Moments** tool (see page 304) use information from the **Media Analyzer** to build their cuts.

To ensure that the **Auto Analyzer/Media Analyzer** is activated, go to the Organizer's **Preferences** (under the **Edit** menu on a PC or under **Preferences** on a Mac) and go to the **Media Analysis** page.

To set the **Auto Analyzer/Media Analyzer** to run automatically, check all of the boxes on the preferences panel, as illustrated above.

(Likewise, if you've got a slower computer and you find the **Auto Analyzer** too intrusive, you can uncheck the **Analyze Photos** and **Analyze Media** checkboxes to turn the feature off.)

Even if you've disabled the automatic **Auto Analyzer/Media-Analyzer**, you can *manually* run it on clips in either the Elements Organizer's **Media Browser** or in the Premiere Elements **Project Assets** panel.

To do this, **right-click** on a clip or clips in the Organizer's **Media Browser** or the Premiere Elements **Project Assets** panel and select **Run Media Analyzer** from the context menu.

The Search Bar

The quickest way to search for a media file is to type the name of the file, any **Keyword Tag** that applies to it or the name of the **Album** that contains it in the **Search Box** along the top right of the interface. The **Media Browser** will then display all media files that match that criteria.

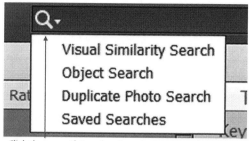

Click the magnifying glass for advanced search options.

This **Search Bar** also includes a number of more advanced search features. These can be selected from the drop-down menu that appears when you click on the magnifying class, as indicated above.

> **Visual Similarity** will search your media for photos similar to the photo that you've currently selected in the **Media Browser**. It will also list below each photo it finds how closely the program feels it matches your selected photo. This can be very helpful for locating all photos that you shot at sunset on a beach, for instance, or other photos that share a similar composition and mix of colors.

> **Object Search** is a more specific way to search for visually similar photos. When you select the **Object Search** option, your selected photo will display with a rectangle over it that can be used to indicate the specific object, animal or face you want to locate. The program will do its best to find all photos which include that indicated object.

With Object Search, you designate a specific object for the Organizer to search.

> **Duplicate Photo Search** is a tool that's designed to help you locate redundant photo files. When you select this option, the program will find photos it considers similar, which you can then choose to keep or remove from your **Catalog**.

> **Saved Searches** will give you access to any custom search criteria you've saved.

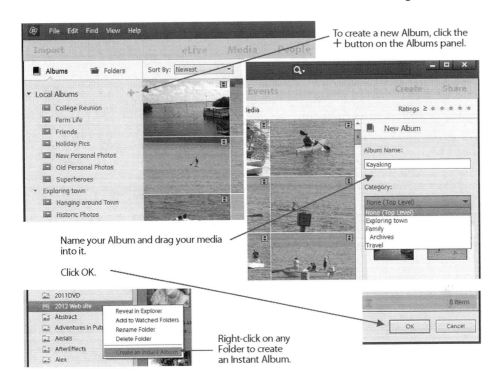

To create a new Album, click the + button on the Albums panel.

Name your Album and drag your media into it.

Click OK.

Right-click on any Folder to create an Instant Album.

Assign your media files to Albums

Albums are collections of media files that you create and assign your photos and videos to.

When an **Album** is selected in the panel to the left of the **Media Browser,** only the files assigned to that **Album** appear in the **Media Browser.**

Albums are a simple way to gather photos, for instance, for creating slideshows or to gather media for a photo or video project.

To create an **Album:**

> Select the media files you'd like to add to your **Album** in the **Media Browser** (by holding down the **Shift, Ctrl** or, on a Mac, the ⌘ key as you click on the files). Click the green **Create Album** button at the top right of the **Albums** panel, as illustrated above. An **Edit Album** panel will open to the right of the **Media Browser,** from which you can name your **Album,** select a sub-category for it and add files to it or remove files from it. When you're done, click **OK.**

> If you switch to **Folder** view (see page 437), you can also turn any **Folder** into an **Album** just by **right-clicking** on it and selecting the **Instant Album** option.

Additional media files can be added to an **Album** by dragging the photo or video from the **Media Browser** onto that **Album's** icon in the **Albums** panel. To re-open an **Album** in the **Edit Album** panel, **right-click** on it and select **Edit.** (And, yes, a media file can be in more than one **Album** at the same time.)

To delete an **Album, right-click** on it and select **Delete.**

You can create new Tags, or sub-Tags, by clicking the New Keyword Tag button.

Tagged media files are indicated with blue tags. (You may need to zoom in the Details view on the Media Browser to see them.)

Selecting one or more Keyword Tags filters the audio, photo and video so that only the media files with those tags are displayed in the Media Browser.

The Image Keywords panel lists all Tags applied to a file selected in the Media Browser.

If the Keyword Tags panel isn't visible, click the button in the lower rigth of the interface.

Manage your files with Keyword Tags

Tagging is a way to manually add custom search metadata to your media files.

At first adding **Keyword Tags** to hundreds of accumulated digital photos and videos may seem like a lot of housekeeping – but the payoff is great!

Creating a new **Tag** is as simple as clicking on the **+** symbol at the top right of this panel. You can create as many **Tags** and as many **Categories** – and **Sub-Categories** under them – as you'd like. You can, for instance, create a **Sub-Category** under Places and name it France. Then, within that **Sub-Category**, create **Tags** for Cousin Pierre, Landmarks, The Louvre, etc. (You can also drag your **Keyword** sub-categories in an out of categories on the **Keyword Tags** panel!)

To assign a **Tag** to a media file, drag the **Tag** from the **Keyword Tags** panel onto the selected file or files in the **Media Browser** (or drag selected media files onto the **Keyword Tag**). You can assign as many **Tags** as you'd like to a file. And you can assign the same **Tag** to as many files as you'd like.

In addition to **Keyword Tags**, the Organizer also includes **People, Places** and **Events Tags**. As you assign a media file to a person, place or event (as discussed on the following pages of this chapter) your file will automatically be tagged in the corresponding category.

If you select a **Tag** in the **Tags** panel, only the photos, video or audio files you've assigned that **Tag** to will appear in the **Media Browser**.

If you select a major category of **Tags**, the files assigned to all of that category's subcategories of **Tags** will appear.

To further refine your search, you can select several **Tags** at once.

Find People in your files

One of the most powerful tools for managing and searching your photo files in the Elements Organizer – and one which Adobe has clearly invested a lot of effort into developing – is the **People Finder**.

The **People Finder** will work with you to identify the people in your photos (identifying as many as it can on its own) so that you can easily locate all of the photos that include one or several individuals.

Once you've identified the faces in your photos, you'll be able to retrieve any photos identified with any name or names by using the **Keyword Tag** filter, as discussed on the facing page.

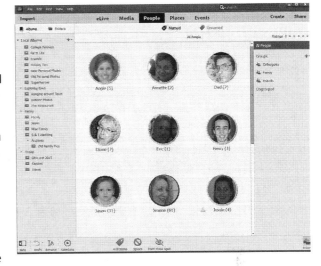

It can take a while to work through all of your photos, but it's actually kind of fun – and the program does a lot of the work for you!

To begin the process:

1　Click the **People** tab at the top of the **Media Browser**.

Under the **Named** tab, the **Media Browser** will display photos grouped by people you've identified.

Under the **Unnamed** tab, the **Media Browser** will display photos grouped by faces the Organizer thinks are similar. (If faces are not displayed, uncheck the **Hide Small Stacks** option in the upper left of the workspace.)

2　Identify **Unnamed** people.

To identify a face in the **Unnamed** workspace, click on **Add Name** below the photo and type in a name.

If the name you are typing has already been tagged to photos in your catalog, the program will offer it to you has an option. Select the name from the list offered.

If you type a name and then click the check mark (or press **Enter** on your keyboard), the name will be added to your list of **People**. If you type in a name of someone already in your **People** list and click the check mark rather than selecting the name from the list the Organizer offers, an additional instance of that name will appear in your **People**.

If you'd like this face not to be added to your list of **People**, **right-click** on the face displayed and select **Ignore This Person**.

An exclamation point indicates that the Organizer has new suggestions for faces to be tagged with an existing name.

Click on the face to open the confirmation workspace.

Hover your mouse over each suggested face and select whether to confirm or reject it from the group.

Click the X in the upper right of the panel to return to the main People worskspace.

Unnamed people are "discovered" by the Organizer, working in the background while you're not using your computer.

To confirm that all of the faces in the set are actually the same person, click on the face displayed. A workspace will open showing all of the faces the Organizer has grouped.

To remove faces that don't belong in the group from a set, hover your mouse over the face and then click on the **Remove** button which appears, as illustrated above.

The Organizer actually "learns" from its mistakes, and it gets more accurate the more you help it identify People.

3 Confirm **Named** people.

As you add **People** to your **Named** files, you may notice that occasionally the **Media Browser** displays an exclamation next to a name. This is an indication that the Organizer has found more faces that it things should be tagged with this same name.

Click on the face above the name and a workspace will open up in which you can confirm or reject the Organizer's selections.

To remove faces from this list, hover your mouse over each face and click the **Remove** indicator.

When you're happy with the faces that appear under a given name, click the **X** in the upper corner of the confirmation workspace to return to the main **People** workspace.

You can begin or end a work session at any time. The Organizer always saves all your work as you work.

Add People to Groups

Your **People** stacks are listed in alphabetic order. But, to make them a bit easier to manage (especially if you've got dozens of them!) you can also arrange them into **Groups.**

The groups **Colleagues, Family** and **Friends** are listed by default. To add someone to an existing **Group**, drag the **Group** onto his or her face.

To create a new **Group**, click the **Add Group** button at the top right of the **Groups** panel.

An option panel will open in which you can name your new **Group** and select whether it will be a main **Group** (select **None**) or it will be a sub-category of an existing **Group**.

To see the **People** in a specific **Group**, click the **Group's** name in the **Groups** panel.

To add a person to a group, drag the Group name onto their face.

Manage your photos by Place

Just as you can manage your photo files using **Albums, Keyword Tags** and the **People** in them, you can also manage your photos or video by the location at which they were shot. Locating media shot at a given location is as simple as clicking on a pin on a map.

Even cooler, if your camera has a built-in GPS (and virtually all smartphone cameras do!), the Elements Organizer reads this metadata and adds the media to your map automatically!

To tag photos with a **Place**:

1. Click the **Places** tab at the top of the interface.

   A map will be displayed on the right side of the **Media Browser**.

If you select the **Pinned** tab, photos already tagged with **Place** metadata will appear on the map as thumbnails. The number on each thumbnails indicates the number of photos tagged to a given **Place**.

The more you zoom in on the map, the more precise their placement will be displayed.

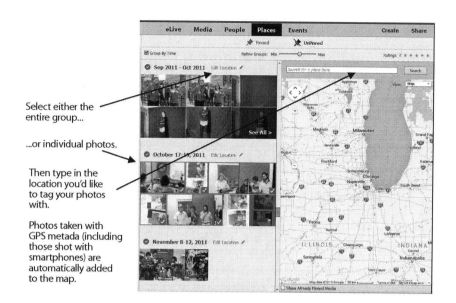

Select either the entire group...

...or individual photos.

Then type in the location you'd like to tag your photos with.

Photos taken with GPS metadata (including those shot with smartphones) are automatically added to the map.

If you select the **Unpinned** tab, you'll have option to tag your photos to **Places**.

2 Under the **Unpinned** tab, select photos to add to a **Place**.

Under the **Unpinned** tab, the **Media Browser** will display photos not yet assigned to **Places**, grouped by date.

To add an entire group of photos to a **Place**, click on the **Edit Location** link above the group.

You have the option of adding the entire group to a location or you can add individual photos.

To add an individual photo or photos to a location, click on the thumbnail displayed or click **See All** to select from the entire group.

A checkmark will appear on your selected photo(s). To select several photos, hold down the **Shift** or **Ctrl** key (the ⌘ key on a Mac) as you click.

3 Indicate a **Place**.

Once you've selected the photos you want to tag with a location, enter the name of the location in the **Search For A Place Here** search box above the map and click **Search** (or press **Enter** in your keyboard). You can enter the name of a city, an address or the zip code of the location.

As you type, the search box will suggest the location. Click to select the location.

Your photo(s) will be linked to that location on the map.

Alternatively, you can simply drag your selected photos onto the map – although this will not give you as accurate a placement. By typing a location into the search box, **you can designate a location as precise as a street address**.

In fact, if your photos have GPS metadata embedded in them, their locations may even be more accurate than that!

Once you've tagged your photos will Place metadata, you can locate all photos shot at that location by zooming in on the map or by filtering the location **Keyword Tags**, as described on page 444.

Manage your media files by Date or Event

Finally, you can manage your media files according to specific dates or events.

1   Click the **Events** tab at the top of the interface.

     If you have media files tagged to **Events**, they will appear as stacks under the **Named** tab.

     Under the **Suggested** tab, the **Media Browser** will display media files not yet assigned to **Events**, grouped by date.

By adjusting the **Refine Groups** slider or by selecting options from the **Calendar** menu to the right, you can adjust how precisely the **Suggested** media files are displayed by date.

To tag **Suggested** media files by **Event**:

2   Select the media files you'd like to add to an **Event**.

     To add an entire group of media files to an **Event**, click on the **Name Event** link above the group.

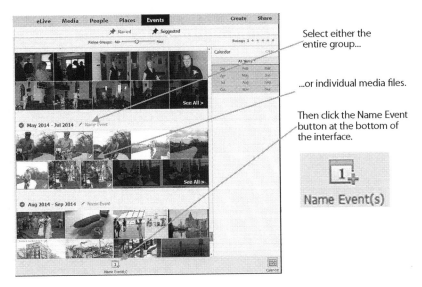

Select either the entire group...

...or individual media files.

Then click the Name Event button at the bottom of the interface.

You have the option of adding the entire group to a location or you can add individual media files.

To add an individual media file or files to a location, click on the thumbnail displayed or click **See All** to select from the entire group.

A checkmark will appear on your selected media file(s). To select several files, hold down the **Shift** or **Ctrl** key (the ⌘ key on a Mac) as you click.

3   Name the **Event**.

Once you've selected the media files, click the **Name Event(s)** button at the bottom of the interface.

In the **Name Event** option panel that opens, you can add the name of the event, the range of dates the event represents and a description of the event.

Once you've tagged your media files with **Event** metadata, you can gather all photos related to that event by clicking on the stack under the **Named** tab or by filtering the **Event**

Keyword Tags, as described on page 444.

Chapter 35

Create Fun Pieces
The Organizer's project templates

The Elements Organizer includes a number of tools for creating everything from a photo scrapbook to a greeting card, DVD cover or a CD or DVD disc label.

Using the templates and wizards in the Organizer (and sometimes Photoshop Elements), creating these photo pieces is as simple as selecting your artwork and following the prompts.

The **Create** tab on the upper right of the Elements Organizer's interface gives you access to an array of tools for creating projects from your media files.

A number of these options are actually links to tools in Premiere Elements or Photoshop Elements, and selecting them will launch the workspace in that program. In fact, **if you do not have Photoshop Elements installed on your computer, some of these options may not even be available to you.**

Create Photo Prints

The **Photo Prints** option under the **Create** tab gives you access to several ways to output your photos.

Print Individual Prints on your local printer

As you'd expect, this option sends your selected photo(s) to your printer. But you may be surprised at the number of possible print layouts this option screen includes!

1. Select the photo or photos you'd like to print in the **Media Browser** and click to select the **Photo Prints** option under the **Create** tab.

    Then, on the **Photo Prints** option panel that appears, select **Local Printer**, as illustrated to the left.

    The **Prints** preview panel will open. The program will automatically arrange the photos you've selected so that it can print as many as possible on each page printed out.

    How many photos it fits on a page depends on the **Print Size** you've selected for photos (as in **Step 2**, below).

    The complete set of photos you've selected to print are displayed as thumbnails along the left side of the panel, and you may add or remove photos from this list.

2. Select your photo print-out options.

    As illustrated on the facing page, the **Select Print Size** drop-down allows you to set how large each photo prints. You can also select from this menu the option to print each photo at its **Actual Size**.

Whenever you print any photo, it's important to consider the resolution of the image. Printing photos smaller than their actual size will usually not be a problem. However, if you set your photo to print at a size in which its final output resolution is less than 150-200 ppi, you will likely see reduced quality and fuzziness in your output. This could definitely be a problem if you selected the **Individual Print** option and you then selected a print size much larger than the actual photo.

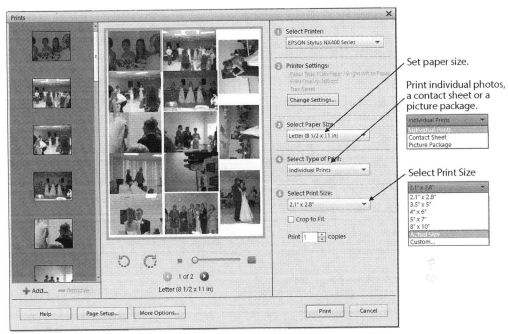

The Print preview panel includes settings for printing your photos in a variety of sizes and layouts as well as options for adding cool custom frames.

Select Type of Print

The **Type of Print** menu on the **Prints** option panel (illustrated above) arranges the photos in your print-out page in one of three patterns.

Individual Prints prints photos to your printer at the size you designate.

Contact Sheet prints proof-style thumbnails of your photos, according to the layout settings you provide.

Picture Package sends an arrangement of photos to your printer based on the number of photos you designate per page. This **Type of Print** also gives you the option of printing these photos with a **Frame** around each.

Print a Picture Package or Contact Sheet on your local printer

The main difference between the **Picture Package** and the **Individual Prints** print-out options is in how you set the size and number of photos that will appear on your print-out page.

When **Type of Print** is set to **Individual Prints**, you will have the option of selecting the *size* your photos will print out at. When you set the **Type of Print** option to **Picture Package** (or **Contact Sheet**), you will have the option of selecting the *number* of photos you want to print on each page.

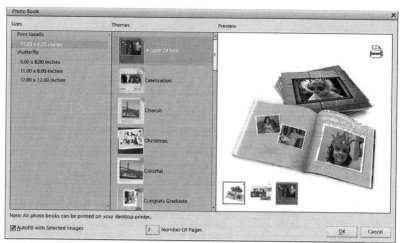

The Photo Book option panel.

Create a Photo Book

A **Photo Book** is a collection of photos laid out in 20 to 80 custom-designed pages. The wizard takes you through the basic steps of setting up the book. Once the book is initially set up, you can add more photos to it and tweak the design and layout. (This tool is only available if you have Photoshop Elements.)

A **Photo Book** can be sent to **Shutterfly** for professional printing and binding, or it can be printed out on your home printer.

1   Select the photos in the **Media Browser** you'd like to include in your **Photo Book.** Then select the **Photo Book** button under the **Create** tab.

    The **Photo Book** option panel will open in Photoshop Elements.

2   Select a size and output options for your book from the **Photo Book** option panel (illustrated above). If you plan to have your book professionally printed and bound, select one of the **Shutterfly** options.

3   On this same panel, select a **Theme** for your book.

    You can designate any number of pages for your book. However, if you plan to have **Shutterfly** produce your book, there must be a minimum of 20 pages.

    Click **OK**

The photos you have selected when you launch this tool will automatically be loaded into your **Photo Book** in the order that they appear in the **Media Browser.**

The first of your selected photos will become your **Title Page Photo.**

The program will fill as many pages as possible with the photos you've selected.

Click a block of text to customize it.

Right-click on photo to modify or replace it.

Select a page for editing from the Page bin.

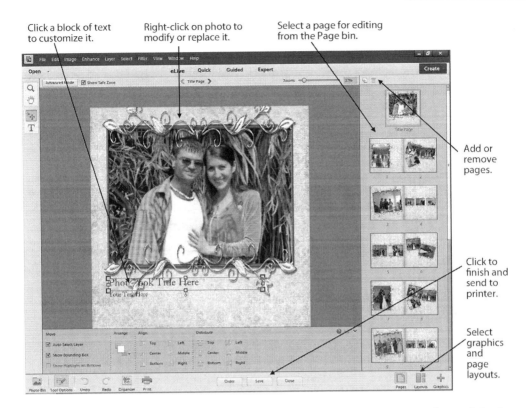

Add or remove pages.

Click to finish and send to printer.

Select graphics and page layouts.

You can add pages to or remove pages from your book by clicking the icons in the top left of the **Page Bin**.

You may also change the theme and/or frames for the individual pages or add graphics by selecting options at the bottom right.

To add, edit or replace photos, **right-click** on the photo frame:

- If the frame is blank, you'll be prompted to browse for a photo on your hard drive.

- If a photo is already in the frame, options will be displayed to resize the photo or **Position Photo Within Frame**, rotate it or replace it.

By dragging on their corner handles, photos and their frames can be resized and repositioned on the page.

Along the bottom of the **Photo Book** workspace panel, you will find the options to **Order** your book professionally produced, to save the project file or to **Print** it on your home printer.

Zoom photo in/out

Rotate photo

Replace photo

Accept/Cancel

The Greeting Card option panel.

Create a Greeting Card

Once completed, your **Greeting Card** can be printed on your home printer. (This tool is available only if you have Photoshop Elements.)

1   Select the **Greeting Card** button under the **Create** tab.

The photos you have in your **Project Bin** – whether because they are open in the **Editor** or selected in the **Organizer** – will automatically be loaded into your **Greeting Card.** Photos may also be added or removed after the book is created.

2   Select a size and output option for your book from the **Greeting Card** option screen (illustrated above). You can send your card to Shutterfly for professional production or print it out on your home printer.

3   On this same panel, select a **Theme** for your card. (These features can be modified later.)

Click **OK**.

The program will generate your card.

As with the **Photo Book**, you may swap out photos and modify your **Greeting Card's** layout, graphics or text, as described on page 455.

After the program generates your card, you can modify its theme, text, photos and effects.

The Calendar option panel.

Create a Photo Calendar

Once completed, your **Photo Calendar** can be printed on your home printer. (This tool is only available if you have Photoshop Elements.)

1 Select the photos you'd like to use in your calendar in the **Media Browser**

2 Select the **Photo Calendar** button under the **Create** tab.

3 Select a starting date, size and output options for your book from the **Photo Calendar** option screen (illustrated above). You can send your card to Kodak for professional production or print it out on your home printer.

4 On this same panel, select a **Theme** for your card. (These features can be modified later.)

The photos you have in your **Media Browser** will automatically be loaded into your **Photo Calendar.** Photos may also be added or removed after the book is created.

Click **OK**.

The program will generate your card.

As with the **Photo Book**, you may swap out photos and modify your **Photo Calendar's** layout, graphics or text, as described on page 455.

After the program generates your calendar, you can modify its layout, graphics, text and photos.

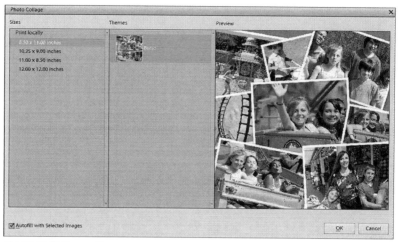

The Photo Collage option screen.

Create a Photo Collage

A **Photo Collage** is an arrangement of photos gathered together in an artful or playful way. Once you create your **Photo Collage**, you'll be able to print it out on your home printer. (This tool is only available if you have Photoshop Elements.)

1   Select the photos you'd like to use in your collage in the **Media Browser**

2   Select the **Photo Collage** button under the **Create** tab.

3   Select a size for your **Photo Collage** from the option screen (illustrated above).

4   On this same panel, select a **Theme** for your collage. (These features can be modified later.)

Click **OK**.

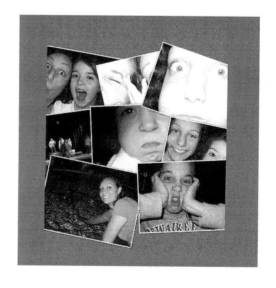

The photos you have in your **Media Browser** will automatically be loaded into your **Photo Collage**. Photos may also be added or removed after the book is created.

The program will generate your card.

As with the **Photo Book**, you may swap out photos and modify your **Photo Calendar's** layout, graphics or text, as described on page 455.

Create an InstantMovie

Selecting the option to create an **InstantMovie** gathers the photos and video clips you've selected in the Organizer's **Media Browser** and ports them to Premiere Elements, where an **InstantMovie Theme** is applied. For more information on **InstantMovies** and **Themes**, see **Chapter 22, Create an InstantMovie or a Video Story**.

Create a Video Story

Selecting the option to create an **Video Story** gathers the photos and video clips you've selected in the Organizer's **Media Browser** and ports them to Premiere Elements and into the **Video Story** workspace. For more information on the **Video Story** tool, see **Chapter 22, Create an InstantMovie or a Video Story**.

Create a DVD with Menu

Selecting the option to create a **DVD With Menu** gathers the photos and video clips you've selected in the Organizer's **Media Browser** and ports them to a Premiere Elements project for further editing. For information on adding a menu to a DVD or BluRay disc project, see **Chapter 31, Create Movie Menus**.

Create a Facebook Cover

Selecting the option to create a **Facebook Cover** opens a Photoshop Elements workspace for creating a cover illustration for your Facebook home page. For more information on the tools in this workspace, see the sidebar on page 463.

Create a CD Jacket

This tool creates a 9¾" x 4¾" image that you can print out and fit into a CD or DVD "jewel case." (Note that disc jewel cases are 4¾" x 4¾", so this artwork is designed to wrap around the case and include a ¼" spine.)

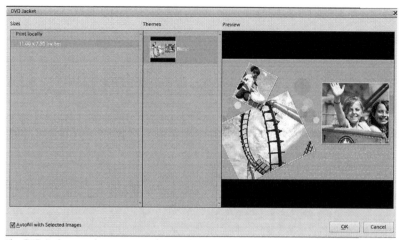

The DVD Jacket template creates an image that wraps around a DVD case that has 5.25" x 7.50" faces and a .5" spine.

The CD/DVD Label template creates art that can be printed onto a 4.75" disc.

Create a DVD Jacket

This tool creates an 11" x 7½" label for a DVD case. This template is made to fit a 5¼" x 7½" case with a ½" wide spine.

Print a CD/DVD Label

This tool creates 4¾", circular-shaped artwork for printing onto discs. It includes the necessary spindle hole through the center. (At Muvipix, we recommend never using glue-on labels for your DVDs and CDs. They can cause any number of problems. Use this template only for printable discs and inkjet printers designed to print them.)

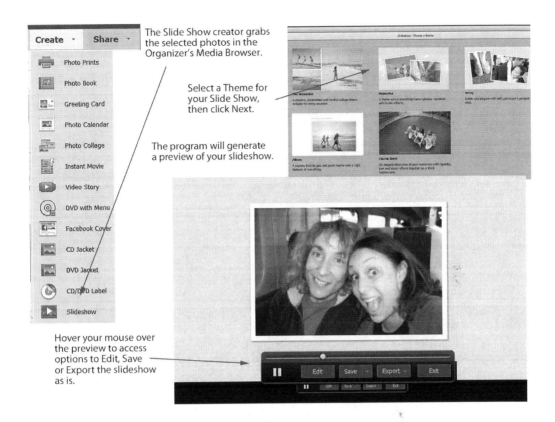

The Slide Show creator grabs the selected photos in the Organizer's Media Browser.

Select a Theme for your Slide Show, then click Next.

The program will generate a preview of your slideshow.

Hover your mouse over the preview to access options to Edit, Save or Export the slideshow as is.

Create an Organizer Slideshow

There are actually several ways to create a slideshow in Premiere Elements and Photoshop Elements (including using the tool in the **Project Assets** panel, as we discuss on page 265.) But the Organizer's new and improved **Slide Show creator** is perhaps the most intuitive option – and includes some very nice looking themes to give your slideshow a real professional look!

1   Select the photos you'd like to include in your slideshow in the **Media Browser**. (You can add or remove photos later.)

2   Select the **Slide Show** option from under the Elements Organizer's **Create** tab.

A **Theme** library window will open.

3   Select a **Theme** for your slideshow.

Click **Next**.

The tool will generate a preview of your slideshow.

Hover your mouse over the slideshow preview.

Add slides.   Re-sort slides by dragging.

Export to
Facebook
or an MP4.

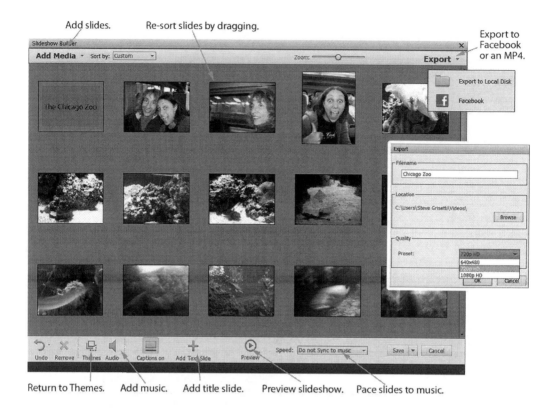

Return to Themes.   Add music.   Add title slide.   Preview slideshow.   Pace slides to music.

An option panel will appear.

Click **Exit** or **Edit** to leave the preview.

4   Edit your slideshow in the **Slideshow Builder** workspace.

Drag your slides in the **Slideshow Builder** to rearrange their order.

Click the **Add Media** button in the upper left of the panel to add more slides.

Right-click on any slide to **Remove Image** from the slideshow.

5   Add production elements.

As illustrated above, click **Add Text Slide** to add a title slide.

Click the **Audio** button to add custom music to your sideshow and select a timing option from the **Speed** drop-down menu.

6   Output your slideshow.

Click **Save** to save your slideshow in a format that will allow you to re-open it and re-edit it later.

Click **Export** to save your slideshow as an MP4 or to upload it directly to your Facebook page.

Create a Facebook cover page

Available only if you have Photoshop Elements installed, the **Create Facebook Cover** workspace offers you templates and tools for creating your own stylish cover illustration for your Facebook home page.

To use this tool, click the **Create** button in the upper right of the interface and select **Facebook Cover**. An option screen will offer you a number of templates for your cover page. Select one and click **OK**.

In the **Facebook Cover** workspace, add photos to the template by clicking on one of the photo placeholders and then browsing to a photo on your hard drive.

A zoom slider at the top right the workspace can be used to zoom in and out on your work. **Double-clicking** on a photo that you've added to the template launches a tool for changing the scale and orientation of your photo, as in the illustration below.

The **Text** tool on the left side of the workspace can be used to add custom text, and the **Move** tool can be used to select, reposition and remove any of the template's elements. The **Graphics** button in the lower right will open a library of clip art options.

When you're ready to upload your finished cover to Facebook, click the **Upload** button on the bottom center of the workspace. (The first time you use this tool, you'll need to follow the prompts to authorize the program's link to your Facebook account.)

Sharing Your Photos as E-mail Attachments
Sharing to Facebook, Flickr, Vimeo and Twitter
Sharing Your Photos or Videos to a CD or DVD
Sharing Your Photos to a PDF Slideshow

Chapter 36

Share Your Photos and Videos
The Organizer's output tools

The Elements Organizer includes a number of tools for outputting your photo and video files – from posting them online or e-mailing them to creating a DVD or PDF slideshow.

In addition to tools for creating photo and video projects, the Elements Organizer includes a number of tools for sharing your photos and videos.

Share your photos and videos on Facebook

If you have a Facebook account, you can upload your photos and videos directly from the Organizer's **Media Browser** to your page.

To upload to Facebook:

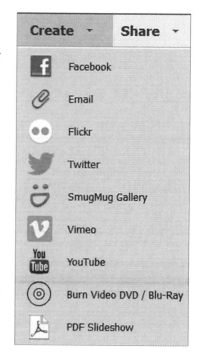

1 Select a media file in the **Media Browser** you'd like to include in your **Photo Book.** Then select the **Facebook** option under the **Share** tab.

The Organizer will prepare your file(s) for upload.

If this is the first time uploading to Facebook from the Organizer, an option screen will ask you to **Authorize** the upload. (It will also ask you if you want to download your Facebook friends to your Organizer **Contacts**. This is, of course, optional.)

2 Click **Authorize**.

After you click the **Authorize** button, your web browser will open to your Facebook page. If you are already logged into Facebook, you're done with the authorization. You can close your web browser now. If not, you will need to log in first.

The Facebook option screen.

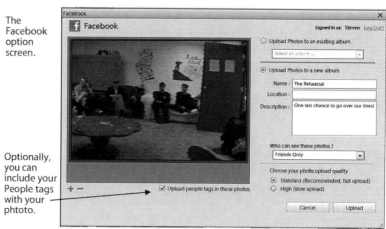

Optionally, you can include your People tags with your phtoto.

3   Back in the Organizer, click the **Complete Authorization** button.

The program will finish preparing your files. An option panel will then open, asking you to name your file(s) and set who can see them.

4   Once you've set your options, as illustrated below, click **Upload**. Your file(s) will load to Facebook.

Share your photos via e-mail

The **E-mail sharing** option optimizes your selected photo files and then sends them off, with a brief note, to the person or group of people you designate as **Recipients**.

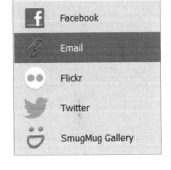

As with any **Share** tool, you can pre-select your media files before starting the tool or add your media files later.

1   Select the photo(s) you want to attach to your e-mail in your **Media Browser**.

2   Select the **E-mail** option under the **Share** tab in the Organizer.

The **E-mail** share panel will open.

3   Drag any more photo(s) you'd like to add to your e-mail attachments from the Organizer's **Media Browser** into the **E-mail Attachments Items** bin.

Remove any photos you'd like to delete by selecting them in the panel and clicking the **trashcan** button below the photos.

You can add photos in any file format. The program will convert whatever you add to this bin into a JPEG for e-mailing.

Set the **Photo Size** and **Quality** by using the slider and selecting a photo size from the **Maximum Photo Size** drop-down menu.

Set up e-mail sharing for the Elements Organizer

In order to use the Elements Organizer's e-mail **Share** options, you must have an active e-mail profile and address listed on the **Email** page of the Organizer's **Preferences** (under the **Edit** drop-down on the Organizer Menu Bar on a PC).

On this **Email Preferences** page, under **Configure Email Client**, select a name for your **Email Profile**, then fill in your e-mail address and password.

Click the **Validate** button. The program will indicate that your validation was successful.

E-mails sent directly from the Organizer will use this e-mail address as their output path.

Naturally, the more photos you're including in your e-mail, the more you'll need to decrease the photo size or quality.

The panel displays an **Estimated Size** and, in order to ensure your e-mail doesn't choke your recipients' e-mail services, you'll probably want to keep your total e-mail size below 1 megabyte or so.

When you are happy with your settings for this panel, click **Next**.

4   Create a message to accompany your photos and then **Select Recipients** from your list of contacts.

(See the sidebar on page 470 – **Create an Elements Organizer Contact Book** – for information on creating your **Contacts** list.)

When you are happy with your settings for this panel, click **Next**.

Your e-mail and optimized attachments will be sent to your selected recipients.

Share your photos on Flickr

When you select photos in your **Media Browser** and select the **Flickr** option under the **Share** tab, your photos will be prepared, then uploaded to your account at www.flickr.com – very much like the process described in **Share Your Videos and Photos to Facebook** on page 466.

The first time you use the tool, you will need to log in to Flickr and **Authorize** the upload, as described in **Share Your Videos and Photos to Facebook**.

Share your photos on Twitter

When you select photos in your **Media Browser** and select the **Twitter** option under the **Share** tab, your photos will be prepared, then uploaded to your account at www.Twitter.com – very much like the process described in **Share Your Videos and Photos to Facebook** on page 466.

The first time you use the tool, you will need to **Authorize** the upload, as described in **Share Your Videos and Photos to Facebook**.

Share your photos in a SmugMug Gallery

A higher-end gallery for displaying your photos, SmugMug offers a wide variety of attractive and stylish templates for displaying your pictures. SmugMug offers their services at prices ranging from $39.95 to $149.95 per year, with a 20% discount for Photoshop Elements users.

When you select your photos in the **Media Browser** and then select the **SmugMug** option under the **Share** tab and follow the prompts, your photos will be displayed as an online slideshow – at a quality worthy of a professional portfolio.

Share your video on Vimeo

When you select a video in your **Media Browser** and select the **Vimeo** option under the **Share** tab, your video will be prepared, then uploaded to your account at www.vimeo.com – very much like the process described in **Share Your Videos and Photos to Facebook** on page 466.

The first time you use this tool, you will be prompted to log in to Vimeo and **Authorize** the upload, as described in **Share Your Videos and Photos to Facebook**.

Share your video on YouTube

When you select a video in your **Media Browser** and select the **YouTube** option under the **Share** tab, your video will be prepared, then uploaded to your account at YouTube – very much like the process described in **Share Your Videos and Photos to Facebook** on page 466.

Create an Elements Organizer Contact Book

In order to have the options to **Select Recipients** for your **E-mail Attachments,** you will need to have these potential recipients listed in your Elements Organizer's **Contact Book**.

To create and add your contacts to this book, go to the **Edit** drop-down on the Organizer Menu Bar and select **Contact Book**:

Click **New Contacts** to manually add your contacts' names and e-mail addresses.

Before you can send out Photo Mail or an e-mail using Adobe's services, you'll need to build a Contact Book, an option available under the Organizer's Edit menu.

Or click the **Import** button to automatically add contacts from your e-mail program.

Once they have been added to your **Contact Book, these names** will be listed under **Select Recipients** whenever you select the **E-mail Attachment** or **Photo Mail** option.

The first time you use the tool, you will be prompted to log in to YouTube and **Authorize** the upload, as described in **Share Your Videos and Photos to Facebook**.

Videos created in Premiere Elements can also be uploaded to YouTube using Premiere Elements' **Export & Share/Online** option described on page 412.

Burn a Video DVD or BluRay disc

When you click on the **Share** option to **Burn Video DVD/BluRay disc**, the program will launch Premiere Elements and the files you have selected in the Organizer's **Media Browser** will be ported to a Premier Elements project.

For information on creating menus for a DVD or BluRay disc in Premiere Elements, see **Chapter 31, Create Movie Menus**.

Share as a PDF Slide Show

Selecting the **PDF Slide Show** option under the **Share** tab creates a dynamic slideshow of the photo files you have selected in the **Media Browser** and outputs them in the PDF (Portable Document File) format, which it then e-mails to your selected recipients.

The slideshow can be viewed on any computer using the free utility Acrobat Reader.

Index